D1134993

Letters to My Brother Priests

Complete Collection of Holy Thursday Letters (1979–2005)

Pope John Paul II

Edited by
James Socias

Midwest Theological Forum
Woodridge, Illinois

This edition of *Letters to My Brother Priests* is published by:

Midwest Theological Forum
1420 Davey Road
Woodridge, IL 60517
phone: (630) 739-9750
fax: (630) 739-9758
e-mail: mail@mwtf.org

The **Midwest Theological Forum** is an educational service
organized by priests of the Prelature of Opus Dei
and other diocesan priests.

Fifth Edition 2006

Printed in Canada

Midwest Theological Forum   ISBN 1-890177-58-X

Contents

1981

1986

1987

1990

1991

1992

1993

1994

1995

1996

2001

2002

2003

2004

2005

Abbreviations

Used for the Books of the Bible

Old Testament

Genesis	Gen	Tobit	Tb	Ezekiel	Ez
Exodus	Ex	Judith	Jdt	Daniel	Dn
Leviticus	Lv	Esther	Est	Hosea	Hos
Numbers	Nm	1 Maccabees	1 Mc	Joel	Jl
Deuteronomy	Dt	2 Maccabees	2 Mc	Amos	Am
Joshua	Jos	Job	Jb	Obadiah	Ob
Judges	Jgs	Psalms	Ps(s)	Jonah	Jon
Ruth	Ru	Proverbs	Prv	Micah	Mi
1 Samuel	1 Sm	Ecclesiastes	Eccl	Nahum	Na
2 Samuel	2 Sm	Song of Songs	Sg	Habakkuk	Hab
1 Kings	1 Kgs	Wisdom	Wis	Zephaniah	Zep
2 Kings	2 Kgs	Sirach	Sir	Haggai	Hg
1 Chronicles	1 Chr	Isaiah	Is	Zechariah	Zec
2 Chronicles	2 Chr	Jeremiah	Jer	Malachi	Mal
Ezra	Ezr	Lamentations	Lam		
Nehemiah	Neh	Baruch	Bar		

New Testament

Matthew	Mt	Ephesians	Eph	Hebrews	Heb
Mark	Mk	Philippians	Phil	James	Jas
Luke	Lk	Colossians	Col	1 Peter	1 Pt
John	Jn	1 Thessalonians	1 Thes	2 Peter	2 Pt
Acts of the Apostles	Acts	2 Thessalonians	2 Thes	1 John	1 Jn
Romans	Rom	1 Timothy	1 Tm	2 John	2 Jn
1 Corinthians	1 Cor	2 Timothy	2 Tm	3 John	3 Jn
2 Corinthians	2 Cor	Titus	Ti	Jude	Jud
Galatians	Gal	Philemon	Phlm	Revelation	Rv

Foreword

by the Most Reverend Gabriel Montalvo
Apostolic Nuncio to the United States

Each year the liturgy of Holy Thursday draws priests, in every part of the world and in every diocese, to gather with their bishops in the shared celebration of the Eucharist. During this Mass, those priests will renew, in the presence of their bishops and together with them, the promises that they made at the time of their ordination. There was no better moment than this for our Holy Father, Pope John Paul II, to speak about the awesome and wonderful gift of the priesthood. In almost every year of his Pontificate, the Holy Father addressed a Letter to the Priests of the Church on the occasion of Holy Thursday. On that day, the Pope reminded us, the Church celebrates "the day of the birth of the Eucharist and the birthday of our priesthood." (p. 102)

Reading this collection of letters, one easily recognizes John Paul II's great love for the Church and the priesthood. Such love extends also, in expressions of paternal affection, for each of the bishops and priests throughout the world. His introductory words in the Letter of 1986 beautifully capture his thoughts and sentiments, which are implicit in almost all of these letters:

"As you know, I feel particularly close to each one of you on this occasion. And, the same as every year, as a sign of our sacramental union in the same priesthood, and impelled by my affectionate esteem for you and by my duty to confirm all my brothers in their service of the Lord, I wish to send you this letter to help you to stir up the wonderful gift that was conferred on you through the laying on of hands." (p. 114)

The Holy Father wanted each priest to know and believe that the gift of the priesthood draws each ordained man into a sacramental union with each other, with their bishops and with the Pope himself. In his Letter of 1994 he spoke of this "sacramental brotherhood" and urged priests to "pray for one another—priests for priests!" (p. 210)

Such unity flows from and is nourished by the Eucharist, which is at the heart of the gift and mystery of the priesthood. The ordained priest enjoys the privilege of being configured to the One Priest, Jesus Christ. It is this privilege that admits the priest to a unique and special relationship with the Lord. In several letters John Paul II recalls the words spoken by Jesus in the Upper Room, "no longer do I call you servants . . . but I have called you friends" (Jn 15: 15). He eloquently captures the significance of such a declaration by the Lord:

"Christ made known to the Apostles, and to all those who inherit from them the ordained priesthood, that in this vocation and for this ministry they must become *his friends*—they must become the *friends of that mystery* which he came to accomplish. To be a priest means to enjoy special friendship with the mystery of Christ, with the mystery of the Redemption, in which he gives his flesh 'for the life of the world.'" (pp. 86–87)

The Eucharist has the power to continually form and transform the priest, who having been called "friend" by the Lord, is marked with that priestly character of Holy Orders. The *mandatum* of Holy Thursday recalls that the priest stands with Christ not only at the altar, but also in the continual action of ministerial service. John Paul II reminds the priest that this is his vocation, "a vocation which must be lived according to the examples of the Master, who before the Last Supper washed the feet of the Apostles." (p. 178)

In both sacrament and ministry the priest acts in the presence and in the name of Christ to strengthen and build his Body, the Church. The priest must never cease to realize, however, that only the Eucharistic Christ can create the one, true and lasting community among so many countless men and women throughout the world. Each person, unique and individual, is brought into communion with Christ and with all those who faithfully share in the celebration of the Eucharist.

John Paul II, writing in 1986, points to St. John Mary Vianney, the Curé of Ars, as an extraordinary model of sacramental life and ministerial service. Weaving together the many fibers of the life of this pastor and saint, he offers an exquisite meditation on the priestly ministry and the holiness of the minister. Through prayer, a spirit of poverty, chastity and obedience, this saintly priest ceaselessly conformed himself to Christ, the High Priest. The Pope reminds his sons in the priesthood that "[O]bedience to Christ consisted, for John Mary Vianney, in obedience to the Church and especially to the bishop." (p. 124)

Such obedience is integral to the priesthood and essential for that unity which must flourish among priests, together with their bishops and with the Holy Father.

It is not surprising that John Paul II, who from his youth has seen himself as a son of the Blessed Virgin Mary, presents Mary as a Mother of priests in many of these letters. St. John, the Beloved Disciple, stood at the foot of the cross and was encouraged by the Crucified Christ to take Mary as his mother. He reminds priests of this gracious, filial status and urges them to turn to Mary as Mother of the Lord and to embrace her as their mother. In 1995 John Paul II closes his letter imploring Mary to bestow her maternal attention upon the priests of the Church:

"May the Blessed Virgin look with special affection upon us all, her well-beloved sons, on this annual celebration of our priesthood. May she especially inspire in our hearts a burning desire for holiness." (p. 223)

Mary is the Mother of the Incarnate Word. She is Mother of Jesus and Mother of priests. In this expression of love for the Blessed Mother John Paul II underscores, once again, his fraternal relationship with all priests.

This collection of Holy Thursday Letters is yet another witness to John Paul II's love for the Church, for the priesthood and for his brother bishops and priests throughout the world. May they, reading this book, not only be grateful to this great Pontiff, but also pray for him.

1979

First Year of Pontificate

On October 16, 1978, Karol Cardinal Wojtyla, Archbishop of Krakow, was elected pope and chose the name John Paul II. "It was to Christ the Redeemer that my feelings and my thoughts were directed . . . when, after the canonical election, I was asked: 'Do you accept?'" he wrote some months later. "I then replied: 'With obedience in faith to Christ, my Lord, and with trust in the Mother of Christ and of the Church, in spite of the great difficulties, I accept.' Today I wish to make that reply known publicly" (*Redemptor hominis*, n. 2).

On the day after his election he celebrated Mass together with the College of Cardinals in the Sistine Chapel. At the end of the Mass he spoke to the cardinals and to the world: "We wish to point out the unceasing importance of the Second Vatican Ecumenical Council and we accept the definite duty of assiduously bringing it into effect." (Address, October 17, 1978)

A few days later, in the homily at the solemn Mass marking the beginning of his new ministry, the Holy Father said: "The new successor of Peter in the See of Rome today makes a fervent, humble and trusting prayer: Christ, make me become and remain the servant of your unique power, the servant of your sweet power, the servant of your power that knows no eventide. Make me a servant; indeed the servant of your servants. Brothers and sisters, do not be afraid to welcome Christ and accept his power. . . . Do not be afraid. Open wide the doors for Christ" (Homily, October 22, 1978, nn. 4-5).

About half a year after his election to the pontificate, Pope John Paul II wrote a short letter to all the bishops and a longer letter to all the priests of the Church on the occasion of Holy Thursday, both dated on Palm Sunday, April 8. It was the first time he celebrated Holy Week as the successor of Peter. "At the beginning of my new ministry in the Church, I feel the deep need to speak to you, to all of you without exception, priests both diocesan and religious, who are my brothers by virtue of the Sacrament of Orders. . . . To all of you . . . I have addressed my thoughts and my heart from the moment when Christ called me to this See, where St. Peter, with his life and his death, had to respond until the end to the question: Do you love me? Do you love me more than these others do?" (cf. Jn 21: 15-17). Those were the first words of the first Holy Thursday Letter to Priests.

The Holy Father opened his heart to the priests: "I think of you all the time, I pray for you, with you I seek the ways of spiritual union and collaboration, because by virtue of the Sacrament of Orders . . . you are my brothers. . . . It is on this day [Holy Thursday] that all priests are invited to renew, before their own bishop and together with him, the promises they made at their priestly ordination; and this fact enables me, together with all my brothers in the episcopate, to be joined to you in a special unity, and especially to be in the very heart of the mystery of Jesus Christ, the mystery in which we all share" (1979 Letter, n. 1).

During this year the Holy Father published his first encyclical, *Redemptor hominis* (March 4). He also released the Apostolic Exhortation *Catechesi tradendæ* (October 16, the first anniversary of his election) on the topic of the 1977 Synod of Bishops, catechesis in our time, the work of three popes.

John Paul's first encyclical opened with these words:"The Redeemer of man, Jesus Christ, is the center of the universe and of history. To him go my thoughts and my heart in this solemn moment of the world that the Church and the whole family of present-day humanity are now living" (*Redemptor hominis*, n. 1). And later on:"While the ways on which the council of this century has set the Church going . . . will continue to be for a long time the ways that all of us must follow, we can at the same time rightly ask at this new stage: How, in what manner should we continue? . . . To this question, dear brothers, sons and daughters, a fundamental and essential response must be given. Our response must be: Our spirit is set in one direction; the only direction for our intellect, will and heart is—towards Christ our Redeemer, towards Christ, the Redeemer of man" (*Redemptor hominis*, n. 7).

Already in 1979 the pope made several pastoral visits to different countries, including Mexico (January 15-31), Poland (June 2-10), Ireland and the United States (September 23–October 7), and Turkey (November 29-30). A few days after his return from the United States he spoke about"my brothers and sisters beyond the ocean. Their Church is still young, because their great society is young: there have passed only two centuries of its history on the political map of the globe. I wish to thank them all, for the welcome they gave me; for their response to this visit. . . . We persisted in pouring rain during the Mass for the young, the first evening, at Boston. . . . Unforgettable for me are the districts of Harlem, with its Black population in the majority; South Bronx, with the newcomers from Latin American countries; the meeting with the young in Madison Square Garden and in Battery Park in torrential rain and a raging storm, and in the stadium at Brooklyn, when the sun finally appeared. . . . And then: illustrious Philadelphia . . . with its bell of freedom. . . . And the meeting with rural America at Des Moines. Afterwards Chicago, in which it was possible, in a more appropriate way, to develop the analogy on the subject *e pluribus unum*. Finally, the city of

Washington, the capital of the United States, with all its heavy program, up to the last Mass with the Capitol in the background" (General Audience, October 17, n. 3).

His love for the Church in the United States, still young, was obvious. On one occasion Cardinal Medeiros mentioned how the Holy Father sitting next to him in the motorcade to the cardinal's residence late in the evening of his first day in the country—the rain still persisting—commented repeatedly: "These are a free people." At the same time, the pope spoke often about the challenge of freedom. In Philadelphia he said: "The Liberty Bell, which I visited on another occasion, proudly bears the words of the Bible: 'Proclaim liberty throughout the land' (Lv 25: 10). This tradition poses for all future generations of America a noble challenge. . . . Freedom can never be construed without relation to the truth as revealed by Jesus Christ and proposed by his Church, nor can it be seen as a pretext for moral anarchy, for every moral order must remain linked to truth" (Homily at Logan Circle, Philadelphia, October 3, nn. 2, 6).

While addressing the American bishops, the pope confirmed to them the clear teaching on difficult issues: "With the candor of the Gospels, the compassion of pastors and the charity of Christ, you faced the question of the indissolubility of marriage. . . . In exalting the beauty of marriage you rightly spoke against both the ideology of contraception and contraceptive acts. . . . You reaffirmed the right to life and the inviolability of every human life, including the life of unborn children. . . . One of the greatest rights of the faithful is to receive the word of God in its purity and integrity as guaranteed by the magisterium of the universal Church" (Address to the Episcopal Conference, Chicago, October 5, nn. 6-7).

During the General Audiences at the beginning of his pontificate, Pope John Paul II dealt with a variety of topics, including a series on the cardinal virtues, following a theme started by his predecessor, and an Advent series. On September 5, 1979, he began what was to be a long sequence on the theme of human love to be developed over several years.

LETTER
OF THE HOLY FATHER
POPE JOHN PAUL II
TO ALL THE BISHOPS OF THE CHURCH
ON THE OCCASION OF HOLY THURSDAY 1979

Venerable Brothers in the Episcopate!

The great day is drawing near when we shall share in the liturgy of Holy Thursday together with our brothers in the priesthood and shall meditate together on the priceless gift in which we have become sharers by virtue of the call of Christ the eternal Priest. On that day, before we celebrate the liturgy *in cena Domini*, we shall gather together in our cathedrals to renew before him who became for us "obedient unto death"[1] in total self-giving to the Church, his spouse, our giving of ourselves to the exclusive service of Christ in his Church.

On this holy day, the liturgy takes us inside the Upper Room, where, with grateful hearts, we set ourselves to listen to the words of the divine Teacher, words full of solicitude for every generation of bishops called, after the Apostles, to take upon themselves care for the Church, for the flock, for the vocation of the whole People of God, for the proclamation of God's word, for the whole sacramental and moral order of Christian living, for priestly and religious vocations, for the fraternal spirit in the community. Christ says: "I will not leave you orphans; I will come back to you."[2] It is precisely this sacred triduum of the passion, death and resurrection of the Lord that re-evokes in us, in a vivid way, not only the memory of his departure, but also faith in his return, in his continuous coming. Indeed, what is the meaning of the words: "I am with you always; yes, to the end of time"?[3]

Venerable and dear brothers, in the spirit of this faith, which fills the entire triduum, it is my desire that, in our vocation and our episcopal ministry, we should feel in a special way this year—the first of my Pontificate—that unity which the Twelve shared in when together with our Lord they were assembled for the Last Supper. It was precisely there that they heard those words that were most complimentary and at the same time most binding: "I shall not call you servants any more, because a servant does not know his master's business; I call you friends, because I have made known to you everything I have learned from my Father. You did not choose me, no, I chose you; and I commissioned you to go out and to bear fruit, fruit that will last."[4]

Can anything be added to those words? Should one not rather pause in humility and gratitude before them, given the greatness of the mystery we are about to celebrate? There then takes root even deeper within us our awareness of the gift that we have received from the Lord through our vocation and our episcopal ordination. In fact the gift of the sacramental fullness of the priesthood is greater than all the toils and also all the sufferings involved in our pastoral ministry in the episcopate.

The Second Vatican Council reminded us and clearly showed us that this ministry, while being a personal duty of each one of us, is nevertheless something that we carry out in the brotherly communion of the whole of the Church's episcopal college or "body." While it is right that we should address every human being, and especially every Christian as "brother," this word takes on an altogether special meaning with regard to us bishops and our mutual relationship: in a certain sense it goes back directly to that brotherhood which gathered the Apostles about Christ; it goes back to that friendship with which Christ honored them and through which he united them to one another, as is attested by the words of John's Gospel quoted above.

Therefore, venerable and dear brothers, we must express the wish, today especially, that everything that the Second Vatican Council so wonderfully renewed in our awareness should take on an ever more mature character of collegiality, both as the principle of our collaboration (*collegialitas effectiva*) and as the character of a cordial fraternal bond (*collegialitas affectiva*), in order to build up the Mystical Body of Christ and to deepen the unity of the whole People of God.

As you gather in your cathedrals, with the diocesan and religious priests who make up the *presbyterium* of your local churches, your dioceses, you will receive from them—as is provided for—the renewal of the promises that they placed in the hands of you, the bishops, on the day of their priestly ordination. With this in mind, I am sending to the priests another letter that—as I hope—will enable you and them to live even more deeply this unity, this mysterious bond that joins us in the one Priesthood of Jesus Christ, brought to completion with the sacrifice of the Cross, which merited for him entrance "into the sanctuary."[5] Venerable brothers, I hope that these words of mine addressed to the priests, at the beginning of my ministry in the See of

St. Peter, will also help you to strengthen ever more that communion and unity of the whole *presbyterium*[6] which have their basis in our collegial communion and unity in the Church.

And may there be a renewal of your love for the priests whom the Holy Spirit has given and entrusted to you as the closest collaborators in your pastoral office. Take care of them like beloved sons, brothers and friends. Be mindful of all their needs. Have particular solicitude for their spiritual advancement, for their perseverance in the grace of the sacrament of the priesthood. Since it is into your hands they make—and each year renew—their priestly promises, and especially the commitment to celibacy, do everything in your power to ensure that they remain faithful to these promises, as is demanded by the holy tradition of the Church, the tradition that sprang from the very spirit of the Gospel.

May this solicitude for our brothers in the priestly ministry also be extended to the seminaries, which constitute, in the Church as a whole and in each of her parts, an eloquent proof of her vitality and spiritual fruitfulness, which are expressed precisely in readiness to give oneself exclusively to the service of God and of souls. Today, every possible effort must again be made to encourage vocations, to form new generations of priests. This must be done in a genuinely evangelical spirit, and at the same time by "reading" properly the signs of the times, to which the Second Vatican Council gave such careful attention. The full reconstitution of the life of the seminaries throughout the Church will be the best proof of the achievement of the renewal to which the council directed the Church.

Venerable and dear brothers: everything that I am writing to you, as I prepare to live Holy Thursday intensely—the "feast of priests"—I wish to link up closely with the desire that the Apostles heard expressed that day by the lips of their beloved Teacher: "Go out and bear fruit, fruit that will last."[7] We can bear this fruit only if we remain in him: in the vine.[8] He told us this clearly in his words of farewell on the day before his Passover: "Whoever remains in me, with me in him, bears fruit in plenty; for cut off from me you can do nothing."[9] Beloved brothers, what more could I wish you, what more could we wish one another, than precisely this: to remain in him, Jesus Christ, and to bear fruit, fruit that will last?

Accept these good wishes. Let us strive to deepen ever more our unity; let us strive to live ever more intensely the sacred triduum of the Passover of our Lord Jesus Christ.

From the Vatican, April 8, Passion Sunday (Palm Sunday), in the year 1979, the first of the Pontificate.

Endnotes

1. Phil 2: 8.
2. Jn 14: 18.
3. Mt 28: 20.
4. Jn 15: 15-16.
5. Cf. Heb 9: 12.
6. Cf. *Lumen gentium*, 28.
7. Jn 15: 16.
8. Cf. Jn 15: 1-8.
9. Jn 15: 5.

LETTER
OF THE HOLY FATHER
POPE JOHN PAUL II
TO ALL THE PRIESTS OF THE CHURCH
ON THE OCCASION OF HOLY THURSDAY 1979

Dear Brother Priests!

1.   For You I Am a Bishop, with You I Am a Priest

At the beginning of my new ministry in the Church, I feel the deep
need to speak to you, to all of you without any exception, priests
both diocesan and religious, who are my brothers by virtue of the
Sacrament of Orders. From the very beginning I wish to express my
faith in the vocation that unites you to your bishops, in a special
communion of sacrament and ministry, through which the Church,
the Mystical Body of Christ, is built up. To all of you therefore, who,
by virtue of a special grace and through a singular gift of our Savior, bear "the burden of the day and the heat"[1] in the midst of the
many tasks of the priestly and pastoral ministry, I have addressed my
thoughts and my heart from the moment when Christ called me to
this See, where St. Peter, with his life and his death, had to respond
until the end to the question: Do you love me? Do you love me more
than these do?[2]

I think of you all the time, I pray for you, with you I *seek the ways of
spiritual union and collaboration*, because by virtue of the Sacrament
of Orders, which I also received from the hands of my bishop (the
Metropolitan of Krakow, Adam Stephen Cardinal Sapieha, of unforgettable memory), you are my brothers. And so, adapting the words
of St. Augustine,[3] I want to say to you today: "For you I am a bishop,
with you I am a priest." Today, in fact, there is a special circumstance
that impels me to confide to you some thoughts that I enclose in this
letter: it is the nearness of Holy Thursday. It is this, the annual feast
of our priesthood, that unites the whole presbyterium of each diocese
about its bishop in the shared celebration of the Eucharist. It is on
this day that all priests are invited to renew, before their own bishop
and together with him, the promises they made at their priestly ordination; and this fact enables me, together with all my brothers in
the episcopate, to be joined to you in a special unity, and especially

to be in the very heart of the mystery of Jesus Christ, the mystery in which we all share.

The Second Vatican Council, which so explicitly highlighted the collegiality of the episcopate in the Church, also gave a new form to the life of the priestly communities, joined together by a special bond of brotherhood, and united to the bishop of the respective local church. The whole priestly life and ministry serve to deepen and strengthen that bond; and a particular responsibility for the various tasks involved by this life and ministry is taken on by the Priests' Councils, which, in conformity with the thought of the council and the Motu Proprio *Ecclesiæ sanctæ*[4] of Paul VI, should be functioning in every diocese. All this is meant to ensure that each bishop, in union with his presbyterium, can serve ever more effectively the great cause of evangelization. Through this service the Church realizes her mission, indeed her very nature. The importance of the unity of the priests with their own bishop on this point is confirmed by the words of St. Ignatius of Antioch: "Strive to do all things in the harmony of God, with the bishop presiding to represent God, the presbyters representing the council of the apostles, and the deacons, so dear to me, entrusted with the service of Jesus Christ."[5]

2. Love for Christ and the Church Unites Us

It is not my intention to include in this letter everything that makes up the richness of the priestly life and ministry. In this regard I refer to the whole tradition of the magisterium and of the Church, and in a special way to the doctrine of the Second Vatican Council, contained in the council's various documents, especially in the Constitution *Lumen gentium* and the Decrees *Presbyterorum ordinis* and *Ad gentes*. I also wish to recall the encyclical of my predecessor Paul VI, *Sacerdotalis cælibatus*. Finally, I wish to place great importance upon the Document *De sacerdotio ministeriali*, which Paul VI approved as the fruit of the labors of the 1971 Synod of Bishops, because I find in this document—although the session of the synod that elaborated it had only a consultative form—a statement of essential importance regarding the specific aspect of the priestly life and ministry in the modern world.

Referring to all these sources, which you are familiar with, I wish in the present letter *only to mention a number of points* which seem to me to be of extreme importance at this moment in the history of the Church and of the world. These are words that are dictated to me by my love for the Church, which will be able to carry out her mission to the world only if—in spite of all human weakness—she maintains her fidelity to Christ. I know that I am addressing those whom only the love of Christ has enabled, by means of a specific vocation, to give themselves to the service of the Church and, in the Church, to the service of man for the solution of the most important problems, and especially those regarding man's eternal salvation.

Although at the beginning of these considerations I refer to many written sources and official documents, nevertheless I wish to refer especially to that living source which is our shared love for Christ and his Church, a love that springs from the grace of the priestly vocation, the love that is the greatest gift of the Holy Spirit.[6]

3.   Chosen from Among Men
"Appointed to Act on Behalf of Men"[7]

The Second Vatican Council deepened the idea of the priesthood and presented it, throughout its teaching, as the expression of the inner forces, those "dynamisms," whereby the mission of the whole People of God in the Church is constituted. Here one should refer especially to the Constitution *Lumen gentium*, and reread carefully the relevant paragraphs. The mission of the People of God is carried out through the sharing in the office and mission of Jesus Christ himself, which, as we know, has a triple dimension: it is the mission and office of Prophet, Priest and King. If we analyze carefully the conciliar texts, it is obvious that one should speak of a triple dimension of Christ's service and mission, rather than of three different functions. In fact, these functions are closely linked to one another, explain one another, condition one another and clarify one another. Consequently, it is from this threefold unity that our sharing in Christ's mission and office takes its origin. As Christians, members of the People of God, and subsequently, as priests, sharers in the hierarchical order, we take our origin from the combination of the mission and office of our Teacher, who is Prophet, Priest and King, in order to witness to him in a special way in the Church and before the world.

The priesthood in which we share through the Sacrament of Orders, which has been forever "imprinted" on our souls through a special sign from God, that is to say the "character," *remains in explicit relationship with the common priesthood of the faithful*, that is to say the priesthood of all baptized, but at the same time it differs from that priesthood "essentially and not only in degree."[8] In this way the words of the author of the Letter to the Hebrews about the priest, who has been "chosen from among men . . . appointed to act on behalf of men,"[9] take on their full meaning.

At this point, it is better to reread once more the whole of this classical conciliar text, which expresses the basic truths on the theme of our vocation in the Church:

> Christ the Lord, high priest taken from among men (cf. Heb 5: 1), made the new people "a kingdom of priests to God, his Father" (Rv 1: 6, cf. 5: 9-10). The baptized, by regeneration and the anointing of the Holy Spirit, are consecrated to be a spiritual house and a holy priesthood, that through all the works of Christian men they may offer spiritual sacrifices and proclaim the perfection of Him who has called them out of darkness into His marvelous light (cf. 1 Pt 2: 4-10). Therefore all the disciples of Christ, persevering in prayer and praising God together (cf. Acts 2: 42-47), should present themselves as a sacrifice, living, holy and pleasing to God (cf. Rom 12: 1). They should everywhere on earth bear witness to Christ and give an answer to everyone who asks a reason for the hope of an eternal life which is theirs (cf. 1 Pt 3: 15).
>
> Though they differ essentially and not only in degree, the common priesthood of the faithful and the ministerial or hierarchical priesthood are nonetheless ordered one to another; each in its own proper way shares in the one Priesthood of Christ. The ministerial priest, by the sacred power that he has, forms and rules the priestly people; in the person of Christ he effects the Eucharistic Sacrifice and offers it to God in the name of all the people. The faithful indeed, by virtue of their royal priesthood, participate in the offering of the Eucharist. They exercise that priesthood, too, by the reception of the sacraments, prayer and thanksgiving, the witness of a holy life, abnegation and active charity.[10]

4. The Priest As a Gift of Christ for the Community

We must consider down to the smallest detail not only the theoretical meaning but also the existential meaning of the mutual "relation" that exists between the hierarchical priesthood and the common priesthood of the faithful. The fact that they differ not only in degree but also in essence is a fruit of a particular aspect of the richness of the very Priesthood of Christ, which is the one center and the one source both of that participation which belongs to all baptized and of that other participation which is reached through a distinct sacrament, which is precisely the Sacrament of Orders. This sacrament, dear brothers, which is specific for us, which is the fruit of the special grace of vocation and the basis of our identity, by virtue of its very nature and of everything that it produces in our life and activity, serves to make the faithful aware of their common priesthood and to activate it: [11] the sacrament reminds them that they are the People of God and enables them "to offer spiritual sacrifices,"[12] through which Christ himself makes us an everlasting gift to the Father.[13] This takes place, above all, when the priest "by the sacred power that he has . . . in the person of Christ (*in persona Christi*) effects the Eucharistic Sacrifice and offers it to God in the name of all the people,"[14] as we read in the conciliar text quoted above.

Our sacramental priesthood, therefore, is a "hierarchical" and at the same time "ministerial" priesthood. It constitutes a special ministerium, that is to say "service," in relation to the community of believers. It does not, however, take its origin from that community, as though it were the community that "called" or "delegated." The sacramental priesthood is truly a gift for this community and comes from Christ himself, from the fullness of his Priesthood. This fullness finds its expression in the fact that Christ, while making everyone capable of offering the spiritual sacrifice, calls some and enables them to be ministers of his own sacramental sacrifice, the Eucharist—in the offering of which all the faithful share—in which are taken up all the spiritual sacrifices of the People of God.

Conscious of this reality, we understand how our priesthood is "hierarchical," that is to say connected with the power of forming and governing the priestly people[15] and *precisely for this reason "ministerial."* We carry out this office, through which Christ himself unceasingly "serves" the Father in the work of our salvation. Our whole priestly existence is and must be deeply imbued with this service, if we wish to effect in an adequate way the Eucharistic Sacrifice *in persona Christi.*

The priesthood calls for a particular integrity of life and service, and precisely such integrity is supremely fitting for our priestly identity. In that identity there are expressed, at the same time, the greatness of our dignity and the "availability" proportionate to it: it is a question of the humble readiness to accept the gifts of the Holy Spirit and to transmit to others the fruits of love and peace, to give them that certainty of faith from which derive the profound understanding of the meaning of human existence and the capacity to introduce the moral order into the life of individuals and of the human setting.

Since the priesthood is given to us so that we can unceasingly serve others, after the example of Christ the Lord, the priesthood cannot be renounced because of the difficulties that we meet and the sacrifices asked of us. Like the Apostles, "we have left everything to follow Christ,"[16] therefore we must persevere beside him also through the cross.

5. In the Service of the Good Shepherd

As I write, there pass before the eyes of my soul the vast and varied areas of human life, areas into which you are sent, dear brothers, like laborers into the Lord's vineyard.[17] But for you there holds also the parable of the flock,[18] for, thanks to the priestly character, you share in the *pastoral charism*, which is a sign of a special relationship of *likeness to Christ, the Good Shepherd.* You are precisely marked with this quality in a very special way. Although care for the salvation of others is and must be a task of every member of the great community of the People of God, that is to say also of all our brothers and sisters who make up the laity—as the Second Vatican Council so amply declared[19]—nevertheless you priests are expected to have a care and commitment which are far greater and different from those of any lay person. And this is because your sharing in the Priesthood of Jesus Christ differs from their sharing, "essentially and not only in degree."[20] In fact, the Priesthood of Jesus Christ is the first source and expression of an unceasing and ever effective care for our salvation, which enables us to look to him precisely as the Good Shepherd. Do not the words "the Good Shepherd is one who lays down his life for his sheep"[21] refer to the Sacrifice of the Cross, to the definitive act of Christ's Priesthood? Do they not show all of us that Christ the Lord, through the Sacrament of Orders, has made us sharers in his Priesthood, the road that we too must travel? Do these words not tell us that our vocation is a singular *solicitude for the salvation of our neighbor*? that this solicitude is a special *raison d'être* of our priestly life? that it is precisely this solicitude that gives it meaning, and that only through this solicitude can we find the full significance of our own life, perfection and holiness? This theme is taken up, at various places, in the conciliar Decree *Optatam totius*.[22]

However, this matter becomes more comprehensible in the light of the words of our same Teacher, who says: "For anyone who wants to save his life will lose it; but anyone who loses his life for my sake, and for the sake of the Gospel, will save it."[23] These are mysterious words, and they seem like a paradox. But they cease to be mysterious if we try to put them into practice. Then the paradox disappears, and the profound simplicity of their meaning is fully revealed. May all of us be granted this grace in our priestly life and zealous service.

6. "The Supreme Art Is the Direction of Souls"[24]

The special care for the salvation of others, for truth, for the love and holiness of the whole People of God, for the spiritual unity of the Church this care that has been entrusted to us by Christ, together with the priestly power, is exercised in various ways. Of course there is a difference in the ways in which you, dear brothers, fulfill your priestly vocation: some in the ordinary pastoral work of parishes; others in mission lands; still others in the field of activities connected with the teaching, training and education of youth, or working in the various spheres and organizations whereby you assist in the development of social and cultural life; yet others near the suffering, the sick, the neglected, and sometimes, you yourselves bedridden and in pain. These ways differ from one another, and it is just impossible to name them all one by one. They are necessarily numerous and different, because of the variety in the structure of human life, in social processes, and in the heritage and historical traditions of the various cultures and civilizations. Nevertheless, within all these differences, *you are always and everywhere the bearers of your particular vocation*: you are bearers of the grace of Christ, the eternal Priest, and bearers of the charism of the Good Shepherd. And this you can never forget; this you can never renounce; this you must put into practice at every moment, in every place and in every way. In this consists that "supreme art" to which Jesus Christ has called you. "The supreme art is the direction of souls," wrote St. Gregory the Great.

I say to you therefore, quoting these words of his: Strive to be "artists" of pastoral work. There have been many such in the history of the Church. There speak to each of us, for example, St. Vincent de Paul, St. John of Avila, the holy Curé of Ars, St. John Bosco, Blessed Maximilian Kolbe, and many, many others. Each of them was different from the others, was himself, was the son of his own time and was "up to date" with respect to his own time. But this "bringing up to date" of each of them was an original response to the Gospel, a response needed precisely for those times; it was the response of holiness and zeal. There is no other rule apart from this for "bringing ourselves up to date," in our priestly life and activity, with our time and with the world as it is today. Without any doubt, the various attempts and projects aimed at the "secularization" of the priestly life cannot be considered an adequate "bringing up to date."

7. Steward and Witness

The priestly life is built upon the foundation of the Sacrament of Orders, which imprints on our soul the mark of an indelible character. This mark, impressed in the depths of our being, has its "personalistic" dynamism. *The priestly personality must be for others a clear and plain sign and indication.* This is the first condition for our pastoral service. The people from among whom we have been chosen and for whom we have been appointed[25] want above all to see in us such a sign and indication, and to this they have a right. It may sometimes seem to us that they do not want this, or that they wish us to be in every way "like them"; at times it even seems that they demand this of us. And here one very much needs a profound "sense of faith" and "the gift of discernment." In fact, it is very easy to let oneself be guided by appearances and fall victim to a fundamental illusion in what is essential. Those who call for the secularization of priestly life and applaud its various manifestations will undoubtedly abandon us when we succumb to temptation. We shall then cease to be necessary and popular. Our time is characterized by different forms of "manipulation" and "exploitation" of man, but we cannot give in to any of these.[26] In practical terms, the only priest who will always prove necessary to people is the priest who is conscious of the full meaning of his priesthood: the priest who believes profoundly, who professes his faith with courage, who prays fervently, who teaches with deep conviction, who serves, who puts into practice in his own life the program of the Beatitudes, who knows how to love disinterestedly, who is close to everyone, and especially to those who are most in need.

Our pastoral activity demands that we should be close to people and all their problems, whether these problems be personal, family or social ones, but it also demands that we should be close to all these problems "in a priestly way." Only then, in the sphere of all those problems, do we remain ourselves. Therefore if we are really of assistance in those human problems, and they are sometimes very difficult ones, then we keep our identity and are really faithful to our vocation. With great perspicacity we must seek, together with all men, truth and justice, the true and definitive dimension of which we can only find in the Gospel, or rather in Christ himself. Our task is to serve *truth and justice* in the dimensions of human "temporal-ity," but *always in a perspective that is the perspective of eternal salvation*. This salvation takes into account the temporal achievements of the human spirit in the spheres of knowledge and morality, as the Second Vatican Council wonderfully recalled,[27] but it is not identical with them, and in fact it goes higher than them: "The things that no eye has seen and no ear has heard . . . all that God has prepared for those who love him."[28] Our brethren in the faith, and unbelievers too, expect us always to be able to show them this perspective, to become real witnesses to it, to be dispensers of grace, to be servants of the word of God. They expect us to be men of prayer.

Among us there are also those who have united their priestly vocation in a special way with an intense life of prayer and penance in the strictly contemplative form of their religious orders. Let them remember that their priestly ministry also in this form is—in a special way—"ordered" to the great solicitude of the Good Shepherd—solicitude for the salvation of every human being.

And this we must all remember: that it is not lawful for any of us to deserve the name of "hireling," that is to say, the name of one "to whom the sheep do not belong," one who, "since he is not the shepherd and the sheep do not belong to him, abandons the sheep and runs away as soon as he sees the wolf coming, and then the wolf attacks and scatters the sheep; this is because he is only a hired man and has no concern for the sheep."[29] The solicitude of every good shepherd is that all people "May have life and have it to the full,"[30] so that none of them may be lost,[31] but should have eternal life. Let us endeavor to make this solicitude penetrate deeply into our souls; let us strive to live it. May it characterize our personality and be at the foundation of our priestly identity.

8. Meaning of Celibacy

Allow me at this point to touch upon the question of priestly celibacy. I shall deal with it summarily, because it has already been considered in a profound and complete way during the council, and subsequently in the Encyclical *Sacerdotalis cælibatus*, and again at the ordinary session of the 1971 Synod of Bishops. This reflection has shown itself to be necessary both in order to present the matter in a still more mature way, and also in order to explain even more deeply the meaning of the decision that the Latin Church took so many centuries ago and to which she has sought to be faithful, and desires to maintain this fidelity also in the future. The importance of the question under consideration is so great, and its link with the language of the gospel itself so close, that in this case we cannot reason with categories different from those used by the council, the Synod of Bishops and the great Pope Paul VI himself. We can only seek to understand this question more deeply and to respond to it more maturely, freeing ourselves from the various objections that have always—as happens today too—been raised against priestly celibacy, and also freeing ourselves from the different interpretations that appeal to criteria alien to the gospel, to tradition and to the Church's magisterium—criteria, we would add, whose "anthropological" correctness and basis in fact are seen to be very dubious and of relative value.

Nor must we be too surprised at all the objections and criticisms which have intensified during the postconciliar period, even though today in some places they seem to be growing less. Did not Jesus Christ, after he had presented the disciples with the question of the renunciation of marriage "for the sake of the kingdom of heaven," add these significant words: "Let anyone accept this who can"?[32] The Latin Church has wished, and continues to wish, referring to the example of Christ the Lord himself, to the apostolic teaching and to the whole tradition that is proper to her, that *all those who receive the Sacrament of Orders should embrace this renunciation "for the sake of the kingdom of heaven."* This tradition, however, is linked with respect for different traditions of other churches. In fact, this tradition constitutes a characteristic, a peculiarity and a heritage of the Latin Catholic Church, a tradition to which she owes much and in which she is resolved to persevere, in spite of all the difficulties to which such fidelity could be exposed, and also in spite of the various symptoms of weakness and crisis in individual priests. We are all aware that "we have this treasure in earthen vessels,"[33] yet we know very well that it is precisely a treasure.

Why is it a treasure? Do we wish thereby to reduce the value of marriage and the vocation to family life? Or are we succumbing to a Manichean contempt for the human body and its functions? Do we wish in some way to devalue love, which leads a man and a woman to marriage and the wedded unity of the body, thus forming "one flesh"?[34] How could we think and reason like that, if we know, believe and proclaim, following St. Paul, that marriage is a "great mystery" in reference to Christ and the Church?[35] However, none of the reasons whereby people sometimes try to "convince us" of the inopportuneness of celibacy corresponds to the truth, the truth that the Church proclaims and seeks to realize in life through the commitment to which priests oblige themselves before ordination.

The essential, proper and adequate reason, in fact, is contained in the truth that Christ declared when he spoke about the renunciation of marriage for the sake of the kingdom of heaven, and which St. Paul proclaimed when he wrote that each person in the Church has his or her own particular gifts.[36] Celibacy is precisely a "gift of the Spirit." A similar though different gift is contained in the vocation to true and faithful married love, directed towards procreation according to the flesh, in the very lofty context of the Sacrament of Matrimony. It is obvious that this gift is fundamental for the building up of the great community of the Church, the People of God. But if this community wishes to respond fully to its vocation in Jesus Christ, there will also have to be realized in it, in the correct proportion, that other "gift," the gift of celibacy "for the sake of the kingdom of heaven."[37]

Why does the Latin Catholic Church link this gift not only with the life of those who accept the strict program of the evangelical counsels in religious institutes but also with the vocation to the hierarchical and ministerial priesthood? She does it because celibacy "for the sake of the kingdom" is not only an eschatological sign; it also has a great social meaning, in the present life, for the service of the People of God. Through his celibacy, the priest becomes the man "for others," in a different way from the man who, by binding himself in conjugal union with a woman, also becomes, as husband and father, a man "for others," especially in the radius of his own family: for his wife and, together with her, for the children, to whom he gives life. The priest, by renouncing this fatherhood proper to married men, seeks another fatherhood and, as it were, even another motherhood, re-calling the words of the Apostle about the children whom he begets in suffering.[38] These are children of his spirit, people entrusted to his solicitude by the Good Shepherd. These people are many, more numerous than an ordinary human family can embrace. The pas-toral vocation of priests is great, and the council teaches that it is universal: it is directed towards the whole Church,[39] and therefore it is of a missionary character. Normally, it is linked to the service of a particular community of the People of God, in which each individual expects attention, care and love. The heart of the priest, in order that it may be available for this service, must be free. Celibacy is a sign of a freedom that exists for the sake of service. According to this sign, the hierarchical or ministerial priesthood is, according to the tradition of our Church, more strictly "ordered" to the common priesthood of the faithful.

9. Test and Responsibility

The often widespread view that priestly celibacy in the Catholic Church is an institution imposed by law on those who receive the Sacrament of Orders is the result of a misunderstanding, if not of downright bad faith. We all know that it is not so. Every Christian who receives the Sacrament of Orders commits himself to celibacy with full awareness and freedom, after a training lasting a number of years, and after profound reflection and assiduous prayer. He decides upon a life of celibacy only after he has reached a firm conviction that Christ is giving him this "gift" for the good of the Church and the service of others. Only then does he commit himself to observe celibacy for his entire life. It is obvious that such a decision obliges not only by virtue of a law laid down by the Church but also by virtue of personal responsibility. It is a matter here of *keeping one's word to Christ and the Church*. Keeping one's word is, at one and the same time, a duty and a proof of the priest's inner maturity; it is the expression of his personal dignity. It is shown in all its clarity when this keeping one's promise to Christ, made through a conscious and free commitment to celibacy for the whole of one's life, encounters difficulties, is put to the test, or is exposed to temptation—all things that do not spare the priest, any more than they spare any other Christian. At such a moment, the individual must seek support in more fervent prayer. Through prayer, he must find within himself that attitude of humility and sincerity before God and his own conscience; prayer is indeed the source of strength for sustaining what is wavering. Then it is that there is born a confidence like the confidence expressed by St. Paul in the words: "There is nothing that I cannot master with the help of the One who gives me strength."[40] These truths are confirmed by the experience of many priests and proved by the reality of life. The acceptance of these truths constitutes the basis of fidelity to the promise made to Christ and the Church, and that promise is at the same time the proof of genuine fidelity to oneself, one's own conscience, and one's own humanity and dignity. One must think of all these things especially at moments of crisis, and not have recourse to a dispensation, understood as an "administrative intervention," as though in fact it were not, on the contrary, a matter of a profound question of conscience and a test of humanity. God has a right to test each one of us in this way, since this earthly life is a time of testing for every human being. But God also wishes us all to emerge victorious from such tests, and he gives us adequate help for this.

Perhaps, not without good reason, one should add at this point that the commitment to married fidelity, which derives from the Sacrament of Matrimony, creates similar obligations in its own sphere; this married commitment sometimes becomes a source of similar trials and experiences for husbands and wives, who also have a way of proving the value of their love in these "trials by fire." Love, in fact, in all its dimensions, is not only a call but also a duty. Finally, we should add that our brothers and sisters joined by the marriage bond *have the right to expect from us, priests and pastors, good example and the witness of fidelity* to one's vocation until death, a fidelity to the vocation that we choose through the Sacrament of Orders just as they choose it through the Sacrament of Matrimony. Also in this sphere and in this sense we should understand our ministerial priesthood as "subordination" to the common priesthood of all the faithful, of the laity, especially of those who live in marriage and form a family. In this way, we serve in "building up the body of Christ";[41] otherwise, instead of cooperating in the building up of that body we weaken its spiritual structure. Closely linked to this building up of the body of Christ is the authentic development of the human personality of each Christian—as also of each priest—a development that takes place according to the measure of the gift of Christ. The disorganization of the spiritual structure of the Church certainly does not favor the development of the human personality and does not constitute its proper testing.

10. Every Day We Have to Be Converted Anew

"What must we do, then?":[42] dear brothers, this seems to be your question, just as the disciples and those who listened to Christ the Lord asked him so often. What must the Church do, when it seems that there is a lack of priests, when their absence makes itself felt especially in certain countries and regions of the world? How are we to respond to the immense needs of evangelization, and how can we satisfy the hunger for the Word and the Body of the Lord? The Church, which commits herself to maintaining priestly celibacy as a particular gift for the kingdom of God, *professes faith in and expresses hope in* her Teacher, Redeemer and Spouse, and at the same time in him who is "Lord of the harvest" and "giver of the gift."[43] In fact, "every perfect gift is from above, coming down from the Father of lights."[44] We for our part cannot weaken this faith and confidence with our human doubting or our timidity.

In consequence, we must all be converted anew every day. We know that this is a fundamental exigency of the Gospel, addressed to everyone,[45] and all the more do we have to consider it as addressed to us. If we have the duty of helping others to be converted we have to do the same continuously in our own lives. Being converted means returning to the very grace of our vocation; it means meditating upon the infinite goodness and love of Christ, who has addressed each of us and, calling us by name, has said: "Follow me." Being converted means continually "giving an account" before the Lord of our hearts about our service, our zeal and our fidelity, for we are "Christ's servants, stewards entrusted with the mysteries of God."[46] Being converted also means "giving an account" of our negligences and sins, of our timidity, of our lack of faith and hope, of our thinking only "in a human way" and not "in a divine way." Let us recall, in this regard, the warning that Christ gave to Peter himself.[47] Being converted means, for us, seeking again the pardon and strength of God in the Sacrament of Reconciliation, and thus always beginning anew, and every day progressing, overcoming ourselves, making spiritual conquests, giving cheerfully, for "God loves a cheerful giver."[48]

Being converted means "to pray continually and never lose heart."[49] *In a certain way prayer is the first and last condition for conversion,* spiritual progress and holiness. Perhaps in these recent years—at least in certain quarters—there has been too much discussion about the priesthood, the priest's "identity," the value of his presence in the modern world, etc., and on the other hand there has been too little praying. There has not been enough enthusiasm for actuating the priesthood itself through prayer, in order to make its authentic evangelical dynamism effective, in order to confirm the priestly identity. It is prayer that shows the essential style of the priest; without prayer this style becomes deformed. Prayer helps us always to find the light that has led us since the beginning of our priestly vocation, and which never ceases to lead us, even though it seems at times to disappear in the darkness. Prayer enables us to be converted continually, to remain in a state of continuous reaching out to God, which is essential if we wish to lead others to him. Prayer helps us to believe, to hope and to love, even when our human weakness hinders us.

Prayer likewise enables us continually to rediscover the dimensions of that kingdom for whose coming we pray every day, when we repeat the words that Christ taught us. Then we realize what *our place is in the realization of the petition:* "Thy kingdom come," and we see how necessary we are in its realization. And perhaps, when we pray, we shall see more easily those "fields . . . already white for harvest"[50] and we shall understand the meaning of Christ's words as he looked at them: "So ask the Lord of the harvest to send laborers to his harvest."[51]

We must link prayer with continuous work upon ourselves: this is the *formatio permanens*. As is rightly pointed out by the document on this theme issued by the Sacred Congregation for the Clergy,[52] this formation must be both interior, that is to say directed towards the deepening of the priest's spiritual life, and must also be pastoral and intellectual (philosophical and theological). Therefore since our pastoral activity, the proclamation of the Word and the whole of the priestly ministry depend upon the intensity of our interior life, that activity must also find sustenance in assiduous study. It is not enough for us to stop at what we once learned in the seminary, even in cases where those studies were done at university level, which the Sacred Congregation for Catholic Education resolutely recommends. This process of intellectual formation must last all one's life, especially in modern times, which are marked—at least in many parts of the world— by widespread development of education and culture. To the people who enjoy the benefits of this development we must be witnesses to Jesus Christ, and properly qualified ones. As teachers of truth and morality, we must tell them, convincingly and effectively, of the hope that gives us life.[53] And this also forms part of the process of daily conversion to love, through the truth.

Dear brothers, you who have borne "the burden of the day and the heat,"[54] who have put your hand to the plough and do not turn back,[55] and perhaps even more those of you who are doubtful of the meaning of your vocation or of the value of your service: think of the places where people anxiously await a priest, and where for many years, feeling the lack of such a priest, they do not cease to hope for his presence. And sometimes it happens that they meet in an abandoned shrine, and place on the altar a stole which they still keep, and recite all the prayers of the Eucharistic Liturgy; and then, at the moment that corresponds to the transubstantiation a deep silence comes down upon them, a silence sometimes broken by a sob . . . so ardently do they desire to hear the words that only the lips of a priest can efficaciously utter. So much do they desire Eucharistic Communion, in which they can share only through the ministry of a priest, just as they also so eagerly wait to hear the divine words of pardon: *Ego te absolvo a peccatis tuis*! So deeply do they feel the absence of a priest among them! . . . Such places are not lacking in the world. So if one of you doubts the meaning of his priesthood, if he thinks it is "socially" fruitless or useless, reflect on this!

We must be converted every day, we must rediscover every day the gift obtained from Christ himself in the Sacrament of Orders, by penetrating the importance of the salvific mission of the Church and by reflecting on the great meaning of our vocation in the light of that mission.

11. Mother of Priests

Dear brothers, at the beginning of my ministry I entrust all of you to the Mother of Christ, who in a special way is our Mother: the Mother of priests. In fact, the beloved disciple, who, as one of the Twelve, had heard in the Upper Room the words "Do this in memory of me,"[56] was given by Christ on the cross to his Mother, with the words: "Behold your son."[57] The man who on Holy Thursday received the power to celebrate the Eucharist was, by these words of the dying Redeemer, given to his Mother as her "son." All of us, therefore, who receive the same power through priestly ordination have in a certain sense a prior right to see her as our Mother. And so I desire that all of you, together with me, should find in Mary the Mother of the Priesthood which we have received from Christ. I also desire that you should entrust your priesthood to her in a special way. Allow me to do it myself, *entrusting to the Mother of Christ* each one of you—without any exception—in a solemn and at the same time simple and humble way. And I ask each of you, dear brothers, to do it yourselves, in the way dictated to you by your own heart, especially by your love for Christ the Priest, and also by your own weakness, which goes hand in hand with your desire for service and holiness. I ask you to do this.

The Church of today speaks of herself especially in the Dogmatic Constitution *Lumen gentium.* Here too, in the last chapter, she proclaims that she looks to Mary as to the Mother of Christ, because she calls herself a mother and wishes to be a mother, begetting people for God to a new life.[58] Now, dear brothers, how near you are to this cause of God! How deeply it is imprinted upon your vocation, ministry and mission. In consequence, in the midst of the People of God, who look to Mary with immense love and hope, you must look to her with exceptional hope and love. Indeed, you must proclaim Christ who is her Son; and who will better communicate to you the truth about him than his Mother? You must nourish human hearts with Christ; and who can make you more aware of what you are doing than she who nourished him? "Hail, true Body, born of the Virgin Mary." In our ministerial priesthood there is the *wonderful and penetrating dimension of nearness to the Mother of Christ.* So let us try to live in that dimension. If I may be permitted to speak here of my own experience, I will say to you that in writing to you I am referring especially to my own personal experience.

As I communicate all this to you, at the beginning of my service to the universal Church, I do not cease to ask God to fill you, priests of Jesus Christ, with every blessing and grace, and as a token of this communion in prayer I bless you with all my heart, in the name of the Father and of the Son and of the Holy Spirit.

Accept this blessing. Accept the words of the new successor of Peter, that Peter whom the Lord commanded: "And once you have recovered, you in your turn must strengthen your brothers."[59] Do not cease to pray for me together with the whole Church, so that I may respond to that exigency of a primacy of love that the Lord made the foundation of the mission of Peter, when he said to him: "Feed my lambs."[60] Amen.

From the Vatican, April 9, Passion Sunday (Palm Sunday), in the year 1979, the first of the Pontificate.

Endnotes

1. Cf. Mt 20: 12.
2. Cf. Jn 21: 15ff.
3. *Vobis enim sum episcopus, vobiscum sum Christianus*: Serm. 340, 1: PL 38, 1483.
4. Cf. I art. 15.
5. *Epistula ad Magnesios*, VI, 1: Patres Apostolici I, ed. Funk, p. 235.
6. Cf. Rom 5: 5; 1 Cor 12: 31; 13.
7. Heb 5: 1.
8. *Lumen gentium*, 10.
9. Heb 5: 1.
10. *Lumen gentium*, 10.
11. Cf. Eph 4: 11-12.
12. Cf. 1 Pt 2: 5.
13. Cf. 1 Pt 3: 18.
14. *Lumen gentium*, 10.
15. Cf. *Lumen gentium*, 10.
16. Cf. Mt 19: 27.
17. Cf. Mt 20: 1-16.
18. Cf. Jn 10: 1-16.
19. Cf. *Lumen gentium*, 11.
20. *Lumen gentium*, 10.

21. Jn 10: 11.
22. Cf. 8-11; 19-20.
23. Mk 8: 35.
24. St. Gregory the Great, *Regula Pastoralis*, I, 1: PL 77, 14.
25. Cf. Heb 5: 1.
26. "Let us not deceive ourselves in thinking we serve the Gospel if we try'to dilute' our priestly charism . . . ": Pope John Paul II, Discourse to the Clergy of Rome (November 9, 1978), n. 3:"L'Osservatore Romano"(November 10, 1978), p. 2.
27. Cf. *Gaudium et spes*, 38-39, 42.
28. 1 Cor 2: 9.
29. Jn 10: 12-13.
30. Jn 10: 10.
31. Cf. Jn 17: 12.
32. Mt 19: 12.
33. Cf. 2 Cor 4: 7.
34. Gen 2: 24; cf. Mt 19: 6.
35. Cf. Eph 5: 32.
36. Cf. 1 Cor 7: 7.
37. Mt 19: 12.
38. Cf. 1 Cor 4: 15; Gal 4: 19.
39. Cf. *Presbyterorum ordinis*, 3, 6, 10, 12.
40. Phil 4: 13.
41. Eph 4: 12.
42. Lk 3: 10.
43. Mt 9: 38; cf. 1 Cor 7: 7.
44. Jas 1: 17.
45. Cf. Mt 4: 17; Mk 1: 15.
46. 1 Cor 4: 1.
47. Cf. Mt 16: 23.
48. 2 Cor 9: 7.
49. Lk 18: 1.
50. Jn 4: 35.
51. Mt 9: 38.
52. Cf. Circular Letter of November 4, 1969: AAS 62 (1970), pp. 123ff.
53. Cf. 1 Pt 3: 15.
54. Mt 20: 12.
55. Cf. Lk 9: 62.
56. Lk 22: 19.
57. Jn 19: 26.
58. Cf. *Lumen gentium*, 8.
59. Lk 22: 32.
60. Jn 21: 16.

1980

Second Year of Pontificate

Unlike the previous year when he wrote a letter to bishops and another to priests, in 1980 the Holy Father only wrote a letter on the occasion of Holy Thursday, *Dominicæ cenæ*, addressed to all the bishops of the Church, dated on the First Sunday of Lent, February 24.

At the beginning of the letter the pope recalled that "many priests expressed their joy, both because of the profound and solemn character of Holy Thursday as the annual 'feast of priests' and also because of the importance of the subjects dealt with in the letter addressed to them" (1980 Letter, n. 1). And he added that "those to whom this letter is directly addressed are you, the bishops of the Church; together with you, all the priests; and, in their own rank, the deacons too" (1980 Letter, n. 2).

Early this year the pope published the Apostolic Letter *Patres Ecclesiæ* on the sixteenth centenary of St. Basil (January 2) and the Apostolic Letter *Amantissima Providentia* on the sixth centenary of the death of St. Catherine of Siena.

In 1980 John Paul II made four pastoral journeys outside Italy: to six African countries, Zaire, Congo, Kenya, Ghana, Upper Volta and Ivory Coast (May 2-12); France (May 30–June 2); Brazil (June 30–July 12); and Germany (November 15-19). At the end of the year, the Holy Father spoke about the meaning of his pastoral trips. "There rise before me, at this moment, the faces of the individual nations visited in the pastoral journeys that God has granted me to carry out this year. . . . I already spoke last June of the ecclesial meaning of these journeys, the possibilities they offer of meeting even brothers of other churches, members of other religions, and also non-believers. . . . In the various journeys—which, with God's help, and as I have announced, will soon resume in a worldwide range, touching other peoples of different and ancient civilization—the Church, by means of her visible Head, becomes concretely acquainted with the situations characteristic of the various nations, thus meeting the intense desire that springs up within those same nations" (Address to the College of Cardinals, December 22, nn. 5-6).

The first Synod of Bishops during his pontificate took place from September 26 to October 25. Its theme was the role of the Christian family in the modern world. In an apostolic letter dated August 15 asking for prayers for the synod, the pope said: "When in the near future the Synod of Bishops begins, the whole Church must take part in its work. The whole Church must in a sense be at the synod, present above all by prayer and sacrifice. Let all the Church's children pray and make spiritual offerings for the synod to obtain God's light and strength for the assembled synod Fathers. The family is a cell from which come all the vocations and states of life in the Church" (Apostolic Letter, August 15, n. 2).

In the homily at the opening of the synod, the pope said: "May the Holy Spirit guide and sustain all our work during this assembly which begins today. . . . All our work during the following days will be nothing but a service rendered to humanity: to our brothers and sisters, to spouses and parents, to youth, to children, to generations, to families" (Homily, September 26, n. 7). In the concluding address he remarked: "We are all grateful, because we could complete this synod. . . . We are grateful because we could see the family as it really is in the Church and in the modern world. . . . We are grateful because, with the outlook of faith, we could reexamine the eternal plan of God concerning the family. . . . Finally we are grateful that we could define, according to the eternal plan concerning life and love, the roles of the family in the Church and in the modern world" (Address, October 25, n. 3).

At the end of 1980 the Holy Father issued his second encyclical, *Dives in misericordia*, on the mercy of God (November 30) and the Apostolic Letter *Egregiæ virtutis* (December 31) proclaiming the Apostles of the Slavs, Saints Cyril and Methodius, co-patrons of Europe, along with St. Benedict, whose centennial year just ended.

During most of the General Audiences of the year the pope continued with the subject of human love (nn. 13-51 of the series, January 2–December 17).

LETTER
OF THE HOLY FATHER
POPE JOHN PAUL II
TO ALL THE BISHOPS OF THE CHURCH

On the Mystery and Worship of the Eucharist
Dominicæ cenæ
February 24, 1980

My Venerable and Dear Brothers!

1. Again this year, for Holy Thursday, I am writing a letter to all of you. This letter has an immediate connection with the one which you received last year on the same occasion, together with the Letter to the Priests. I wish in the first place to thank you cordially for having accepted my previous letters with that spirit of unity which the Lord established between us, and also for having transmitted to your priests the thoughts that I desired to express at the beginning of my Pontificate.

During the Eucharistic Liturgy of Holy Thursday, you renewed, together with your priests, the promises and commitments undertaken at the moment of ordination. Many of you, venerable and dear brothers, told me about it later, also adding words of personal thanks, and indeed often sending those expressed by your priests. Furthermore, many priests expressed their joy, both because of the profound and solemn character of Holy Thursday as the annual "feast of priests" and also because of the importance of the subjects dealt with in the letter addressed to them.

Those replies form a rich collection which once more indicates how dear to the vast majority of priests of the Catholic Church is the path of the priestly life, the path along which this Church has been journeying for centuries: how much they love and esteem it, and how much they desire to follow it for the future.

At this point I must add that only a certain number of matters were dealt with in the Letter to Priests, as was in fact emphasized at the beginning of the document.[1] Furthermore, the main stress was laid upon the pastoral character of the priestly ministry; but this certainly does not mean that those groups of priests who are not engaged in direct pastoral activity were not also taken into consideration. In this regard I would refer once more to the teaching of the Second Vatican Council, and also to the declarations of the 1971 Synod of Bishops.

The pastoral character of the priestly ministry does not cease to mark the life of every priest, even if the daily tasks that he carries out are not explicitly directed to the pastoral administration of the sacraments. In this sense, the letter written to the priests on Holy Thursday was addressed to them all, without any exception, even though, as I said above, it did not deal with all the aspects of the life and activity of priests. I think this clarification is useful and opportune at the beginning of the present letter.

I.

THE EUCHARISTIC MYSTERY IN THE LIFE
OF THE CHURCH AND OF THE PRIEST

2. Eucharist and Priesthood

The present letter that I am addressing to you, my venerable and dear brothers in the episcopate—and which is, as I have said, in a certain way a continuation of the previous one—is also closely linked with the mystery of Holy Thursday, and is related to the priesthood. In fact I intend to devote it to the Eucharist, and in particular to certain aspects of the Eucharistic Mystery and its impact on the lives of those who are the ministers of it: and so those to whom this letter is directly addressed are you, the bishops of the Church; together with you, all the priests; and, in their own rank, the deacons, too.

In reality, the ministerial and hierarchical priesthood, the priesthood of the bishops and the priests, and, at their side, the ministry of the deacons—ministries which normally begin with the proclamation of the Gospel—are in the closest relationship with the Eucharist. The Eucharist is the principal and central raison d'être of the sacrament of the priesthood, which effectively came into being at the moment of the institution of the Eucharist, and together with it.[2] Not without reason the words "Do this in memory of me" are said immediately after the words of Eucharistic consecration, and we repeat them every time we celebrate the holy Sacrifice.[3]

Through our ordination—the celebration of which is linked to the holy Mass from the very first liturgical evidence[4]—we are united in a singular and exceptional way to the Eucharist. In a certain way we derive from it and exist for it. We are also, and in a special way, responsible for it—each priest in his own community and each bishop by virtue of the care of all the communities entrusted to him, on the basis of the solicitude *omnium ecclesiarum* that St. Paul speaks of.[5] Thus we bishops and priests are entrusted with the great "mystery of Faith," and while it is also given to the whole People of God, to all believers in Christ, yet to us has been entrusted the Eucharist also "for others," who expect from us a particular witness of veneration and love towards this sacrament, so that they too may be able to be built up and vivified "to offer spiritual sacrifices."[6]

In this way our Eucharistic worship, both in the celebration of Mass and in our devotion to the Blessed Sacrament, is like a life-giving current that links our ministerial or hierarchical priesthood to the common priesthood of the faithful, and presents it in its vertical dimension and with its central value. The priest fulfills his principal mission and is manifested in all his fullness when he celebrates the Eucharist,[7] and this manifestation is more complete when he himself allows the depth of that mystery to become visible, so that it alone shines forth in people's hearts and minds, through his ministry. This is the supreme exercise of the "kingly Priesthood," "the source and summit of all Christian life."[8]

3. Worship of the Eucharistic Mystery

This worship is directed towards God the Father through Jesus Christ in the Holy Spirit. In the first place towards the Father, who, as St. John's Gospel says, "loved the world so much that he gave his only Son, so that everyone who believes in him may not be lost but may have eternal life."[9]

It is also directed, in the Holy Spirit, to the Incarnate Son, in the economy of salvation, especially at that moment of supreme dedication and total abandonment of himself to which the words uttered in the Upper Room refer: "This is my body given up for you. . . .This is the cup of my blood shed for you. . . ."[10] The liturgical acclamation: "We proclaim your death, Lord Jesus" takes us back precisely to that moment; and with the proclamation of his resurrection we embrace in the same act of veneration Christ risen and glorified "at the right hand of the Father," as also the expectation of his "coming in glory." Yet it is the voluntary emptying of himself, accepted by the Father and glorified with the Resurrection, which, sacramentally celebrated together with the Resurrection, brings us to adore the Redeemer who "became obedient unto death, even death on a cross."[11]

And this adoration of ours contains yet another special characteristic. It is compenetrated by the greatness of that human death, in which the world, that is to say each one of us, has been loved "to the end." [12] Thus it is also a response that tries to repay that love immolated even to the death on the cross: it is our "Eucharist," that is to say our giving him thanks, our praise of him for having redeemed us by his death and made sharers in immortal life through his resurrection.

This worship, given therefore to the Trinity of the Father and of the Son and of the Holy Spirit, above all accompanies and permeates the celebration of the Eucharistic Liturgy. But it must fill our churches also outside the timetable of Masses. Indeed, since the Eucharistic Mystery was instituted out of love, and makes Christ sacramentally present, it is worthy of thanksgiving and worship. And this worship must be prominent in all our encounters with the Blessed Sacrament, both when we visit our churches and when the sacred species are taken to the sick and administered to them.

Adoration of Christ in this sacrament of love must also find expression in various forms of Eucharistic devotion: personal prayer before the Blessed Sacrament, Hours of Adoration, periods of exposition— short, prolonged and annual (Forty Hours), Eucharistic benediction, Eucharistic processions, Eucharistic congresses. [13] A particular mention should be made at this point of the Solemnity of the Body and Blood of Christ as an act of public worship rendered to Christ present in the Eucharist, a feast instituted by my predecessor Urban IV in memory of the institution of this great Mystery. [14] All this therefore corresponds to the general principles and particular norms already long in existence but newly formulated during or after the Second Vatican Council. [15]

The encouragement and the deepening of Eucharistic worship are proofs of that authentic renewal which the council set itself as an aim and of which they are the central point. And this, venerable and dear brothers, deserves separate reflection. The Church and the world have a great need of Eucharistic worship. Jesus waits for us in this sacrament of love. Let us be generous with our time in going to meet him in adoration and in contemplation that is full of faith and ready to make reparation for the great faults and crimes of the world. May our adoration never cease.

4.   Eucharist and Church

Thanks to the council we have realized with renewed force the following truth: Just as the Church "makes the Eucharist" so "the Eucharist builds up" the Church; [16] and this truth is closely bound with the mystery of Holy Thursday. The Church was founded, as the new community of the People of God, in the apostolic community of those Twelve who, at the Last Supper, became partakers of the body and blood of the Lord under the species of bread and wine. Christ had said to them: "Take and eat. . . . Take and drink." And carrying out this command of his, they entered for the first time into sacramental communion with the Son of God, a communion that is a pledge of eternal life. From that moment until the end of time, the Church is being built up through that same communion with the Son of God, a communion which is a pledge of the eternal Passover.

Dear and venerable brothers in the episcopate, as teachers and custodians of the salvific truth of the Eucharist, we must always and everywhere preserve this meaning and this dimension of the sacramental encounter and intimacy with Christ. It is precisely these elements which constitute the very substance of Eucharistic worship. The meaning of the truth expounded above in no way diminishes—in fact, it facilitates—the Eucharistic character of spiritual drawing together and union between the people who share in the sacrifice, which then in communion becomes for them the banquet. This drawing together and this union, the prototype of which is the union of the Apostles with Christ at the Last Supper, express the Church and bring her into being.

But the Church is not brought into being only through the union of people, through the experience of brotherhood to which the Eucharistic banquet gives rise. The Church is brought into being when, in that fraternal union and communion, we celebrate the sacrifice of the Cross of Christ, when we proclaim "the Lord's death until he comes,"[17] and later, when, being deeply compenetrated with the mystery of our salvation, we approach as a community the table of the Lord, in order to be nourished there, in a sacramental manner, by the fruits of the holy Sacrifice of propitiation. Therefore in Eucharistic Communion we receive Christ, Christ himself; and our union with him, which is a gift and grace for each individual, brings it about that in him we are also associated in the unity of his body which is the Church.

Only in this way, through that faith and that disposition of mind, is there brought about that building up of the Church, which in the Eucharist truly finds its "source and summit," according to the well-known expression of the Second Vatican Council.[18] This truth, which as a result of the same council has received a new and vigorous emphasis,[19] must be a frequent theme of our reflection and teaching. Let all pastoral activity be nourished by it, and may it also be food for ourselves and for all the priests who collaborate with us, and likewise for the whole of the communities entrusted to us. In this practice there should thus be revealed, almost at every step, that close relationship between the Church's spiritual and apostolic vitality and the Eucharist, understood in its profound significance and from all points of view.[20]

5. Eucharist and Charity

Before proceeding to more detailed observations on the subject of the celebration of the holy Sacrifice, I wish briefly to reaffirm the fact that Eucharistic worship constitutes the soul of all Christian life. In fact, Christian life is expressed in the fulfilling of the greatest commandment, that is to say, in the love of God and neighbor, and this love finds its source in the Blessed Sacrament, which is commonly called the sacrament of love.

The Eucharist signifies this charity, and therefore recalls it, makes it present and at the same time brings it about. Every time that we consciously share in it, there opens in our souls a real dimension of that unfathomable love that includes everything that God had done and continues to do for us human beings, as Christ says: "My Father goes on working, and so do I."[21] Together with this unfathomable and free gift, which is charity revealed in its fullest degree in the saving sacrifice of the Son of God, the sacrifice of which the Eucharist is the indelible sign, there also springs up within us a lively response of love. We not only know love; we ourselves begin to love. We enter, so to speak, upon the path of love and along this path make progress. Thanks to the Eucharist, the love that springs up within us from the Eucharist develops in us, becomes deeper and grows stronger.

Eucharistic worship is therefore precisely the expression of that love which is the authentic and deepest characteristic of the Christian vocation. This worship springs from the love and serves the love to which we are all called in Jesus Christ.[22] A living fruit of this worship is the perfecting of the image of God that we bear within us, an image that corresponds to the one that Christ has revealed in us. As we thus become adorers of the Father "in spirit and truth,"[23] we mature in an ever fuller union with Christ, we are ever more united to him, and—if one may use the expression—we are ever more in harmony with him.

The doctrine of the Eucharist, sign of unity and bond of charity, taught by St. Paul,[24] has been in subsequent times deepened by the writings of very many saints who are living examples for us of Eucharistic worship. We must always have this reality before our eyes, and at the same time we must continually try to bring it about that our own generation too may add new examples to those marvelous examples of the past, new examples no less living and eloquent, that will reflect the age to which we belong.

6.   Eucharist and Neighbor

The authentic sense of the Eucharist becomes of itself the school of active love for neighbor. We know that this is the true and full order of love that the Lord has taught us:"By this love you have for one another, everyone will know that you are my disciples."[25] The Eucharist educates us to this love in a deeper way; it shows us, in fact, what value each person, our brother or sister, has in God's eyes, if Christ offers himself equally to each one, under the species of bread and wine. If our Eucharistic worship is authentic, it must make us grow in awareness of the dignity of each person. The awareness of that dignity becomes the *deepest motive of our relationship with our neighbor*.

We must also become particularly sensitive to all human suffering and misery, to all injustice and wrong, and seek the way to redress them effectively. Let us learn to discover with respect the truth about the inner self that becomes the dwelling place of God present in the Eucharist. Christ comes into the hearts of our brothers and sisters and visits their consciences. How the image of each and every one changes, when we become aware of this reality, when we make it the subject of our reflections! The sense of the Eucharistic Mystery leads us to a love for our neighbor, to a love for every human being.[26]

7.   Eucharist and Life

Since therefore the Eucharist is the source of charity, it has always been at the center of the life of Christ's disciples. It has the appearance of bread and wine, that is to say of food and drink; it is therefore as familiar to people, as closely linked to their life, as food and drink. The veneration of God, who is love, springs, in Eucharistic worship, from that kind of intimacy in which *he himself, by analogy with food and drink*, fills our spiritual being, ensuring its life, as food and drink do. This "Eucharistic" veneration of God therefore strictly corresponds to his saving plan. He himself, the Father, wants the "true worshipers"[27] to worship him precisely in this way, and it is Christ who expresses this desire, both with his words and likewise with this sacrament in which he makes possible worship of the Father in the way most in conformity with the Father's will.

From this concept of Eucharistic worship there then stems the whole *sacramental style of the Christian's life*. In fact, leading a life based on the sacraments and animated by the common priesthood means in the first place that Christians desire God to act in them in order to enable them to attain, in the Spirit, "the fullness of Christ himself."[28] God, on his part, does not touch them only through events and by this inner grace; he also acts in them with greater certainty and power through the sacraments. The sacraments give the lives of Christians a sacramental style.

Now, of all the sacraments it is the Holy Eucharist that brings to fullness their initiation as Christians and confers upon the exercise of the common priesthood that sacramental and ecclesial form that links it—as we mentioned before[29]—to the exercise of the ministerial priesthood. In this way Eucharistic worship is the *center and goal of all sacramental life*.[30] In the depths of Eucharistic worship we find a continual echo of the sacraments of Christian initiation: Baptism and Confirmation. Where better is there expressed the truth that we are not only "called God's children" but "that is what we are"[31] by virtue of the Sacrament of Baptism, if not precisely in the fact that in the Eucharist we become partakers of the body and blood of God's only Son? And what predisposes us more to be "true witnesses of Christ"[32] before the world—as we are enabled to be by the Sacrament of Confirmation—than Eucharistic Communion, in which Christ bears witness to us, and we to him?

It is impossible to analyze here in greater detail the links between the Eucharist and the other sacraments, in particular with the sacrament of family life and the sacrament of the sick. In the Encyclical *Redemptor hominis*[33] I have already drawn attention to the close link between the Sacrament of Penance and the Sacrament of the Eucharist. *It is not only that Penance leads to the Eucharist, but that the Eucharist also leads to Penance.* For when we realize who it is that we receive in Eucharistic Communion, there springs up in us almost spontaneously a sense of unworthiness, together with sorrow for our sins and an interior need for purification.

But we must always take care that this great meeting with Christ in the Eucharist does not become a mere habit, and that we do not receive him unworthily, that is to say, in a state of mortal sin. The practice of the virtue of penance and the Sacrament of Penance are essential for sustaining in us and continually deepening that spirit of veneration which man owes to God himself and to his love so marvelously revealed. The purpose of these words is to put forward some general reflections on worship of the Eucharistic Mystery, and they could be developed at greater length and more fully. In particular, it would be possible to link what has been said about the effects of the Eucharist on love for others with what we have just noted about commitments undertaken towards humanity and the Church in Eucharistic Communion, and then outline the picture of that "new earth"[34] that springs from the Eucharist through every "new self."[35] *In this sacrament* of bread and wine, of food and drink, *everything that is human really undergoes a singular transformation and elevation.* Eucharistic worship is not so much worship of the inaccessible transcendence as worship of the divine condescension, and it is also the merciful and redeeming transformation of the world in the human heart.

Recalling all this only very briefly, I wish, notwithstanding this brevity, to create a wider context for the questions that I shall subsequently have to deal with: These questions are closely linked with the celebration of the holy Sacrifice. In fact, in that celebration there is expressed in a more direct way the worship of the Eucharist. This worship comes from the heart, as a most precious homage inspired by the faith, hope and charity which were infused into us at Baptism. And it is precisely about this that I wish to write to you in this letter, venerable and dear brothers in the episcopate, and with you to the priests and deacons. It will be followed by detailed indications from the Sacred Congregation for the Sacraments and Divine Worship.

II.

THE SACRED CHARACTER
OF THE EUCHARIST AND SACRIFICE

8.   Sacred Character

Beginning with the Upper Room and Holy Thursday, the celebration of the Eucharist has a long history, a history as long as that of the Church. In the course of this history the secondary elements have undergone certain changes, *but there has been no change in the essence of the "Mysterium" instituted* by the Redeemer of the world at the Last Supper. The Second Vatican Council too brought alterations, as a result of which the present liturgy of the Mass is different in some ways from the one known before the council. We do not intend to speak of these differences: It is better that we should now concentrate on what is essential and immutable in the Eucharistic Liturgy.

There is a close link between this element of the Eucharist and its sacredness, that is to say, its being a holy and sacred action. Holy and sacred, because in it are the continual presence and action of Christ, "the Holy One" of God,[36] "anointed with the Holy Spirit,"[37] "consecrated by the Father"[38] to lay down his life of his own accord and to take it up again,[39] and the High Priest of the New Covenant.[40] For it is he who, represented by the celebrant, makes his entrance into the sanctuary and proclaims his Gospel. It is he who is "the offerer and the offered, the consecrator and the consecrated."[41] The Eucharist is a holy and sacred action, because it constitutes the sacred species, the *Sancta sanctis*, that is to say, the "holy things (Christ, the Holy One) given to the Holy," as all the Eastern liturgies sing at the moment when the Eucharistic Bread is raised in order to invite the faithful to the Lord's Supper.

The sacredness of the Mass, therefore, is not a "sacralization," that is to say, something that man adds to Christ's action in the Upper Room, for the Holy Thursday supper was a sacred rite, a primary and constitutive liturgy, through which Christ, by pledging to give his life for us, himself celebrated sacramentally the mystery of his passion and resurrection, the heart of every Mass. Our Masses, being derived from this liturgy, possess of themselves a complete liturgical form, which, in spite of its variations in line with the families of rites, remains substantially the same. The sacred character of the Mass is a sacredness instituted by Christ. The words and actions of every priest, answered by the conscious active participation of the whole Eucharistic assembly, echo the words and actions of Holy Thursday.

The priest offers the holy Sacrifice *in persona Christi*; this means more than offering "in the name of" or "in place of" Christ. *In persona* means in specific sacramental identification with "the eternal High Priest"[42] who is the author and principal subject of this sacrifice of his, a sacrifice in which, in truth, nobody can take his place. Only he—only Christ—was able and is always able to be the true and effective "expiation for our sins and . . . for the sins of the whole world."[43] Only his sacrifice—and no one else's—was able and is able to have a "propitiatory power" before God, the Trinity, and the transcendent holiness. Awareness of this reality throws a certain light on the character and significance of the priest celebrant who, *by confecting the holy Sacrifice and acting "in persona Christi,"* is sacramentally (and ineffably) brought into that most profound *sacredness*, and made part of it, spiritually linking with it in turn all those participating in the Eucharistic assembly.

This sacred rite, which is actuated in different liturgical forms, may lack some secondary elements, but it can in no way lack its essential sacred character and sacramentality, since these are willed by Christ and transmitted and regulated by the Church. Neither can this sacred rite be utilized for other ends. If separated from its distinctive sacrificial and sacramental nature, the Eucharistic Mystery simply ceases to be. It admits of no "profane" imitation, an imitation that would very easily (indeed regularly) become a profanation. This must always be remembered, perhaps above all in our time, when we see a tendency to do away with the distinction between the "sacred" and "profane," given the widespread tendency, at least in some places, to desacralize everything.

In view of this fact, *the Church has a special duty to safeguard and strengthen the sacredness of the Eucharist.* In our pluralistic and often deliberately secularized society, *the living faith* of the Christian community—a faith always aware of its rights vis-à-vis those who do not share that faith—ensures respect for this sacredness. The duty to respect each person's faith is the complement of the natural and civil right to freedom of conscience and of religion.

The sacred character of the Eucharist has found and continues to find expression in the terminology of theology and the liturgy.[44] This sense of the objective sacred character of the Eucharistic Mystery is so much part of the faith of the People of God that their faith is enriched and strengthened by it.[45] Therefore the ministers of the Eucharist must, especially today, be illumined by the fullness of this living faith, and in its light they must understand and perform all that is part, by Christ's will and the will of his Church, of their priestly ministry.

9. Sacrifice

The Eucharist is above all else a sacrifice. It is the sacrifice of the Redemption and also the sacrifice of the New Covenant,[46] as we believe and as the Eastern Churches clearly profess: "Today's sacrifice," the Greek Church stated centuries ago, "is like that offered once by the only-begotten Incarnate Word; it is offered by him (now as then), since it is one and the same sacrifice."[47] Accordingly, precisely by making this single sacrifice of our salvation present, man and the world are restored to God through the paschal newness of Redemption. This restoration cannot cease to be: it is the foundation of the "new and eternal covenant" of God with man and of man with God. If it were missing, one would have to question both the excellence of the sacrifice of the Redemption, which in fact was perfect and definitive, and also the sacrificial value of the Mass. In fact, the Eucharist, being a true sacrifice, brings about this restoration to God.

Consequently, the celebrant, as minister of this sacrifice, is the authentic *priest*, performing—in virtue of the specific power of sacred ordination—a true sacrificial act that brings creation back to God. Although all those who participate in the Eucharist do not confect the sacrifice as he does, they offer with him, by virtue of the common priesthood, their own spiritual sacrifices represented by the bread and wine from the moment of their presentation at the altar. For this liturgical action, which takes a solemn form in almost all liturgies, has a "spiritual value and meaning."[48] The bread and wine become in a sense a symbol of all that the Eucharistic assembly brings, on its own part, as an offering to God and offers spiritually.

It is important that this first moment of the Liturgy of the Eucharist in the strict sense should find expression in the attitude of the participants. There is a link between this and the offertory "procession" provided for in the recent liturgical reform[49] and accompanied, in keeping with ancient tradition, by a psalm or song. A certain length of time must be allowed, so that all can become aware of this act, which is given expression at the same time by the words of the celebrant.

Awareness of the act of presenting the offerings should be maintained throughout the Mass. Indeed, it should be brought to fullness at the moment of the consecration and of the anamnesis offering, as is demanded by the fundamental value of the moment of the sacrifice. This is shown by the words of the Eucharistic Prayer said aloud by the priest. It seems worthwhile repeating here some expressions in the third Eucharistic Prayer that show in particular the sacrificial character of the Eucharist and link the offering of our persons with Christ's offering: "Look with favor on your Church's offering, and see the victim whose death has reconciled us to yourself. Grant that we, who are nourished by his body and blood, may be filled with his Holy Spirit, and become one body, one spirit in Christ. May he make us an everlasting gift to you."

This sacrificial value is expressed earlier in every celebration by the words with which the priest concludes the presentation of the gifts, asking the faithful to pray "that my sacrifice and yours may be acceptable to God, the almighty Father." These words are binding, since they express the character of the entire Eucharistic Liturgy and the fullness of its divine and ecclesial content.

All who participate with faith in the Eucharist become aware that it is a "sacrifice," that is to say, a "consecrated Offering." For the bread and wine presented at the altar and accompanied by the devotion and the spiritual sacrifices of the participants are finally consecrated, so as to become *truly, really and substantially* Christ's own body that is given up and his blood that is shed. Thus, by virtue of the consecration, the species of bread and wine represent[50] in a sacramental, unbloody manner the bloody propitiatory sacrifice offered by him on the cross to his Father for the salvation of the world. Indeed, he alone, giving himself as a propitiatory victim in an act of supreme surrender and immolation, has reconciled humanity with the Father, solely through his sacrifice, "having cancelled the bond which stood against us."[51]

To this sacrifice, which is renewed in a sacramental form on the altar, the offerings of bread and wine, united with the devotion of the faithful, nevertheless bring their unique contribution, since by means of the consecration by the priest they become sacred species.

This is made clear by the way in which the priest acts during the Eucharistic Prayer, especially at the consecration, and when the celebration of the holy Sacrifice and participation in it are accompanied by awareness that "the Teacher is here and is calling for you."[52] This call of the Lord to us through his Sacrifice opens our hearts, so that, purified in the mystery of our redemption, they may be united to him in Eucharistic Communion, which confers upon participation at Mass a value that is mature, complete and binding on human life: "The Church's intention is that the faithful not only offer the spotless victim but also learn to offer themselves and daily to be drawn into ever more perfect union, through Christ the Mediator, with the Father and with each other, so that at last God may be all in all."[53]

It is therefore very opportune and necessary to continue to actuate a new and intense education, in order to discover all the richness contained in the new liturgy. Indeed, the liturgical renewal that has taken place since the Second Vatican Council has given, so to speak, greater visibility *to the Eucharistic Sacrifice*. One factor contributing to this is that the words of the Eucharistic Prayer are said aloud by the celebrant, particularly the words of consecration, with the acclamation by the assembly immediately after the elevation.

All this should fill us with joy, but we should also remember that *these changes demand new spiritual awareness and maturity*, both on the part of the celebrant—especially now that he celebrates "facing the people"—and by the faithful. Eucharistic worship matures and grows when the words of the Eucharistic Prayer, especially the words of consecration, are spoken with great humility and simplicity, in a worthy and fitting way, which is understandable and in keeping with their holiness; when this essential act of the Eucharistic Liturgy is performed unhurriedly; and when it brings about in us such recollection and devotion that the participants become aware of the greatness of the mystery being accomplished and show it by their attitude.

III.

THE TWO TABLES OF THE LORD AND THE COMMON POSSESSION OF THE CHURCH

10. The Table of the Word of God

We are all well aware that from the earliest times the celebration of the Eucharist has been linked not only with prayer but also with the reading of Sacred Scripture and with singing by the whole assembly. As a result, it has long been possible to apply to the Mass the comparison, made by the Fathers, with the two tables, at which the Church prepares for her children the word of God and the Eucharist, that is, the bread of the Lord. We must therefore go back to the first part of the sacred mystery, the part that at present is most often called the *Liturgy of the Word,* and devote some attention to it.

The reading of the passages of Sacred Scripture chosen for each day *has been subjected by the council* to new criteria and requirements.[54] As a result of these norms of the council a new collection of readings has been made, in which there has been applied to some extent the principle of continuity of texts and the principle of making all the sacred books accessible. The insertion of the Psalms with responses into the liturgy makes the participants familiar with the great wealth of Old Testament prayer and poetry. The fact that these texts are read and sung in the vernacular enables everyone to participate with fuller understanding.

Nevertheless, there are also those people who, having been educated on the basis of the old liturgy in Latin, experience the lack of this "one language," which in all the world was an expression of the unity of the Church and through its dignified character elicited a profound sense of the Eucharistic Mystery. It is therefore necessary to show not only understanding but also full respect towards these sentiments and desires. As far as possible these sentiments and desires are to be accommodated, as is moreover provided for in the new disposi-tions.[55] The Roman Church has special obligations towards Latin, the splendid language of ancient Rome, and she must manifest them whenever the occasion presents itself.

The possibilities that the post-conciliar renewal has introduced in this respect are indeed often utilized so as to make us *witnesses of and sharers in the authentic celebration of the word of God.* There is also an increase in the number of people taking an active part in this celebra-tion. Groups of readers and cantors, and still more often choirs of men or women, are being set up and are devoting themselves with great enthusiasm to this aspect. The word of God, Sacred Scripture, is beginning to take on new life in many Christian communities. The faithful gathered for the liturgy prepare with song for listening to the Gospel, which is proclaimed with the devotion and love due it.

All this is noted with great esteem and gratitude, but it must not be forgotten that complete renewal makes yet other demands. These demands consist in a *new sense of responsibility towards the word of God transmitted* through the liturgy in various languages, something that is certainly in keeping with the universality of the Gospel and its purposes. The same sense of responsibility also involves the per-formance of the corresponding liturgical actions (reading or singing), which must accord with the principles of art. To preserve these ac-tions from all artificiality, they should express such capacity, simplicity and dignity as to highlight the special character of the sacred text, even by the very manner of reading or singing.

Accordingly, these demands, which spring from a new responsibility for the word of God in the liturgy,[56] go yet deeper and concern the inner attitude with which the ministers of the Word perform their function in the liturgical assembly.[57] This responsibility also concerns the *choice of texts. The choice has already been made by the competent ecclesiastical authority, which has also made provision for the cases in which readings more suited to a particular situation may be chosen.*[58] Furthermore, it must always be remembered that only the word of God can be used for Mass readings. The reading of Scripture cannot be replaced by the reading of other texts, however much they may be endowed with undoubted religious and moral values. On the other hand such texts can be used very profitably in the homily. Indeed the homily is supremely suitable for the use of such texts, provided that their content corresponds to the required conditions, since it is one of the tasks that belong to the nature of the homily to show the points of convergence between revealed divine wisdom and noble human thought seeking the truth by various paths.

11. The Table of the Bread of the Lord

The other table of the Eucharistic Mystery, that of the Bread of the Lord, also requires reflection from the viewpoint of the present-day liturgical renewal. This is a question of the greatest importance, since it concerns a special act of living faith, and indeed, as has been attested since the earliest centuries,[59] it is a manifestation *of worship of Christ, who in Eucharistic Communion entrusts himself to each one of us,* to our hearts, our consciences, our lips and our mouths, in the form of food. Therefore there is special need, with regard to this question, for the watchfulness spoken of by the Gospel, on the part of the pastors who have charge of *Eucharistic worship* and on the part of the People of God, whose "sense of the faith"[60] must be very alert and acute particularly in this area.

I therefore wish to entrust this question to the heart of each one of you, venerable and dear brothers in the episcopate. You must above all make it part of your care for all the churches entrusted to you. I ask this of you in the name of the unity that we have received from the Apostles as our heritage, collegial unity. This unity came to birth, in a sense, at the table of the Bread of the Lord on Holy Thursday. With the help of your brothers in the priesthood, *do all you can to safeguard the sacred dignity of the Eucharistic ministry and that deep spirit of Eucharistic Communion* which belongs in a special way to the Church as the People of God, and which is also a particular heritage transmitted to us from the Apostles, by various liturgical traditions, and by unnumbered generations of the faithful, who were often heroic witnesses to Christ, educated in "the school of the cross" (Redemption) and of the Eucharist.

It must be remembered that the Eucharist as the table of the Bread of the Lord is a continuous invitation. This is *shown in the liturgy when the celebrant says: "This is the Lamb of God. Happy are those who are called to his supper"*;[61] it is also shown by the familiar Gospel parable about the guests invited to the marriage banquet.[62] Let us remember that in this parable there are many who excuse themselves from accepting the invitation for various reasons.

Moreover our Catholic communities certainly do not lack people who *could participate* in Eucharistic Communion and do not, even though they have no serious sin on their conscience as an obstacle. To tell the truth, this attitude, which in some people is linked with an exaggerated severity, has changed in the present century, though it is still to be found here and there. In fact what one finds most often is not so much a feeling of unworthiness as a certain lack of interior willingness, if one may use this expression, a lack of Eucharistic"hunger" and "thirst," which is also a sign of lack of adequate sensitivity towards the great sacrament of love and a lack of understanding of its nature.

However, we also find in recent years another phenomenon. Sometimes, indeed quite frequently, everybody participating in the Eucharistic assembly goes to Communion; and on some such occasions, as experienced pastors confirm, there has not been due care to approach the Sacrament of Penance so as to purify one's conscience. This can of course mean that those approaching the Lord's table find nothing on their conscience, according to the objective law of God, to keep them from this sublime and joyful act of being sacramentally united with Christ. But there can also be, at least at times, another idea behind this: the idea of the Mass as only a banquet[63] in which one shares by *receiving the body of Christ in order to manifest, above all else, fraternal communion*. It is not hard to add to these reasons a certain human respect and mere "conformity."

This phenomenon demands from us watchful attention and a theological and pastoral analysis guided by a sense of great responsibility. We cannot allow the life of our communities to lose the good quality of sensitiveness of Christian conscience, guided solely by respect for Christ, who, when he is received in the Eucharist, should find in the heart of each of us a worthy abode. This question is closely linked not only with the practice of the Sacrament of Penance but also with a correct sense of responsibility for the whole deposit of moral teaching and for the precise distinction between good and evil, a distinction which then becomes for each person sharing in the Eucharist the basis for a correct judgment of self to be made in the depths of the personal conscience. St. Paul's words, "Let a man examine himself,"[64] are well known; this judgment is an indispensable condition for a personal decision whether to approach Eucharistic Communion or to abstain.

Celebration of the Eucharist places before us many other requirements regarding the ministry of the Eucharistic table. Some of these requirements concern only priests and deacons, others concern all who participate in the Eucharistic Liturgy. Priests and deacons must remember that the service of the table of the Bread of the Lord imposes on them special obligations which refer in the first place to

Christ himself *present in the Eucharist* and secondly to all who actually participate in the Eucharist or who might do so. With regard to the first, perhaps it will not be superfluous to recall the words of the *Pontificale* which on the day of ordination the bishop addresses to the new priest as he hands to him on the paten and in the chalice the bread and wine offered by the faithful and prepared by the deacon: *"Accipe oblationem plebis sanctæ Deo offerendam. Agnosce quod agis, imitare quod tractabis, et vitam tuam mysterio dominicæ crucis conforma."* [65] This last admonition made to him by the bishop should remain as one of the most precious norms of his Eucharistic ministry.

It is from this admonition that the priest's attitude in handling the bread and wine which have become the body and blood of the Redeemer should draw its inspiration. Thus it is necessary for all of us who are ministers of the Eucharist to examine carefully our actions at the altar, in particular the way in which we handle that food and drink which are the body and blood of the Lord our God in our hands: the way in which we distribute Holy Communion; the way in which we perform the purification.

All these actions have a meaning of their own. Naturally, scrupulosity must be avoided, but God preserve us from behaving in a way that lacks respect, from undue hurry, from an impatience that causes scandal. Over and above our commitment to the evangelical mission, our greatest commitment consists in exercising this mysterious power over the body of the Redeemer, and all that is within us should be decisively ordered to this. We should also always remember that to this ministerial power we have been sacramentally consecrated, that we have been chosen from among men "for the good of men." [66] We especially, the priests of the Latin Church, whose ordination rite added in the course of the centuries the custom of anointing the priest's hands, should think about this.

In some countries the *practice of receiving Communion in the hand* has been introduced. This practice has been requested by individual episcopal conferences and has received approval from the Apostolic See. However, cases of a deplorable lack of respect towards the Eucharistic species have been reported, cases which are imputable not only to the individuals guilty of such behavior but also to the pastors of the Church who have not been vigilant enough regarding the attitude of the faithful towards the Eucharist. It also happens, on occasion, that the free choice of those who prefer to continue the practice of receiving the Eucharist on the tongue is not taken into account in those places where the distribution of Communion in the hand has been authorized. It is therefore difficult in the context of this present letter not to mention the sad phenomena previously referred to. This is in no way meant to refer to those who, receiving the Lord Jesus in the hand, do so with profound reverence and devotion, in those countries where this practice has been authorized.

But one must not forget the primary office of priests, who have been consecrated by their ordination to represent Christ the Priest: for this reason their hands, like their words and their will, have become the direct instruments of Christ. Through this fact, that is, as ministers of the Holy Eucharist, they have a primary responsibility for the sacred species, because it is a total responsibility: they offer the bread and wine, they consecrate it, and then distribute the sacred species to the participants in the assembly who wish to receive them. Deacons can only bring to the altar the offerings of the faithful and, once they have been consecrated by the priest, distribute them. How eloquent therefore, even if not of ancient custom, is the rite of the anointing of the hands in our Latin ordination, as though precisely for these hands a special grace and power of the Holy Spirit is necessary!

To touch the sacred species and to *distribute them with their own hands* is a privilege of the ordained, one which indicates an active participation in the *ministry of the Eucharist*. It is obvious that the Church can grant this faculty to those who are neither priests nor deacons, as is the case with acolytes in the exercise of their ministry, especially if they are destined for future ordination, or with any other lay people who are chosen for this to meet a just need, but always after an adequate preparation.

12. A Common Possession of the Church

We cannot, even for a moment, forget that the Eucharist is a special possession belonging to the whole Church. It is *the greatest gift* in the order of grace and of sacrament that the divine Spouse has offered and unceasingly offers to his spouse. And precisely because it is such a gift, all of us should in a spirit of profound faith let ourselves be guided by a sense of truly Christian responsibility. A gift obliges us ever more profoundly because it speaks to us not so much with the force of a strict right as with the force of personal confidence, and thus without legal obligations it calls for *trust and gratitude*. The Eucharist is just such a gift and such a possession. We should remain faithful in every detail to what it expresses in itself and to what it asks of us, namely, thanksgiving.

The Eucharist is a common possession of the whole Church as the sacrament of her unity. And thus the Church has the strict duty to specify everything which concerns participation in it and its celebration. We should therefore act according to the principles laid down by the last council, which, in the Constitution on the Sacred Liturgy, defined the authorizations and obligations of individual bishops in their dioceses and of the Episcopal Conferences, given the fact that both act in collegial unity with the Apostolic See.

Furthermore we should follow the directives issued by the various departments of the Holy See in this field: be it in liturgical matters, in the rules established by the liturgical books in what concerns the Eucharistic Mystery,[67] and in the Instructions devoted to this mystery, be it with regard to *communicatio in sacris*, in the norms of the *Directorium de re oecumenica*[68] and in the *Instructio de peculiaribus casibus admittendi alios christianos ad communionem eucharisticam in Ecclesia catholica*.[69] And although at this stage of renewal the possibility of a certain "creative" freedom has been permitted, nevertheless this freedom must strictly respect the requirements of substantial unity. We can follow the path of this pluralism (which arises in part from the introduction itself of the various languages into the liturgy) only as long as the essential characteristics of the celebration of the Eucharist are preserved, and the norms prescribed by the recent liturgical reform are respected.

Indispensable effort is required everywhere to ensure that within the pluralism of Eucharistic worship envisioned by the Second Vatican Council the unity of which the Eucharist is the sign and cause is clearly manifested.

This task, over which in the nature of things the Apostolic See must keep careful watch, should be assumed not only by each *episcopal conference* but by every minister of the Eucharist, without exception. Each one should also remember that he is responsible for the common good of the whole Church. The *priest as minister*, as celebrant, as the one who presides over the Eucharistic assembly of the faithful, should have a special *sense of the common good of the Church*, which he represents through his ministry, but to which he must also be subordinate, according to a correct discipline of faith. He cannot consider himself a "proprietor" who can make free use of the liturgical text and of the sacred rite as if it were his own property, in such a way as to stamp it with his own arbitrary personal style. At times this latter might seem more effective, and it may better correspond to subjective piety; nevertheless, objectively it is always a betrayal of that union which should find its proper expression in the sacrament of unity.

Every priest who offers the holy Sacrifice should recall that during this sacrifice it is not *only* he with his community that is praying but the whole Church, which is thus expressing in this sacrament her spiritual unity, among other ways by the use of the approved liturgical text. To call this position "mere insistence on uniformity" would only show ignorance of the objective requirements of authentic unity, and would be a symptom of harmful individualism.

This subordination of the minister, of the celebrant, to the *Mysterium* which has been entrusted to him by the Church for the good of the whole People of God, should also find expression in the observance of the liturgical requirements concerning the celebration of the holy Sacrifice. These refer, for example, to dress, and in particular to the vestments worn by the celebrant. Circumstances have of course existed and continue to exist in which the prescriptions do not oblige. We have been greatly moved when reading books written by priests who had been prisoners in extermination camps, with descriptions of Eucharistic celebrations without the above-mentioned rules, that is to say, without an altar and without vestments. But although in those conditions this was a proof of heroism and deserved profound admiration, nevertheless in normal conditions to ignore the liturgical directives can be interpreted as a lack of respect towards the Eucharist, dictated perhaps by individualism or by an absence of a critical sense concerning current opinions, or by a certain *lack of a spirit of faith*.

Upon all of us who, through the *grace of God*, are ministers of the Eucharist, there weighs a particular responsibility for the ideas and attitudes of our brothers and sisters who have been entrusted to our pastoral care. It is our vocation to nurture, above all by personal example, every healthy manifestation of worship towards Christ present and operative in that sacrament of love. May God preserve us from acting otherwise and weakening that worship by "becoming unaccustomed" to various manifestations and forms of Eucharistic worship which express a perhaps "traditional" but healthy piety, and which express above all that "sense of the faith" possessed by the whole People of God, as the Second Vatican Council recalled.[70]

As I bring these considerations to an end, I would like to ask forgiveness—in my own name and in the name of all of you, venerable and dear brothers in the episcopate—for everything which, for whatever reason, through whatever human weakness, impatience or negligence, and also through the at times partial, one-sided and erroneous application of the directives of the Second Vatican Council, may have caused scandal and disturbance concerning the interpretation of the doctrine and the veneration due to this great sacrament. And I pray the Lord Jesus that in the future we may avoid in our manner of dealing with this sacred mystery anything which could weaken or disorient in any way the sense of reverence and love that exists in our faithful people.

May Christ himself help us to follow the path of true renewal towards that fullness of life and of Eucharistic worship whereby the Church is built up in that unity that she already possesses, and which she desires to bring to ever greater perfection for the glory of the living God and for the salvation of all humanity.

13. Conclusion

Permit me, venerable and dear brothers, to end these reflections of mine, which have been restricted to a detailed examination of only a few questions. In undertaking these reflections, I have had before my eyes all the work carried out by the Second Vatican Council, and have kept in mind Paul VI's Encyclical *Mysterium fidei*, promulgated during that council, and all the documents issued after the same council for the purpose of implementing the post-conciliar liturgical renewal. A very close and organic *bond exists between the renewal of the liturgy and the renewal of the whole life of the Church*.

The Church not only acts but also expresses herself in the liturgy, lives by the liturgy and draws from the liturgy the strength for her life. For this reason liturgical renewal carried out correctly in the spirit of the Second Vatican Council is, in a certain sense, the measure and the condition for putting into effect the teaching of that council which we wish to accept with profound faith, convinced as we are that by means of this council the Holy Spirit "has spoken to the Church" the truths and given the indications for carrying out her mission among the people of today and tomorrow.

We shall continue in the future to take special care to promote and follow the renewal of the Church according to the teaching of the Second Vatican Council, in the spirit of an ever living tradition. In fact, to the substance of tradition properly understood belongs also a correct rereading of the "signs of the times," which require us to draw from the rich treasure of Revelation "things both new and old."[71] Acting in this spirit, in accordance with this counsel of the gospel, the

Second Vatican Council carried out a providential effort to renew the face of the Church in the sacred liturgy, most often having recourse to what is "ancient," what comes from the heritage of the Fathers and is the expression of the faith and doctrine of a Church which has remained united for so many centuries.

In order to be able to continue in the future to put into practice the directives of the council in the field of liturgy, and in particular in the field of Eucharistic worship, *close collaboration* is necessary between the competent department of the Holy See and each episcopal conference, a collaboration which must be at the same time *vigilant and creative*. We must keep our sights fixed on the greatness of the most holy Mystery and at the same time on spiritual movements and social changes, which are so significant for our times, since they not only sometimes create difficulties but also prepare us for a new way of participating in that great Mystery of Faith.

Above all I wish to emphasize that the problems of the liturgy, and in particular of the Eucharistic Liturgy, must not be an *occasion for dividing Catholics and for threatening the unity of the Church*. This is demanded by an elementary understanding of that sacrament which Christ has left us as the source of spiritual unity. And how could the Eucharist, which in the Church is the *sacramentum pietatis, signum unitatis, vinculum caritatis*,[72] form between us at this time a point of division and a source of distortion of thought and of behavior, instead of being the focal point and constitutive center, which it truly is in its essence, of the unity of the Church herself?

We are all equally indebted to our Redeemer. We should all listen together to that Spirit of Truth and of love whom he has promised to the Church and who is operative in her. In the name of this truth and of this love, in the name of the crucified Christ and of his Mother, I ask you, and beg you: Let us abandon all opposition and division, and let us all unite in this great mission of salvation which is the price and at the same time the fruit of our redemption. The Apostolic See will continue to do all that is possible to provide the means of ensuring that unity of which we speak. Let everyone avoid anything in his own way of acting which could "grieve the Holy Spirit."[73]

In order that this unity and the constant and systematic collaboration which leads to it may be perseveringly continued, I beg on my knees that, through the intercession of Mary, holy spouse of the Holy Spirit and Mother of the Church, we may all receive the light of the Holy Spirit. And blessing everyone, with all my heart I once more address myself to you, my venerable and dear brothers in the episcopate, with a fraternal greeting and with full trust. In this collegial unity in which we share, let us do all we can to ensure that the Eucharist may become an ever greater source of life and light for the consciences of all our brothers and sisters of all the communities in the universal unity of Christ's Church on earth.

In a spirit of fraternal charity, to you and to all our confreres in the priesthood I cordially impart the apostolic blessing.

From the Vatican, February 24, first Sunday of Lent, in the year 1980, the second of the Pontificate.

Endnotes

1. Cf. Chapter 2: AAS 71 (1979), pp. 395f.
2. Cf. Ecumenical Council of Trent, Session XXII, Can. 2: *Conciliorum Oecumenicorum Decreta*, ed. 3, Bologna 1973, p. 735.
3. Because of this precept of the Lord, an Ethiopian Eucharistic Liturgy recalls that the Apostles "established for us patriarchs, archbishops, priests and deacons to celebrate the ritual of your holy Church": *Anaphora Sancti Athanasii: Prex Eucharistica*, Haenggi-Pahl, Fribourg (Switzerland) 1968, p. 183.
4. Cf. *La Tradition apostolique de saint Hippolyte*, nos. 2-4, ed. Botte, Münster-Westfalen 1963, pp. 5-17.
5. 2 Cor 11: 28.
6. 1 Pt 2: 5.
7. Cf. Second Vatican Council, Dogmatic Constitution on the Church *Lumen gentium*, 28: AAS 57 (1965), pp. 33f.; Decree on the Ministry and Life of Priests *Presbyterorum ordinis*, 2, 5: AAS 58 (1966), pp. 993, 998; Decree on the Missionary Activity of the Church *Ad gentes*, 39: AAS 58 (1966), p. 986.
8. Second Vatican Council, Dogmatic Constitution on the Church *Lumen gentium*, 11: AAS 57 (1965), p. 15.
9. Jn 3: 16. It is interesting to note how these words are taken up by the liturgy of St. John Chrysostom immediately before the words of consecration and introduce the latter: cf. *La divina Liturgia del nostro Padre Giovanni Crisostomo*, Roma-Grottaferrata 1967, pp. 104f.
10. Cf. Mt 26: 26-28; Mk 14: 22-25; Lk 22: 18-20; 1 Cor 11: 23-25; cf. also the Eucharistic Prayers.
11. Phil 2: 8.
12. Jn 13: 1.
13. Cf. John Paul II, Homily in Phoenix Park, Dublin, 7: AAS 71 (1979), pp. 1074ff.; Sacred Congregation of Rites, Instruction *Eucharisticum mysterium*: AAS 59 (1967), pp. 539-573; *Rituale Romanum, De sacra communione et de cultu Mysterii eucharistici extra Missam*, ed. typica, 1973. It should be noted that the value of the worship and the sanctifying power of these forms of devotion to the Eucharist depend not so much upon the forms themselves as upon interior attitudes.
14. Cf. Bull *Trasiturus de hoc mundo* (Aug. 11, 1264): Aemilii Friedberg, *Corpus Iuris Canonici*, Pars II. *Decretalium Collectiones*, Leipzig 1881, pp. 1174-1177; *Studi eucharistici*, VII Centenario della Bolla '*Transiturus*,' 1264-1964, Orvieto 1966, pp. 302-317.

15. Cf. Paul VI, Encyclical Letter *Mysterium Fidei*: AAS 57 (1965), pp. 753-774; Sacred Congregation of Rites, Instruction *Eucharisticum mysterium*: AAS 59 (1967), pp. 539-573; *Rituale Romanum, De sacra communione et de cultu Mysterii eucharistici extra Missam*, ed. typica, 1973.
16. John Paul II, Encyclical Letter *Redemptor hominis*, 20: AAS 71 (1979), p. 311; cf. Second Vatican Council, Dogmatic Constitution on the Church *Lumen gentium*, 11: AAS 57 (1965), pp. 15f; also, note 57 to Schema II of the same dogmatic constitution, in *Acta Synodalia Sacrosancti Concilii Oecumenici Vaticani II*, vol. II, periodus 2a, pars I, public session II, pp. 251f.; Paul VI, Address at the General Audience of September 15, 1965: *Insegnamenti di Paolo VI*, III (1965), p. 103; H. de Lubac, *Méditation sur l'Eglise*, 2 ed., Paris 1963, pp. 129-137.
17. 1 Cor 11: 26.
18. Cf. Second Vatican Council, Dogmatic Constitution on the Church *Lumen gentium*, 11: AAS 57 (1965), pp. 15f.; Constitution on the Sacred Liturgy *Sacrosanctum concilium*, 10: AAS 56 (1964), p. 102; Decree on the Ministry and Life of Priests *Presbyterorum ordinis*, 5: AAS 58 (1966), pp. 997f.; Decree on the Bishops' Pastoral Office in the Church *Christus Dominus*, 30: AAS 58 (1966), pp. 688f.; Decree on the Church's Missionary Activity *Ad gentes*, 9: AAS 58 (1966), pp. 957f.
19. Cf. Second Vatican Council, Dogmatic Constitution on the Church *Lumen gentium*, 26: AAS 57 (1965), pp. 31f.; Decree on Ecumenism *Unitatis redintegratio*, 15: AAS 57 (1965), pp. 101f.
20. This is what the Opening Prayer of Holy Thursday asks for: "We pray that in this Eucharist we may find the fullness of love and life": *Missale Romanum*, ed. typica altera 1975, p. 244; also the communion epiclesis of the Roman Missal: "May all of us who share in the body and blood of Christ be brought together in unity by the Holy Spirit. Lord, remember your Church throughout the world; make us grow in love": Eucharistic Prayer II: *ibid.*, pp. 458f.; Eucharistic Prayer III, p. 463.
21. Jn 5: 17.
22. Cf. Prayer after Communion of the Mass for the Twenty-second Sunday in Ordinary Time: "Lord, you renew us at your table with the bread of life. May this food strengthen us in love and help us to serve you in each other": *Missale Romanum*, ed. cit., p. 361.
23. Jn 4: 23.
24. Cf. 1 Cor 10: 17; commented upon by St. Augustine: *In Evangelium Ioannis* tract. 31, 13; PL 35, 1613; also commented upon by the Ecumenical Council of Trent, Session XIII, can. 8; *Conciliorum Oecumenicorum Decreta*, ed. 3, Bologna 1973, p. 697, 7; cf. Second Vatican Council, Dogmatic Constitution on the Church *Lumen gentium*, 7: AAS 57 (1965), p. 9.
25. Jn 13: 35.
26. This is expressed by many prayers of the Roman Missal: the Prayer over the Gifts from the Common, "For those who work for the underprivileged": "May we who celebrate the love of your Son also follow the example of your saints and grow in love for you and for one another": *Missale Romanum*, ed. cit., p. 721; also the Prayer after Communion of the Mass, "For Teachers": "May this holy meal help us to follow the example of your saints by showing in our lives the light of truth and love for our brothers": *ibid.*, p. 723; cf. also the Prayer after Communion of the Mass for the Twenty-second Sunday in Ordinary Time, quoted in note 22.
27. Jn 4: 23.
28. Eph 4: 13.
29. Cf. above, n. 2.
30. Cf. Second Vatican Council, Decree on the Missionary Activity of the Church *Ad gentes*, 9, 12: AAS 58 (1966), pp. 958-961f.; Decree on the Ministry and Life of Priests *Presbyterorum ordinis*, 5: AAS 58 (1966), p. 997.
31. 1 Jn 3: 1.
32. Second Vatican Council, Dogmatic Constitution on the Church *Lumen gentium*, 11: AAS 57 (1965), p. 15.

33. Cf. n. 20: AAS 71 (1979), pp. 313f.

34. 2 Pt 3: 13.

35. Col 3: 10.

36. Lk 1: 34; Jn 6: 69; Acts 3: 14; Rv 3: 7.

37. Acts 10: 38; Lk 4: 18.

38. Jn 10: 36.

39. Cf. Jn 10: 17.

40. Heb 3: 1, 4: 15, etc.

41. As was stated in the ninth-century Byzantine liturgy, according to the most ancient codex, known formerly as Barberino di San Marco (Florence), and, now that it is kept in the Vatican Apostolic Library, as Barberini Greco 366 f. 8 verso, lines 17-20. This part has been published by F. E. Brightman, Liturgies Eastern and Western, I. Eastern Liturgies, Oxford 1896, p. 318, 34-35.

42. Opening Prayer of the Second Votive Mass of the Holy Eucharist: *Missale Romanum*, ed. cit., p. 858.

43. 1 Jn 2: 2; cf. *ibid.*, 4: 10.

44. We speak of the *Divinum mysterium*, the *Sanctissimum*, the *Sacrosanctum*, meaning what is sacred and holy par excellence. For their part, the Eastern churches call the Mass *raza* or *mysterion, hagiasmos, quddasa, qedasse,* that is to say"consecration"par excellence. Furthermore there are the liturgical rites, which, in order to inspire a sense of the sacred, prescribe silence, and standing or kneeling, and likewise professions of faith, and the incensation of the Gospel book, the altar, the celebrant and the sacred species. They even recall the assistance of the angelic beings created to serve the Holy God, i.e., with the *Sanctus* of our Latin churches and the *Trisagion* and *Sancta Sanctis* of the Eastern liturgies.

45. For instance, in the invitation to receive communion, this faith has been so formed as to reveal complementary aspects of the presence of Christ the Holy One: the epiphanic aspect noted by the Byzantines ("Blessed is he who comes in the name of the Lord: The Lord is God and has appeared to us": *La divina Liturgia del santo nostro Padre Giovanni Crisostomo*, Roma-Grottaferrata 1967, pp. 136f.); the aspect of relation and union sung of by the Armenians (Liturgy of St. Ignatius of Antioch: *"Unus Pater sanctus nobiscum, unus filius sanctus nobiscum, unus Spiritus sanctus nobiscum": Die Anaphora des heiligen Ignatius von Antiochien*, libersetzt von A. Rücker, Oriens Christianus, 3 ser., 5 [1930], p. 76); and the hidden heavenly aspect celebrated by the Chaldeans and Malabars (cf. the antiphonal hymn sung by the priest and the assembly after communion: F. E. Brightman, op. sit., p. 299.

46. Cf. Second Vatican Council, Constitution on the Sacred Liturgy *Sacrosanctum concilium*, 2, 47: AAS 56 (1964), pp. 83f., 113; Dogmatic Constitution on the Church *Lumen gentium*, 3 and 28: AAS 57 (1965), pp. 6, 33f.; Decree on Ecumenism *Unitatis redintegratio*, 2: AAS 57 (1965), p. 91; Decree on the Ministry and Life of Priests *Presbyterorum ordinis*, 13: AAS 58 (1966), pp. 1011f., Ecumenical Council of Trent, Session XXII, chap. I and II: *Conciliorum Oecumenicorum Decreta*, ed. 3, Bologna 1973, pp. 732f. especially: *una eademque est hostia, idem nunc offerens sacerdotum ministerio, qui se ipsum tunc in cruce obtulit, sola offerendi ratione diversa (ibid., p. 733)*.

47. *Synodus Constantinopolita adversus Sotericum* (January 1156 and May 1157): Angelo Mai, Spicilegium romanum, t. X, Rome 1844, p. 77; PG 140, 190; cf. Martin Jugie, Dict. Theol. Cath., t. X, 1338; *Theologia dogmatica christianorum orientalium*, Paris 1930, pp. 317-320.

48. *Institutio Generalis Missalis Romani*, 49c: *Missale Romanum*, ed. cit., p. 39; cf. Second Vatican Council, Decree on the Ministry and Life of Priests *Presbyterorum ordinis*, 5: AAS 58 (1966), pp. 997f.

49. *Ordo Missæ cum populo*, 18: *Missale Romanum*, ed. cit., p. 390.

50. Cf. Ecumenical Council of Trent, Session XXII, chap I, *Conciliorum Oecumenicorum Decreta*, ed. 3, Bologna 1973, pp. 732f.

51. Col 2: 14.

52. Jn 11: 28.

53. *Institutio Generalis Missalis Romani*, 55f.: *Missale Romanum*, ed. cit., p. 40.

54. Cf. Constitution on the Sacred Liturgy *Sacrosanctum concilium*, 35, 51: AAS 56 (1964), pp. 109, 114.
55. Cf. Sacred Congregation of Rites, Instruction *In edicendis normis*, VI, 17-18; VII, 19-20: AAS 57 (1965), pp. 1012f.; Instruction *Musicam Sacram*, IV, 48: AAS 59 (1967), p. 314; Decree *De Titulo Basilicæ Minoris*, II, 8: AAS 60 (1968), p. 538; Sacred Congregation for Divine Worship, Notif. *De Missali Romano, Liturgia Horarum et Calendario*, I, 4: AAS 63 (1971), p. 714.
56. Cf. Paul VI, Apostolic Constitution *Missale Romanum*: "We are fully confident that both priests and faithful will prepare their minds and hearts more devoutly for the Lord's Supper, meditating on the scriptures, nourished day by day with the words of the Lord": AAS 61 (1969), pp. 220f.; *Missale Romanum*, ed. cit., p. 15.
57. Cf. *Pontificale Romanum. De Institutione Lectorum et Acolythorum*, 4, ed. typica, 1972, pp. 19f.
58. Cf. *Institutio Generalis Missalis Romani*, 319-320: *Missale Romanum*, ed. cit., p. 87.
59. Cf. Fr. J. Dölger, *Das Segnen der Sinne mit der Eucharistie. Eine Altchristliche Kommunionsitte: Antike und Christentum*, t. 3 (1932), pp. 231-244; *Das Kultvergehen der Donatistin Lucilla von Karthago. Reliquienkuss vor dem Kuss der Eucharistie, ibid.*, pp. 245-252.
60. Cf. Second Vatican Council, Dogmatic Constitution on the Church *Lumen gentium*, 12, 35: AAS 57 (1965), pp. 16, 40.
61. Cf. Jn 1: 29; Rv 19: 9.
62. Cf. Lk 14: 16ff.
63. Cf. *Institutio Generalis Missalis Romani*, 7-8: *Missale Romanum*, ed. cit., p. 29.
64. 1 Cor 11: 28.
65. *Pontificale Romanum. De Ordinatione Diaconi, Presbyteri et Episcopi*, ed. typica, 1968, p. 93.
66. Heb 5: 1.
67. Sacred Congregation of Rites, Instruction *Eucharisticum Mysterium*: AAS 59 (1967), pp. 539-573; *Rituale Romanum. De sacra communione et de cultu Mysterii eucharistici extra Missam*, ed. typica, 1973; Sacred Congregation for Divine Worship, *Litteræ circulares ad Conferentiarum Episcopalium Præsides de precibus eucharisticis*: AAS 65 (1973), pp. 340-347.
68. nn. 38-63: AAS 59 (1967), pp. 586-592.
69. AAS 64 (1972), pp. 518-525. Cf. also the *Communicatio* published the following year for the correct application of the above-mentioned Instruction: AAS 65 (1973), pp. 616-619.
70. Cf. Second Vatican Council, Dogmatic Constitution on the Church *Lumen gentium*, 12: AAS 57 (1965), pp. 16f.
71. Mt 13: 52.
72. Cf. St. Augustine, *In Evangelium Ioannis* tract. 26, 13: PL 35, 1612f.
73. Eph 4: 30.

1981

Third Year of Pontificate

In the early part of the year Pope John Paul II made a long apostolic journey (February 16-27) to the Far East: the Philippines, Guam and Japan, with brief stops in Pakistan and Alaska.

Shortly after the trip, he commented on it. "I wanted to go to the Far East, to the Philippines and to Japan, to pay tribute to the martyrs of the faith, both to those who had come from old Europe, and to the local inhabitants. . . . It is difficult to say enough about the Philippines and it would be necessary to say a great deal. . . . The Philippines is the country in the Far East in which the Catholic Church has become rooted most deeply. . . . The stay in Japan had a particular eloquence. For the first time, the feet of the Bishop of Rome touched that archipelago in which the history of Christianity goes back to the times of St. Francis Xavier. . . . This recent journey was certainly the longest of those I have undertaken so far, connected with my service in Peter's See. Its itinerary covered nearly the whole globe" (General Audience, March 4, nn. 3, 6, 8-9).

In this year the pope did not write a Letter to Priests specifically for Holy Thursday. However, on March 25 he issued a Letter to the Bishops, *A Concilio Constantinopolitano I*, for the 1600th anniversary of the First Council of Constantinople and the 1550th anniversary of the Council of Ephesus. "I write these things in the first place to you, my dear and venerable brothers in the episcopal service. I address myself at the same time to my brother priests, your closest collaborators in your pastoral care *in virtute Spiritus Sancti*" (1981 Letter, n. 5). The pope referred to Holy Thursday which was to be celebrated on April 16. "I know that on Holy Thursday you renew within the community of the presbyterium of your dioceses the memorial of the Last Supper, during which, by the words of Christ and the power of the Holy Spirit, the bread and wine became the body and blood of our Savior, that is to say, the Eucharist of our redemption" (1981 Letter, n. 12). For this reason, this document has been considered the annual Holy Thursday Letter for 1981.

In the same document, the pope made specific arrangements for the liturgical celebration of Pentecost which "by a singular coincidence . . . will this year fall on June 7, as it did in 431, when on that solemn day, on which the council sessions, later postponed to June 22, were to begin, the first groups of bishops began to arrive in Ephesus" (1981 Letter, n. 11).

Unforeseen circumstances changed somewhat the course of events. May 13, the Feast of Our Lady of Fatima, marked the tragic attempt on the Holy Father's life. After being shot he fell into the arms of his Secretary, Father Stanislaw Dziwisz, and was rushed immediately to the Gemelli Hospital. L'Osservatore Romano followed in detail the news bulletins on the pope's health and the concern of the whole world during his recovery. "He was shot at with the evident intention of killing him," wrote Valerio Volpini, "a thought that is unable to find a motive in our overwhelmed, dismayed minds, which find it almost impossible to believe that this can really have happened. Sorrow and apprehension mingle with prayer. . . . We pray together with the whole Church. . . ."

The following Saturday, May 17, thousands of people crowded St. Peter's Square to hear the pope's *Regina cæli* message which had previously been recorded at his bedside in the hospital: "Praised be Jesus Christ! Beloved brothers and sisters, I know that during these days and especially in this hour of the *Regina cæli* you are united with me. With deep emotion I thank you for your prayers and I bless you all. I am particularly close to the two persons wounded together with me. I pray for that brother of ours who shot me, and whom I have sincerely pardoned. United with Christ, Priest and Victim, I offer my sufferings for the Church and for the world. To you, Mary, I repeat: *Totus tuus ego sum.*"

On June 3, exactly three weeks after the attempt on his life, the Holy Father returned to the Vatican. The liturgical celebrations for Pentecost took place as indicated by the Holy Father on May 25. The celebrant of the Mass was the Cardinal Dean of the Sacred College, Carlo Confalonieri, and, after the proclamation of the Gospel, the Holy Father's prerecorded homily was broadcast in St. Peter's Basilica. Before the conclusion of the Mass, John Paul II appeared at the interior loggia of the Basilica to greet and bless those present. On the same day he appeared at the window of his private study and the *Regina cæli* message, which he had recorded for the occasion, was broadcast in the Square.

In the Angelus message a week later the pope thanked "the young people of my Krakow, of my Rome, of those in Switzerland whom I should have met in the past days, and of the many others in various countries in the world, who have wished to be spiritually close to me and all of whom it is difficult for me to name here. Let them be assured that their messages and their prayers have really been a support and comfort to me, because I have seen in them the true love that Christ revealed to us."

On June 20 the Holy Father was readmitted to the hospital for further tests, treatment for an infection, and a final operation, and he stayed for almost two months. On August 14 he addressed the patients and personnel with a message broadcast throughout the hospital: "On May 13, after the attempt on my life, I immediately found effective help in this house which bears the name 'Gemelli Polyclinic.' Today, after three months, most of which I have spent among you—after the successful and final operation undergone on August 5, the Feast of Our Lady of Snows—I am able to return home. Having been restored to health clinically, I am going home to recuperate the strength that is indispensable for the complete exercise of my ministry in St. Peter's See. . . . I now know better than ever that suffering is a certain dimension of life, in which more than ever the grace of Redemption is deeply engrafted in the human heart."

Before the year was over, two major papal documents were issued, the third encyclical *Laborem exercens* on human work (September 14), which is inserted in the line of the great magisterial documents on social doctrine, and the Apostolic Exhortation *Familiaris consortio* on the mission of the Christian family in the modern world (November 22), following last year's Synod of Bishops. *Familiaris consortio* is addressed "to those who are already aware of the value of marriage and the family and seek to live it faithfully, to those who are uncertain and anxious and searching for the truth, and to those who are unjustly impeded from living freely their family lives. . . . In a particular way the Church addresses the young, who are beginning their journey towards marriage and family life, for the purpose of presenting them with new horizons, helping them to discover the beauty and grandeur of the vocation to love and the service of life" (*Familiaris consortio*, n. 1).

Except for the forced interruption during his recovery, the Holy Father continued the General Audience talks on human love.

LETTER
OF THE HOLY FATHER
POPE JOHN PAUL II
TO ALL THE BISHOPS OF THE CATHOLIC CHURCH
FOR THE 1600ᵗʰ ANNIVERSARY
OF THE FIRST COUNCIL OF CONSTANTINOPLE
AND THE 1550ᵗʰ ANNIVERSARY
OF THE COUNCIL OF EPHESUS

My Dear Brothers in the Episcopate!

I.

1. I am impelled to write you this letter—which is both a theological reflection and a pastoral invitation coming from the depths of my heart—first of all by the 16ᵗʰ centenary of the First Council of Constantinople which was held in the year 381. As I pointed out at the beginning of the New Year in St. Peter's Basilica, "after the Council of Nicæa this was the second ecumenical council of the Church. . . . To it we owe the Credo that is constantly recited in the Liturgy. A particular heritage of that council is the doctrine on the Holy Spirit, thus proclaimed in the Latin liturgy: '*Credo in Spiritum Sanctum, Dominum et vivificantem . . . qui cum Patre et Filio simul adoratur et conglorificatur, qui locutus est per prophetas.*'"[1]

These words repeated in the Creed by so many generations of Christians will have a particular significance both of doctrine and religious sentiment for us this year and will remind us of the profound bonds that link the Church of today—as we look towards the coming of the third millennium of her life, a life so wonderfully rich and tested, continually sharing in the cross and resurrection of Christ, in the power of the Holy Spirit—with the Church of the fourth century, in the one continuity of her first beginnings, and in fidelity to the teaching of the gospel and the preaching of the Apostles.

What has just been said suffices to enable us to understand how the teaching of the First Council of Constantinople is still the *expression of the one common faith* of the Church of the whole of Christianity. As we confess this faith—as we do every time that we recite the Creed—and as we revive it in the forthcoming centenary commemoration, we wish to emphasize the things which unite us with all our brothers, notwithstanding the divisions that have occurred in the course of the centuries. As we do this, 1600 years after the First Council of Constantinople, we give thanks to God for the *truth of the Lord*, which, thanks to the teaching of that council, enlightens the paths of our faith and the paths of life by virtue of that faith. In this anniversary we not only call to mind a formula of faith that has been in force for sixteen centuries in the Church; at the same time we make ever more present to our spirit, in reflection, in prayer, in the contribution of spirituality and theology, that personal divine power which gives life, that hypostatic Gift—*Dominum et vivificantem*—that Third Person of the Most Holy Trinity who in this faith is shared in by each individual soul and by the whole Church. The Holy Spirit continues to vivify the Church and to guide her along the paths to holiness and love. As St. Ambrose pointed out so well in his work *De Spiritu Sancto,*"although he is inaccessible by nature, yet he can be received by us, thanks to his goodness; he fills everything with his power, but only the just share in him; he is simple in his substance, rich in power, present in all, shares that which is his in order to give it to each one, and is wholly present in every place."[2]

2. The memory of the Council of Constantinople, which was the second ecumenical council of the Church, makes us, the Christians of the period towards the end of the second millennium, aware of how lively was the need, in the first centuries of the first millennium, among the growing community of believers, to understand and to proclaim *correctly*, in the confession of the Church, the inscrutable mystery of God in his absolute transcendence: Father, Son and Holy Spirit. This and other key principles of truth and of Christian life first attracted the attention of the faithful; and with regard to these principles there arose numerous interpretations, some of them divergent ones, which made necessary the voice of the Church, her solemn witness given in virtue of the promise made by Christ in the Upper Room: "the Counsellor, the Holy Spirit, whom the Father will send in my name . . . will bring to your remembrance all that I have said to you";[3] he, the Spirit of Truth, "will guide you into all the truth."[4]

Therefore, in the present year 1981, we ought to give thanks to the Holy Spirit in a special way because, in the midst of the many fluctuations of human thought, he has enabled the Church to express her faith, in the manners of expression peculiar to the age, in complete harmony with "all the truth."

"I believe in the Holy Spirit, the Lord, the giver of life, who proceeds from the Father. With the Father and the Son he is worshipped and glorified. He has spoken through the Prophets": these are the words of the Creed of the First Council of Constantinople in 381[5] that elucidated the mystery of the Holy Spirit and his origin from the Father, thus affirming the unity and equality in divinity of the Holy Spirit with the Father and the Son.

II.

3.   As I recall the 16th centenary of the First Council of Constantinople, I cannot pass over in silence yet another significant occasion that concerns 1981: this year, in fact, there also occurs the 1550th anniversary of the Council of Ephesus, which was held in 431. This anniversary is, as it were, overshadowed by the preceding council, but it too has a particular importance for our faith, and is supremely worthy of being remembered.

In that same Creed, in fact, we recite, in the midst of the liturgical community as it prepares to relive the Divine Mysteries, the words: *"Et incarnatus est de Spiritu Sancto ex Maria Virgine, et homo factus est"* (by the power of the Holy Spirit he became incarnate from the Virgin Mary, and was made man). The Council of Ephesus thus had *a value that was above all Christological*, for it defined the two natures in Jesus Christ, the divine and the human, in order to state exactly the authentic doctrine of the Church already expressed by the Council of Nicæa in 325, but which had been imperilled by the spread of certain formulas used in the Nestorian teaching. In close connection with these affirmations, the Council of Ephesus also had a soteriological significance, for it illustrated the fact that—as the well-known axiom has it—"what is not assumed is not saved." But just as closely linked with the value of these dogmatic truths was also the truth concerning the Blessed Virgin, called to the unique and unrepeatable dignity of being the Mother of God, *Theotokos*, as was so clearly shown principally by the letter of St. Cyril to Nestorius[6] and by the splendid *Formula Unionis* of 433.[7] It was a whole hymn raised by those ancient Fathers to the incarnation of the only-begotten Son of God, in the full truth of the two natures in the One Person: it was a hymn to the work of salvation, accomplished in the world through the working of the Holy Spirit; and all of this could not fail to redound to the honor of the Mother of God, the first cooperator with the power of the Almighty, which overshadowed her at the moment of the Annunciation in the luminous coming of the Holy Spirit.[8] And this is how our brothers and sisters of Ephesus understood it, when, on the evening of 22 June, the first day of the council, celebrated in the Cathedral of the "Mother of God," they acclaimed the Virgin Mary with this title and carried the Fathers in triumph at the end of that first session.

It therefore seems to me very opportune that this ancient council too, the third in the history of the Church, should be remembered by us in its rich theological and ecclesial context. The Most Blessed Virgin is she who, by the overshadowing of the power of the Trinity, was the creature most closely associated with the work of salvation. The incarnation of the Word took place beneath her heart, by the power of the Holy Spirit. In her there dawned the new humanity which with Christ was presented in the world in order to bring to completion the original plan of the covenant with God, broken by the disobedience of the first man. *Et incarnatus est de Spiritu Sancto ex Maria Virgine.*

4.   These two anniversaries, though for different reasons and with differing historical relevance, redound to the honor of the Holy Spirit. All was accomplished *by the power of the Holy Spirit.* One can see how profoundly these two great commemorations, to which it is proper to make reference in this year of the Lord 1981, are linked to one another in the teaching and in the profession of faith of the Church, of the faith of all Christians. Faith in the Most Holy Trinity: faith in the Father, from whom all gifts come.[9] Faith in Christ the Redeemer of man. Faith in the Holy Spirit. And, in this light, veneration of the Blessed Virgin, who "by thus consenting to the divine utterance . . . became the Mother of Jesus. Embracing God's saving will with a full heart and impeded by no sin, she devoted herself totally as a hand-maid of the Lord to the person and work of her Son" and "the holy Fathers see her as used by God not merely in a passive way, but as cooperating in the work of human salvation through free faith and obedience."[10] And it is wonderful that, just as Mary awaited with faith the coming of the Lord, so also in this last part of the second millennium she should be present to illuminate our faith as we await this "advent."

All this is for us a *source* of immense *joy*, a source of *gratitude* for the light of this faith, whereby we share in the inscrutable mysteries of God, making them the living content of our souls, expanding thereby the horizons of the understanding of our spiritual dignity and of our individual destinies. And so, these great anniversaries too cannot remain for us merely a memory of the distant past. They must take on fresh life in the faith of the Church, they must re-echo anew in her spirituality, indeed they must find an external manifestation of their ever living relevance for the entire community of believers.

5. I write these things in the first place to you, my dear and venerable *brothers in the episcopal service*. I address myself at the same time to my *brother priests*, your closest collaborators in your pastoral care *in virtute Spiritus Sancti*. I address the brothers and sisters of all the religious families of men and women, in the midst of which there should be a particularly lively witness of the Spirit of Christ and likewise a particular love for the mission of her who consented to be the handmaid of the Lord.[11] I finally address myself to all my brothers and sisters *of the laity* of the Church, who, in professing her faith together with all the other members of the ecclesial community, have so often and for so many generations rendered ever living the memory of the great councils. I am convinced that they will accept with gratitude the evocation of these dates and anniversaries, especially when together we realize how relevant are, at the same time, the mysteries to which the two councils gave authoritative expression as long ago as the first half of the first millennium of the history of the Church.

I also venture to hope that the commemoration of the Councils of Constantinople and Ephesus, which were expressions of the faith taught and professed by the undivided Church, will make us grow in mutual understanding with our beloved brothers in the East and in the West, with whom we are still not united by full ecclesial communion but together with whom we seek in prayer, with humility and with trust, the paths to unity in truth. What indeed can more effectively hasten the journey toward that unity than the memory and, at the same time, the reliving of that which for so many centuries has been the content of the faith professed in common, indeed which has not ceased to be so, even after the sad divisions which have occurred in the course of the centuries?

III.

6. It is therefore my aim that these events should be lived within the whole of their *ecclesiological context*. We should not merely commemorate these great anniversaries as things that happened in the past: we must give them life in our own times and establish a deep link between them and the life and role *of the Church of our period*, as that life and role have been given expression throughout the message of *the council* of our period, the Second Vatican Council. How deeply rooted in that teaching are the truths defined in the two councils that we are commemorating! To how great an extent those truths have permeated the Second Vatican Council's central doctrine on the Church! How substantial and constitutive they are for that doctrine! And likewise how intensely these fundamental and central truths of our faith live, so to speak, a new life and shine with a new light throughout the teaching of the Second Vatican Council!

While the chief task of our generation, and perhaps also of future generations in the Church, will be to carry out and make part of life the teaching and guidance of this great council, the anniversaries this year of the First Council of Constantinople and the Council of Ephesus give us an opportunity for performing this task in the living context of the truth that lasts throughout the ages to eternity.

7.   "When the Son had accomplished the work that the Father gave him to do on earth,[12] the Holy Spirit was sent on the day of Pentecost, in order that he might continually sanctify the Church and that through Christ those who believe might thus have access in one Spirit to the Father.[13] He is the Spirit of life, aspring of water welling up to eternal life;[14] through him the Father gives life to people who are dead because of sin, until the day when, in Christ, he raises to life their mortal bodies.[15] The Spirit dwells in the Church and in the hearts of the faithful, as in a temple.[16] In them he prays and bears witness to their adoption as children.[17] He guides the Church into all the truth,[18] unifies her in communion and ministry, provides her with varied hierarchic and charismatic gifts, through which he directs her, and adorns her with his fruits.[19] He rejuvenates the Church by the power of the Gospel, continually renews her and leads her to perfect union with her Bridegroom. For the Spirit and the Bride say to the Lord Jesus:'Come.'[20] Thus the universal Church is seen to be'a people brought into unity from the unity of the Father, the Son and the Holy Spirit.'"[21] This is certainly the richest and most synthetic text, although not a unique one, indicating how the *truth about the Holy Spirit*, to which expression was given so authoritatively 1600 years ago by the First Council of Constantinople, lives with new life and shines with new splendor throughout the teaching of the Second Vatican Council.

The whole *work of renewal of the Church*, so providentially set forth
and initiated by the Second Vatican Council—a renewal that must be
both an updating and a consolidation of what is eternal and constitutive of the Church's mission—can be carried out only *in the Holy
Spirit*, that is to say, with the aid of his light and his power. This is
important, so important, for the whole of the universal Church and
also for each particular Church in its communion with all the other
particular Churches. This is important also for the ecumenical process
within Christianity and for the Church's path in the modern world,
which must extend in the direction of justice and peace. This is important also for activity in favor of priestly or religious vocations, as
well as for the apostolate of the laity, as the fruit of a new maturity
in their faith.

8.   The two phrases in the Nicene-Constantinopolitan Creed, "*Et
incarnatus est de Spiritu Sancto*" and "*Credo in Spiritum Sanctum, Dominum et vivificantem*," remind us that the greatest work of the Holy
Spirit, one to which all the others unceasingly refer as a source from
which they draw, is that of the *incarnation of the Eternal Word* by the
power of the Spirit from the Virgin Mary.

Christ, the Redeemer of man and the world, is the center of
history: "Jesus Christ is the same yesterday and today and forever."[22]
Our thoughts and our hearts are turned to him in view of the approaching end of the second millennium separating us from his first
coming into the world, but for that very reason they turn to the *Holy
Spirit*, through whose power his human conception took place, and
to the *Virgin Mary*, by whom he was conceived and from whom he
was born. The anniversaries of the two great councils this year direct
our thoughts and hearts in a special way to the Holy Spirit and to
Mary, the Mother of God. While we recall the joy and exultation that
the profession of faith in the divine motherhood of the Virgin Mary
(*Theotokos*) aroused 1550 years ago at Ephesus, we understand that
that profession of faith also glorified the *particular work of the Holy
Spirit*, the work composed of both the human conception and birth
of the Son of God by the power of the Holy Spirit and, again by the
power of the Holy Spirit, the holy motherhood of the Virgin Mary.
This motherhood is not only the source and foundation of all her
exceptional holiness and her very special participation in the whole
plan of salvation; it also establishes a permanent maternal link with
the Church, as a result of the fact that she was chosen by the Holy
Trinity as the Mother of Christ, who is "the head of the body, the

Church."[23] This link was revealed especially beneath the cross, where she, "enduring with her only-begotten Son the intensity of his suffering, associated herself with his Sacrifice in her mother's heart . . . she was given by the same Christ Jesus dying on the cross as a Mother to his disciple, with these words: 'Woman, behold, your son!'"[24]

The Second Vatican Council summarizes in felicitous words Mary's unbreakable relationship with Christ and with the Church: "Since it had pleased God not to manifest solemnly the mystery of the salvation of the human race before he would pour forth the Spirit promised by Christ, we see the Apostles before the day of Pentecost 'with one accord devoting themselves to prayer, together with the women and Mary the Mother of Jesus, and with his brethren,'[25] and we also see Mary by her prayers imploring the gift of the Spirit, who had already overshadowed her in the Annunciation."[26] With these words the council text links the two moments in which Mary's motherhood is most closely united with the work of the Holy Spirit: firstly, the moment of the Incarnation, and secondly, that of the birth of the Church in the Upper Room in Jerusalem.

IV.

9.   Accordingly, all these great and important motives and the coincidence of such meaningful circumstances are reasons for giving particular emphasis throughout the Church this year, which is the jubilee of two events, to the solemnity of Pentecost.

I therefore invite all the Episcopal Conferences of the Catholic Church and the Patriarchates and Metropolitan Provinces of the Eastern Catholic Churches to send the representatives they wish to Rome for that day, in order that we may together renew the inheritance that we have received from the Pentecost Upper Room in the power of the Holy Spirit. It is he who showed the Church, at the moment of her birth, the way that leads to all nations, all peoples and tongues, and to the heart of every individual.

Finding ourselves gathered in collegial unity, as inheritors of the apostolic solicitude for all the Churches,[27] we shall draw from the abundant source of the same Spirit, who guides the Church's mission on the paths of present-day humanity, at the close of the second millennium after the Word became incarnate by the power of the Holy Spirit in the womb of the Virgin Mary.

10. First, on the morning of the solemnity we shall come together in the *Basilica of St. Peter in the Vatican* to sing with all our hearts our belief *"in Spiritum Sanctum, Dominum et vivificantem . . . qui locutus est per prophetas . . . Et unam sanctam catholicam et apostolicam Ecclesiam."* We are prompted to do this by the 1600th anniversary of the First Council of Constantinople. Like the Apostles in the Upper Room and the Fathers of that council, we shall be brought together by the one who "rejuvenates the Church by the power of the Gospel" and "constantly renews her."[28]

Thus, this year's solemnity of Pentecost will be a sublime and grateful profession of the faith in the Holy Spirit, the Lord, the giver of life, that we owe in a particular way to that council. It will also be a humble and ardent prayer that the Holy Spirit will help us "renew the face of the earth"—among other ways by means of the Church's work of renewal in accordance with the thought of the Second Vatican Council. It will be a prayer that this work may be carried out maturely and in a regular way in all the Churches and Christian communities, and that the work may, first and foremost, be carried out within people's souls, since no true renewal is possible without continual conversion to God. We shall ask the Spirit of Truth that we may, *on the path of this renewal*, remain *perfectly faithful to what the Spirit says* to us at the present time in the teaching of the Second Vatican Council, not abandoning this way at the prompting of a certain regard for the spirit of the world. We shall also ask him who is *"fons vivus, ignis, caritas"* (living water, fire and love) to permeate us and the whole Church, and also the human family, with the love that "hopes all things, endures all things" and "never ends."[29]

There is no doubt that at the present stage of the history of the Church and of humanity a special need is felt to go deeper into and give new life to the truth about the Holy Spirit. The commemoration at Pentecost of the sixteenth centenary of the First Council of Constantinople will give us an occasion for doing this. May the Holy Spirit accept our manifestation of faith. In the liturgical function of the solemnity of Pentecost may he accept us as we humbly open our hearts to him, the Consoler, in whom the gift of unity is revealed and brought to realization.

11. In the second part of the celebration, we shall gather in the late afternoon of the same day in the *Basilica of St. Mary Major*. There the morning part will be completed by the thoughts presented by the 1550th anniversary of the Council of Ephesus. We shall also be prompted to do this because by a singular coincidence Pentecost will this year fall on 7 June, as it did in 431, when on that solemn day, on which the council sessions, later postponed to 22 June, were to begin, the first groups of bishops began to arrive in Ephesus.

These thoughts will also be reflected on in the light of the Second Vatican Council, with special attention to the marvelous seventh chapter of the Constitution *Lumen gentium*. Just as the Council of Ephesus's Christological and soteriological teaching made it possible to confirm the truth about the divine motherhood of Mary, *Theotokos*, so too the Second Vatican Council enables us to recall that, when the Church was born by the power of the Holy Spirit in the Upper Room in Jerusalem, she began to look to Mary as the example for her own spiritual motherhood and therefore as her archetype. On that day the one whom Paul VI called *Mother of the Church* irradiated the power of her intercession over the *Church as Mother* and protected the apostolic zeal by which the Church still lives, generating for God the believers of all times and all geographical areas.

Accordingly, the afternoon liturgy of the solemnity of Pentecost will gather us in the chief Marian Basilica of Rome, in order thus to recall in a special way that in the Upper Room at Jerusalem the Apostles "with one accord devoted themselves to prayer, together with . . . Mary the Mother of Jesus . . .",[30] in preparation for the coming of the Holy Spirit. We too likewise wish on that important day to devote ourselves with one accord to prayer, together with her who, as Mother of God, is, in the words of the Second Vatican Council's Dogmatic Constitution on the Church, "a type of the Church in the order of faith, charity, and perfect union with Christ."[31] Thus, devoting ourselves to prayer, together with her, and full of trust in her, we shall entrust to the power of the Holy Spirit the Church and her mission among all the nations of the world of today and tomorrow. For we have within us the heritage of those who were commanded by the Risen Christ to go into all the world and preach the Gospel to all creation.[32]

On the day of Pentecost, gathered in prayer, together with Mary the Mother of Jesus, they became convinced that they could carry out this command with the power of the Holy Spirit that had come upon them, as the Lord had foretold.[33] On the same day we, their heirs, shall join together in the same act of faith and prayer.

V.

12. Dear brothers, I know that on Holy Thursday you renew within the community of the presbyterium of your dioceses the memorial of the Last Supper, during which, by the words of Christ and the power of the Holy Spirit, the bread and wine became the body and blood of our Savior, that is to say, the Eucharist of our redemption.

On that day, or also on other suitable occasions, speak to all the People of God about these important anniversaries and events, in order that in every local church and every community of the Church they may similarly be recalled and lived as they deserve, in the manner that will be decided by the individual bishops in accordance with the indications of the respective Episcopal Conferences or of the Patriarchates or Metropolitan Provinces of the Eastern Churches.

Looking forward eagerly to the celebrations that I have announced, I gladly impart my special Apostolic Blessing to all of you, venerable and dear brothers in the episcopate, and together with you to your ecclesial communities.

Given in Rome, at St. Peter's on 25 March 1981, the Solemnity of the Annunciation of the Lord, the third year of the Pontificate.

Endnotes

1. L'Osservatore Romano, 2-3 January 1981.
2. St. Ambrose, *De Spiritu Sancto*, I, V, 72; ed. O. Faller; CSEL 79, Vindobonæ 1964, p. 45.
3. Jn 14: 26.
4. Jn 16: 13.
5. Thus quoted for the first time in the Acts of the Council of Chalcedon, act. II: ed. E. Schwartz, *Acta Conciliorum Oecumenicorum, II Concilium universale Chalcedonense, Berolini et Lipsiæ* 1917-32 I, 2, p. 80; cf. also *Conciliorum Oecumenicorum Decreta*, Bologna 1973, p. 24.
6. *Acta Conciliorum Oecumenicorum, I Concilium universale Ephesinum*: ed. E. Schwartz, I, 1, pp. 25-28 and 223-242; cf. also *Conciliorum Oecumenicorum Decreta*, Bologna 1973, pp. 40-44; 50-61.
7. *Acta Conciliorum Oecumenicorum*, I, I, 4, pp. 8ff. (A); cf. also *Conciliorum Oecumenicorum Decreta*, pp. 69f.
8. Cf. Lk 1: 35.
9. Cf. Jas 1: 17.
10. *Lumen gentium*, 56.
11. Cf. Lk 1: 38.
12. Cf. Jn 17: 4.
13. Cf. Eph 2: 18.

14. Cf. Jn 4: 14; 7: 38-39.
15. Cf. Rom 8: 10-11.
16. Cf. 1 Cor 3: 16; 6: 19.
17. Cf. Gal 4: 6; Rom 8: 15-16, 26.
18. Cf. Jn 16: 13.
19. Cf. Eph 4: 11-12; 1 Cor 12: 4; Gal 5: 22.
20. Cf. Rv 22: 17.
21. *Lumen gentium*, 4.
22. Heb 13: 8.
23. Col 1: 18.
24. *Lumen gentium*, 58.
25. Cf. Acts 1: 14.
26. *Lumen gentium*, 59.
27. Cf. 2 Cor 11: 28.
28. Cf. *Lumen gentium*, 4.
29. 1 Cor 13: 7-8.
30. Acts 1: 14.
31. *Lumen gentium*, 63.
32. Cf. Mk 16: 15.
33. Cf. Acts 1: 8.

1982

Fourth Year of Pontificate

Early in this year the Holy Father made another apostolic journey to Africa during which he visited four countries: Nigeria, Benin, Gabon and Equatorial Guinea (February 12-19). In May he made a short trip to Portugal (May 12-15) to pray before Our Lady of Fatima on the anniversary of the attempt on his life. "I come here today because on this very day last year, in St. Peter's Square in Rome, the attempt on the pope's life was made, in mysterious coincidence with the anniversary of the first apparition at Fatima. . . . I seemed to recognize in the coincidence of the dates a special call to come to this place. And so, today I am here. I have come in order to thank Divine Providence in this place which the Mother of God seems to have chosen in a particular way" (Homily, May 13, n. 4).

On the occasion of Holy Thursday the pope sent to all the priests of the Church the text of a prayer. "This year I am not writing you a letter," he said. "Instead I am sending you the text of a prayer dictated by faith and coming from my heart, so as to share with you in offering it to Christ on the birthday of my priesthood and yours, and to suggest a shared meditation in the light and with the support of this prayer" (1982 Letter, Introduction).

Later in the year the Holy Father visited England, Scotland and Wales (May 28–June 2); Rio de Janeiro and Argentina (June 11-12), Switzerland (June 15), and made a long trip to Spain (October 31–November 9). On his return from Switzerland he commented: "Fulfilling a commitment that I had made last year . . . I went to the city of Geneva in Switzerland to visit the International Labor Conference. . . . I was thus able to carry out a part of the program that had been postponed by what happened on May 13 of last year. . . . I thank God for the pastoral duty that was given me to fulfill in line with the mission that the Church is called to carry out in today's world. This mission concerns not only eternal goods, but is also directed with particular concern toward 'earthly realities,' namely the goods of culture, economy, the arts, the professions, the political and social institutions in which man's life on earth is summed up" (General Audience, June 16, n. 1).

On November 26 John Paul II proclaimed a Holy Year: "It seems opportune . . . to proclaim for the coming year 1983 the Holy Year of the Redemption, which will begin in the course of next Lent. We ask the Lord that this celebration may bring a gust of spiritual renewal at all levels!" (Address to the College of Cardinals, November 26, n. 6). On

November 28 he erected Opus Dei as a Personal Prelature. "The pontifi-cal act erecting Opus Dei as a Personal Prelature . . . is directly aimed at promoting the apostolic activity of the Church, inasmuch as it puts into operation a new pastoral instrument, which up to now was only foreseen and desired in the law of the Church, and it does so through an institution which offers proven guarantees of apostolic vigor, discipline and faithfulness to the teaching of the Church" (Sacred Congregation for Bishops, Declaration, August 23, 1982).

In the General Audiences of the year the Holy Father continued with the theme of human love (nn. 69-103 of the series, January 13-Decem-ber 15).

LETTER
OF THE HOLY FATHER
POPE JOHN PAUL II
TO ALL THE PRIESTS OF THE CHURCH
ON THE OCCASION OF HOLY THURSDAY 1982

A Prayer Dictated by Faith and Coming from My Heart

Dear Brothers in the Priesthood!

From the beginning of my ministry as Pastor of the universal Church, I have wished Holy Thursday each year to be a day of special spiritual communion with you, in order to share with you in prayer, in pastoral care and in hope, to encourage you in your generous and faithful service, and to thank you in the name of the whole Church.

This year I am not writing you a letter. Instead I am sending you the text of a prayer dictated by faith and coming from my heart, so as to share with you in offering it to Christ on the birthday of my priesthood and yours, and to suggest a shared meditation in the light and with the support of this prayer.

May each one of you rekindle the gift of God that is within you through the laying on of hands (cf. 2 Tm 1: 6), and may you experience with renewed fervor the joy of having given yourselves totally to Christ.

From the Vatican, on the 25th day of March, the Solemnity of the Annunciation of the Lord, in the year 1982, the fourth of the Pontificate.

I.

1.   We turn to You, O Christ of the Upper Room and of Calvary, on this day which is the feast of our priesthood.

To You we turn, all of us, bishops and priests, gathered together in the priestly assemblies of our churches, and at the same time joined together in the universal unity of the holy and apostolic Church.

Holy Thursday is the *birthday of our priesthood*. It is on this day that we were all born. As a child is born from its mother's womb, thus were we born, O Christ, from Your one and eternal Priesthood. We were born in the grace and strength of the new and eternal Covenant from the body and blood of Your redeeming sacrifice: from the body that was given for us,[1] and from the blood that was poured out for us all.[2]

We were born at the Last Supper, and at the same time at the foot of the cross on Calvary: the place which is *the source* of new life and of all the sacraments of the Church is also the place where our priest-hood begins.

We were also born together with the whole People of God of the New Covenant, whom You, the beloved of the Father,[3] made "a kingdom, priests to your God and Father."[4]

We have been called to be *servants* of this people, which brings to the eternal tabernacles of the thrice holy God its "spiritual sacrifices."[5]

The Eucharistic Sacrifice is the "source and summit of all Christian life."[6] It is a single sacrifice that embraces everything. It is the greatest treasure of the Church. It is her life.

We thank You, O Christ:

— because You Yourself have chosen us, associating us in a special way with Your Priesthood and marking us with an indelible character which makes each of us able to offer Your own sacri-fice as the sacrifice of the whole people: a sacrifice of reconcili-ation, in which You unceasingly offer to the Father Your own self, and, in You, man and the world;

— because You have made us ministers of the Eucharist and of Your pardon; sharers in Your mission of evangelization; servants of the people of the New Covenant.

II.

2. Lord Jesus Christ, when on the day of Holy Thursday You had to separate Yourself from those whom You had "loved to the end,"[7] You promised them the Spirit of Truth. You said: "It is to your advantage that I go away, for if I do not go away, the Counselor will not come to you; but if I go, I will send him to you."[8]

You went away by means of the cross, becoming "obedient unto death,"[9] and *"emptying Yourself"*[10] through the love with which You loved us to the end; and so, after Your resurrection, *the Holy Spirit was given to the Church,* the Holy Spirit who came to dwell in her "forever."[11]

It is the Spirit who "by the power of the Gospel preserves the Church's youth, continually renews her and leads her to perfect union" with You.[12]

Each one of us is aware that through the Holy Spirit, working through the power of Your cross and resurrection, we have received the ministerial priesthood in order to serve the cause of man's salvation in Your Church; and

— we ask today, on this day which is so holy for us, that Your Priesthood may be *continually renewed* in the Church, through Your Spirit who in every epoch of history must "preserve the youth" of this beloved Bride of yours;

— we ask that each one of us will find again in his heart, and will unceasingly confirm through his life, the genuine meaning that his personal priestly vocation has both for himself and for all people,

— so that in an ever more mature way we may see with the eyes of faith the true dimension and beauty of the priesthood,

— so that we may persevere in giving thanks for the gift of his vocation, as for an undeserved grace,

— so that, giving thanks unceasingly, we may be strengthened in fidelity to this holy gift, which, precisely because it is completely gratuitous, imposes a proportionately greater obligation.

3.   We thank You for having likened us to You as ministers of Your Priesthood, by calling us to build up Your Body, the Church, not only through the administration of the sacraments, but also, and even before that, through the proclamation of Your "message of salvation,"[13] making us sharers in Your responsibility as Pastor.

We thank You for having had confidence in us, in spite of our weakness and human frailty, infusing into us at Baptism the vocation and grace of perfection to be acquired day by day.

We ask that we may always be able to carry out our sacred duties according to the measure of a pure heart and an upright conscience. May we be *faithful "to the end" to You, who loved us "to the end."*[14]

May no place be found in our souls for those currents of ideas which diminish the importance of the ministerial priesthood, those opinions and tendencies which strike at the very nature of the holy vocation and service to which You, O Christ, call us within Your Church.

When on Holy Thursday, as You instituted the Eucharist and the priesthood, You were leaving those whom You had loved to the end, You promised them the new "Counselor."[15] May this Counselor, the "Spirit of Truth,"[16] be with us through his holy gifts! May there be with us wisdom and understanding, knowledge and counsel, fortitude, piety and the holy fear of God, so that we may always know how to discern what comes from You and distinguish what comes from the "spirit of the world"[17] or even from the "ruler of this world."[18]

4.   Save us from *"grieving Your Spirit"*: [19]

— by our lack of faith and lack of readiness to witness to Your Gospel "in deed and in truth";[20]

— by secularism and by wishing at all costs to conform to the mentality of this world;[21]

— by a lack of that love which is "patient and kind . . . ," which "is not boastful . . ." and which "does not insist on its own way . . . ," which "bears all things, believes all things, hopes all things, endures all things . . ." and that which "rejoices in the right" and only in the right.[22]

Save us from *"grieving Your Spirit"*:

— by everything that brings inward sadness and is an obstacle for the soul;

— by whatever causes complexes and divisions;

— by whatever makes us a fertile soil for all temptations;

— by whatever shows itself as a desire to hide one's priesthood before men and to avoid all external signs of it;

— by whatever can in the end bring one to the temptation to run away, under the pretext of the "right to freedom."

Save us from demeaning the fullness and richness of our freedom, which we have ennobled and realized by giving ourselves to You and accepting the gift of the priesthood.

Save us from separating our freedom from You, to whom we owe the gift of this inexpressible grace.

Save us from *"grieving Your Spirit."*

Enable us to *love with that love with which Your Father* "loved the world" when He gave "his only Son, that whoever believes in him should not perish but have eternal life."[23]

Today, which is the day on which You Yourself promised to the Church the Spirit of Truth and love, joining with those who at the Last Supper were the first to receive from You the charge to celebrate the Eucharist, all of us cry out:

"Send forth Your Spirit . . . and renew the face of the earth."[24] Renew too the face of that priestly earth which You made fruitful by the sacrifice of Your body and blood, the sacrifice which You renew through our hands every day on the altars, in the vineyard of Your Church.

III.

5.   Today everything speaks of this love whereby You loved the Church and gave Yourself up for her, in order to make her holy.[25]

Through the redeeming love of Your definitive giving You made the Church Your bride, leading her along the paths of her earthly experiences, in order to prepare her for the eternal "marriage of the Lamb"[26] in the "Father's house."[27]

This spousal love of Yours as Redeemer, this saving love of Yours as Bridegroom, makes fruitful all the "hierarchical and charismatic gifts" by which the Holy Spirit "provides for and guides" the Church.[28]

Is it permissible for us, Lord, to doubt this love of Yours?

Can anyone who lets himself be guided by living faith in the Founder of the Church doubt this love, to which the Church owes all her spiritual vitality?

Is it permissible to doubt:

— that You can and will give Your Church true "stewards of the mysteries of God,"[29] and, especially, true ministers of the Eucharist?

— that You can and will kindle in the souls of men, especially the young, the charism of priestly service, as it has been received and actuated in the tradition of the Church?

— that You can and will kindle in those souls not only a desire for the priesthood but also that readiness to accept the gift of celibacy for the sake of the kingdom of heaven of which both in the past and still today whole generations of priests in the Catholic Church have given proof?

Is it proper to continue, in opposition to the voice of the recent ecumenical council and the Synod of Bishops, to declare that the Church ought to give up this tradition and heritage?

Is it not rather the duty of us priests to live out our commitment with generosity and joy, helping by our witness and by our action to spread this ideal? Is it not our task to cause an increase in the number of future priests in the service of the People of God, by working with all our strength for the reawakening of vocations and by supporting the irreplaceable work of the seminaries, where those called to the ministerial priesthood can properly prepare for the total gift of themselves to Christ?

6.   In this Holy Thursday meditation I boldly put this far-reaching question to my brothers, precisely because this sacred day seems to demand of us *complete and absolute sincerity before You*, the Eternal Priest and the Good Shepherd of our souls.

Indeed yes. It saddens us that the years following the council, for all their undoubted wealth of beneficial leaven, their abundance of edifying initiatives and their fruitfulness for the spiritual renewal of all sections of the Church, have also seen the occurrence of a crisis and the appearance of not a few rifts.

But, in any crisis, can we doubt Your love? The love with which You loved the Church and gave Yourself up for her?[30]

Are not this love and the power of the Spirit of Truth greater than any human weakness, even when this weakness seems to gain the upper hand, even claiming to be a sign of "progress"?

The love that You bestow on the Church is always meant for the man who is weak and exposed to the consequences of his weakness. And yet *You never renounce this love,* which raises man and the Church, placing before both of them precise demands. May we "curtail" this love? Do we not do so whenever, because of man's weakness, we decree that the demands that this love makes must be renounced?

IV.

7.   "Pray therefore the Lord of the harvest to send out laborers into his harvest."[31]

On Holy Thursday, the birthday of the priesthood of each one of us, we see with the eyes of faith all the immensity of this love, which in the Paschal Mystery commanded You to become "obedient unto death" and in this light we also see more clearly our own unworthiness. We feel the need to say, today more than ever: "Lord, I am not worthy. . . . "

Indeed "we are *unworthy servants.*"[32]

But let us make sure that we see this "unworthiness" of ours with a simplicity that makes us *men of great hope.* "Hope does not disappoint us, because God's love has been poured into our hearts through the Holy Spirit who has been given to us."[33]

This Gift is precisely the fruit of Your love: the fruit of the Upper Room and of Calvary. Faith, hope and charity must be the proper standard of our judgment and initiatives.

Today, the day on which the Eucharist was instituted, we beg You with the greatest humility and all the fervor of which we are capable that the Eucharist may be celebrated throughout the world by the ministers called to do so, so that *no community of Your disciples and confessors may lack* this holy sacrifice and spiritual food.

8.   The Eucharist is first and foremost a gift made to the Church. An inexpressible gift. The priesthood too is *a gift* to the Church, *for the sake of the Eucharist.*

Today, when it is said that the community has a right to the Eucharist, it must be remembered in particular that You urged Your disciples to "pray . . . the Lord of the harvest to send out laborers into his harvest."[34]

If people do not "pray" with fervor, if they do not strive with all their strength to ensure that the Lord sends to communities good ministers of the Eucharist, can they say with inner conviction that "the community has a right . . . "?

If it has a right, then it has a right to the gift! And a gift cannot be treated as if it were not a gift. Unceasing prayers must be offered to obtain that gift. We must ask for it on our knees.

And so, since the Eucharist is the Lord's greatest gift to the Church, we must *ask for priests,* because the priesthood too is a gift to the Church.

On this Holy Thursday, as we are gathered with the bishops in our priestly assemblies, we beg You, Lord, to grant that we may always be intensely aware of the greatness of the gift which is the sacrament of Your body and blood.

Grant that, in inner accord with the economy of grace and the law that governs gifts, we may continually "pray the Lord of the harvest," and that our cry may come from a pure heart, a heart that has the simplicity and sincerity of true disciples. Then, *Lord, You will not reject our plea.*

9.   We must cry to You with a voice as loud as is demanded by the greatness of the cause and the eloquence of the needs of our time. And so let us raise our imploring cry.

And yet we are aware that "we do not know how to pray as we ought."[35] Is it not perhaps so because we are dealing with an issue that is so much above us? Nevertheless the issue is ours. There is no other issue as much ours as this one.

The day of Holy Thursday is our feast day.

Let us also think of the fields that "are already white for harvest."[36] Let us therefore be confident that *the Spirit will* "help us in our weakness . . . interceding for us with sighs too deep for words."[37] For it is always the Spirit that "preserves the Church's youth, continually renews her and leads her to perfect union with her Bridegroom."[38]

10.   We are not told that Your *Mother* was present in the Upper Room on Holy Thursday. Nevertheless we pray to You especially through her intercession. What can be dearer to her than the body and blood of her own son, entrusted to the Apostles in the Eucharistic Mystery, the body and blood that our priestly hands unceasingly offer as a sacrifice "for the life of the world"?[39]

And so, *through her,* especially on this day, we thank You, and *through her* we beg:

— that our priesthood may be renewed by the power of the Holy Spirit;
— that it may be ever vibrant with a humble but solid certainty of our vocation and mission;
— that our readiness for the sacred service may increase.

O Christ of the Upper Room and of Calvary! Accept us all, the priests of the Year of Our Lord 1982, and by the mystery of Holy Thursday sanctify us anew. Amen.

Endnotes

1. Cf. Lk 22: 19.
2. Cf. Mt 26: 28.
3. Cf. Col 1: 13.
4. Cf. Rv 1: 6.
5. 1 Pt 2: 5.
6. *Lumen gentium,* 11.
7. Cf. Jn 13: 1.
8. Jn 16: 7.
9. Phil 2: 8.
10. Cf. Phil 2: 7.
11. Cf. Jn 14: 16.
12. Cf. *Lumen gentium,* 4.
13. Cf. Acts 13: 26.
14. Cf. Jn 13: 1.
15. Jn 14: 16.
16. Jn 14: 17.
17. 1 Cor 2: 12.
18. Jn 16: 11.
19. Cf. Eph 4: 30.
20. 1 Jn 3: 18.
21. Cf. Rom 12: 2.
22. Cf. 1 Cor 13: 4-7.
23. Jn 3: 16.
24. Cf. Ps 104 (103): 30.
25. Cf. Eph 5: 25-26.
26. Rv 19: 7.
27. Jn 14: 2.
28. *Lumen gentium,* 4.
29. 1 Cor 4: 1.
30. Cf. Eph 5: 25.
31. Mt 9: 38.
32. Lk 17: 10.
33. Rom 5: 5.
34. Mt 9: 38.
35. Rom 8: 26.
36. Jn 4: 35.
37. Cf. Rom 8: 26.
38. *Lumen gentium,* 4.
39. Jn 6: 51.

1983

Fifth Year of Pontificate

The early part of this year witnessed the beginning of the Holy Year of the Redemption convoked by the Holy Father in the Bull of Indiction *Aperite portas* (January 6) and the promulgation of the new Code of Canon Law by the Apostolic Constitution *Sacræ disciplinæ leges* (January 25).

The thirteen-month-long Jubilee began March 25, the Solemnity of the Annunciation of the Lord. "Let this be a Year that is truly Holy," the pope said on January 6. "Let it be a time of grace and salvation, by being more intensely sanctified by the acceptance of the graces of the Redemption on the part of the people of our time, through a spiritual renewal of the whole People of God, which has for its head Christ" (*Aperite portas*, n. 2). In the same document: "The practice of sacramental confession, in the context of the Communion of Saints . . . is an act of faith in the mystery of Redemption and of its realization in the Church. . . . It is a demand of the very mystery of Redemption that the ministry of reconciliation, entrusted by God to the Shepherds of the Church, should find its natural accomplishment in the Sacrament of Penance" (*Aperite portas*, n. 7).

On January 25 John Paul II addressed a Letter to All the Bishops of the World on the occasion of the presentation of the *Instrumentum laboris* for this year's synod: "I write to you from the depths of my heart, and I ask you to accept my words as though in a sincere and fraternal conversation. . . . I see a providential coincidence in the fact that the synod will be celebrated, precisely in the Jubilee Year of the Redemption, on the subject 'Reconciliation and Penance in the Mission of the Church'" (1983 Letter to Bishops, n. 1). Among the practical considerations, the pope mentioned the fact that "one of the main purposes of the Holy Year of the Redemption is to ensure that the renewing power of the Church's sacramental life be lived especially intensely and indeed, if necessary, that this power be rediscovered. . . . This will include devoting very special attention to the Sacrament of Penance" (1983 Letter to Bishops, n. 5).

The Letter to Priests on the occasion of Holy Thursday was dated March 27, Palm Sunday, two days after the inauguration of the Jubilee. "I wish to address myself to you," the pope said, "at the beginning of the Holy Year. . . . A few days after its opening, there occurs Holy Thursday 1983. As we know, this day reminds us of the day on which, together with the Eucharist, the ministerial priesthood was instituted by

Christ. The priesthood was instituted for the Eucharist . . ." (1983 Letter to Priests, n. 1).

The main theme of the letter was the Sacrament of Penance. "How eloquent is the fact," the pope commented, "that Christ, after his resurrection, once more entered that Upper Room in which on Holy Thursday he had left to the Apostles, together with the Eucharist, the sacrament of the ministerial priesthood, and that he then said to them: 'Receive the Holy Spirit; whose sins you shall forgive, they are forgiven them; and whose sins you shall retain, they are retained' (Jn 20: 22f.). Just as he had previously given them the power to celebrate the Eucharist, or to renew in a sacramental manner his own Paschal Sacrifice, so on this second occasion he gave them the power to forgive sins. During the Jubilee Year, when you meditate on how your ministerial priesthood has been inscribed in the mystery of Christ's redemption, you should have this constantly before your eyes! . . . May you succeed in being, during this Holy Year, in a particularly willing and generous way, the ministers of the Sacrament of Penance . . ." (1983 Letter to Priests, n. 3).

During this year John Paul II travelled to America, Costa Rica, Nicaragua, Panama, El Salvador, Guatemala, Honduras, Belize and Haiti (March 2-9); Poland (his second visit to his homeland, June 16-22); Lourdes, France (August 14-15); and Austria (September 10-13).

In the Consistory of February 2, the Holy Father created eighteen new cardinals, including Joseph Cardinal Bernardin, Archbishop of Chicago. Also during this year the American bishops made their *ad limina* visits, the first time in the pontificate of John Paul II.

In the General Audiences at the beginning of the year, the Holy Father continued his catechetical addresses on human love (nn. 104-108, January 5–February 9) and then continued with themes especially related to the Holy Year, including a series on principles of morality.

LETTER
OF THE HOLY FATHER
POPE JOHN PAUL II
TO ALL THE PRIESTS OF THE CHURCH
ON THE OCCASION OF HOLY THURSDAY 1983

Year of Renewal of the Priestly Vocations

Dear Brothers in the Priesthood of Christ!

1. I wish to address myself to you, at the beginning of the Holy Year of the Redemption and of the special Jubilee, which was opened both in Rome and throughout the Church on March 25. The choice of this day, the Solemnity of the Annunciation of the Lord and at the same time of the Incarnation, has a particular eloquence of its own. In fact, the mystery of the Redemption had its beginning when the Word became flesh in the womb of the Virgin of Nazareth through the power of the Holy Spirit, and it reached its climax in the Paschal event with the death and resurrection of the Redeemer. And it is from those days that we calculate our Jubilee Year, because we desire that precisely in this year the *mystery of the Redemption* should become *particularly present and fruitful* in the life of the Church. We know that this mystery is always present and fruitful, and that it always accompanies the earthly pilgrimage of the People of God, permeating it and shaping it from within. Nevertheless, the custom of making special reference to the periods of fifty years in this pilgrimage corresponds to an ancient tradition. We wish to remain faithful to that tradition, and we are also sure that it bears within itself a part of the mystery of the time chosen by God: that *kairos* in which the economy of salvation is accomplished.

And thus, at the beginning of this new Year of the Redemption and of the special Jubilee, a few days after its opening, there occurs *Holy Thursday 1983*. As we know, this day reminds us of the day on which, together with the Eucharist, the ministerial priesthood was instituted by Christ. The priesthood was instituted for the Eucharist, and therefore for the Church, which, as the community of the People of God, is formed by the Eucharist. This priesthood—ministerial and hierarchical—is shared by us. We received it on the day of our ordination through the ministry of the bishop, who transmitted to each one of us the *sacrament begun with the Apostles*—begun at the Last Supper, in the Upper Room, on the Holy Thursday. And therefore, though the dates of our ordination differ, Holy Thursday remains each year the birthday of our ministerial priesthood. On this holy day, each one of us, as priests of the New Covenant, was born into the priesthood of the Apostles. Each one of us was born in the revelation of the one and eternal Priesthood of the same Jesus Christ. In fact, this revelation took place in the Upper Room on Holy Thursday, on the eve of Golgotha. It was precisely there that Christ began his Paschal Mystery: He "opened" it. And he opened it precisely with the key of the Eucharist and the priesthood.

For this reason, on Holy Thursday we, the "ministers of the New Covenant,"[1] *gather together* with the bishops in the cathedrals of our local churches; *we gather together* before Christ—the one and eternal Source of our priesthood. In this union of Holy Thursday *we find him once more,* and, at the same time—through him, with him and in him—*we once more find ourselves.* Blessed be God the Father, the Son and the Holy Spirit for the grace of this union.

2.   Therefore, at this important moment, I wish once more to proclaim the Year commemorating the Redemption and the special Jubilee. I wish to proclaim it in a special way to you and before you, venerable and dear brothers in the Priesthood of Christ—and I wish to meditate, at least briefly, together with you upon its meaning. In fact, this Jubilee refers in a special way to all of us, as priests of the New Covenant. If the Jubilee means *an invitation* to all believers, the sons and daughters of the Church, to reexamine their own lives and vocations *in the light of the mystery of the Redemption,* then a similar invitation is offered to us with, I would say, an even stronger insistence. The Holy Year of the Redemption, therefore, and the special Jubilee mean that we should see our ministerial priesthood afresh in that light in which it is inscribed by Christ himself in the mystery of the Redemption.

"No longer do I call you servants . . . but I have called you friends."[2] It was precisely in the Upper Room that those words were spoken, in the immediate context of the institution of the Eucharist and of the ministerial priesthood. Christ made known to the Apostles, and to all those who inherit from them the ordained priesthood, that in this vocation and for this ministry they must become *his friends*—they must become the *friends of that mystery* which he came to accomplish. To be a priest means to enjoy special friendship with the mystery of Christ, with the mystery of the Redemption, in which he gives his flesh"for the life of the world."[3] We who celebrate the Eucharist each day, the saving sacrament of the body and blood, must have a particular intimacy with the mystery from which this sacrament takes its beginning. The ministerial priesthood is explainable only and exclusively in the framework of this divine mystery—and only within this framework is it accomplished.

In the depths of our priestly being, thanks to what each one of us became at the moment of our ordination, we are "friends": *we are witnesses who are particularly close to this love,* which manifests itself in the Redemption."For God so loved the world that he gave his only Son, that whoever believes in him should not perish but have eternal life."[4] This is the definition of love in its redemptive meaning. This is the mystery of the Redemption, defined by love. It is the only-begotten Son who takes this love from the Father and who gives it to the Father by bringing it to the world. It is the only-begotten Son who, through this love, gives himself for the salvation of the world: for the eternal life of all individuals, his brothers and sisters.

And we priests, *the ministers of the Eucharist,* are "friends": we find ourselves particularly close to this redeeming love which the Son has brought to the world—and which he brings continuously. Even if this fills us with a holy fear, we must nevertheless recognize that, together with the Eucharist, the mystery of this redeeming love is, in a sense, in our hands. We must recognize that it returns each day upon our lips, that it is lastingly inscribed in our vocation and our ministry.

How very deeply each one of us is *constituted* in his own priestly being *through the mystery of the Redemption!* It is precisely this that the liturgy of Holy Thursday brings home to us. It is precisely this that we must meditate upon during the Jubilee Year. It is upon this that our personal interior renewal must be concentrated, for the Jubilee Year is understood by the Church as a time of spiritual renewal for everyone. If we must be witnesses of this renewal for others, for our brothers and sisters in the Christian vocation, then we must be witnesses to it, and spokesmen for it, to ourselves: the Holy Year of the Redemption is *a year of renewal in the priestly vocation.*

By bringing about such an interior renewal in our holy vocation, we shall be able better and more effectively to preach "a year of favor from the Lord."[5] In fact, the mystery of the Redemption is not just a theological abstraction, but an unceasing reality, through which God embraces man in Christ with his eternal love—and man recognizes this love, allows himself to be guided and permeated by it, to be inte-

riorly transformed by it, and through it he becomes "a new creation."[6]
Man, thus created anew by love, the love that is revealed to him in
Jesus Christ, raises the eyes of his soul to God and together with the
psalmist declares: "With him is plenteous redemption!"[7]

In the Jubilee Year this declaration must rise with special power from
the heart of the whole Church. And this must come about, dear
brothers, through your witness and your priestly ministry.

3.   The Redemption remains connected in the closest possible way
with forgiveness. God has redeemed us in Jesus Christ; God has
caused us to become, in Christ, a "new creation," for in him he has
granted us the gift of forgiveness.

God has reconciled the world to himself in Christ.[8] And precisely
because he has reconciled it in Jesus Christ, as the firstborn of all
creation,[9] *the union of man with God has been irreversibly consolidated*.
This union—which the "first Adam" had, in himself, once consented
to be taken away from the whole human family—cannot be taken
from humanity by anyone, since it has been rooted and consolidated
in Christ, the "second Adam." And therefore humanity becomes continually, in Jesus Christ, a "new creation." It becomes this, because
in him and through him the grace of the remission of sins remains
inexhaustible before every human being: "With him is plenteous redemption."

Dear brothers, during the Jubilee Year we must become particularly
aware of the fact that we are *at the service of this reconciliation with
God*, which was accomplished once and for all in Jesus Christ. We
are the servants and ministers of this sacrament, in which the Redemption is made manifest and is accomplished as forgiveness, as
the remission of sins.

How eloquent is the fact that Christ, after his resurrection, once more
entered that Upper Room in which on Holy Thursday he had left
to the Apostles, together with the Eucharist, the sacrament of the
ministerial priesthood, and that he then said to them: "Receive the
Holy Spirit; whose sins you shall forgive, they are forgiven them; and
whose sins you shall retain, they are retained."[10]

Just as he had previously given them the power to celebrate the
Eucharist, or to renew in a sacramental manner his own Paschal
Sacrifice, so on this second occasion he gave them the power to
forgive sins.

During the Jubilee Year, when you meditate on how your ministerial priesthood has been inscribed in the mystery of Christ's redemption, you should have this constantly before your eyes! The Jubilee is in fact that special time when the Church, according to a very ancient tradition, renews within the whole community of the People of God an awareness of the Redemption *through a singular intensity of the remission and forgiveness of sins*: precisely that remission of sins of which we, the priests of the New Covenant, have become, after the Apostles, the legitimate ministers.

As a consequence of the remission of sins in the Sacrament of Penance, all those who, availing themselves of our priestly service, receive this sacrament can draw even more fully from the generosity of Christ's redemption, obtaining the remission of the *temporal punishment* which, after the remission of sins, still remains to be expiated in the present life or in the next. The Church believes that each and every act of forgiveness comes from the redemption accomplished by Christ. At the same time, she also believes and hopes that Christ himself accepts the mediation of his Mystical Body in the remission of sins and of temporal punishment. And since, upon the basis of the mystery of the Mystical Body of Christ, which is the Church, there develops, in the context of eternity, the *mystery of the Communion of Saints*, in the course of the Jubilee Year the Church looks with special confidence towards that mystery.

The Church wishes to make use, more than ever, of the merits of Mary, of the martyrs and saints, and also of their mediation, in order to make still more present, in all its saving effects and fruits, the redemption accomplished by Christ. In this way the practice of the indulgence, connected with the Jubilee Year, *reveals its full evangelical meaning*, insofar as the good deriving from Christ's redeeming Sacrifice, through the entire generations of the Church's martyrs and saints, from the beginning up to the present time, once more bears fruit, by the grace of the remission of sins and of the effects of sin, in the souls of people today.

My dear brothers in the Priesthood of Christ! During the Jubilee Year, may you succeed in being in a special way *the teachers of God's truth* about forgiveness and remission, as this truth is constantly proclaimed by the Church. Present this truth in all its spiritual richness. Seek the ways to impress it upon the minds and consciences of the men and women of our time. And together with this teaching, may you succeed in being, during this Holy Year, in a particularly willing and generous way, the *ministers of the Sacrament of Penance*, in which the sons and daughters of the Church gain the remission of their sins. May you find, in the service of the confessional, that irreplaceable manifestation and proof of the ministerial priesthood, the model of which has been left to us by so many holy priests and pastors of souls in the history of the Church, down to our own times. And may *the toil of this sacred ministry* help you to understand still more how much the ministerial priesthood of each one of us is inscribed in the mystery of Christ's redemption through the cross and the resurrection.

4. By the words that I am writing to you, I wish to proclaim in a special way for you the Jubilee of the Holy Year of the Redemption. As you know from the documents already published, the Jubilee is being celebrated simultaneously in Rome and throughout the Church, from March 25, 1983, and continuing until Easter of next year. In this way the particular grace of the Year of the Redemption is *being entrusted* to all my brothers in the episcopate, as the pastors of the local churches in the universal community of the Catholic Church. At the same time the same grace of the special Jubilee is being entrusted also to you, dear brothers in the Priesthood of Christ. In fact, you, in union with your bishops, *are the pastors of the parishes* and *of the other communities* of the People of God in all parts of the world.

In fact, the Year of the Redemption is to be lived in the Church *beginning* precisely *from these basic communities* of the People of God. In this regard, I wish to refer at this point to certain passages in the Bull of Indiction of the Jubilee Year, passages which explicitly state that this is necessary:

"The Year of the Redemption," as I wrote,[11] "should leave a special imprint *on the Church's whole life,* so that Christians may learn to rediscover *in their daily experience* all the riches of the salvation which is communicated to them from the time of their Baptism." In fact, "the profound meaning and hidden beauty of this Year that the Lord enables us to celebrate is to be seen in the rediscovery and lived practice of the sacramental economy of the Church, through which the grace of God in Christ reaches *individuals and communities.*"[12]

To sum up, the Jubilee Year is meant to be "a call to repentance and conversion," for the purpose of "bringing about a spiritual renewal of *individuals, families, parishes and dioceses, of religious communities and the other centers of Christian life and apostolate.*"[13] If this call is generously received, it will bring about a sort of movement "from below," which, beginning with the parishes and various communities, as I recently said to my dear presbyterate of the diocese of Rome, will give fresh life to the dioceses and thus cannot fail to exercise a positive influence on the whole Church. Precisely in order to favor this *dynamic movement*, in the Bull I limited myself to offering some guidelines of a general character, and I left "to the episcopal conferences and to the bishops of the individual dioceses" the task of *laying down "more concrete pastoral regulations and suggestions . . . ,* in accordance with local attitudes and customs as well as with the objectives of the 1950th anniversary of Christ's death and resurrection."[14]

5.   For this reason, dear brothers, I ask you with all my heart to reflect on the way in which the holy Jubilee of the Year of the Redemption *can and should be celebrated* in each parish, as also in the other communities of the People of God in which you exercise your priestly and pastoral ministry. I ask you to reflect on how it can and should be celebrated in the framework of these communities and, at the same time, in union with the local and universal Church. I ask you to devote special attention to these *sectors* which the Bull expressly mentions, such as cloistered men and women religious, the sick, the imprisoned, the old and those suffering in other ways.[15] We know in fact that the words of the Apostle: "In my flesh I complete what is lacking in Christ's afflictions for the sake of his body, that is, the Church"[16] are accomplished ceaselessly and in different ways.

May the special Jubilee, thanks to this pastoral *solicitude* and *zeal*, thus truly become, in the words of the prophet, "the year of the Lord's favor"[17] for each one of you, dear brothers, as also for all those whom Christ, Priest and Pastor, has entrusted to your priestly and pastoral ministry.

Accept for the sacred day of Holy Thursday 1983 my present words, as a manifestation of my heartfelt love; and also pray for the one who writes to you, that *he may never lack* this love, about which Christ the Lord three times questioned Simon Peter.[18] With these sentiments I bless you all.

Given in Rome, at St. Peter's, on March 27, Passion (Palm) Sunday, 1983, the fifth year of the Pontificate.

Endnotes

1. Cf. 2 Cor 3: 6.
2. Jn 15: 15.
3. Jn 6: 51.
4. Jn 3: 16.
5. Lk 4: 19; cf. Is 61: 2.
6. 2 Cor 5: 17.
7. Ps 130 (129): 7.
8. Cf. 2 Cor 5: 19.
9. Cf. Col 1: 15.
10. Jn 20: 22f.
11. Bull *Aperite portas Redemptori*, n. 3.
12. *Ibid.*
13. *Loc. cit.*, n. 11.
14. *Ibid.*
15. *Loc. cit.*, n. 11, A and B.
16. Col 1: 24.
17. Is 61: 2; cf. Lk 4: 19.
18. Cf. Jn 21: 15ff.

1984

Sixth Year of Pontificate

In this year, which concluded the Jubilee of the Redemption, officially closed on Easter Sunday, April 22, the Holy Father consecrated the world to the Immaculate Heart of Mary (March 25).

On Ash Wednesday, March 7, John Paul II addressed all the priests: "As Holy Thursday draws near, the day on which each of us is invited to reflect once more with deep gratitude upon the priceless gift bestowed on us by Christ, I feel the need to speak to you, in order to make known to you the sincere affection and lively solicitude with which I follow, in my thoughts and in my prayers, your daily work in the service of the Lord's flock." With the brief letter he sent the text of the homily he gave on February 23 in the celebration of the Jubilee of the Redemption with a large number of priests who had come to Rome from all over the world. "May what I said then bring to each of you spiritual comfort, and renew in your hearts the resolve to persevere generously in your vocation as ministers of the merciful love of God" (1994 Letter, Introduction).

The pope made apostolic visits to Alaska, Korea, Papua New Guinea, the Solomon Islands and Thailand (May 2-12); Switzerland (June 12-17); Canada (September 9-20); and Spain, the Dominican Republic, and Puerto Rico (October 10-12). During the last trip he inaugurated "a special novena. It is the period of nine years which separates us from the fifth centenary of the discovery of America. This date, one of the most important in the history of mankind, also marks the beginning of the faith and the Church on this continent" (Homily during the Mass in Santo Domingo, October 11).

The following pontifical documents were published: the Apostolic Exhortation *Salvifici doloris* on the Christian meaning of human suffering (February 11), the Apostolic Exhortation *Redemptionis donum* to men and women religious on their consecration in the light of the mystery of the Redemption (March 25), and the Post-Synodal Exhortation *Reconciliatio et pænitentia* on the theme of the 1983 Synod of Bishops, reconciliation and penance in the mission of the Church today (December 2). The Sacred Congregation for the Doctrine of the Faith issued the Instruction *Libertatis nuntius* on certain aspects of liberation theology (August 6).

In the General Audience addresses at the beginning of the year, the Holy Father dealt primarily with topics related to the Holy Year, including a series of nine addresses on the Sacrament of Penance (February 22–April 18). On May 23 he said: "During the Holy Year I postponed the treatment of the theme of human love in the divine plan. I would now like to conclude that topic with some considerations especially about the teaching of *Humanæ vitæ*, premising some reflections on the Song of Songs and the Book of Tobit. It seems to me, indeed, that what I intend to explain in the coming weeks constitutes, as it were, the crowning of what I have illustrated" (General Audience, May 23). He continued with this topic until November 28, when in the last and 128th address of the long series he stated: "As a whole, the catechesis which I began over four years ago and which I am concluding today can be summed up under the title 'Human love in the divine plan,' or more precisely, 'The Redemption of the body and the sacramentality of marriage'" (General Audience, November 28). A week later, on December 5, Pope John Paul II began a new series on the truths of the faith, which was to be extended for a number of years.

LETTER
OF THE HOLY FATHER
POPE JOHN PAUL II
TO ALL THE PRIESTS OF THE CHURCH
ON THE OCCASION OF HOLY THURSDAY 1984

Dear Brothers in the Grace of the Priesthood!

As Holy Thursday draws near, the day on which each of us is invited to reflect once more with deep gratitude upon the priceless gift bestowed on us by Christ, I feel the need to speak to you, in order to make known to you the sincere affection and lively solicitude with which I follow, in my thoughts and in my prayers, your daily work in the service of the Lord's flock.

On last February 23, I had the joy of celebrating the Jubilee of the Redemption with a large number of priests who had come to Rome from all over the world. It was a very beautiful experience and one that filled my soul with profound emotion, the echo of which remains with me in undiminished intensity. Wishing in some way to share this experience of communion with all the "stewards of the mysteries of God" (1 Cor 4: 1), I have thought of sending you the text of the homily which I gave on that occasion.

May what I said then bring to each of you spiritual comfort, and renew in your hearts the resolve to persevere generously in your vocation as ministers of the merciful love of God. May you also be sustained by my blessing which I send you with particular affection in Christ Jesus.

From the Vatican, March 7, 1984, Ash Wednesday, the sixth year of the Pontificate.

*Homily for Priests
at the Jubilee of Redemption*
(February 23, 1984)

1. "The Spirit of the Lord God is upon me,
    because the Lord has anointed me
    to bring good tidings to the afflicted;
    he has sent me to bind up the brokenhearted,
    to proclaim liberty to the captives,
    and the opening of the prison to those who are bound;
    to proclaim the year of the Lord's favor."[1]

Dear Brothers in the Grace of the Sacrament of the Priesthood!

A year ago I addressed to you *the Letter for Holy Thursday* 1983, asking you to *proclaim,* together with myself and all the bishops of the Church, *the Year of the Redemption:* the extraordinary Jubilee, the Year of the Lord's favor.

Today I wish to *thank you* for what *you have done* in order to ensure that this Year, which recalls to us the 1950th anniversary of the Redemption, should really be "the year of the Lord's favor," the Holy Year. At the same time, as I meet you *at this concelebration,* the climax of your Jubilee pilgrimage to Rome, I wish to *renew* with you and *make still more vivid the awareness of the mystery of the Redemption,* the living and life giving source of the sacramental priesthood in which each one of us shares.

In you who have gathered here, not only from Italy but also from other countries and continents, I see all priests: *the entire presbyterate of the universal Church.* And I address myself to all with the words of encouragement and exhortation of the Letter to the Ephesians: Brothers, "I . . . beg you to lead a life worthy of the calling to which you have been called."[2]

We too—who have been called to serve others in the spiritual renewal of the Year of the Redemption—need *to be renewed,* through the grace of this Year, in our blessed vocation.

2. *"I will sing of your steadfast love, O Lord, forever."*
This verse of the Responsorial Psalm (89: 1) of today's liturgy reminds us that we are in a special way "servants of Christ and stewards of the mysteries of God,"[3] that we are *men of the divine economy of salva-*

tion, that we are conscious *"instruments" of grace,* that is, of the Holy Spirit's action in the power of Christ's cross and resurrection.

What is this divine economy, what is the grace of our Lord Jesus Christ—the grace which it was his wish to link sacramentally *to our* priestly *life* and to our priestly *service,* even though it is performed by men who are so poor, so unworthy?

Grace, as the psalm of today's liturgy proclaims, is a *proof of the fidelity of God himself to that eternal Love* with which he has loved creation, and in particular man, in his eternal Son.

The psalm says:"For your steadfast love was established forever, your faithfulness is firm as the heavens."[4]

This faithfulness of his love—his merciful love—is also *faithfulness to the Covenant* that God made, from the beginning, with man, and which he renewed many times, even though man so many times was not faithful to it.

Grace is thus *a pure gift of Love,* which only in Love itself, and in nothing else, finds its reason and motivation.

The psalm exalts *the Covenant* which God made *with David,* and at the same time, through its messianic content, it shows how that historical Covenant is only a stage and *a foretelling of the perfect Covenant in Jesus Christ:* "He shall cry to me,'You are my Father, my God, and the Rock of my salvation.'"[5]

Grace, as a gift, is the foundation *of the elevation of man to the dignity of an adopted child of God* in Christ, the only-begotten Son.

"My faithfulness and my steadfast love shall be with him and in my name shall his power be exalted."[6]

Precisely this power that *makes us become children of God,* as is spoken of in the prologue to St. John's Gospel—the entire salvific power—is conferred upon humanity in Christ, in the Redemption, in the cross and Resurrection.

And *we*—Christ's servants—are its stewards.

> The priest: *the man of the economy of salvation.*
> The priest: *the man formed by grace.*
> The priest: *the steward of grace!*

3.   *"I will sing of your steadfast love, O Lord, forever."*
Our vocation is precisely this. In this consists the specific nature, the originality of the priestly vocation. It *is* in a special way *rooted* in the mission of Christ himself, Christ the Messiah.

"The Spirit of the Lord God is upon me,
because the Lord *has anointed me*
to bring good tidings to the afflicted;
he has sent me to bind up the brokenhearted,
to proclaim liberty to the captives,
and the opening of the prison to those who are bound . . .
to comfort all who mourn."[7]

In the very heart of this messianic mission of Christ the Priest *is rooted our vocation and mission too:* the vocation and mission of the priests of the new and eternal Covenant. It is the vocation and mission of the proclaimers *of the Good News;*

— of those who must *bind up* the wounds of human hearts;

— of those who must proclaim liberation in the midst of all the many afflictions, in the midst of the evil that in so many ways "holds" man prisoner;

— of those who must console.

This is our vocation and mission *as servants.* Our vocation, dear brothers, includes a great and fundamental *service to be offered to every human being! Nobody can take our place. With the sacrament of the new and eternal Covenant* we must go to the very roots of human existence on earth.

Day by day, we must bring into that existence *the dimension of the Redemption and the Eucharist.*

We must strengthen awareness *of divine filiation* through *grace.* And what higher prospect, what finer destiny could there be for man than this?

Finally, we must administer the sacramental reality of Reconciliation with God, and the sacramental reality of Holy Communion, in which the deepest longing of the "insatiable" human heart is met.

Truly, our *priestly anointing* is deeply rooted in the very *messianic anointing of Christ.*

Our priesthood is ministerial. Yes, we must serve. And "to serve" means to bring man to the very foundations of his humanity, to the deepest essence of his dignity.

It is precisely there that—through our service—*the song "of praise instead of a faint spirit"* must ring out, to use once more the words of the text of Isaiah.[8]

4. *Dearly beloved brothers! Day after day, year after year, we discover the content and substance,* which are truly inexpressible, of our priesthood in the depths of the mystery of the Redemption. And I hope that the present Year of the extraordinary Jubilee will serve this purpose in a special way!

Let us open our eyes ever wider—the eyes of our soul—in order to understand better what it means to celebrate the Eucharist, *the sacrifice of Christ himself,* entrusted to our priestly lips and hands in the community of the Church.

Let us open our eyes ever wider—the eyes of our soul—in order to understand better what it means *to forgive sins and reconcile human consciences with* the infinitely holy *God,* with the God of Truth and Love.

Let us open our eyes ever wider—the eyes of our soul—in order to understand better what it means to act *"in persona Christi," in the name of Christ;* to act *with his power,* with the power which, in a word, is rooted in the salvific ground of the Redemption.

Let us open our eyes ever wider—the eyes of our soul—in order to understand better what *the mystery of the Church* is. *We are men of the Church!*

"There is one body and one Spirit, just as you were called to the one hope that belongs to your call, *one Lord, one faith, one baptism, one God and Father* of us all, who is above all and through all and in all."[9]

Therefore: seek *"to maintain the unity of the Spirit* in the bond of peace."[10] Yes. Precisely this in a special way depends on you: *"to maintain the unity of the Spirit."*

At a time of great tensions that affect the earthly body of humanity, *the Church's most important service* springs from the "unity of the Spirit," so that not only she herself will not suffer division coming from outside but she will also *reconcile and unite* people in the midst of the adversities that increase around them and within themselves in today's world.

My brothers! To each of us "*grace* was given . . . according to the measure of Christ's gift . . . *for building up* the body of Christ."[11]

May we be faithful to this grace! May we be heroically faithful to this grace!

My brothers! It is a great gift that God has given to us, to each of us! So great that every priest can discover in himself the signs of a divine predilection.

Let each one of us basically preserve his gift in all the wealth of its expressions: including the magnificent gift of celibacy voluntarily consecrated to the Lord—and received from him—for our sanctification and for the building up of the Church.

5.   *Jesus Christ* is in our midst and he says to us:"I am the Good Shepherd."[12]

It is precisely he who has *"made" shepherds* of us too. And it is he who goes about all the cities and villages,[13] *wherever we are sent* in order to perform our priestly and pastoral service.

It is he, Jesus Christ, who teaches, . . . preaches the gospel of the kingdom and heals every human disease and infirmity,[14] wherever *we are sent for the service of the gospel and the administration of the sacraments.*

It is precisely he, Jesus Christ, who continually feels compassion for the crowds and for every tired and exhausted person, like a "sheep without a shepherd."[15] Dear brothers! In this liturgical assembly of ours *let us ask Christ* for just one thing: that each of us may learn to *serve* better, more clearly and more effectively, *his presence as Shepherd* in the midst of the people of today's world!

This is also most important for ourselves, so that we may not be ensnared by the temptation of "uselessness," that is to say, the temptation to feel that we are not needed. Because it is not true. *We are more necessary than ever, because Christ is more necessary than ever!* The Good Shepherd is more than ever necessary!

We have in our hands—precisely in our "empty hands"—the power of the means of action that the Lord has given to us.

Think of the word of God, sharper than a two-edged sword;[16] think of liturgical prayer, especially the prayer of the Hours, in which Christ himself prays with us and for us; and think of the sacraments, in particular the Sacrament of Penance, the true life buoy for so many consciences, the haven towards which so many people also of our own time are striving. Priests should once more give great importance to this sacrament, for the sake of their own spiritual life and that of the faithful.

There is no doubt about it, dear brothers: with the good use of these "poor means" (but divinely powerful ones) you will see blossoming along your path the wonders of the infinite Mercy.

And also the gift of new vocations!

With this awareness, in this shared prayer, let us listen once more to the words which the Master addressed to his disciples: "The harvest is plentiful, but the laborers are few; *pray* therefore *the Lord of the harvest* to send out laborers into his harvest."[17]

How relevant these words are in our time too!

So let us pray! And let the whole Church pray with us! And in this prayer may there be manifested *awareness,* renewed by the Jubilee, *of the mystery of the Redemption.*

Endnotes

1. Is 61: 1-2.
2. Eph 4: 1.
3. 1 Cor 4: 1.
4. Ps 89 (88): 2.
5. Ps 89 (88): 26.
6. Ps 89 (88): 24.
7. Is 61: 1-2.
8. Is 61: 3.
9. Eph 4: 4-6.
10. Eph 4: 3.
11. Eph 4: 7, 12.
12. Jn 10: 11, 14.
13. Cf. Mt 9: 35.
14. Cf. *ibid.*
15. Cf. Mt 9: 36.
16. Cf. Heb 4: 12.
17. Mt 9: 37-38.

1985

Seventh Year of Pontificate

In this International Year of Youth, Pope John Paul II addressed his apostolic letter to all the youth of the world, dated Palm Sunday, March 31.

On the same date he also published his now customary Letter to Priests. "In the liturgy of Holy Thursday," he said at the beginning of the letter, "we unite ourselves in a particular way with Christ, who is the eternal and unceasing source of our priesthood in the Church. He alone is the Priest of his own sacrifice, as he is also the ineffable victim of his own Priesthood in the sacrifice of Golgotha" (1985 Letter, n. 1). He referred explicitly to his Letter to Youth "which I am enclosing with this annual message for Holy Thursday" in which he wished "to express some thoughts on the theme of youth in the pastoral work of priests and in general in the apostolate proper to our vocation. Also in this field Jesus Christ is the most perfect model" (1985 Letter, nn. 3-4).

The Holy Father published his fourth encyclical, *Slavorum Apostoli,* on the eleventh centenary of the evangelizing work of Saints Cyril and Methodius (June 2).

The pope's travels brought him to Venezuela; Ecuador; Peru, Trinidad and Tobago (January 26–February 6); the Netherlands; Luxembourg and Belgium (May 11-21); several African countries: Togo, Ivory Coast, Cameroon, Central Africa, Zaire, Kenya, and Morocco (August 8-19); and Liechtenstein (September 8).

In the Consistory of May 25 the Holy Father created twenty-eight new cardinals, including Bernard Cardinal Law, Archbishop of Boston, and John Cardinal O'Connor, Archbishop of New York.

In the General Audiences of the year John Paul II continued the series on the Creed, including the topics of revelation and Faith (nn. 7-20 of the series, March 13–June 26); the One God (nn. 21-32, July 3-October 2) and the Trinity (nn. 33-43, October 9-December 18).

At the end of the year the second Extraordinary Assembly of the Synod of Bishops took place in Rome (November 24–December 8) to commemorate the twentieth anniversary of the closing of Vatican II. In the homily at the solemn Mass of December 8 concelebrated by the pope and the synod Fathers, John Paul II said: "Twenty years ago, on this very day, December 8, the Fathers of the council, under the presidency of Pope Paul VI, offered to the Blessed Trinity, through the heart of Immaculate Mary, the fruits of their four years of work. The central theme of the council had been the Church. . . . We come out of the synod with an intense desire to spread ever wider in the body of the Church the climate of that new Pentecost that animated us during the celebration of the council and that during these last two weeks we have once more happily experienced" (Homily, December 8). In the closing address on the day before the Holy Father wished to underline some of the suggestions made during the synod, including"the desire expressed to prepare a compendium or catechism of all Catholic doctrine to serve as a point of reference for catechisms or compendia in all the particular churches; this desire responds to a real need both of the universal Church and of the particular churches."A message to the people of God and a final report of the synod were released at its conclusion.

LETTER
OF THE HOLY FATHER
POPE JOHN PAUL II
TO ALL THE PRIESTS OF THE CHURCH
ON THE OCCASION OF HOLY THURSDAY 1985

Dear Brother Priests!

1.   In the liturgy of Holy Thursday we unite ourselves in a particular way *with Christ,* who is the eternal and unceasing source of our
priesthood in the Church. He alone is *the Priest* of his own sacrifice,
as he is also the ineffable *victim* of his own Priesthood in the sacrifice
of Golgotha.

During the Last Supper, he left to the Church this sacrifice of his
—the sacrifice of the new and eternal Covenant—as the *Eucharist:* the
sacrament of his body and blood under the appearances of bread and
wine "after the order of Melchizedek."[1]

When he says to the Apostles: "Do this in remembrance of me!"[2] he
constitutes *the ministers of this sacrament* in the Church, in which for
all time the sacrifice offered by him for the redemption of the world
must continue, be renewed and be actuated; and he commands these
same ministers to act—by virtue of their sacramental priesthood—in
his place: *"in persona Christi."*

All this, dear brothers, through the apostolic succession is granted to
us in the Church. Holy Thursday is every year *the day of the birth of the
Eucharist* and *the birthday of our priesthood,* which is above all ministerial and at the same time hierarchical. It is ministerial, because by
virtue of Holy Orders we perform in the Church that service which is
given only to priests to perform, first of all *the service of the Eucharist.*
It is also hierarchical, because this service enables us, by serving, to
guide pastorally the individual *communities* of the People of God, in
communion with the bishops, who have inherited from the Apostles
the pastoral power and charism in the Church.

2.   On the solemn occasion of Holy Thursday the community of
priests—the presbyterate—of each church, beginning with the Church
in Rome, gives a particular *expression to its unity* in the Priesthood of
Christ. And also on this day I address myself—not for the first time
and in collegial union with my brothers in the episcopate—to you

who are *my and our brothers in the ministerial Priesthood of Christ,* in every place on earth, in every nation and people, language and culture. As I wrote to you on another occasion, adapting the well-known words of St. Augustine, I repeat to you, *"Vobis sum episcopus,"* and at the same time *"vobiscum sum sacerdos."*[3] On the solemn occasion of Holy Thursday, together with all of you, dear brothers, I renew—like every bishop in his own church—with the most profound humility and gratitude *the awareness of the reality of the Gift,* which through priestly ordination has become our lot, the lot of each and every one of us in the presbyterate of the universal Church.[4]

The sentiment of humble gratitude ought to prepare us better every year *for the increase of that talent* which the Lord bestowed on us on the day of his departure, that we may be able to present ourselves before him on the day of his second coming, we to whom he said: "No longer do I call you servants, . . . *but I have called you friends. . . .* You did not choose me, but I chose you and appointed you that you should go and bear fruit and that your fruit should abide."[5]

3. Referring to these words of our Master, which contain the most marvelous *good wishes* for the birthday of our priesthood, I desire to deal in this Holy Thursday Letter with one of the subjects that we necessarily meet along the way of our priestly vocation and apostolic mission.

This subject is spoken of more fully in the Letter to Youth, which I am enclosing with this annual message for Holy Thursday. The current year, 1985, through the initiative of the United Nations, is in fact being celebrated throughout the world as International Youth Year. It has seemed to me that this initiative should not remain on the margins of the Church, any more than other noble initiatives of an international character, as for example the initiative of the Year for the Aged, or the Year of the Handicapped and others. In all these initiatives *the Church cannot remain on the sidelines,* for the essential reason that they are at the heart of her mission and service, which is to be built up and *to grow* as the community of believers, as the Dogmatic Constitution *Lumen gentium* of the Second Vatican Council well notes. Each of these initiatives in its own way also confirms the reality of the Church's presence in the modern world, a fact to which the last council gave magisterial expression in the Pastoral Constitution *Gaudium et spes.*

I therefore wish also in this year's Letter for Holy Thursday to express some thoughts *on the theme of youth in the pastoral work of the priests* and in general in the apostolate proper to our vocation.

4.   *Also* in this field *Jesus Christ is the most perfect model.* His *conversation with the young man,* which we find in the text of all three synoptic Gospels,[6] constitutes an inexhaustible source of reflection on this theme. To this source I refer especially in this year's Letter to Youth. But it is also fitting that we should use it, especially when we consider our *priestly and pastoral commitment regarding youth.* In this concern Jesus Christ must remain for us the first and fundamental source of inspiration.

The Gospel text indicates that the young man had *easy access to Jesus.* For him, the Teacher from Nazareth was someone to whom he could turn with confidence; *someone to whom he could entrust his essential questions;* someone from whom he could expect a true response. All this is for us too an indication of fundamental importance. Each one of us must be distinguished by *an accessibility* similar to that of Christ. Young people should not find difficulty in approaching the priest, and should discover in him the same *openness, benevolence* and *availability* with regard to the problems troubling them. Even when by temperament they are a little shy or reserved, the priest's attitude should help them to overcome the resistances which derive from that. Moreover, there are various ways of beginning and forming the contact which can be summed up as *"the dialogue of salvation."* On this theme priests engaged in pastoral work among youth could *themselves* say much. I therefore desire simply to address myself to their experience. *The experience of the saints* naturally has a special importance, and we know that among the generations of priests there are not lacking "saintly pastors of youth."

The priest's *accessibility* to young people means not only *ease of contact with them,* both inside and outside church, wherever young people feel drawn in harmony with the healthy characteristics of their age (I am thinking for example of tourism, sport and in general the sphere of cultural interests). The *accessibility* of which Christ gives us an example consists in something more. The priest, not only through his training for the ministry but also through the skill he has gained in the *educational sciences,* ought to evoke in young people trust as the *confidant of their problems of a fundamental nature,* questions regarding their spiritual life and questions of conscience. The young man who approaches Jesus of Nazareth asks directly: "Good Teacher, what must I do to inherit eternal life?"[7]The same question can be asked in a different way, not always as explicit as this; often it is asked in an indirect and apparently detached way. Yet the question reported by the Gospel determines, in a certain sense, *a wide area* within which our pastoral dialogue with youth develops. Very many problems come into this area, and many possible questions and answers; for human life, especially during youth, is full of different questions, and the Gospel, for its part, is full *of possible answers.*

5.   The priest who is in contact with youth *should know how to listen and how to answer.* Both of these acts should be the fruit of his interior maturity; this should be reflected in a clear consistency between life and teaching; still more, it should be the fruit of prayer, of union with Christ the Lord and of docility to the action of the Holy Spirit. Naturally an adequate training is important in this regard, but what is most important is *a sense of responsibility with regard to the truth* and *to one's questioner.* The conversation reported by the synoptics proves first of all that the Master whom the young man questions has in the latter's eyes a special *credibility* and *authority: moral authority.* The young man expects from him the truth, and accepts his response as an expression of a truth that imposes an obligation. This truth can be demanding. We must not be afraid of demanding much from the young. It can happen that one of them may go away "saddened," when he or she seems unable to face some demand. Nevertheless, sadness of this sort can also be "salvific." Sometimes the young *must make progress* through such experiences of *salvific sadness,* so as gradually to reach the truth and *that joy* which truth gives.

Besides, the young know that the true good cannot be had "cheaply"; it must "cost." They possess a certain healthy instinct when it is a question of values. If the soul has not yet yielded to corruption, they react directly with this *health judgment.* If moral corruption has gained a hold the ground must be broken up again, and this cannot be done otherwise than by giving true answers and proposing true values.

In Christ's way of acting there is one element which is very instructive. When the young man addresses him ("Good Teacher"), *Jesus in a certain sense* puts himself "to one side," because he replies: "No one is good but God alone."[8] In effect, in all our contacts with the young this seems especially important. We must be more than ever *personally committed,* we ought to act with all the naturalness of the questioner, friend, and guide; and at the same time we cannot for a moment *obscure God by placing ourselves before him.* We cannot obscure him"who alone is good,"who is invisible and at the same time totally present: *"Interior intimo meo,"* as St. Augustine says.[9] Acting in the most natural manner, in the"first person,"we cannot forget that the"first person"in every dialogue of salvation can only be *the One who alone saves and alone sacrifices.* Our every contact with the young, our pastoral work in whatever form—also the type which is externally most"secular"—must serve in all humility to create and to *make more room for God,* for Jesus Christ, since"my Father is working still, and I am working."[10]

6.   In the Gospel account of Christ's conversation with the young man there is an expression that we must assimilate in a particular way. The Evangelist says that Jesus"looked at him and loved him."[11] We touch here the truly crucial point. If we were to question those among the generations of priests who have done the most for young lives, for boys and girls—those who have borne the most lasting fruit in work with the young—we would realize *that the first and most profound source* of their effectiveness has been that"loving look" of Christ.

We must *clearly identify this love* in our hearts as priests. It is simply love"of neighbor": love of man in Christ, directed to every individual, including every single one. With regard to young people, this love *is not something exclusive,* as if it did not also concern others, such as adults, the old, the sick. Indeed, love for the young has a specifically evangelical character only when it *flows from love for every single person and for all.* At the same time, as love it has its own specific and one might say charismatic quality. It flows from *a particular concern for what being young means in human life.* Young people undoubtedly have a great attraction, proper to their age; but sometimes they also have not a few weaknesses and defects. The young man in the Gospel with whom Christ speaks appears on the one hand as an Israelite *faithful* to God's commandments, but then he appears as one who is *too conditioned* by his wealth and too attached to his possessions.

Love for young people—this love which is an essential quality of every honest educator and every good pastor—is fully conscious both of the qualities and of the defects proper to youth and to young people. At the same time, this love—just like Christ's love—reaches the person directly *precisely through these qualities and defects.* It reaches the individual who is at an extremely *important phase of life.* Many things, in fact, are determined and decided at this phase (sometimes in an irreversible way). *The future of a person depends* to a great extent upon the nature of that person's youth: the future, that is, of a concrete and unique human being. The time of youth therefore in the life of every person is *a particularly responsible phase.* Love for young people is above all awareness of this responsibility and *readiness to share it.*

Such love is truly free from self-interest. It evokes trust from young people. And they have *an immense need* of that love in the phase of life which they are experiencing. Each one of us priests should be especially *prepared to offer such a disinterested love.* It can be said that the whole ascetical endeavor of the priestly life, the daily effort to grow in holiness, the spirit of prayer, of union with Christ, the offering of oneself to Christ's Mother—all of this is daily put to the test on this point. Young lives are particularly sensitive. Young minds are sometimes very critical. For this reason the intellectual formation of the priest is important. But at the same time experience shows that even more important are *goodness, dedication* and also *firmness:* the qualities of character and heart.

I believe, dear brothers, that each one of us should earnestly ask the Lord Jesus that our contact with youth may be essentially *a sharing of that gaze with which he "looked at"* his young questioner in the Gospel, and a sharing *in the love* with which he "loved" him. We must also earnestly pray that this priestly and disinterested love may really match the expectations of all young people, *both male and female, boys and girls.* For we are aware of the rich diversity constituted by masculinity and femininity for the development of a concrete and unique human person. *In relation to each individual young person* we must learn from Christ that same love with which he himself "loved."

7.   Love enables us to *propose what is good.* Jesus "looked" at his young questioner in the Gospel "with love" and said to him: "Follow me."[12] This good that we can propose to young people is always expressed in this exhortation: *Follow Christ!* We have no other good to propose; no one has a better good to propose. To say "Follow Christ!" means, above all, try to *find yourself as a person.* For—as the council teaches—it is precisely Christ who *"fully reveals man to himself* and brings to light his highest calling."[13]

And so, *Follow Christ!* which means try *to discover the calling* that Christ makes known to man: that calling which is the realization of *man* and of his unique *dignity.* Only in the light of Christ and of his Gospel can we fully understand what it means that man has been created *in the image and likeness of God himself.* Only by following him can we *fill* this eternal image with a content of actual life. This content is very diversified: many are the vocations and duties of life before which young people must decide their *own path.* But on each of these paths it is a question of following a fundamental vocation: to be a person! to be so in a Christian way! to be a person *"in the measure of the gift of Christ."*[14]

If there is love of young people in our priestly hearts, we shall know how to help them to find the answer to what constitutes the life vocation of each one. *We will know how to help them* while leaving them fully free to seek and *choose,* and at the same time we shall show them the essential *value*—in the human and Christian sense—of *each* of these *choices.*

We shall also know how to be *with them,* with each young man or woman, *in the midst of the trials and sufferings* from which youth is certainly not exempt. Yes, sometimes it is even burdened beyond measure. There are sufferings and trials of various kinds, *disappointments* and *disillusionments:* they are real *crises.* Youth is particularly sensitive and not always prepared for the blows that life inflicts. *Today many young people are rightly perturbed* by the threat to human existence at the level of whole societies, indeed at the level of the whole human race. They must be helped in these anxieties to discover their own vocation. They must also be supported and strengthened *in their desire to transform the world,* to make it *more human* and *more fraternal.* And these are not just words; it is a question of the whole reality of the "path" that Christ points out for a world made in just this way. In the gospel this world is called the kingdom of God. The *kingdom of God* is at the same time the true "kingdom of man": the new world in which his authentic "kingship" is achieved.

Love is capable *of proposing good.* When Christ says to the young man: "Follow me," in that concrete Gospel circumstance it is a call to "leave everything" and to follow the path taken by Christ's Apostles. *Christ's conversation with the young man* is the *prototype* of countless other conversations in which *the prospect of a vocation to the priesthood or religious life* opens up before a young soul. Dear brother priest and pastors, we must know how to recognize these vocations. Truly, "the harvest is plentiful but the laborers are few!" Here and there they are extremely few! Let us ask "the Lord of the harvest to send out laborers into his harvest."[15] *Let us pray ourselves,* and let us ask others to pray for this. And above all, let us endeavor to make our very lives a *concrete point of reference* for priestly and religious vocations: a concrete *model.* Young people have an extreme need of such a concrete model in order to discover in themselves the possibility of following a similar path. In this area *our priesthood can bear fruit* in an extraordinary way. Work for this, and pray that the gift which you have received may become the source of a similar gift to others: precisely to the young!

8.   Much more could be said and written on this theme. The education and pastoral care of youth have been made the subject of many systematic studies and publications. Writing to you on Holy Thursday, my dear brother priests, *I wish to limit myself to a few points only.* I wish, in a certain sense, to "point out" one of the themes belonging to the manifold treasure of our priestly vocation and mission. More is said of this theme in the Letter to Young People, which together with this present letter I am putting at your disposal, so that you can use it especially in this Youth Year.

In the old liturgy which the older priests still remember, Holy Mass began with the prayers at the foot of the altar, and the first words of the psalm were: *"Introibo ad altare Dei—ad Deum qui lætificat iuventutem meam"*[16] ("I will go to the altar of God—to God who gives joy to my youth").

On Holy Thursday we all return *to the source of our priesthood:* the *Upper Room.* Let us meditate on how our priesthood was born from the heart of Jesus Christ during the Last Supper. Let us meditate too on how it was born in the heart of each one of us.

On this day, dear brothers, my wish for each and every one of you— independently of your age and of the generation to which you belong—is that the "going to the altar of God" (as the psalm says) may be the source of that supernatural *youthfulness of spirit* that comes from God himself. He "makes us rejoice with the youthfulness" of his eternal mystery in Jesus Christ. As priests of this saving mystery, we have a share *in the very source* of the *youthfulness of God:* this inexhaustible *"newness of life"* which with Christ is poured out in human hearts.

May this "newness of life" become for all of us, and *through us for others* and especially for *the young,* a source of life and holiness. I place this good wish in the heart of her about whom we think when we sing: *"Ave verum Corpus, natum de Maria Virgine. Vere passum, immolatum in Cruce pro homine. Esto nobis prægustatum mortis in examine."*

With all the affection of my heart and with my Apostolic Blessing, as a pledge of strength in your ministry.

From the Vatican, on 31 March, Palm Sunday and the Sunday of the Lord's Passion, in the year 1985, the seventh of my Pontificate.

Endnotes

1. Ps 110 (109): 4; cf. Heb 7: 17.
2. Lk 22: 19; cf. 1 Cor 11: 24f.
3. *"Vobis enim sum episcopus, vobiscum sum Christianus": Serm.* 340, 1: PL 38, 1483.
4. Cf. Ps 16 (15): 5:*"Dominus pars hereditatis meæ et calicis mei."*
5. Jn 15: 15f.
6. Cf. Mt 19: 16-22; Mk 10: 17-22; Lk 18: 18-23.
7. Mk 10: 17.
8. Cf. Mt 19: 17; Mk 10: 18; Lk 18: 19.
9. St. Augustine, *Confess.* III, VI, 11: CSEL 33, p. 53.
10. Jn 5: 17.
11. Mk 10: 21.
12. Mt 19: 21; Mk 10: 21; Lk 18: 22.
13. Pastoral Constitution on the Church in the Modern World *Gaudium et spes,* 22.
14. Eph 4: 7.
15. Mt 9: 37f.
16. Ps 43 (42): 4 (Vulgate); cf. St. Ambrose, *Exposit. Evang. sec. Lucam* VIII, 73; cf. also Council of Trent, Session XXIII, c. I, *De institutione sacerdotii Novæ Legis:* DS 1764.

1986

Eighth Year of Pontificate

This year's Letter to Priests on the occasion of Holy Thursday was dated March 16, the fifth Sunday of Lent. The letter is a reflection on the figure, the life and the ministry of the holy Curé of Ars. "St. John Mary Vianney never ceases to be a witness, ever living, ever relevant, to the truth about the priestly vocation and service. We recall the convincing way in which he spoke of the greatness of the priest and of the absolute need for him. . . . Dear brothers, may these reflections renew your joy at being priests, your desire to be priests more profoundly!" (1986 Letter, nn. 11-12).

During this year the Holy Father published his fifth encyclical, *Dominum et vivificantem,* on the Holy Spirit in the life of the Church and the world (May 18, Solemnity of Pentecost) and the Apostolic Letter *Augustinum Hipponensem* on the occasion of the sixteenth centenary of the conversion of St. Augustine (August 28). The Sacred Congregation for the Doctrine of the Faith issued the Instruction *Libertatis conscientia* on Christian freedom and liberation (March 22).

John Paul II visited India (February 1-10); Colombia and St. Lucia (July 1-8); France (October 4-7); and Bangladesh, Singapore, Fiji, New Zealand, and Australia (November 18-December 1).

The Holy Father spoke on several occasions during the October 27 day of prayer for peace in Assisi, Italy, to which he had invited world religious leaders. In one of those addresses he said: "The way of peace passes in the last analysis through love. Let us implore the Holy Spirit, who is the love of the Father and the Son, to take possession of us with all his power, to enlighten our minds and to fill our hearts with his love." And in the Christmas address to the Roman Curia, the pope said referring to the day at Assisi: "With this day, and by means of it, we have succeeded, by the grace of God, in realizing this conviction of ours, inculcated by the council, about the unity of the origin and goal of the human family, and about the meaning and the value of non-Christian religions—without the least shadow of confusion or syncretism" (Address to Roman Curia, December 22, n. 9).

In most of the General Audiences of this year the pope continued his catechesis on the Creed, dealing with creation, divine providence, the angels, and original sin (nn. 44-79 of the series, January 8–December 17).

LETTER
OF THE HOLY FATHER
POPE JOHN PAUL II
TO ALL THE PRIESTS OF THE CHURCH
ON THE OCCASION OF HOLY THURSDAY 1986

Dear Brother Priests!

1. Holy Thursday, the Feast of Priests

Here we are again, about to celebrate Holy Thursday, the day on which Christ Jesus instituted the Eucharist and at the same time our ministerial priesthood."Having loved his own who were in the world, he loved them to the end."[1] As the Good Shepherd, he was about to give his life for his sheep,[2] to save man, to reconcile him with his Father and bring him into a new life. And already at the Last Supper he offered to the Apostles as food his own body given up for them, and his blood shed for them.

Each year this day is an important one for all Christians: like the first disciples, they come to receive the Body and Blood of Christ in the evening liturgy that renews the Last Supper. They receive from the Savior his testament of fraternal love which must inspire their whole lives, and they begin to watch with him, in order to be united with him in his Passion. You yourselves gather them together and guide their prayer.

But this day is especially important for us, dear brother priests. It is the feast of priests. It is the birthday of our priesthood, which is a sharing in the one Priesthood of Christ the Mediator. On this day the priests of the whole world are invited to concelebrate the Eucharist with their bishops and with them to renew the promises of their priestly commitment to the service of Christ and his Church.

As you know, I feel particularly close to each one of you on this occasion. And, the same as every year, as a sign of our sacramental union in the same priesthood, and impelled by my affectionate esteem for you and by my duty to confirm all my brothers in their service of the Lord, I wish to send you this letter to help you to stir up the wonderful gift that was conferred on you through the laying on of hands.[3] This ministerial priesthood which is our lot is also our vocation and our grace. It marks our whole life with the seal of the most necessary and most demanding of services, the salvation of souls. We are led to it by a host of predecessors.

2. The Matchless Example of the Curé of Ars

One of those predecessors remains particularly present in the memory of the Church, and he will be especially commemorated this year, on the second centenary of his birth: *St. John Mary Vianney, the Curé of Ars.*

Together we wish to thank Christ, the Prince of Pastors, for this extraordinary model of priestly life and service which the saintly Curé of Ars offers to the whole Church, and above all to us priests.

How many of us prepared ourselves for the priesthood, or today exercise the difficult task of caring for souls, having before our eyes the figure of St. John Mary Vianney! His example cannot be forgotten. More than ever we need his witness, his intercession, in order to face the situations of our times when, in spite of a certain number of hopeful signs, evangelization is being contradicted by a growing secularization, when spiritual discipline is being neglected, when many are losing sight of the kingdom of God, when often, even in the pastoral ministry, there is a too exclusive concern for the social aspect, for temporal aims. In the last century the Curé of Ars had to face difficulties which were perhaps of a different kind but which were no less serious. By his life and work he represented, for the society of his time, a great evangelical challenge that bore astonishing fruits of conversion. Let us not doubt that he still presents to us today the *great evangelical challenge.*

I therefore invite you now to meditate on our priesthood in the presence of this matchless pastor who illustrates both the fullest realization of the priestly ministry and the holiness of the minister.

As you know, John Mary Baptist Vianney died at Ars on 4 August 1859, after some 40 years of exhausting dedication. He was 73 years of age. When he arrived, Ars was a small and obscure village in the Diocese of Lyons, now in the Diocese of Belley. At the end of his life, people came from all over France, and his reputation for holiness, after he had been called home to God, soon attracted the attention of the universal Church. St. Pius X beatified him in 1905, Pius XI canonized him in 1925 and then in 1929 declared him patron saint of the parish priests of the whole world. On the centenary of his death, Pope John XXIII wrote the encyclical *Nostri sacerdotii primitias*, to present the Curé of Ars as a model of priestly life and asceticism, a model of piety and Eucharistic worship, a model of pastoral zeal, and this in the context of the needs of our time. Here, I would simply like to draw your attention to certain essential points so as to help us to rediscover and live our priesthood better.

3.   The Truly Extraordinary Life of the Curé of Ars: *His tenacious will in preparing for the priesthood*

The Curé of Ars is truly a model of strong will for those preparing for the priesthood. Many of the trials which followed one after another could have discouraged him: the effects of the upheaval of the French Revolution, the lack of opportunities for education in his rural environment, the reluctance of his father, the need for him to do his share of work in the fields, the hazards of military service. Above all, and in spite of his intuitive intelligence and lively sensitivity, there was his great difficulty in learning and memorizing, and so in following the theological courses in Latin, all of which resulted in his dismissal from the seminary in Lyons. However, after the genuineness of his vocation had finally been acknowledged, at 29 years of age he was able to be ordained. Through his tenacity in working and praying, he overcame all obstacles and limitations, just as he did later in his priestly life, by his perseverance in laboriously preparing his sermons or spending the evenings reading the works of theologians and spiritual writers. From his youth he was filled with a great desire to "win souls for the good God" by being a priest, and he was supported by the confidence placed in him by the parish priest of the neighboring town of Ecully, who never doubted his vocation and took charge of a good part of his training. What an example of courage for those who today experience the grace of being called to the priesthood!

4.   The Depth of His Love for Christ and for Souls

The Curé of Ars is a model of priestly zeal for all pastors. The secret of his generosity is to be found without doubt in *his love of God*, lived without limits, in constant response to the love made manifest *in Christ crucified*. This is where he bases his desire to do everything to save the souls ransomed by Christ at such a great price, and to bring them back to the love of God. Let us recall one of those pithy sayings which he had the knack of uttering: "The priesthood is the love of the Heart of Jesus."[4] In his sermons and catechesis he continually returned to that love: "O my God, I prefer to die loving you than to live a single instant without loving you. . . . I love you, my divine

Savior, because you were crucified for us . . . because you have me crucified for you."[5]

For the sake of Christ, he seeks to conform himself exactly to the radical demands that Jesus in the Gospel puts before the disciples whom he sends out: prayer, poverty, humility, self-denial, voluntary penance. And, like Christ, he has a love for his flock that leads him to extreme pastoral commitment and self-sacrifice. Rarely has a pastor been so acutely aware of his responsibilities, so consumed by a desire to wrest his people from their sins or their lukewarmness."O my God, grant me the conversion of my parish: I consent to suffer whatever you wish, for as long as I live."

Dear brother priests, nourished by the Second Vatican Council which has felicitously placed the priest's consecration within the framework of his pastoral mission, let us join St. John Mary Vianney and seek the dynamism of our pastoral zeal in the Heart of Jesus, in his love for souls. If we do not draw from the same source, our ministry risks bearing little fruit!

5. The Many Wonderful Fruits of His Ministry

In the case of the Curé of Ars, the results were indeed wonderful, somewhat as with Jesus in the Gospel. Through John Mary Vianney, who consecrates his whole strength and his whole heart to him, Jesus saves souls. The Savior entrusts them to him, in abundance.

First *his parish*—which numbered only 230 people when he arrived —was profoundly changed. One recalls that in that village there was a great deal of indifference and very little religious practice among the men. The bishop had warned John Mary Vianney:"There is not much love of God in that parish, you will put some there."But quite soon, far beyond his own village, the Curé becomes *the pastor of a multitude* coming from the entire region, from different parts of France and from other countries. It is said that 80,000 came in the year 1858! People sometimes waited for days to see him, to go to confession to him. What attracted them to him was not merely curiosity nor even a reputation justified by miracles and extraordinary cures, which the saint would wish to hide. It was much more the realization of meeting a saint, amazing for his penance, so close to God in prayer, remarkable for his peace and humility in the midst of popular acclaim, and above all so intuitive in responding to the inner disposition of souls and in freeing them from their burdens, especially in the confessional. Yes, God chose as a model for pastors one who could have appeared poor, weak, defenseless and contemptible in the eyes of men.[6] He graced him with his best gifts as a guide and healer of souls.

While recognizing the special nature of the grace given to the Curé of Ars, is there not here a sign of hope for pastors today who are suffering from a kind of spiritual desert?

6. The Main Acts of the Ministry of the Curé of Ars:
Different apostolic approaches to what is essential

John Mary Vianney dedicated himself essentially to teaching the faith and to purifying consciences, and these two ministries were directed towards the Eucharist. Should we not see here, today also, the three objectives of the priest's pastoral service?

While the purpose is undoubtedly to bring the People of God together around the Eucharistic Mystery by means of catechesis and penance, other apostolic approaches, varying according to circumstances, are also necessary. Sometimes it is a simple presence, over the years, with the silent witness of faith in the midst of non-Christian surroundings; or being near to people, to families and their concerns; there is a preliminary evangelization that seeks to awaken to the faith unbelievers and the lukewarm; there is the witness of charity and justice shared with Christian lay people, which makes the faith more credible and puts it into practice. These give rise to a whole series of undertakings and apostolic works which prepare or continue Christian formation. The Curé of Ars himself taxed his ingenuity to devise initiatives adapted to his time and his parishioners. However, all these priestly activities were centered on the Eucharist, catechesis and the Sacrament of Reconciliation.

7. The Sacrament of Reconciliation

It is undoubtedly his untiring devotion to the Sacrament of Reconciliation which revealed the principle charism of the Curé of Ars and is rightly the reason for his renown. It is good that such an example should encourage us today to restore to the ministry of reconciliation all the attention which it deserves and which the Synod of Bishops of 1983 so justly emphasized.[7] Without the step of conversion, penance and seeking pardon that the Church's ministers ought untiringly to encourage and welcome, the much desired renewal will remain superficial and illusory.

The first care of the Curé of Ars was to teach the faithful to desire repentance. He stressed the beauty of God's forgiveness. Was not all his priestly life and all his strength dedicated to the conversion of sinners? And it was above all in the confessional that God's mercy manifested itself. So he did not wish to get rid of the penitents who came from all parts and to whom he often devoted ten hours a day, sometimes fifteen or more. For him this was undoubtedly the greatest of his mortifications, a form of martyrdom. In the first place it was a martyrdom in the physical sense from the heat, the cold or the suffocating atmosphere. Secondly in the moral sense, for he himself suffered from the sins confessed and even more the lack of repentance:"I weep because you do not weep." In the face of these indifferent people, whom he welcomed as best he could and tried to awaken in them the love of God, the Lord enabled him to reconcile great sinners who were repentant, and also to guide to perfection souls thirsting for it. It was here above all that God asked him to share in the Redemption.

For our own part, we have rediscovered, better than during the last century, the community aspect of penance, preparation for forgiveness and thanksgiving after forgiveness. But sacramental forgiveness will always require a personal encounter with the crucified Christ through the mediation of his minister.[8] Unfortunately it is often the case that penitents do not fervently hasten to the confessional, as in the time of the Curé of Ars. Now, just when a great number seem to stay away from confession completely, for various reasons, it is a sign of the urgent need to develop a whole pastoral strategy of the Sacrament of Reconciliation. This will be done by constantly reminding Christians of the need to have a real relationship with God, to have a sense of sin when one is closed to God and to others, the need to be converted and through the Church to receive forgiveness as a free gift of God. They also need to be reminded of the conditions that enable the sacrament to be celebrated well, and in this regard to overcome prejudices, baseless fears and routine.[9] Such a situation at the same time requires that we ourselves should remain very available for this ministry of forgiveness, ready to devote to it the necessary time and care, and I would even say giving it priority over other activities. The faithful will then realize the value that we attach to it, as did the Curé of Ars.

Of course, as I wrote in the Post-Synodal Exhortation on Penance,[10] the ministry of reconciliation undoubtedly remains the most difficult, the most delicate, the most taxing and the most demanding of all—especially when priests are in short supply. This ministry also presupposes on the part of the confessor great human qualities, above all an intense and sincere spiritual life; it is necessary that the priest himself should make regular use of this sacrament.

Always be convinced of this, dear brother priests: this ministry of mercy is one of the most beautiful and most consoling. It enables you to enlighten consciences, to forgive them and to give them fresh vigor in the name of the Lord Jesus. It enables you to be for them a spiritual physician and counsellor; it remains "the irreplaceable manifestation and the test of the priestly ministry."[11]

8. The Eucharist: Offering the Mass, Communion and Adoration

The two Sacraments of Reconciliation and the Eucharist remain closely linked. Without a continually renewed conversion and the reception of the sacramental grace of forgiveness, participation in the Eucharist would not reach its full redemptive efficacy.[12] Just as Christ began his ministry with the words "Repent and believe in the Gospel,"[13] so the Curé of Ars generally began each of his days with the ministry of forgiveness. But he was happy to direct his reconciled penitents to the *Eucharist*.

The Eucharist was at the very center of his spiritual life and pastoral work. He said: "All good works put together are not equivalent to the Sacrifice of the Mass, because they are the works of men and the Holy Mass is the work of God."[14] It is in the Mass that the sacrifice of Calvary is made present for the redemption of the world. Clearly, the priest must unite the daily gift of himself to the offering of the Mass: "How well a priest does, therefore, to offer himself to God in sacrifice every morning!"[15] "Holy Communion and the Holy Sacrifice of the Mass are the two most efficacious actions for obtaining the conversion of hearts."[16]

Thus the Mass was for John Mary Vianney the great joy and comfort of his priestly life. He took great care, despite the crowds of penitents, to spend more than a quarter of an hour in silent preparation. He celebrated with recollection, clearly expressing his adoration at the consecration and communion. He accurately remarked: "The cause of priestly laxity is not paying attention to the Mass!"[17]

The Curé of Ars was particularly mindful of the permanence of Christ's real presence in the Eucharist. It was generally before the tabernacle that he spent long hours in adoration, before daybreak or in the evening; it was towards the tabernacle that he often turned during his homilies, saying with emotion: "He is there!" It was also for this reason that he, so poor in his presbytery, did not hesitate to spend large sums on embellishing his church. The appreciable result was that his parishioners quickly took up the habit of coming to pray before the Blessed Sacrament, discovering, through the attitude of their pastor, the grandeur of the mystery of faith.

With such a testimony before our eyes, we think about what the Second Vatican Council says to us today on the subject of priests: "They exercise this sacred function of Christ most of all in the Eucharistic Liturgy."[18] And more recently, the Extraordinary Synod in December 1985 recalled: "The liturgy must favor and make shine brightly the sense of the sacred. It must be imbued with reverence, adoration and glorification of God. . . . The Eucharist is the source and summit of all the Christian life."[19]

Dear brother priests, the example of the Curé of Ars invites us to a serious examination of conscience: what place do we give to the Mass in our daily lives? Is it, as on the day of our ordination—it was our first act as priests!—the principle of our apostolic work and personal sanctification? What care do we take in preparing for it? And in celebrating it? In praying before the Blessed Sacrament? In encouraging our faithful people to do the same? In making our churches the House of God to which the divine presence attracts the people of our time who too often have the impression of a world empty of God?

9. Preaching and Catechesis

The Curé of Ars was also careful never to neglect in any way the ministry of the word, which is absolutely necessary in predisposing people to faith and conversion. He even said: "Our Lord, who is truth itself, considers his word no less important than his body."[20] We know how long he spent, especially at the beginning, in laboriously composing his Sunday sermons. Later on he came to express himself more spontaneously, always with lively and clear conviction, with images and comparisons taken from daily life and easily grasped by his flock. His catechetical instructions to the children also formed an important part of his ministry, and the adults gladly joined the children so as to profit from this matchless testimony which flowed from his heart.

He had the courage to denounce evil in all its forms; he did not keep silent, for it was a question of the eternal salvation of his faithful people: "If a pastor remains silent when he sees God insulted and souls going astray, woe to him! If he does not want to be damned, and if there is some disorder in his parish, he must trample upon

human respect and the fear of being despised or hated."This responsibility was his anguish as parish priest. But as a rule, "he preferred
to show the attractive side of virtue rather than the ugliness of vice,"
and if he spoke sometimes in tears about sin and the danger for salvation, he insisted on the tenderness of God who has been offended,
and the happiness of being loved by God, united to God, living in
his presence and for him.

Dear brother priests, you are deeply convinced of the importance
of proclaiming the gospel, which the Second Vatican Council placed
in the first rank of the functions of a priest.[21] You seek, through
catechesis, through preaching and in other forms which also include
the media, to touch the hearts of our contemporaries, with their
hopes and uncertainties, in order to awaken and foster faith. Like
the Curé of Ars and in accordance with the exhortation of the council,[22] take care to teach the word of God itself which calls people to
conversion and holiness.

10. The Identity of the Priest
The specific ministry of the priest

St. John Mary Vianney gives an eloquent answer to certain *question-
ings of the priest's identity*, which have manifested themselves in the
course of the last twenty years; in fact it seems that today a more
balanced position is being reached.

The priest always, and in an unchangeable way, finds the source of
his identity in Christ the Priest. It is not the world which determines
his status, as though it depended on changing needs or ideas about
social roles. The priest is marked with the seal of the Priesthood of
Christ, in order to share in his function as the one Mediator and
Redeemer.

So, because of this fundamental bond, there opens before the priest
the immense field of the service of souls, for their salvation in Christ
and in the Church. This service must be completely inspired by love
of souls in imitation of Christ, who gives his life for them. It is God's
wish that all people should be saved, and that none of the little ones
should be lost.[23]"The priest must always be ready to respond to the
needs of souls," said the Curé of Ars.[24]"He is not for himself, he is
for you."[25]

The priest is for the laity: he animates them and supports them in the
exercise of the common priesthood of the baptized—so well illustrated by the Second Vatican Council—which consists in their making

their lives a spiritual offering, in witnessing to the Christian spirit in the family, in taking charge of the temporal sphere and sharing in the evangelization of their brethren. But the service of the priest belongs to another order. He is ordained to act in the name of Christ the Head, to bring people into the new life made accessible by Christ, to dispense to them the mysteries—the word, forgiveness, the Bread of Life—to gather them into his body, to help them to form themselves from within, to live and to act according to the saving plan of God. In a word, our identity as priests is manifested in the "creative" exercise of the love for souls communicated by Christ Jesus.

Attempts to make the priest more like the laity are damaging to the Church. This does not mean in any way that the priest can remain remote from the human concerns of the laity: he must be very near to them, as John Mary Vianney was, but as a priest, always in a perspective which is that of their salvation and of the progress of the kingdom of God. He is the witness and dispenser of a life other than earthly life.[26] It is essential to the Church that the identity of the priest be safeguarded, with its vertical dimension. The life and personality of the Curé of Ars are a particularly enlightening and vigorous illustration of this.

11. His Intimate Configuration to Christ and His Solidarity with Sinners

St. John Mary Vianney did not content himself with the ritual carrying out of the activities of his ministry. It was his heart and his life which he sought to conform to Christ.

Prayer was the soul of his life: silent and contemplative prayer, generally in his church at the foot of the tabernacle. Through Christ, his soul opened to the three divine Persons, to whom he would entrust "his poor soul" in his last will and testament. "He kept a constant union with God in the middle of an extremely busy life." And he did not neglect the office or the rosary. He turned spontaneously to the Virgin.

His *poverty* was extraordinary. He literally stripped himself of everything for the poor. And he shunned honors. *Chastity* shone in his face. He knew the value of purity in order "to rediscover the source of love which is God." *Obedience* to Christ consisted, for John Mary Vianney, in obedience to the Church and especially to the bishop. This obedience took the form of accepting the heavy charge of being a parish priest, which often frightened him.

But the gospel insists especially on *renouncing self*, on accepting the cross. Many were the crosses which presented themselves to the Curé of Ars in the course of his ministry: calumny on the part of the people, being misunderstood by an assistant priest or other confrères, contradictions, and also a mysterious struggle against the powers of hell, and sometimes even the temptation to despair in the midst of spiritual darkness.

Nonetheless he did not content himself with just accepting these trials without complaining; he went beyond them by *mortification*, imposing on himself continual fasts and many other rugged practices in order "to reduce his body to servitude," as St. Paul says. But what we must see clearly in this penance, which our age unhappily has little taste for, are his motives: love of God and the conversion of sinners. Thus he asks a discouraged fellow priest: "You have prayed . . . , you have wept . . . , but have you fasted, have you kept vigil . . . ?"[27] Here we are close to the warning of Jesus to the Apostles: "But this kind is cast out only by prayer and fasting."[28]

In a word, John Mary Vianney sanctified himself so as to be more able to sanctify others. Of course, conversion remains the secret of hearts, which are free in their actions, and the secret of God's grace. By his ministry, the priest can only enlighten people, guide them in the internal forum and give them the sacraments. The sacraments are of course actions of Christ, and their effectiveness is not diminished by the imperfection or unworthiness of the minister. But the results depend also on the dispositions of those who receive them, and these are greatly assisted by the personal holiness of the priest, by his perceptible witness, as also by the mysterious exchange of merits in the Communion of Saints. St. Paul said: "In the flesh I complete what is lacking in Christ's afflictions for the sake of his body, that is, the Church."[29] John Mary Vianney in a sense wished to force God to grant these graces of conversion, not only by his prayer but by the sacrifice of his whole life. He wished to love God for those who did not love him, and even do the penance which they would not do. He was truly a pastor completely at one with his sinful people.

Dear brother priests, let us not be afraid of this very personal commitment—marked by asceticism and inspired by love—which God asks of us for the proper exercise of our priesthood. Let us remember the recent reflections of the synodal Fathers: "It seems to us that in the difficulties of today God wishes to teach us more deeply the value, importance and central place of the Cross of Jesus Christ."[30] In the priest, Christ relives his Passion, for the sake of souls. Let us give thanks to God who thus permits us to share in the Redemption, in our hearts and in our flesh!

For all these reasons, St. John Mary Vianney never ceases to be a witness, ever living, ever relevant, to the truth about the priestly vocation and service. We recall the convincing way in which he spoke of the greatness of the priest and of the absolute need for him. Those who are already priests, those who are preparing for the priesthood and those who will be called to it must fix their eyes on his example and follow it. The faithful too will more clearly grasp, thanks to him, the mystery of the priesthood of their priests. No, *the figure of the Curé of Ars does not fade.*

12. Conclusion: for Holy Thursday

Dear brothers, may these reflections renew your joy at being priests, your desire to be priests more profoundly! The witness of the Curé of Ars contains still other treasures to be discovered. We shall return to these themes at greater length during the pilgrimage which I shall have the joy of making next October, since the French bishops have invited me to Ars in honor of the second centenary of the birth of John Mary Vianney.

I address this first meditation to you, dear brothers, for the Solemnity of Holy Thursday. In each of our diocesan communities we are going to gather together, on this birthday of our priesthood, to renew the grace of the Sacrament of Orders, to stir up the love which is the mark of our vocation.

We hear Christ saying to us as he said to the Apostles: "Greater love has no man than this, that a man lay down his life for his friends. . . . No longer do I call you servants . . . , I have called you friends."[31]

Before him who manifests love in its fullness, we, priests and bishops, renew our priestly commitments.

We pray for one another, each for his brother, and all for all.

We ask the eternal Father that the memory of the Curé of Ars may help to stir up our zeal in his service.

We beseech the Holy Spirit to call to the Church's service many priests of the calibre and holiness of the Curé of Ars: in our age she has so great a need of them, and she is no less capable of bringing such vocations to full flower.

And we entrust our priesthood to the Virgin Mary, the Mother of priests, to whom John Mary Vianney ceaselessly had recourse with

tender affection and total confidence. This was for him another reason for giving thanks: "Jesus Christ," he said, "having given us all
that he could give us, also wishes to make us heirs of what is most
precious to him, his holy Mother."[32]

For my part, I assure you once more of my great affection, and, with
your bishop, I send you my Apostolic Blessing.

From the Vatican, 16 March 1986, the fifth Sunday of Lent, in the
eighth year of my Pontificate.

Endnotes

1. Jn 13: 1.
2. Cf. Jn 10: 11.
3. Cf. 2 Tm 1: 6.
4. Cf. *Jean-Marie Vianney, Curé d'Ars, sa pensé e, son coeur,* présentés par l'Abbé Bernard Nodet, editions Xavier Mappus, Le Puy, 1958, p. 100; henceforth quoted as: Nodet.
5. Nodet, p. 44.
6. Cf. 1 Cor 1: 28-29.
7. Cf. John Paul II, Post-Synodal Apostolic Exhortation *Reconciliatio et pænitentia* (2 Decembe r 1984): AAS 77 (1985), pp. 185-275.
8. Cf. John Paul II, Encyclical Letter *Redemptor hominis* (4 March 1979), n. 20: AAS 71 (1979), pp. 313-316.
9. Cf. John Paul II, Post-Synodal Apostolic Exhortation *Reconciliatio et pænitentia* (2 December 1984), n. 28: AAS 77 (1985), pp. 250-252.
10. Cf. *ibid.,* n. 29: AAS 77 (1985), pp. 252-256.
11. John Paul II, Letter to Priests for Holy Thursday 1983, n. 3: AAS 75 (1983), par. 1, p. 419.
12. Cf. John Paul II, Encyclical Letter *Redemptor hominis* (4 March 1979), n. 20: AAS 71 (1979), pp. 309-313.
13. Mk 1: 15.
14. Nodet, p. 108.
15. Nodet, p. 107.
16. Nodet, p. 110.
17. Nodet, p. 108.
18. Second Vatican Council, Dogmatic Constitution on the Church *Lumen gentium,* n. 28.
19. II, B, b/1, and C/1; cf. Second Vatican Council, Dogmatic Constitution on the Church *Lumen gentium,* n. 11.
20. Nodet, p. 126.
21. Second Vatican Council, Decree on the Ministry and Life of Priests *Presbyterorum ordinis,* n. 4.
22. Cf. *ibid.*
23. Cf. Mt 18: 14.
24. Nodet, p. 101.
25. Nodet, p. 102.
26. Cf. Second Vatican Council, Decree on the Ministry and Life of Priests *Presbyterorum ordinis,* n. 3.
27. Nodet, p. 193.

28. Mt 17: 21.
29. Col 1: 24.
30. Final Report, D/2.
31. Jn 15: 13-15.
32. Nodet, p. 252.

1987

Ninth Year of Pontificate

On the first day of the year Pope John Paul II announced a Marian Year, which would begin on Pentecost, June 7, 1987, and end on the Solemnity of the Assumption, August 15, 1988. As a preparation for it, he published his sixth encyclical *Redemptoris Mater* on the Blessed Virgin Mary in the life of the pilgrim Church (March 25).

On April 13, the Monday of Holy Week, the Holy Father addressed once again all priests. Referring to Holy Thursday, he said: "On this extraordinary day, I wish—the same as every year—to be with you all, as also with your bishops, since we all feel a deep need to renew in ourselves the awareness of the grace of this sacrament which unites us closely to Christ, Priest and Victim." The theme of his letter is "the importance of prayer in our lives, especially in relationship with our vocation and mission" (1987 Letter, n. 1).

His apostolic travels carried the pope to several countries of Latin America: Uruguay, Chile, and Argentina (March 31-April 12); Germany (April 30-May 1); Poland for the third time (June 8-14); and the United States (September 10-20).

Regarding his visit to the United States, these are his own words: "The previous visit in 1979 was to the northeastern and central parts of the country. This time my journey was directed especially to the regions of the American South and West. The stages were successively: Miami (Florida), Columbia (South Carolina), New Orleans (Louisiana), San Antonio (Texas), Phoenix (Arizona), and then along the Pacific coast: Los Angeles, Monterey, San Francisco (California), concluding eventually in the Northeast with the stop at Detroit (Michigan). . . . I must reserve words of special gratitude for the way in which the Church in the United States, and particularly its pastors, welcomed this visit. It did not turn into a merely liturgical meeting during Holy Mass (which, however, had always a central and solemn place, as is obvious), but it also comprised 'work' sessions, which enabled one to see how the Church in America carries out its activity in the different sectors of her own proper mission" (General Audience, September 23, nn. 2 and 7).

In most of the General Audiences during this year the Holy Father continued his catechetical series on the Creed, speaking about Jesus Christ, true God and true Man (January 7-December 16).

The seventh Ordinary Synod of Bishops on "the vocation and mission of the laity in the Church and in the world" took place in Rome, October 1-30.

LETTER
OF THE HOLY FATHER
POPE JOHN PAUL II
TO ALL THE PRIESTS OF THE CHURCH
ON THE OCCASION OF HOLY THURSDAY 1987

The Prayer of Jesus
Rediscovering the Priesthood in the light
of the Upper Room and Gethsemane

I.

BETWEEN THE UPPER ROOM AND GETHSEMANE

1. "And when they had sung a hymn, they went out to the Mount of Olives."[1]

Dear Brothers in the Priesthood, allow me to begin my Letter for Holy Thursday this year with these words, which take us back to the moment when, after the Last Supper, Jesus Christ set out to go to the Mount of Olives.

All of us who, through the Sacrament of Holy Orders, enjoy a special ministerial sharing in the Priesthood of Christ, on Holy Thursday concentrate our inner thoughts *upon the memory of the institution of the Eucharist.* For this event marks the beginning and source of everything that we are, by the grace of God, in the Church and the world. Holy Thursday is the birthday of our priesthood, and so is also our yearly feast day.

This is an important and holy day not only for ourselves but for the whole Church, for all those whom God has made for himself in Christ "a kingdom of priests."[2] For us, this is particularly important and decisive, since the common priesthood of the whole People of God is linked with *the service of the ministers of the Eucharist,* which is our holiest task. And so today, dear brothers, as you gather around your bishops, together with them *renew* in your hearts *the grace given to you* "through the laying on of the hands"[3] *in the sacrament of the priesthood.*

On this extraordinary day, I wish—the same as every year—to be with you all, as also with your bishops, since we all feel a deep need to renew in ourselves the awareness of the grace of this sacrament which unites us closely to Christ, Priest and Victim.

Precisely for this purpose, in this letter I wish to express a few *thoughts on the importance of prayer in our lives,* especially in relationship with our vocation and mission.

2.   After the Last Supper, Jesus sets out with the Apostles for the Mount of Olives. In the series of the saving events of Holy Week, the Supper constitutes for Christ the beginning of *"his hour."* Precisely during the Supper the definitive accomplishment of everything that is to make up this "hour" begins.

In the Upper Room, Jesus institutes the sacrament, the sign of a reality that is still to take place in the series of events. Therefore he says: "This is *my body which is given for you,"*[4] "This cup which is poured out for you is the new covenant in my blood."[5] Thus is born the sacrament of the Body and Blood of the Redeemer, to which is intimately linked the sacrament of the priesthood, by virtue of the mandate given to the Apostles: "Do this in memory of me."[6]

The words which institute the Eucharist not only anticipate what will happen on the following day, they also deliberately emphasize that this imminent *accomplishment* possesses *the meaning and significance of a sacrifice.* For, "the Body is given . . . and the Blood *is poured out for you."*

In this way, at the Last Supper Jesus places in the hands of the Apostles and of the Church the true sacrifice. That which at the moment of the institution still represents a prophecy, even though a definitive one, but is also the actual anticipation of the sacrificial reality of Calvary will then become, through the ministry of priests, *"the memorial" which perpetuates in a sacramental manner* the same redeeming reality. It is a central reality in the order of the whole divine economy of salvation.

3.   Setting out with the Apostles and going towards the Mount of Olives, Jesus goes forward precisely to meet the reality of his "hour," which is the time of the Paschal fulfillment of God's plan and of all the prophecies, both ancient and more recent, contained in the Scriptures in this regard.[7]

This "hour" also marks the time when the *priesthood* is endowed with a new and definitive content as a *vocation,* on the basis of revelation and divine institution. We shall be able to find a fuller exposition of this truth above all in the Letter to the Hebrews, a fundamental text for knowledge of Christ's and our own priesthood.

But in the context of the present considerations, the essential fact seems to be that it is *through prayer that Jesus goes forward* towards the accomplishment of the reality that came to a climax in "his hour."

4.   *The prayer in Gethsemane* is to be understood not only in reference to everything that follows it during the events of Good Friday, namely Christ's Passion and death on the cross, it is also to be understood, and no less intimately, in reference to the Last Supper.

During the Last Supper Jesus accomplished what was the Father's eternal will for him, and which was also his own will, his will as the Son: "For this purpose I have come to this hour."[8] The words which institute the sacrament of the new and eternal Covenant, the Eucharist, constitute *in a certain way the sacramental seal of that eternal will of the Father and of the Son,* the will which has now reached that "hour" of its definitive accomplishment.

In Gethsemane the name "Abba," which on Jesus' lips always has a Trinitarian depth (for it is the name which he uses in speaking to or about the Father, and especially in prayer), casts upon the pains of the Passion a reflection of the meaning of the words of the institution of the Eucharist. Indeed, Jesus comes to Gethsemane to reveal a further aspect of the truth concerning himself, the Son, and he does so especially through this word: Abba. And this truth, this unheard-of truth about Jesus Christ, consists in the fact that *"being equal to the Father"* as the Father's consubstantial Son, he is at the same time *true man.* In fact he frequently calls himself the "Son of Man." Never so much as at Gethsemane is the reality of the Son of God revealed, the reality of him who "takes the form of a servant"[9] in accordance with Isaiah's prophecy.[10]

The prayer in Gethsemane equals and even exceeds any other prayer of Jesus in revealing the truth about the identity, vocation and mission of the Son, who came into the world to fulfill the fatherly will of God to the very end, when he says "it is finished."[11] This is important for all who enter Christ's "school of prayer"; it is especially important for us priests.

5.   Jesus Christ, then, the consubstantial Son, presents himself to the Father and says "Abba." And what do we find? As he reveals, in a way that we could call radical, his condition as true man, as the "Son

of Man," he *asks that the bitter chalice be taken away:* "My Father, if it be possible, let this cup pass from me."[12]

Jesus knows that this is "not possible" and that "the chalice" is given to him to "drink" to the very last drop. Yet he still says precisely this: "if it be possible, let it pass from me." He says it at the very moment when this "chalice," which he earnestly desired,[13] has now become the sacramental seal of the new and eternal Covenant in the Blood of the Lamb when everything which has been *"ordained"* from eternity is at last sacramentally *"instituted"* in time: introduced into the Church's whole future.

Jesus, who had accomplished this institution in the Upper Room, certainly cannot wish to revoke the reality signified by the sacrament of the Last Supper. On the contrary, with all his heart he desires its fulfillment. If, despite everything, he prays that "this chalice pass from him," he thus reveals before God and mankind all the weight of the task he has to assume: to substitute himself for all of us in the expiation of sin. He also shows the immensity of the suffering which fills his human heart. In this way the Son of Man shows his oneness with all his brothers and sisters who make us the great human family from the beginning until the end of time. Suffering *is an evil* for mankind at Gethsemane. Jesus Christ experiences its whole weight, which fits our common experience, our spontaneous inner attitude. Before the Father he remains *in all the truth of his humanity,* the truth of a human heart oppressed by a suffering which is about to reach its tragic conclusion: "My soul is very sorrowful, even to death."[14] And yet, no one is in a position to adequately express the depth of this suffering using only human criteria. For in Gethsemane the One who beseeches the Father is a Man who at the same time is God, *consubstantial* with the Father.

6.   The words of the Evangelist, "he began to be sorrowful and troubled,"[15] and the whole development of the prayer in Gethsemane, seem to indicate not only fear in the face of suffering, but also the dread which is characteristic of mankind—a sort of dread *associated with the sense of responsibility.* Is not man that unique being whose vocation is "constantly to surpass himself"?

Jesus Christ, the "Son of Man," in the prayer with which he begins his Passion expresses the typical anguish of responsibility associated with taking on tasks in which the individual must "surpass himself."

The Gospels often record that Jesus prayed, indeed that he "spent the night in prayer";[16] but none of these prayers has been presented in as deep and penetrating a way as the prayer in Gethsemane. This is understandable. The fact is that no other moment in Jesus' life was so decisive. No other *prayer* so fully *formed part of what was to be "his hour."* No decision in his life was as important as this one for the fulfillment of his Father's will, the Father who "so loved the world that he gave his only Son, that whoever believes in him should not perish but have eternal life."[17]

When in Gethsemane Jesus says: "Not my will, but yours, be done,"[18] he reveals the truth about the Father and the Father's salvific love for mankind. The "will of the Father" is precisely salvific love: the salvation of the world is to be accomplished through the *redemptive sacrifice of the Son.* It is very understandable that the Son of Man, taking this task upon himself, shows in his crucial dialogue with the Father the awareness that he has of the superhuman dimension of this task, in which he fulfills the Father's will in the divine depths of his filial union with him.

"I have accomplished the work which you gave me to do."[19] The Evangelist says: *"And being in an agony he prayed more earnestly."*[20] And this mortal anguish also showed itself in the sweat which, like drops of blood, streamed down Jesus' face.[21] This is the ultimate expression of a suffering that is translated into prayer, and of a prayer that, in its turn, knows sorrow, accompanying the sacrifice sacramentally anticipated in the Upper Room, deeply experienced in the spirit of Gethsemane, and about to be consummated on Calvary.

It is precisely to these moments of Jesus' priestly and sacrificial prayer that I wish to call your attention, dear brothers, in relation to our own prayer and life.

II.

PRAYER AT THE CENTER OF PRIESTLY EXISTENCE

7. If in our Holy Thursday meditation this year we link the Upper Room with Gethsemane, it is in order to understand how deeply our priesthood must be linked with prayer, *rooted in prayer.*

Surely this statement is obvious, but it does need to be continually pondered in our minds and hearts, so that the truth of it can be realized ever more deeply in our lives.

For it is a question of our life, *our priestly existence itself,* in all its richness, encompassed first of all in the call to priesthood and then shown in that service of salvation which flows from it.

We know that the priesthood, sacramental and ministerial, is a special sharing in the Priesthood of Christ. It does not exist without him or apart from him. It neither develops nor bears fruit unless it is rooted in him. *"Apart from me you can do nothing,"*[22] Jesus said during the Last Supper at the conclusion of the parable about the vine and the branches.

When later, during his solitary prayer in the garden of Gethsemane, Jesus goes to Peter, James and John and finds them overcome with sleep, he awakens them saying:"Watch and pray that you may not enter into temptation."[23]

For the Apostles therefore prayer was to be the concrete and effective *means of sharing in "Jesus' hour,"* of taking root in him and in his Paschal mystery. Thus it will always be for us priests. Without prayer, the danger of that"temptation"threatens us, the temptation to which the Apostles sadly succumbed when they found themselves face to face with"the scandal of the cross."[24]

8.   In our priestly life prayer has a variety of forms and meanings: *personal, communal* and *liturgical* (public and official). However, at the basis of these many forms of prayer there must always be that *most profound foundation* which corresponds to our priestly existence in Christ, insofar as it is a specific realization of Christian existence itself and even with a wider radius of human existence. For prayer is a connatural expression of the awareness that we have been created by God and still more as we clearly see from the Bible that *the Creator* has manifested himself to man as the *God of the Covenant.*

The prayer which corresponds to our priestly existence naturally includes everything that derives from our being Christians, or even simply from our being men made"in the image and likeness"of God. It also includes our awareness of our *being men and Christians as priests.* And it seems we can more fully discover this on Holy Thursday, as we go with Christ, after the Last Supper, to Gethsemane. For here we are witnesses *of the prayer of Jesus himself,* the prayer which *immediately precedes the supreme fulfillment of his Priesthood through the sacrifice of himself on the cross.* "As a high priest of the good things to come . . . he entered once for all into the Holy Place . . . by his own blood."[25] In fact, if he was a priest from the beginning of his existence, nevertheless he"became"in a full way the unique priest of the new and eternal Covenant through the redemptive sacrifice which had its beginning in Gethsemane. This beginning took place in a context of prayer.

9.   For us, dear brothers, this is a discovery of fundamental importance on Holy Thursday, which we rightly consider the birthday of our ministerial priesthood in Christ. Between the words of institution: "This is my body which is given for you"; "This cup which is poured out for you is the new covenant in my blood," and the effective fulfillment of what these words express, *the prayer of Gethsemane* is interposed.

Is it not true that, in the course of the Paschal events, it is this prayer which *leads to the reality* which is also visible and which *the sacrament both signifies and renews?*

The priesthood, which has become our inheritance by virtue of a sacrament so closely linked to the Eucharist, is always a call to share in the same divine-human, salvific and redemptive reality which precisely by means of our ministry must bear ever new fruit in the history of salvation: "that you should go and bear fruit and that your fruit should abide."[26] *The saintly Curé of Ars,* the second centenary of whose birth we celebrated last year, appears to us precisely as a man of this call, reviving the awareness of it in us too. In his heroic life, prayer was the means which enabled him to remain constantly in Christ, *to "watch" with Christ as his "hour" approached.* This "hour" does not cease to decide the salvation of the many people entrusted to the priestly service and pastoral care of every priest. In the life of St. John Mary Vianney, this "hour" was realized particularly by his service in the confessional.

10.   The prayer in Gethsemane is *like a cornerstone,* placed by Christ at the foundation of the service of the cause "entrusted to him by the Father" at the foundation of the work of the world's redemption through the sacrifice offered on the cross.

As sharers in the Priesthood of Christ, which is inseparably connected with his sacrifice, we too must place at the foundation of our priestly existence the cornerstone of prayer. It will enable us to harmonize our lives with our priestly service, preserving intact the *identity and authenticity* of this vocation which has become our special inheritance in the Church as the community of the People of God.

Priestly prayer, in particular that of the Liturgy of the Hours and of Eucharistic Adoration, will help us first of all to preserve the profound

awareness that, as "servants of Christ," we are in a special and exceptional way *"stewards of the mysteries of God."*[27] Whatever our actual
task may be, whatever the type of work by which we carry out our
pastoral service, prayer will ensure our awareness of those divine
mysteries of which we are "stewards," and will cause that awareness
to express itself in everything that we do. In this way too we shall be
for people a *clear sign* of Christ and his Gospel.

Dear brothers! We need prayer, profound and in a sense "organic"
prayer, in order to be able to be such a sign. "By this all men will
know that you are my disciples, if you have love for one another."[28]
Yes! *In a word, this is a question of love,* love *"for others"*; in fact "to be,"
as priests, "stewards of the mysteries of God" means to place oneself
at the disposal of others, and in this way to bear witness to that supreme love which is in Christ, that love which is God himself.

11. If priestly prayer renews such an awareness and attitude in the
life of each of us, at the same time, according to the inner "logic" of
being stewards of the mysteries of God, this prayer must constantly
broaden and extend to all those whom "the Father has given us."[29]

This is what stands out clearly in the priestly prayer of Jesus in the
Upper Room: "I have manifested your name to the men whom you
gave me out of the world; yours they were, and you gave them to
me, and they have kept your word."[30]

Following Jesus' example, *the priest,* "the steward of the mysteries of
God," is truly himself *when he is "for others."* Prayer gives him a special *sensitivity to these "others,"* making him attentive to their needs,
to their lives and destiny. Prayer also enables the priest to recognize
those whom "the Father has given to him." These are, in the first
place, those whom the Good Shepherd has as it were placed on the
path of his priestly ministry, *of his pastoral care.* They are children,
adults and the aged. They are the youth, married couples, families,
but also those who are alone. They are the sick, suffering, the dying;
they are those who are spiritually close and willing to collaborate in
the apostolate, but also those who are distant, those who are absent
or indifferent, though many of them may be searching and reflecting.
Those who for different reasons are negatively disposed, *those who
find themselves in difficulties of various sorts,* those who are struggling
against vices and sins, those who are fighting for faith and hope.
Those who seek the priest's help, and those who reject it.

How can one be "for" all of these people and "for" each one of them
according to the model of Christ? How can we be "for" those whom

"the Father has given to us," committing them to us in trust? Ours will always be *a test of love*—a test that we must accept, first of all, in the realm of prayer.

12. We are all well aware, dear brothers, that *this test is "costly."* How demanding at times are those seemingly ordinary conversations with different people! How demanding the service to consciences in the confessional! How demanding the solicitude "for all the churches"[31] *(sollicitudo omnium ecclesiarum):* when it is a question of the "domestic churches,"[32] namely families, especially in their present difficulties and crises; or a question of each individual "temple of the Holy Spirit": [33] of all individuals in their human and Christian dignity; when it is a question of a *church-community* such as the parish which always remains the fundamental community, or of those groups, movements or associations which *serve* the renewal of individuals and of society according to the spirit of the gospel, which are flourishing today in the Church and for which we must be grateful to the Holy Spirit who gives rise to so many wonderful initiatives. Such a commitment has its cost, and we must bear that cost with the help of prayer.

Prayer is essential for maintaining pastoral sensitivity to everything that comes from the "Spirit," for *correctly "discerning"* and properly employing those charisms that lead to union and are linked to priestly service in the Church. For it is the task of priests *"to gather together the People of God,"* not to divide them. And they fulfill this task above all as ministers of the Holy Eucharist.

Prayer, then, in spite of the many obstacles we meet, will enable us *to give that proof of love* that must be offered by the life of every individual but especially the life of the priest. And when it appears that this proof is beyond our strength, let us remember what the Evangelist says of Jesus in Gethsemane: *"Being in an agony, he prayed more earnestly."*[34]

13. The Second Vatican Council presents the life of the Church as *a pilgrimage of faith.*[35] Each one of us, dear brothers, by reason of our priestly vocation and ordination, has a special part in this pilgrimage. As ministers of the Good Shepherd we are called to go forward guiding others, helping them along their way. As stewards of the mysteries of God we must therefore possess *a maturity of faith* corresponding to our vocation and our tasks. Indeed, "it is required of stewards that they be found trustworthy,"[36] since the Lord commits his inheritance to them.

It is appropriate, then, that on this *pilgrimage of faith* each one of us should *fix his soul's gaze on the Virgin Mary, the Mother of Jesus Christ*, the Son of God. For as the council teaches, following the Fathers of the Church she "precedes" us in this pilgrimage,[37] and she offers us a sublime example, as I have sought to show in the recent encyclical published for the Marian Year which we are preparing to celebrate.

In Mary, who is the Immaculate Virgin, we also discover *the mystery* of that supernatural *fruitfulness through the power of the Holy Spirit*, which makes her *the "figure" of the Church*. For the Church "becomes herself a mother . . . because by her preaching and by Baptism she brings forth to a new and immortal life children who are conceived of the Holy Spirit and born of God,"[38] as witnessed to by the Apostle Paul: "My children, I must go through the pain *of giving birth to you all over again*."[39] This the Church does, suffering as a mother who "has sorrow, because her hour has come; but when she is delivered of her child, she no longer remembers the anguish, for joy that a child is born into the world."[40]

Is not his witness related also to the essence of our special vocation in the Church? And yet let us say it in conclusion in order that the Apostle's testimony may becomes ours too, we must *constantly return to the Upper Room and to Gethsemane*, and rediscover *the very center of our priesthood in prayer* and through prayer.

When with Christ we pray: "Abba, Father" then "it is the Spirit himself bearing witness with our spirit that we are children of God."[41] "Likewise the Spirit helps us in our weakness; for we do not know how to pray as we ought, but *the Spirit himself intercedes for us* with sighs too deep for words, and he who searches the hearts of men knows what is the mind of the Spirit."[42]

Accept, dear brothers, my Easter greeting and the kiss of peace in Jesus Christ our Lord.

From the Vatican, 13 April 1987, Monday of Holy Week, in the ninth year of my Pontificate.

Endnotes

1. Mk 14: 26.
2. Rv 1: 6.
3. Cf. 2 Tm 1: 6.
4. Lk 22: 19.
5. Lk 22: 20.
6. Lk 22: 19.
7. Cf. Lk 24: 27.
8. Jn 12: 27.
9. Cf. Phil 2: 7.
10. Cf. Is 53.
11. Jn 19: 30.
12. Mt 26: 39; Cf. Mk 14: 36; Lk 22: 42.
13. Cf. Lk 22: 15.
14. Mk 14: 34.
15. Mt 26: 37.
16. Cf. Lk 6: 12.
17. Jn 3: 16.
18. Lk 22: 42.
19. Cf. Jn 17: 4.
20. Lk 22: 44.
21. Cf. Lk 22: 44.
22. Jn 15: 5.
23. Mt 26: 41.
24. Cf. Gal 5: 11.
25. Heb 9: 11-12.
26. Jn 15: 16.
27. 1 Cor 4: 1.
28. Jn 13: 35.
29. Cf. Jn 17: 6.
30. Jn 17: 6.
31. Cf. 2 Cor 11: 28.
32. Cf. *Lumen gentium,* 11.
33. 1 Cor 6: 19.
34. Lk 22: 44.
35. Cf. *Lumen gentium,* 48ff.
36. 1 Cor 4: 2.
37. Cf. *Lumen gentium,* 58.
38. *Lumen gentium,* 64.
39. Gal 4: 19.
40. Jn 16: 21.
41. Rom 8: 15-16.
42. Rom 8: 26-27.

1988

Tenth Year of Pontificate

This year began with the publication of the seventh encyclical of Pope John Paul II *Sollicitudo rei socialis* on the occasion of the twentieth anniversary of *Populorum progressio* (dated December 30, 1987, it was released in January) and the Apostolic Letter *Euntes in mundum* to celebrate the first millennium of the faith in Russia (January 25).

The pope's Letter to Priests on the occasion of Holy Thursday was dated March 25, the Solemnity of the Annunciation of the Lord. "It is appropriate during this year, being lived in the whole Church as a Marian Year, to recall the reality of the Incarnation as it relates to the institution of the Eucharist and also to the institution of the sacrament of the priesthood. The Incarnation was brought about by the Holy Spirit when he came down upon the Virgin of Nazareth and she spoke her fiat in response to the angel's message" (1988 Letter, n. 1).

The whole letter is an encouragement to a greater closeness to Mary: "When, acting *in persona Christi*, we celebrate the sacrament of the one same sacrifice of which Christ is and remains the only priest and victim," the Holy Father said, "we must not forget this suffering of his Mother, in whom were fulfilled Simeon's words in the Temple at Jerusalem. . . . When we celebrate the Eucharist and stand each day on Golgotha, we need to have near us the one who through heroic faith carried to its zenith her union with her Son, precisely then on Golgotha" (1988 Letter, n. 2). A little later in the same letter: "Let us strive to be close to that Mother in whose heart is inscribed in a unique and incomparable way the mystery of the world's redemption" (1988 Letter, n. 3).

This year witnessed the promulgation of the Apostolic Constitution *Pastor bonus* on the work of the Roman Curia (June 28), the Apostolic Letter *Ecclesia Dei* on Archbishop Lefebvre (July 2) and the Apostolic Letter *Mulieris dignitatem* on the dignity and vocation of women, dated on the day of the conclusion of the fourteen-month-long Marian Year, August 15. On the same day, in the homily of the Mass in St. Peter's Basilica, the Holy Father said: "All this year which is now ending was a time for 'turning the eyes' to you, Virgin Mother of God, constantly present in the mystery of Christ and of the Church. The Marian Year finishes today. But the time for 'turning the eyes' to Mary, that does not finish" (Homily, August 15, n. 6). It also included the set of *ad limina* visits of American bishops and the corresponding series of addresses given by the pope to the different groups of bishops.

In the consistory of June 28 the Holy Father created twenty-four new cardinals, including James Cardinal Hickey, Archbishop of Washington, and Edmund Cardinal Szoka, Archbishop of Detroit.

The pilgrimages of the pope during this year carried him to several Latin American countries: Uruguay, Bolivia, Peru and Paraguay (May 7-18); Austria (June 23-27); five African countries: Zimbabwe, Bostwana, Lesotho, Swaziland and Mozambique (September 10-19); and France (his fourth apostolic journey to that country).

During most of the General Audiences the pope continued his catechetical addresses on Jesus Christ (nn. 119-154 of the series on the Creed, January 13-December 14).

LETTER
OF THE HOLY FATHER
POPE JOHN PAUL II
TO ALL THE PRIESTS OF THE CHURCH
ON THE OCCASION OF HOLY THURSDAY 1988

Mary in the Life of the Priest: "Behold, your Mother"

Dear Brothers in the Priesthood!

1.   Today we all return to the Upper Room. Gathering at the altar in so many places throughout the world, we celebrate in a special way the memorial of the Last Supper in the midst of the community of the People of God whom we serve. The words which Christ spoke on "the day before he suffered" re-echo on our lips at the evening liturgy of Holy Thursday as they do every day; yet they do so in a particular way since they refer back to that special evening which is recalled by the Church *precisely today.*

Like our Lord, and at the same time *in persona Christi,* we say the words: "Take this, all of you, and eat it: *this is my body.* . . . Take this, all of you, and drink from it: *this is the cup of my blood."* Indeed, the Lord himself commanded us to do so, when he said to the Apostles: "Do this in memory of me."[1]

And as we do this, the *whole mystery of the Incarnation* must be alive in our minds and hearts. Christ, who on Holy Thursday announces that his body will be "given up" and his blood "shed," is the eternal Son, who "coming into the world" says to the Father: *"A body you prepared for me. . . . Behold, I come to do your will."*[2]

It is precisely that Passover which is drawing near, when the Son of God, as Redeemer of the world, will fulfill the Father's will through the offering and *the immolation of his body and blood* on Golgotha. It is by means of this sacrifice that he "entered once for all into the Holy Place, taking . . . his own blood, thus securing an eternal redemption."[3] Indeed, this is the sacrifice of the "new and everlasting" covenant. See how it is intimately connected with the mystery of the Incarnation: the Word who became flesh[4] immolates his humanity as *homo assumptus* in the unity of the divine Person.

It is appropriate during this year, being lived by the whole Church as a Marian Year, to recall the reality of the Incarnation as it relates to the institution of the Eucharist and also to the institution of the sacrament of the priesthood. The Incarnation was brought about by the Holy Spirit when he came down upon *the Virgin of Nazareth* and she spoke her *fiat* in response to the angel's message.[5]

Hail, true Body, born of the Virgin Mary: you truly suffered and were immolated on the cross for man.

Yes, the same Body! When we celebrate the Eucharist, through our priestly ministry there is made present the mystery of the Incarnate Word, the Son who is of one being with the Father, who as a man "born of woman" is the Son of the Virgin Mary.

2.   There is no indication that the Mother of Christ was present in the Upper Room at the Last Supper. *But she was present on Calvary*, at the foot of the cross, where as the Second Vatican Council teaches, "she stood, in accordance with the divine plan,[6] suffering grievously with her only-begotten Son, uniting herself with a maternal heart to his sacrifice, and lovingly consenting to the immolation of this victim which she herself had brought forth."[7] How far the *fiat* uttered by Mary at the annunciation had taken her!

When, acting *in persona Christi*, we celebrate the sacrament of the one same sacrifice of which Christ is and remains the only priest and victim, *we must not forget this suffering of his Mother*, in whom were fulfilled Simeon's words in the Temple at Jerusalem: "A sword will pierce through your own soul also."[8] They were spoken directly to Mary forty days after Jesus' birth. On Golgotha, beneath the cross, these words were completely fulfilled. When on the cross Mary's Son revealed himself fully as the "sign of contradiction," it was then that this immolation and mortal agony also reached her maternal heart.

Behold the agony of the heart of the Mother who suffered together with him, "consenting to the immolation of this victim which she herself had brought forth." Here we reach *the high point of Mary's presence in the mystery of Christ and of the Church* on earth. This high point is on the path of the *pilgrimage of faith* to which we make special reference in the Marian Year.[9]

Dear brothers: who more than we has an absolute need of a deep and unshakable faith, we who by virtue of the apostolic succession begun in the Upper Room celebrate the sacrament of Christ's sacrifice? We must therefore constantly deepen our spiritual bond with the Mother of God *who on the pilgrimage of faith "goes before" the whole People of God.*

And in particular, when we celebrate the Eucharist and stand each day on Golgotha, we need to have near us the one who through heroic faith carried to its zenith her union with her Son, precisely then on Golgotha.

3. Moreover, has Christ not left us a special sign of this? See how during his agony on the cross he spoke the words which have for us the meaning of a testament: "When Jesus saw his mother, and the disciple whom he loved standing near, he said to his mother, 'Woman, behold, your son!' Then he said to the disciple, 'Behold, your mother!' And from that hour the disciple took her to his own home."[10]

That disciple, the Apostle John, was with Christ at the Last Supper. He was one of the "Twelve" to whom the Master addressed, together with the words instituting the Eucharist, the command: "Do this in memory of me." He received the power to celebrate the Eucharistic Sacrifice instituted in the Upper Room on the eve of the Passion, as the Church's most holy sacrament.

At the moment of death, Jesus gives his own Mother to this disciple. John "took her to his own home." He took her as the first witness to the mystery of the Incarnation. And he, as an evangelist, expressed in the most profound yet simple way the truth about the Word who "became flesh and dwelt among us,"[11] the truth about the Incarnation and the truth about Emmanuel.

And so, by taking "to his own home" the Mother who stood beneath her Son's cross, he also made his own *all that was within her on Golgotha*: the fact that she "suffered grievously with her only-begotten Son, uniting herself with a maternal heart in his sacrifice, and lovingly consenting to the immolation of this victim that she herself had brought forth." All this—the superhuman *experience of the sacrifice of our redemption, inscribed in the heart of Christ the Redeemer's own Mother*—was entrusted to the man who in the Upper Room received the power to make this sacrifice present through the priestly ministry of the Eucharist in the Church!

The reality of Golgotha is truly an amazing one: the reality of Christ's sacrifice for the redemption of the world! Equally amazing is *the mystery of God of which we are ministers in the sacramental order*.[12] But are we not threatened by the danger of being unworthy ministers? By the danger of not presenting ourselves with sufficient fidelity at the foot of Christ's cross as we celebrate the Eucharist?

Let us strive to be close to that Mother in whose heart is inscribed in a unique and incomparable way the mystery of the world's redemption.

4.   The Second Vatican Council proclaims:"Through the gift and role of her divine motherhood, by which the Blessed Virgin is united with her Son, . . . she is also intimately united with the Church. As St. Ambrose taught, *the Mother of God is a 'type' of the Church* in the matter of faith, charity and perfect union with Christ. For in the mystery of the Church, herself rightly called mother and virgin, the Blessed Virgin stands out in eminent and singular fashion as exemplar of both virginity and motherhood."[13]

The council text goes on to develop this typological analogy: *"The Church,* moreover, contemplating Mary's mysterious sanctity, imitating her charity and faithfully fulfilling the Father's will, *becomes herself a mother* by faithfully accepting God's word. For by her preaching and by baptism, she brings forth to a new and immortal life children who are conceived of the Holy Spirit and born of God. *The Church herself is a virgin,* who keeps whole and pure the fidelity she has pledged to her Spouse."The Church, therefore,"imitating the Mother of her Lord, and by the power of the Holy Spirit, preserves with virginal purity an integral faith, a firm hope and a sincere charity."[14]

At the foot of the cross on Golgotha,"the disciple took to his own home"Mary, whom Christ had pointed out to him with the words, "Behold, your mother."The council's teaching demonstrates how much *the whole Church* has taken Mary into"the Church's own home," how profoundly the mystery of this Virgin Mother belongs to the mystery of the Church, to the Church's intimate reality.

All this is of fundamental importance for all the sons and daughters of the Church. *It has special significance for us* who have been marked with the sacramental sign of the priesthood which, while being"hierarchical,"is at the same time"ministerial,"in keeping with the example of Christ, the first servant of the world's redemption.

If everyone in the Church—the people who participate in Christ's priestly function—possesses the common"royal priesthood"of which the Apostle Peter speaks,[15] then all must apply to themselves the words of the conciliar constitution just quoted. But these words refer in a special way to us.

The council sees *the Church's motherhood,* which is modeled on Mary's, *in the fact that the Church*"brings forth to a new and immortal life

children who are conceived of the Holy Spirit and born of God." Here
we find echoed St. Paul's words about "the children with whom I am
again in travail,"[16] in the same way as a mother gives birth. When,
in the Letter to the Ephesians, we read about Christ as the Spouse
who "nourishes and cherishes" the Church as his body,[17] we cannot
fail to link this spousal solicitude on the part of Christ above all with
the gift of Eucharistic Food, similar to the many maternal concerns
associated with "nourishing and cherishing" a child.

It is worth recalling these scriptural references so that the truth about
the Church's motherhood, founded on the example of the Mother of
God, may become more and more a part of our priestly consciousness. If each of us lives the equivalent of this *spiritual motherhood* in a
manly way, namely, as a *"spiritual fatherhood,"* then Mary, as a "figure"
of the Church, has a part to play in this experience of ours. The passages quoted show how profoundly this role is inscribed at the very
center of our priestly and pastoral service. Is not Paul's analogy on
"pain in childbirth" close to all of us in the many situations in which
we too are involved in the spiritual process of *man's "generation" and
"regeneration"* by the power of the Holy Spirit, the Giver of life? The
most powerful experiences in this sphere are had by confessors all
over the world and not by them alone.

On Holy Thursday we need to deepen once again this mysterious
truth of our vocation: this "spiritual fatherhood" which on the human
level is similar to motherhood. Moreover, does not God himself, the
Creator and Father, make the comparison between his love and the
love of a human mother?[18] Thus we are speaking of a characteristic
of our priestly personality that expresses precisely *apostolic maturity and spiritual "fruitfulness."* If the whole Church "learns her own
motherhood from Mary,"[19] do we not need to do so as well? Each
of us, then, has to "take her to our own home" like the Apostle John
on Golgotha; that is to say, each of us should allow Mary to dwell
"within the home" of our sacramental priesthood, as mother and
mediatrix of that "great mystery"[20] which we all wish to serve with
our lives.

5.   *Mary is the Virgin Mother,* and when the Church turns to Mary,
figure of the Church, she recognizes herself in Mary because the
Church too is "called mother and virgin." The Church is virgin, because *"she guards whole and pure the faith given to the Spouse."* Christ,
according to the teaching contained in the Letter to the Ephesians,[21]
is the Spouse of the Church. The nuptial meaning of Redemption

impels each of us to guard our fidelity to this vocation, by means of which we are made sharers of the saving mission of Christ, priest, prophet and king.

The analogy between the Church and the Virgin Mother has a special eloquence for us, who link our *priestly vocation to celibacy*, that is, to "making ourselves eunuches for the sake of the kingdom of heaven." We recall the conversation with the Apostles, in which Christ explained to them the meaning of this choice[22] and we seek to understand the reasons fully. We freely renounce marriage and establishing our own family in order to be better able to serve God and neighbor. It can be said that we renounce fatherhood "according to the flesh" in order that there may grow and develop in us fatherhood "according to the Spirit,"[23] which, as has already been said, possesses at the same time maternal characteristics. Virginal fidelity to the Spouse, which finds its own particular expression in this form of life, enables us to share in the intimate life of the Church, which, following the example of the Virgin, seeks to keep "whole and pure the fidelity she has pledged to her Spouse."

By reason of this model—of the prototype which the Church finds in Mary—it is necessary that our *priestly choice of celibacy* for the whole of our lives *should also be placed within her heart.* We must have recourse to this Virgin Mother when we meet difficulties along our chosen path. With her help we must seek always a more profound understanding of this path, an ever more complete affirmation of it in our hearts. Finally, in fact, there must be developed in our life this fatherhood "according to the Spirit," which is one of the results of "making ourselves eunuches for the sake of the kingdom of God."

From Mary, who represents the singular "fulfillment" of the biblical "woman" of the Proto-evangelium[24] and of the Book of Revelation,[25] let us seek also *a proper relationship with women* and the attitude toward them *shown by Jesus of Nazareth himself.* We find this expressed in many passages of the Gospel. This theme is an important one in the life of every priest, and the Marian Year impels us to take it up again and to develop it in a special way. By reason of his vocation and service, the priest must discover in a new way *the question of the dignity and vocation of women* both in the Church and in today's world. He must understand thoroughly what Christ intended to say to all of us when he spoke to the Samaritan woman;[26] when he defended the adulteress threatened with stoning;[27] when he bore witness to her whose many sins were forgiven because she had loved much;[28] when he conversed with Mary and Martha at Bethany;[29] and, finally, when he conveyed to the women, before others, "the Easter Good News" of his resurrection.[30]

The Church's mission, from apostolic times, was taken up in different ways *by men and by women*. In our own times, since the Second Vatican Council, this fact involves a new call addressed to each one of us, if the priesthood which we exercise in the different communities of the Church is to be truly ministerial and by this very fact effective and fruitful at the apostolic level.

6.   Meeting today, on Holy Thursday, at the birthplace of our priesthood, we desire to read its fullest meaning through the prism of the council teaching about the Church and her mission. The figure of the Mother of God belongs to this teaching in its entirety, as do the reflections of the present meditation.

Speaking from the cross on Golgotha, Christ said to the disciple: "Behold, your mother." And the disciple "took her to his own home" as Mother. Let us also *take Mary as Mother into the interior "home" of our priesthood*. For we belong to the "faithful in whose re-birth and development" the Mother of God "cooperates with a maternal love."[31] Yes, we have, in a certain sense, a special "right" to this love in consideration of the mystery of the Upper Room. Christ said: "No longer do I call you servants . . . , but I have called you friends."[32] Without this "friendship" it would be difficult to think that, after the Apostles, he *would entrust to us* the Sacrament of his Body and Blood, the sacrament of his redeeming death and resurrection, in order that we might celebrate this ineffable sacrament in his name, indeed, *in persona Christi*. Without this special "friendship" it would also be difficult to think about Easter evening, when the Risen Lord appeared in the midst of the Apostles, saying to them: "Receive the Holy Spirit. Whose sins you forgive are forgiven them, and whose sins you retain are retained."[33]

Such a friendship involves a commitment. Such a friendship should instill a holy fear, a much greater sense of responsibility, a much greater readiness to give of oneself all that one can, with the help of God. In the Upper Room such a friendship has been profoundly sealed with the promise of the Paraclete: "He will teach you all things, and bring to your remembrance all that I have said to you. . . . He will bear witness to me, and you also are witnesses."[34]

We always feel unworthy of Christ's friendship. But it is a good thing that we should have a holy fear of not remaining faithful to it.

The Mother of Christ knows all this. She herself has understood most completely the meaning of the words spoken to her during his agony on the cross:"Woman, behold, your son . . . Behold, your mother."They referred to her and to the disciple—one of those to whom Christ said in the Upper Room:"You are my friends";[35] they referred to John and to all those who, through the mystery of the Last Supper, share in the same"friendship." *The Mother of God,* who (as the council teaches) cooperates, with a mother's love, in the rebirth and the training of all those who become brothers of her Son—who become his friends—*will do everything in her power so that they may not betray this holy friendship,* so that they may be worthy of it.

7.   Together with John, the Apostle and Evangelist, we turn the gaze of our soul *towards* that *"woman clothed with the sun,"* who appears on the eschatological horizon of the Church and the world in the Book of Revelation.[36] It is not difficult to recognize in her the same figure who, at the beginning of human history, after original sin, was foretold as the Mother of the Redeemer.[37] In the Book of Revelation we see her, on the one hand, as the exalted woman in the midst of visible creation and, on the other, as the one who continues to *take part in the spiritual battle for the victory of good over evil.* This is the combat waged by the Church in union with the Mother of God, her "model,""against the world rulers of this present darkness, against the spiritual hosts of wickedness," as we read in the Letter of the Ephesians.[38] The beginning of this spiritual battle goes back to the moment when man"abused his liberty at the urging of personified Evil and set himself against God and sought to find fulfillment apart from God."[39] One can say that *man,* blinded by the prospect of being raised beyond the measure of the creature which he was—in the words of the tempter:"you will become as God"[40]—has ceased to seek the truth of his own existence and progress in him who is "the firstborn of all creation,"[41] and has ceased to give this creation and himself in Christ to God, from whom everything takes its origin. Man *has lost the awareness of being the priest of the whole visible world,* turning the latter exclusively towards himself.

The words of the Proto-evangelium at the beginning of the Scriptures and the words of the Book of Revelation at the end refer to the same battle in which man is involved. In the perspective of this spiritual battle which takes place in history, the Son of the woman is the Redeemer of the world. The Redemption is accomplished through the sacrifice in which Christ—the Mediator of the new and eternal covenant—"entered once for all into the Holy Place . . . with his own blood," making room in the "house of the Father"—in the bosom of the Most Holy Trinity—for all "those who are called to the eternal inheritance."[42] It is precisely for this reason that the crucified and risen Christ is "the high priest of the good things to come"[43] and his *sacrifice means a new orientation of man's spiritual history towards God*—the Creator and Father, towards whom the firstborn of all creation leads all in the Holy Spirit.

The priesthood, which has its beginning in the Last Supper, enables us to share in this essential transformation of man's spiritual history. For in the Eucharist we present the sacrifice of Redemption, the same sacrifice which Christ offered on the cross "with his own blood." Through this sacrifice we too, as its sacramental dispensers, together with all those whom we serve through its celebration, *continually touch the decisive moment of that spiritual combat* which, according to the Books of Genesis and Revelation, is linked with the "woman." In this battle she is entirely united with the Redeemer. And therefore our priestly ministry too unites us with her: with her who is the Mother of the Redeemer and the "model" of the Church. In this way all remain united with her in this spiritual battle which takes place throughout the course of human history. In this battle we have a special part by virtue of our sacramental priesthood. We fulfill a special service in the work of the world's redemption.

The council teaches that *Mary advanced in her pilgrimage of faith* through her perfect union with her Son unto the cross and goes before, presenting herself in an eminent and singular way to the whole People of God, which follows the same path, in the footsteps of Christ in the Holy Spirit. Should not we priests unite ourselves with her in a special way, we who as *pastors* of the Church must also lead the communities entrusted to us along the path which from the Upper Room of Pentecost follows Christ throughout human history?

8.   Dear brothers in the priesthood: as we come together today with our bishops in so many different places on earth, it has been my wish to develop in this annual letter precisely the motif which also seems to me particularly linked with the subject of the Marian Year.

As we celebrate the Eucharist at so many altars throughout the world, *let us give thanks* to the Eternal Priest *for the gift* which he has bestowed on us in the sacrament of the priesthood. And in this thanksgiving may there be heard the words which the Evangelist puts on Mary's lips on the occasion of her visit to her cousin Elizabeth: "The

Almighty *has done great things for me,* and holy is his name."[44] Let us also give thanks to Mary for the indescribable gift of the priesthood, whereby we are able to serve in the Church every human being. *May gratitude also reawaken our zeal!* Is it not through our priestly ministry that there is accomplished what the next verses of Mary's *Magnificat* speak of? Behold, the Redeemer, the God of the Cross and of the Eucharist, indeed "lifts up the lowly" and "fills the hungry with good things." He who was rich, yet for our sake became poor, so that by his poverty we might become rich,[45] has entrusted to the humble Virgin of Nazareth the admirable *mystery of his poverty* which makes us rich. And he entrusts the same mystery to us too through the sacrament of the priesthood.

Let us unceasingly give thanks for this. Let us give thanks with the whole of our lives. Let us give thanks with all our strength. Let us give thanks together with Mary, the Mother of priests. *"How can I repay the Lord for his goodness to me?* The cup of salvation I will raise; I will call on the Lord's name."[46]

With fraternal charity I send to all my brothers in the priesthood and in the episcopate, for the day of our common celebration, my heartfelt greetings and my Apostolic Blessing.

From the Vatican, on March 25, the Solemnity of the Annunciation of the Lord, in the year 1988, the tenth of my Pontificate.

Endnotes

1. Lk 22: 19.
2. Cf. Heb 1: 5-7.
3. Heb 9: 12.
4. Cf. Jn 1: 14.
5. Cf. Lk 1: 38.
6. Cf. Jn 19: 25.
7. *Lumen gentium,* n. 58.
8. Lk 2: 35.
9. Cf. *Redemptoris Mater,* n. 33: AAS 79 1987, p. 42.
10. Jn 19: 26-27.
11. Jn 1: 14.
12. Cf. 1 Cor 4: 1.
13. *Lumen gentium,* n. 63.
14. *Ibid.,* n. 64.
15. Cf. 1 Pt 2: 9.
16. Cf. Gal 4: 19.
17. Cf. 5: 29.

18. Cf. Is 49: 15; 66: 13.
19. Cf. *Redemptoris Mater*, n. 43: AAS 79 1987, p. 42.
20. Cf. Eph 5: 32.
21. *Ibid.*
22. Cf. Mt 19: 12.
23. Cf. Jn 1: 13.
24. Cf. Gen 3: 15.
25. Rv 12: 1.
26. Cf. Jn 4: 1-42.
27. Cf. Jn 8: 1-11.
28. Cf. Lk 7: 36-50.
29. Cf. Lk 1: 38-42; Jn 11: 1-44.
30. Cf. Mt 28: 9-10.
31. Cf. *Lumen gentium*, n. 63.
32. Jn 15: 15.
33. Jn 2: 22-23.
34. Jn 14: 26; 15: 26-27.
35. Jn 15: 14.
36. Cf. 12: 1ff.
37. Cf. Gen 3: 15.
38. Eph 6: 12.
39. *Gaudium et spes*, n. 13.
40. Cf. Gen 3: 5.
41. Col 1: 15.
42. Cf. Heb 9: 12, 15.
43. Heb 9: 11.
44. Lk 1: 49.
45. Cf. 2 Cor 8: 9.
46. Ps 115 (116): 12-13.

1989

Eleventh Year of Pontificate

The beginning of the year marked the release of the Post-Synodal Apostolic Exhortation *Christifideles laici*, dated December 30, 1988, on the vocation and mission of the laity in the Church and in the world, the topic of the 1987 Synod of Bishops.

The customary Holy Thursday Letter to Priests was dated March 12, the Fifth Sunday of Lent. The subject of the letter was the common priesthood of all the faithful and the ministerial priesthood of the ordained priests, their intimate link, and the essential differences between the two. "By virtue of their own vocation the lay faithful—our brothers and sisters—are united with this 'world' in a way that differs from ours. The world is given to them as a task by God in Christ the Redeemer. Their apostolate must lead directly to the transformation of the world in the spirit of the gospel (cf. *Christifideles laici*, 36). In the Eucharist of which we are ministers through Christ's grace, they come to discover light and strength for carrying out this task" (1989 Letter, n. 8).

Other pontifical documents included the Apostolic Letter *Vicesimus quintus annus*, released in May of this year, although dated December 4, 1988, on the twenty-fifth anniversary of *Sacrosanctum concilium*, the Conciliar Constitution on the Liturgy; the Apostolic Letter for the fiftieth anniversary of the outbreak of the Second World War (August 27) and the Apostolic Letter *Redemptoris custos* on the person and mission of St. Joseph in the life of Christ and of the Church (August 15).

The pope visited four African countries: Madagascar, Réunion, Zambia, and Malawi (his fifth African pilgrimage, April 28-May 6); five countries of Northern Europe: Norway, Iceland, Finland, Denmark, and Sweden (June 1-10); Spain (August 19 21), where he gave an address for World Youth Day; and Korea, Indonesia, East Timor, and Mauritius (October 6-16). On the last trip he participated in the close of the forty-fourth International Eucharistic Congress in Seoul.

In most of the General Audiences of the year John Paul II continued his catechetical reflections on the Creed, completing the considerations on Jesus Christ (nn. 155-164 in the series, January 11-April 19) and beginning a new section on the Holy Spirit (nn. 165-190, April 26-December 20).

LETTER
OF THE HOLY FATHER
POPE JOHN PAUL II
TO ALL THE PRIESTS OF THE CHURCH
ON THE OCCASION OF HOLY THURSDAY 1989

1. Once again this year I wish to call attention to the greatness of this day, which unites all of us around Christ. During the sacred triduum the whole Church deepens her awareness of the Paschal Mystery. Holy Thursday is meant for us in a particular way. It is the memorial of the Last Supper, which is renewed and represented on this day. In it we find what we live by; we find what we are by the grace of God. We return to the very beginning of the sacrifice of the new and everlasting Covenant as well as to the beginning of our priesthood, which is whole and complete in Christ. During the Paschal Supper he said: "This is my body, which will be given up for you"; "this is the cup of my blood which will be shed for you and for all so that sins may be forgiven."[1] Through these sacramental words, Christ reveals himself as the redeemer of the world and also as priest of the new and everlasting Covenant.

The Letter to the Hebrews expresses this truth most completely, re-ferring to Christ as "high priest of the good things that have come," who "entered once for all into the holy place" through "his own blood, thus securing an eternal redemption." Through his blood shed on the cross he "offered himself without blemish to God" through the "eternal Spirit."[2]

The one Priesthood of Christ is eternal and definitive, just as the sacrifice he offered is definitive and eternal. Every day and always, especially during the sacred triduum, this truth lives in the Church's consciousness: "We have a great high priest."[3]

And at the same time, what was accomplished at the Last Supper has made Christ's Priesthood into a sacrament of the Church. Until the end of time it is the sign of her identity and the source of that life in the Holy Spirit which the Church is constantly receiving from Christ. This life is shared by all who in Christ make up the Church. All share in the Priesthood of Christ, and this sharing signifies that already through Baptism "of water and the Holy Spirit"[4] they are consecrated to offer spiritual sacrifices in union with the one redeeming sacrifice offered by Christ himself. In him all become a "royal priesthood"[5] as the messianic people of the New Covenant.

2.   It is very timely to recall this truth on the occasion of the recent publication of the Apostolic Exhortation *Christifideles laici*. This document contains the results of the work done by the Synod of Bishops, which met in ordinary session in 1987 to discuss the theme of the vocation and mission of the laity in the Church and in the world.

We all need to become familiar with this important document. We also need to meditate on our own vocation in light of it. This kind of reflection is very opportune, especially on the day which recalls the origin of the Eucharist and of that sacramental service of priests which is connected with the Eucharist.

In the Dogmatic Constitution *Lumen gentium*, the Second Vatican Council pointed out the difference between the common priesthood of all the baptized and the priesthood which we receive in the Sacrament of Orders. The council calls the latter the "ministerial priesthood," which means both "office" and "service." It is also "hierarchical" in the sense of sacred service. For "hierarchy" means sacred governance, which in the Church is service.

We recall the often-quoted conciliar text: "Although they differ essentially and not only in degree, the common priesthood of the faithful and the ministerial or hierarchical priesthood are nonetheless ordered one to another; each in its own proper way shares in the one Priesthood of Christ. The ministerial priest, by the sacred power that he has, forms and rules the priestly people; in the person of Christ (*in persona Christi*) he effects the Eucharistic Sacrifice and offers it to God in the name of all the people. The faithful, by virtue of their royal priesthood, participate in the offering of the Eucharist. They exercise that priesthood too by the reception of the sacraments, by prayer and thanksgiving, by the witness of a holy life, by self-denial and active charity."[6]

3.   During the sacred triduum, the one priesthood of the new and everlasting Covenant is made visible to the eyes of our faith, the Priesthood which is in Christ himself. To him indeed can be applied the words about the high priest who, "chosen from among men, is appointed to act on their behalf."[7] As man, Christ is Priest; he is "high priest of the good things that have come." At the same time, however, this man-priest is the Son, of one being with the Father. For this reason his Priesthood—the Priesthood of his redemptive

sacrifice—is one and unrepeatable. It is the transcendent fulfillment of all that priesthood is.

This very same Priesthood of Christ is shared by everyone in the Church through the Sacrament of Baptism. Although the words "a priest chosen from among men" are applied to each of us who shares in the ministerial priesthood, they refer first of all to membership in the messianic people, in the royal priesthood. They point to our roots in the common priesthood of the faithful, which lies at the base of our individual call to the priestly ministry.

The "lay faithful" are those from among whom each one of us "has been chosen," from among whom our priesthood has been born. First of all, there are our parents, then our brothers and sisters as well as the many people of different backgrounds, sometimes de-Christian-ized, from which each of us comes. The priestly vocation, in fact, does not always emerge in an atmosphere favorable to it; sometimes the grace of vocation passes through an unfavorable environment and even through occasional resistance by parents or family.

Besides all those whom we know and whom we can personally iden-tify along the road of our own vocation, there are still others who remain unknown. We are never able to say with certainty to whom we owe this grace, to whose prayers and sacrifices we are indebted, in the mystery of the divine plan.

In any case, the words "a priest chosen from among men" have a broad application. If we meditate today on the birth of Christ's Priesthood, first of all in our own hearts (even before we received it through the imposition of hands by the bishop), we must live this day as debtors. Yes, brothers, we are debtors! It is as debtors to God's inscrutable grace that we are born to the priesthood, both from the heart of the Redeemer himself in the midst of his sacrifice and from the womb of the Church, the priestly people. For these people are, as it were, the spiritual seedbed of vocations; the earth tilled by the Holy Spirit, who is the Church's Paraclete for all time.

The People of God rejoices in the priestly vocation of its sons. In this vocation it finds the confirmation of its own vitality in the Holy Spirit, the confirmation of the royal priesthood, by means of which Christ, the "high priest of the good things that have come," is pres-ent in every generation of individuals and in Christian communities. He too was "chosen from among men." He is "the Son of Man," the son of Mary.

4. Wherever vocations are scarce, the Church must be attentive. And she is indeed attentive, very attentive. This concern is shared also by the laity in the Church. At the 1987 synod we heard touching words in this regard not only from the bishops and priests, but also from the lay people who were there.

This concern shows in the best possible way who the priest is for the laity. It testifies to his identity, and here we are talking of a community testimony, a social testimony, for the priesthood is a "social" sacrament: the priest "chosen from among men is appointed to act on behalf of men in relation to God."[8]

Jesus washed the feet of the Apostles at the Last Supper on the day before his passion and death on the cross, and he did this to stress the fact that he came "not to be served but to serve."[9] All that Christ did and taught was at the service of our redemption. The ultimate and most complete expression of this messianic service was to be the cross on Calvary. The cross confirmed in the fullest possible way that the Son of God became man "for us men and for our salvation" (*Credo* of the Mass). And this salvific service, which embraces the whole universe, is "inscribed" forever in the Priesthood of Christ. The Eucharist, the sacrament of Christ's redeeming sacrifice, contains in itself this "inscription." Christ, who came to serve, is sacramentally present in the Eucharist precisely in order to serve. At the same time this service is the fullness of salvific mediation: Christ has entered an eternal sanctuary, "into heaven itself, now to appear in the presence of God on our behalf."[10] In truth, he was "appointed to act on behalf of men in relation to God."

Each of us who shares by sacramental ordination in Christ's Priesthood must constantly reread this "inscription" of Christ's redeeming service. For we too, each one of us, are appointed "to act on behalf of men in relation to God." The council rightly affirms that "the laity have the right to receive in abundance from their pastors the spiritual goods of the Church, especially the assistance of the word of God and the sacraments."[11]

This service is at the very heart of our mission. Certainly our brothers and sisters, the lay faithful, look to us as "servants of Christ and stewards of the mysteries of God."[12] Here is found the full authenticity of our vocation, of our place in the Church. During the Synod of Bishops, in its discussion on the very question of the laity's apostolate, it was frequently mentioned that the laity have very much at heart the authenticity of vocations and priestly life. Indeed this is the first condition for the vitality of the lay state and for the apostolate proper to the laity. It is not at all a matter of "laicizing" the clergy any more than it is a matter of "clericalizing" the laity. The Church develops organically according to the principle of the multiplicity and diversity of "gifts," that is to say, charisms.[13] Each one "has his own special gift"[14] "for the common good."[15] "As each one has received a gift, employ it for one another, as good stewards of God's varied grace."[16] These statements by the Apostles are fully relevant in our own time. Likewise the exhortation "to lead a life worthy of the calling"[17] to which each one has been called is directed to everyone, both the ordained and the laity.

5.   Today therefore on a day so holy and filled with deep spiritual meaning for us, we should meditate once more, and in detail, on the particular character of our vocation and of our priestly service. Concerning priests, the council teaches that "their ministry itself by a special title forbids them to be conformed to this world. Yet at the same time this ministry requires that they live in this world among men."[18] In the priestly vocation of a pastor there must always be a special place for these people, the lay faithful and their "lay state," which is also a great asset of the Church. Such an interior place is a sign of the priest's vocation as a pastor.

The council has shown with great clarity that the lay state, which is rooted in the Sacraments of Baptism and Confirmation, has a common dimension of sharing in the Priesthood of Christ, which constitutes the essential vocation of all the lay faithful. Priests "cannot be ministers of Christ unless they are witnesses and dispensers of a life other than this earthly one," yet at the same time "they cannot be of service to men if they remain strangers to the life and conditions of men."[19] This indicates precisely that interior place given to the lay state, which is deeply inscribed in the priestly vocation of every pastor: It is the place for everything in which this "secularity" expresses itself. In all this the priest must try to recognize the "true Christian dignity"[20] of each of his lay brothers and sisters; indeed, he must make every effort to convince them of it, to educate them in it through his own priestly service.

Recognizing the dignity of the lay faithful and "the role which is proper to them in the mission of the Church," "priests are brothers among brothers . . . members of one and the same body of Christ, whose upbuilding is entrusted to all."[21]

6.   Cultivating such an attitude toward all the lay faithful, the laity and their lay state who themselves have been marked by the gift of a vocation received from Christ, the priest can carry out this social task which is linked with his vocation as a pastor, that is to say, he can "gather together" the Christian communities to which he is sent. The council on several occasions emphasizes this task. For example, its says that priests "exercising . . . the function of Christ . . . gather together God's family as a brotherhood all of one mind and lead them in the Spirit, through Christ, to God the Father." [22]

This "gathering together" is service. Each of us must be aware of gathering the community together not around ourselves but around Christ, and not for ourselves but for Christ, so that he can act in this community and at the same time in each person. He acts by the power of his Spirit, the Paraclete, in the measure of the "gift" which each person receives in this Spirit "for the common benefit." Consequently, this "gathering together" is service, and all the more service, to the extent that the priest "presides" over the community. In this regard the council emphasizes that "priests should preside in such a way that they seek the things of Jesus, not the things which are their own. They must work together with the lay faithful." [23]

This "gathering together" is not to be understood as something occasional but as a continuous and coherent "building up" of the community. It is precisely here that the cooperation of which the council speaks is essential. Priests must "discover with the instinct of faith, acknowledge with joy and foster with diligence the various humble and exalted charisms of the laity," as we read in the council's decree. [24] "Priests should also confidently entrust to the laity duties in the service of the Church, allowing them freedom and room for action." [25]

Referring to the words of St. Paul, the council reminds priests that they "have been placed in the midst of the laity to lead them to the unity of charity, so that they May 'love one another with fraternal charity, anticipating one another with honor.'" [26]

7.   At the present time, many groups within the Church are studying the Post-Synodal Exhortation *Christifideles laici*, which expresses the collegial solicitude of the bishops assembled in the synod. The synod was indeed echoing the council by attempting to indicate in the light of years of experience the direction in which the implementation of the council's teaching in the laity should proceed. Everyone knows that the council's teaching has proved to be especially rich and stimulating as well as responsive to the needs of the Church in the modern world.

We are aware of these needs in all their importance and variety. Thus knowledge of the post-synodal document will enable us to face these needs and in many cases will help us to improve our priestly service. For as we read in the Constitution *Lumen gentium:* "Sacred pastors know how much the laity contribute to the welfare of the entire Church. Pastors also know that they themselves were not meant by Christ to shoulder alone the entire saving mission of the Church toward the world."[27]

Upholding the dignity and responsibility of the laity, "let pastors willingly make use of their prudent advice."[28] All the pastors, "bishops and priests" reveal the face of the Church to the world. People will judge the power and truth of the Christian message thereby."[29] In this way there is "a strengthened sense of personal responsibility, a renewed enthusiasm, a more ready application of their talents to the projects of their pastors."[30]

This too will be an object of study for the meeting of the Synod of Bishops on the theme of priestly formation which has been announced for the year 1990. This sequence of themes in itself helps us to understand that in the Church there exists a profound link between the vocation of the laity and the vocation of priests.

8.   In mentioning all these things in this year's Letter for Holy Thursday, it has been my wish to touch upon a subject which is essentially linked to the Sacrament of Holy Orders. Today we gather around our bishops as the *presbyterium* of the individual local churches in so many places round the world. We concelebrate the Eucharist and renew the priestly promises connected with our vocation and our service of Christ's Church. It is the great priestly day of all the particular churches of the world within the one universal Church. We offer one another the sign of peace, and through this sign we reach out to all our brothers in the priesthood, even those farthest away in the vastness of the visible world.

It is precisely this world that we offer together with Christ to the Father in the Holy Spirit: the world of today, "the whole human family together with the sum of those realities in the midst of which that family lives."[31] Acting *in persona Christi*, as "stewards of the mysteries of God,"[32] we are conscious of the universal dimension of the Eucharistic Sacrifice.

By virtue of their own vocation the lay faithful—our brothers and sisters—are united with this "world" in a way that differs from ours. The world is given to them as a task by God in Christ the Redeemer. Their apostolate must lead directly to the transformation of the world in the spirit of the gospel.[33] In the Eucharist of which we are the ministers through Christ's grace, they come to discover light and strength for carrying out this task.

Let us remember them at all the altars of the Church in today's world as we renew the redeeming service of Christ. Let us renew it, as "good and faithful" servants "whom the master finds awake when he comes."[34]

To all my dear brothers in the Priesthood of Christ I send my cordial greeting and my Apostolic Blessing.

From the Vatican, on March 12, the fifth Sunday of Lent, in the year 1989, the eleventh of my Pontificate.

Endnotes

1. Cf. Mt 26: 26-28; Lk 22: 19-20.
2. Cf. Heb 9: 11-14.
3. Heb 4: 14.
4. Jn 3: 5.
5. 1 Pt 2: 9.
6. *Lumen gentium,* 1; cf. *Christifideles laici,* 22.
7. Cf. Heb 5: 1.
8. Heb 5: 1.
9. Mk 1: 45.
10. Heb 9: 24.
11. *Lumen gentium,* 37.
12. 1 Cor 4: 1.
13. Cf. *Christifideles laici,* 21-24.
14. 1 Cor 7: 7.
15. *Ibid.,* 12: 7.
16. 1 Pt 4: 10.
17. Eph 4: 1.
18. *Presbyterorum ordinis,* 3.
19. *Ibid.*
20. *Lumen gentium,* 18.
21. *Presbyterorum ordinis,* 9.
22. *Lumen gentium,* 28.
23. *Presbyterorum ordinis,* 9.
24. *Ibid.*
25. *Ibid.*
26. Rom 12: 1

27. *Lumen gentium,* 30.
28. *Ibid.,* 37.
29. *Gaudium et spes,* 43.
30. *Lumen gentium,* 37.
31. *Gaudium et spes,* 2.
32. 1 Cor 4: 1.
33. Cf. *Christifideles laici,* 36.
34. Cf. Lk 19: 17; 12: 37.

1990

Twelfth Year of Pontificate

This year's Letter to All the Priests of the Church was dated on Holy Thursday, April 12. "As the sacred triduum of the year of the Lord 1990 begins, we remember together the day of our ordination. We go to the Upper Room with Christ and the Apostles to celebrate the Eucharist *in cena Domini* and to rediscover that root which joins the Eucharist of Christ's Passover to our sacramental priesthood, inherited from the Apostles" (1990 Letter, n. 1).

The main theme of the letter was the Synod of Bishops to be celebrated at the end of the year. "*Veni, Creator Spiritus*! A few months from now these same words of the liturgical hymn will open the assembly of the Synod of Bishops, which is to be devoted to the priesthood and the training and continuing formation of priests in the Church" (1990 Letter, n. 3). And later on: "The synod for which we are preparing must be marked by prayer. Its work must indeed be conducted in an atmosphere of prayer by those actually taking part. But this is not enough. The work of the synod must be accompanied by the prayer of all the priests and of the whole Church" (1990 Letter, n. 4).

During this year the Holy Father made a trip to Cape Verde, Guinea, Bissau, Mali, Burkina Faso, and Chad (January 25-29); a short historic visit to Czechoslovakia (April 21-22), only a few days after the Holy See and that country reestablished diplomatic relations; a journey to Mexico and Curacao (May 6-13) and another to Tanzania, Burundi, Rwanda, and Ivory Coast (September 1-10).

The 1990 Synod of Bishops on "The Formation of Priests in Circumstances of the Present Day" opened September 30 and concluded October 28. It marked the first time since the synods began in 1967 that bishops were present from all countries of Eastern Europe. In the homily during the synod's opening Mass, the Holy Father spoke of formation as the response to the call of the Lord. "It is always a personal call: The Lord calls by name just as he called the Prophets and Apostles. At the same time it is a call within the community: in the Church and by the Church" (Homily, September 30, n. 1).

At the closing address the pope said: "During the work of this eighth ordinary assembly of the world Synod of Bishops, the Holy Spirit has permitted us to serve a cause of very great importance for the life of the Church: priestly formation. . . . It is the very life of the Church which points the way out of the crisis of priestly identity. This crisis was born in the years immediately following the council. It was based on an erroneous understanding—and sometimes even consciously biased—of the doctrine of the conciliar magisterium. Herein lies undoubtedly one of the reasons for the great number of defections experienced then by the Church, losses which did serious harm to pastoral ministry and priestly vocations, especially missionary vocations"(Address, October 27, nn. 3-4). In the matter of vocations, the pope called for "a total act of faith in the Holy Spirit." Praising the synod's reaffirmation of priestly celibacy, the Holy Father said that "the suggestion to consider ordaining *viri probati*," an expression used to refer to ordination of non-celibates, "is too often evoked within the framework of systematic propaganda which is hostile to celibacy. Such propaganda finds support and complicity in some of the mass media" (Address, October 27, nn. 5-6). On October 28 the Synod Message was proclaimed.

During this year several important papal documents were issued: the Apostolic Constitution on Catholic Universities *Ex corde Ecclesiæ* on August 15; the Apostolic Letter for the fourth centenary of the death of St. John of the Cross on December 14; the eighth encyclical of Pope John Paul II *Redemptoris missio*, dated December 7, although released the following month. The Sacred Congregation for the Doctrine of the Faith published the Instruction on the Ecclesial Vocation of the Theologian on May 24, and the Pontifical Council for Justice and Peace issued a circular letter dated May 15, the ninety-ninth anniversary of *Rerum novarum*, urging adequate celebrations of the centenary of the landmark social encyclical of Pope Leo XIII.

In most of the General Audiences the pope continued his talks on the Holy Spirit as part of the long series of catechetical addresses on the Creed (nn. 191-228 of the series, January 3-December 12).

LETTER
OF THE HOLY FATHER
POPE JOHN PAUL II
TO ALL THE PRIESTS OF THE CHURCH
ON THE OCCASION OF HOLY THURSDAY 1990

Come, Holy Spirit

1. *Veni, Creator Spiritus!*

In these words the Church prayed on the day of our priestly ordination. Today, as the sacred triduum of the year of the Lord 1990 begins, we remember together the day of our ordination. We go to the Upper Room with Christ and the Apostles to celebrate the Eucharist *in cena Domini* and to rediscover that *root which joins the Eucharist* of Christ's Passover *to our sacramental priesthood, inherited from the Apostles:* "When Jesus knew that his hour had come to depart out of this world to the Father, having loved his own who were in the world, he loved them to the end."[1]

Veni, Creator Spiritus!

On this Holy Thursday, as we go back to the origin of the priesthood of the new and everlasting Covenant, each one of us recalls, at the same time, that day which is inscribed in the history of our personal lives as the beginning of our sacramental priesthood, which is service in Christ's Church. *The voice of the Church, which invokes the Holy Spirit* on that day so decisive for each of us, alludes to Christ's promise in the Upper Room: "I will pray the Father, and he will give you another Counselor, to be with you forever, even the Spirit of Truth."[2] The Counselor—the Paraclete! The Church is certain of his saving and sanctifying presence. It is he "who gives life."[3] *The Spirit of Truth*, who proceeds from the Father . . . , whom I shall send to you from the Father,"[4] is he who has generated in us that new life which is called and which really is the ministerial Priesthood of Christ. He says: "*He will take what is mine and declare it to you.*"[5] It happened exactly like this. The Spirit of Truth, the Paraclete, "has taken" from that one Priesthood which is in Christ and has revealed it to us as the path of our vocation and our life. It was on that day that each of us saw himself, in the Priesthood of Christ in the Upper Room, as a minister of the Eucharist and, seeing ourselves in this way, we began to walk along this path. *It was on this day* that each of us, by virtue of the sacrament, saw this Priesthood as accomplished in himself, as imprinted on his soul in the form of an indelible seal: "You are a priest forever, after the order of Melchizedek."[6]

2.   All this is set before our eyes each year on the *anniversary of our ordination*, but it is also put forward again *on Holy Thursday*. For today, in the morning liturgy of the Chrism Mass, we gather, within our various priestly communities, around our bishops, *in order to rekindle the sacramental grace of Orders*. We gather together so as to renew, before the priestly people of the New Covenant, those promises which since the day of our ordination have been the basis of the special character of our ministry in the Church.

And, as we renew those promises, we invoke the Spirit of Truth—the Paraclete, that he may grant saving and sanctifying power to the words which the Church utters in her hymn of invocation:

> *Mentes tuorum visita,*
> *imple superna gratia,*
> *quæ tu creasti pectora*

Yes! Today let us open our hearts—these hearts which he has created anew by his divine power. He has created them anew with the grace of the priestly vocation, and within them he is continually at work. Every day he creates: he creates in us, ever anew, that reality which constitutes the essence of our priesthood—which confers upon each of us full identity and authenticity in priestly service—which enables us to "go and bear fruit" and which ensures that this fruit "abides."[7]

It is he, the Spirit of the Father and the Son, who enables us *to re-discover ever more deeply the mystery of that friendship* to which Christ the Lord called us in the Upper Room: "No longer do I call you servants . . . , but I have called you friends."[8] For while the servant does not know what his master is doing, the friend is familiar with the secrets of his Lord. The servant can only be obliged to work. The friend rejoices that he has been chosen by the one who has entrusted himself to him and to whom he too entrusts himself, entrusts himself totally.

So today let us pray to the Holy Spirit and ask him always to visit our thoughts and our hearts. *His visit is the prerequisite for remaining in Christ's friendship*. It also guarantees for us an ever deeper, ever more stirring knowledge of the mystery of our Master and Lord. We share in the mystery in a singular way: *we are its heralds*, and, above all, *its stewards*. This mystery fills us and, through us, like the vine, brings to birth the branches of divine life. How desirable therefore is the time of the coming of this Spirit who "gives life"! How closely our priesthood must be united to him in order to "abide in the vine which is Christ"!⁹

3.   *Veni, Creator Spiritus!*

A few months from now these same words of the liturgical hymn will open the assembly of the Synod of Bishops, *which is to be devoted to the priesthood and to the training and continuing formation of priests in the Church.* This subjects appeared on the horizon of the previous assembly of the synod three years ago, in 1987. The result of the work of that session of the synod was the Apostolic Exhortation *Christifideles laici*, which in many places has been received with great satisfaction.

This was a subject that needed to be explored, and the work of the synod, carried out with notable participation by the Catholic laity—men and women from every continent—proved particularly useful regarding the problems of the apostolate in the Church. It is worth adding that the Document *Mulieris dignitatem*, which in a way was the completion of the Marian Year, owes its inspiration to the synod.

But already at that time, there was emerging on the horizon of the work completed *the subject of the priesthood and the formation of priests.* "Without priests who are able to call upon the laity to play their role in the Church and in the world, and who can assist in the laity's formation for the apostolate, supporting them in their difficult vocation, an essential witness in the life of the Church would be lacking." With these words a highly regarded and expert representative of the laity commented on what was to become the subject of the next meeting of the Synod of Bishops of the whole world. Nor was this a solitary voice. The same need is felt by the People of God both in the countries where Christianity and the Church have existed for many centuries and in the mission countries where the Church and Christianity are beginning to take root. Although in the first years after the council a certain disorientation was felt in this area, both by the laity and by pastors of souls, nowadays the need for priests has become obvious and urgent for everyone.

Also implicit in this entire issue is the need for a careful rereading of the *council's teaching concerning the relationship between the "priesthood and the faithful,"* which results from their basic insertion through Baptism into the reality of the priestly mission of Christ, *and the "ministerial priesthood,"* shared in different degrees by bishops, priests and deacons.[10] This relationship corresponds to the structure of the Church as a community. The priesthood is not an institution that exists "alongside" the laity, or "above" it. The priesthood of bishops and priests, as well as the ministry of deacons, is *"for" the laity*, and precisely for this reason it possesses a "ministerial" character, that is to say one "of service." Moreover, it highlights the "baptismal priest-hood," the priesthood common to all the faithful. It highlights this priesthood and at the same time helps it to be realized in the sac-ramental life.

We can thus see how *the subject of the priesthood and the formation of priests* emerges from the very heart of the topics discussed at the last meeting of the Synod of Bishops. We can also see how this subject, within this framework, is all the more *justified and needed* the more *pressing* it becomes.

4.   It is therefore appropriate that this year's sacred triduum, and Holy Thursday in particular, should be a special time of prepara-tion for the autumn assembly of the Synod of Bishops. During the preparatory phase, which began about two years ago, diocesan and religious priests have been asked to speak up and to present observa-tions, suggestions and conclusions. Although the topic concerns the Church as a whole, it is nonetheless the priests of the entire world who first and foremost have the right and also the duty to consider this synod as "their own": indeed, *res nostra agitur*!

And since at the same time the entire matter is *res sacra*, it is ap-propriate that the preparation of the synod should be based not only on an exchange of reflections, experiences and suggestions, but also that it should have a sacred character. Much prayer is needed for the work of the synod. Much depends on that work for the continuing process of renewal begun by the Second Vatican Council. In this field much depends on the "laborers" whom "the Lord will send out into his harvest."[11] Perhaps today, as we approach the third millennium of Christ's coming, we are experiencing more deeply both the vastness and the difficulties of the harvest: "*The harvest is plentiful*"; but we also notice the lack of laborers: "*The laborers are few.*"[12] "Few": and this in regard not only to quantity but also quality! Hence the need for formation! Hence also the Master's next words: "*Pray therefore the Lord of the harvest to send out laborers into his harvest.*"[13]

The synod for which we are preparing must be marked by prayer. Its work must indeed be conducted in an atmosphere of prayer by those actually taking part. But this is not enough. The work of the synod must be accompanied by the prayer of all priests and of the whole Church. For some weeks now, my Sunday Angelus reflections have been directed toward fostering such prayer.

5. For these reasons *Holy Thursday 1990*—the *dies sacerdotalis* of the whole Church—*has a fundamental significance* for the course of the synod's preparation. From this day forward, we must call upon the Holy Spirit, the Giver of life: *Veni, Creator Spiritus!* No other period affords us such an intimate grasp of the profound truth about Christ's Priesthood. He who "entered once for all into the holy place with his own blood, thus securing us an eternal redemption,"[14] who is himself the priest of the new and everlasting Covenant, at the same time "loved his own who were in the world and loved them to the end."[15] And the measure of this love is *the gift of the Last Supper: the Eucharist and the priesthood.*

Gathered together around this gift through today's liturgy, and looking forward to the synod devoted to the priesthood, let us allow the Holy Spirit to work within us, so that the Church's mission will continue to mature *according to the measure found in Christ.*[16] May it be granted us to know ever more perfectly "the love of Christ which surpasses all knowledge!"[17] In him and through him may we be "filled with all the fullness of God"[18] in our priestly service.

To all my brothers in the Priesthood of Christ I send the assurance of my esteem and love, with my special Apostolic Blessing.

From the Vatican, on April 12, Holy Thursday, in the year 1990, the twelfth of my Pontificate.

Endnotes

1. Jn 13: 1.
2. Jn 14: 16-17.
3. Jn 6: 63.
4. Cf. Jn 15: 26.
5. Jn 16: 14.
6. Heb 5: 6.
7. Cf. Jn 15: 16.
8. Jn 15: 15.
9. Cf. Jn 15: 5.
10. Cf. *Lumen gentium,* nn. 1 and 28.
11. Cf. Mt 9: 38.
12. Mt 9: 37.
13. Mt 9: 38.
14. Cf. Heb 9: 12.
15. Cf. Jn 13: 1.
16. Cf. Eph 4: 13.
17. Eph 3: 19.
18. *Ibid.*

1991

Thirteenth Year of Pontificate

Although dated December 7 of the previous year, the Encyclical *Redemptoris missio* on the permanent validity of the Church's missionary mandate was made public on January 22. Jozef Cardinal Tomko, Prefect of the Congregation for the Evangelization of Peoples, presented the document at a press conference in the Vatican.

"The Encyclical *Redemptoris missio*," Cardinal Tomko said, "is a cry on behalf of the mission which calls to mind the memorable loud cry which John Paul II expressed to all people at the beginning of his Pontificate: 'Open wide the doors to Christ.' . . . The encyclical *synthesizes and vigorously expresses the essential line of this Pontificate.*" After explaining the reasons for and the novelties of the document, as well as giving a brief summary of its content, the cardinal concluded: "*Redemptoris missio* is totally filled with a *vigorous optimism.* . . . The great jubilee of the Redemption is at hand, and the third millennium is about to begin. Today the Church has as *her guide for the 'mission of the year 2000'* a modern, sure, complete and vibrant *'vademecum,' Redemptoris missio.*"

As the first reason given in the encyclical itself for its promulgation, the Holy Father mentions "an interior renewal of faith and Christian life. For missionary activity renews the Church, revitalizes faith and Christian identity, and offers fresh enthusiasm and new incentive. Faith is strengthened when it is given to others" (*Redemptoris missio,* n. 2).

The same theme, faith is a gift to be shared, was in the pope's mind at the ordination, on the Solemnity of the Epiphany, of thirteen bishops from various continents, including Archbishop Jean-Louis Tauran, Secretary of the Secretariat of State's Section for Relations with States, and Bishop Alvaro del Portillo, Prelate of Opus Dei. "Epiphany is the feast of living faith," the Holy Father said in the homily. "Receiving the mystery of God as a gift, people must share it with others. They must give it to others" (Homily, January 6, n. 2).

The war in the Persian Gulf region was a continuing source of sorrow for the Holy Father throughout its duration. He repeatedly appealed for peace in his weekly reflections before praying the Angelus on Sundays. "At this time," he said at the very start of the hostilities, "I cannot neglect to mention that for several days a war is being fought in the Gulf region which is a cause of concern and sorrow for everyone. Together with many people of goodwill, I did what I could that this tragic experience might be avoided. . . . May the Virgin Mary comfort all those who are suffering because of this war" (Angelus reflection, January 20).

The pope's sorrow continued to be expressed as the war continued. "The anxiety and sadness which unfortunately have been voiced more than once over the war in progress in the Gulf region continue to be increased by the prolonged fighting. . . . *Let us pray first of all for peace. . . . Let us pray for the civilian populations. . . . Let us pray that the tragedy in progress will not be made even greater and more inhumane* through acts that are unacceptable to the natural law and the international agreements in effect. . . . *Let us pray again for and with all believers* belonging to the three religions which have their historical roots in the Middle East: Jews, Christians and Muslims. . . . With confidence we entrust these intentions to the Virgin Most Holy, Queen of Peace" (Angelus reflection, January 27). "*Life must always be defended,* welcomed with love and accompanied with constant respect. . . . We must proclaim the inviolability of the right to life—and to a life with dignity—against abortion, an aberrant crime which has the qualities of totalitarianism in regard to the most defenseless human beings. We must proclaim this right against genetic manipulation which threatens the development of the person; against euthanasia and the rejection of those who are most feeble; against racism and homicidal violence of every kind. We must proclaim such right against war—against this war which is continuing to be fought in the Persian Gulf region with increasing threat to all humanity. . . . With confidence we turn to you, Mother of mercy, Mother of life" (Angelus reflection, February 3). "I invite everyone present for the Angelus and all those who hear my voice to join in our fervent and confident prayer to God, Father of all mankind, that he may grant our heartfelt plea for peace. . . . O Mary, Queen of Peace, pray for us" (Angelus reflection, February 10).

As Lent started, the Holy Father made it the occasion for a renewed request of prayer for peace: "The season of Lent, which we have just begun, is an occasion for more intense prayer and more generous penance in order to implore God for the grace of conversion of hearts and the gift of *peace in justice* for all peoples. I ask all the faithful of the Catholic Church—the dioceses, parishes and various ecclesiastical organizations—to devote this time of preparation for Easter to prayer for peace and to concrete acts of fraternal solidarity with those who are suffering because of the war and injustices existing in the vast, tired region of the Middle East" (Angelus reflection, February 17). "War has never seemed so much like the seeds of death as it does in these hours. . . . This Apostolic See has done everything possible to avoid this terrible war. Now all that is left for us to do is to work and pray that it may end as soon as possible and that similar tragedies never again appear on mankind's horizon. O Mary, Queen of Peace, intercede for us" (Angelus reflection, February 24).

On March 3, the pope thanked God for the end of the fighting and requested prayers for the meeting of Eastern patriarchs and representatives of the episcopal conferences of countries more directly involved in the conflict.

The meeting with the Holy Father of the patriarchs of the Catholic Churches of the Middle East and the bishops of the countries most directly involved in the Gulf conflict took place on March 4-5. During the General Audience on March 6 they celebrated the solemn conclusion of the meeting. "Our meeting," the Holy Father said in his final address, "has been first of all a deep experience of ecclesial communion encouraged by our common sensitivity and responsibility which derive from the ministry entrusted to us by Christ. . . . The Gulf war has wrought death, destruction and enormous economic and environmental damage: we have expressed the hope that, for the people of Kuwait, the population of Iraq and all their neighbors, the desire for material reconstruction may be accompanied by a desire for faithful collaboration with one another and the great family of the nations. It will be necessary to overcome the rancor and cultural divisions and especially those which have been created between diverse religious worlds. . . . The reference to the land where Christ was born directed our thoughts to the city where he preached, died and rose: Jerusalem, with its holy places which are also dear to the Jews and Muslims and their communities. Jerusalem, called to be a crossroads of peace, cannot continue to be the cause of discord and dispute" (General Audience, March 6).

The pope's Letter to Priests on occasion of Holy Thursday was dated March 10, the Fourth Sunday of Lent. The Holy Father made reference to last year's letter and to the 1990 Synod of Bishops and announced the document which will present its results. "But today, even before that document is published, I wish to tell you that the synod itself was a great blessing. For the Church, every synod is always a blessing, because the collegiality of the bishops of the whole Church is expressed in a special way" (1991 Letter, n. 2).

Addressing the topic of priestly identity, the Holy Father writes that "it is difficult to say why in the period following the council the awareness of this identity has in some quarters become less sure. The fact could depend on an incorrect reading of the Church's conciliar magisterium in the context of certain ideological premises inapplicable to the Church and of certain trends coming from the cultural environment." However, the pope observes that "it appears that lately . . . a significant transformation in the ecclesial communities themselves is taking place. Lay people are seeing the indispensable need for priests as a condition for their own authentic Christian life and their own apostolate." And the growing need for priests "should help to overcome the crisis of priestly identity."

In regard to the shortage of priests, the Holy Father points out that *"the gradual revival of priestly vocations* only partially compensates for the shortage of priests. Even if this process is positive on a worldwide scale, nevertheless there are imbalances between different parts of the Church community throughout the world,"and the pope recalls that"during the synod this picture was analyzed in great detail, not only for statistical purposes but also with a view to a possible 'exchange of gifts,' that is to say, mutual assistance"which is appropriate due to the above-mentioned imbalance (1991 Letter, n. 2).

The pope's letter was made public at the Vatican along with a document drawn up by a committee consisting of members of the Congregation for Bishops, the Congregation for Institutes of Consecrated Life and Societies of Apostolic Life, the Congregation for Catholic Education, the Pontifical Commission for Latin America and the General Secretariat of the Synod of Bishops. The document presents the basic data:"In Latin America . . . about 43 percent of the Catholics of the world are served by . . . 13 percent of the priests of the world, while the Catholics of Europe and North America, who constitute 38.81 percent of the Catholics of the world, are served by . . . 73.14 percent of the priests worldwide," and it offers both short-term and long-range plans to solve the geographic inequity in the distribution of priests, including the sharing of priests between countries, new vocation programs, and the development of new national and international seminaries.

An extraordinary consistory, the fourth convoked by John Paul II, took place April 4-7 in Vatican City; 112 cardinals from every part of the world participated. Two topics were on its agenda: threats to human life and the challenge of the sects in the proclamation of Christ, the only Savior.

A Vatican Press communique outlined the conclusions of the meeting. In regard to the first topic,"the College of Cardinals first of all reaffirmed that they are with the Holy Father in the struggle on behalf of life, thanking him for the prophetic service which he tirelessly gives all mankind. . . . Today many states allow and promote abortion, and some others propose to legalize euthanasia too. Therefore, in such a renewed context, respect for human life in the person who is weak and defenseless is not only a problem of an individual morality, but it becomes a topic of social morality and political ethics. . . . The cardinals expressed a desire that the Holy Father solemnly reaffirm in a document (the majority of the cardinals favor an encyclical) the Church's constant teaching on the value of human life and its intangibility in the light of present circumstances and the attacks which threaten it today." Shortly afterwards, the pope addressed a Letter to All the Bishops of the World, dated Pentecost, May 19, in which referring to the extraordinary consistory, he asks the bishops to make public declarations, be vigilant about teaching in seminaries and universities, and ensure right practices in Catholic hospitals.

In regard to the second topic, the proclamation of Christ and the challenge of sects, "the cardinals affirmed that the Church . . . is today faced not only with the urgent task of reaching those who have never known the Gospel, but also with the phenomenon which leads many Catholics to join religious communities which are extraneous to their tradition and contrary to their membership in the Church. . . . The cardinals particularly emphasized the need for a new evangelization which responds to current needs, helping Christians rediscover their identity and the richness of their faith in Christ. . . . The participants in the consistory insisted on the necessity of promoting a knowledge of Sacred Scripture rooted in the Church's tradition and capable of nourishing authentic spirituality and personal prayer."

Already at the very beginning of the year, on the Solemnity of Mary, Mother of God, Pope John Paul declared 1991 the Year of the Social Teaching of the Church: "In this year of the Lord 1991," the Holy Father said, "the Church commemorates *a great event of worldwide importance,* whose prophetic value has been confirmed with the passing of time: *the publication of the Encyclical Rerum novarum* by Pope Leo XIII on May 15, 1891. . . . I wish therefore to proclaim the year beginning today the *Year of the Social Teaching of the Church,* and thereby to invite the faithful, within the context of commemorating the Encyclical *Rerum novarum,* to become better acquainted with the Church's teaching on social matters, and to develop and spread that teaching. I am pleased to announce in this regard, the publication of an encyclical commemorating the one hundredth anniversary of that of my predecessor." (Homily, January 1, n. 6)

The new encyclical, *Centesimus annus,* Pope John Paul's third social encyclical, is dated May 1, the Memorial of St. Joseph the Worker, and was presented to the press by Roger Cardinal Etchegaray, president of the Pontifical Council for Justice and Peace. "The announcement of a new encyclical, made at the beginning of January by the Pope himself," Cardinal Etchegaray said, "aroused curiosity, interest and expectation— everyone had his own little idea about the baby to be born. Today the encyclical's birth certificate removes all doubt about what Pope John Paul II wanted: an encyclical which 'overprints' that of Pope Leo XIII, an encyclical meant to commemorate the publication one hundred years ago of *Rerum novarum.*"

Cardinal Etchegaray indicated the three viewpoints of the new document: a retrospective view, through a rereading of *Rerum novarum;* a contemporary viewpoint of the "new things" which surround us today;

a forward-looking viewpoint"at a time when we can already glimpse the third millennium of the Christian era, so filled with uncertainties but also with promises" (*Centesimus annus*, n. 3). After giving a brief summary of each of the six chapters of the document, he concluded:"The Encyclical *Centesimus annus* restores fresh youth to the one-hundred-year-old Encyclical *Rerum novarum*. . . . It is not European; it embraces all people because it embraces the whole person. It does not allow for a 'diagonal reading'; we must read it line by line. It does not lend itself to selective quotations; it has to be taken as a whole, like a living body. It comes from a pope whose clear-sightedness has the profundity of the gospel."

The pope's second visit to Portugal took place May 10-13, with stops in Lisbon, the Azores, Madeira, and Fatima. It was the fiftieth trip beyond Italy during his pontificate, and one of its highlights was his visit to the Marian shrine of Fatima, where he thanked Our Lady for her protection during the attempt made on his life ten years earlier. At the General Audience following the trip, the Holy Father commented:"The pilgrimage this year had a particular purpose: to give thanks *for saving the Pope's life on May 13, 1981*. . . . I consider this entire decade to be a free gift, given to me in a special way by Divine Providence—a special responsibility was given to me that I might continue to serve the Church by exercising the ministry of Peter. . . . My pilgrimage began with the holy sacrifice of the Mass, celebrated in Lisbon, the capital city, as a *thanksgiving* for the five hundred years of Portugal's participation in the Church's mission of evangelization. At the same time, this thanksgiving is an ardent appeal and prayer for a new evangelization. Our age is waiting for this. The recent Encyclical *Redemptoris missio* speaks of this in a most convincing way" (General Audience, May 15, nn. 1-2).

On June 1 the pope began a nine-day pilgrimage to his native Poland for the fourth time since his election as supreme pontiff. A few days later he spoke about his visit:"This trip was first of all a 'pilgrimage of thanks.' . . . The year 1989 will remain an important date not only for my homeland, but also for all of Europe, particularly the countries of eastern and central Europe. . . . The *leitmotiv* 'Do not quench the Spirit' has a contemporary relevance. . . . This phrase focused my *teaching* in Poland *by basing it on the Ten Commandments and the Gospel commandment of love*" (General Audience, June 12, nn. 1, 5).

On June 28 the Holy Father celebrated an ordinary public consistory for the creation of twenty-two new cardinals, including Roger Cardinal Mahony, Archbishop of Los Angeles, and Anthony Cardinal Bevilacqua, Archbishop of Philadelphia.

In August the pope visited Poland again, this time for World Youth Day. The day after his return to Rome he commented:"This World Youth Day has become a tradition, not a long one, but one that has been going on for several years. . . . Several times this special day has been celebrated on a world scale, an international scale: first in Rome in 1985, then in Buenos Aires, Argentina, in 1987, and then in Santiago de Compostela, Spain, in 1989, and this year in Czestochowa. . . . It was an experience of prayer, a spiritual experience, in which a great increase in the number of participants was noted: actually more than a million people gathered at the shrine of Jasna Gora" (Address, August 21). After his stay in Poland (August 13-16), the second part of this pastoral visit was in Hungary (August 16-20), marking the first time in modern times that the pope had visited Hungary. "This," the Holy Father said, "fulfilled my desire, after so many years, of visiting a nation which, from the beginning of its recent history, has been closely tied to the See of Peter by a special bond, the sign of which is the baptism and royal crown which the King of Hungary, St. Stephen, received from Pope Sylvester II in the year 1000" (Address, August 28, n. 1).

The second papal visit to Brazil (October 12-21) included the celebration of the Mass that marked the close of the twelfth National Eucharistic Congress. "The fact that for the first time in Brazilian soil a beatification was celebrated," that of Blessed Mother Pauline, foundress of the Congregation of the Little Sisters of the Immaculate Conception, "deserves special mention" (Address, October 23, n. 6).

During most of the General Audiences of the first part of the year the pope continued with his reflections on the Holy Spirit (January 2-July 3). On July 10 he began a new set of talks on the Church that continued for the rest of the year (July 10-December 18).

LETTER
OF THE HOLY FATHER
POPE JOHN PAUL II
TO ALL THE PRIESTS OF THE CHURCH
ON THE OCCASION OF HOLY THURSDAY 1991

Priestly Identity and the Need for Priests

1.   "The Spirit of the Lord is upon me."[1]

As we gather around the bishop in the cathedrals of our dioceses for the liturgy of the Chrism Mass, we hear these words which Christ spoke in the synagogue at Nazareth. Standing for the first time before the people of his native village, Jesus reads from the book of the prophet Isaiah the words foretelling the coming of the Messiah: "The Spirit of the Lord is upon me; because he has anointed me. . . . He has sent me."[2] In their immediate setting these words point to the prophetic mission of the Lord as the one who proclaims the Gospel. But we can also apply them to the manifold grace which he communicates to us.

The renewal of priestly promises on Holy Thursday is linked to the rite of the blessing of the holy oils, which in some of the Church's sacraments express that anointing with the Holy Spirit which comes from the fullness which is in Christ. The anointing with the Holy Spirit first brings about the supernatural gift of sanctifying grace by which we become, in Christ, sharers in the divine nature and in the life of the most holy Trinity. In each of us, this gift is the interior source of our Christian vocation and of every vocation within the community of the Church, as the People of God of the New Covenant.

Today, then, we look to Christ, who is the fullness, the source and the model of all vocations and in particular of the vocation to priestly service as a special sharing, through the priestly character of Holy Orders, in his own Priesthood.

In Christ alone is the fullness of anointing, the fullness of the gift; a fullness destined to one and all, an inexhaustible fullness. At the beginning of the sacred triduum, when the whole Church, through the liturgy, enters in a special way into Christ's Paschal Mystery, we see before us the depth of our vocation to be ministers, a vocation which must be lived according to the example of the Master, who before the Last Supper washed the feet of the Apostles.

During this supper, from the fullness of the Father's gift—which is in Christ and which, through him, is bestowed upon mankind—Jesus will institute the sacrament of his body and blood under the appearances of bread and wine. He will place it—the Sacrament of the Eucharist—in the hands of the Apostles and, through them, in the hands of the Church, for all time, until his final coming in glory.

In the power of the Holy Spirit, at work in the Church since the day of Pentecost, this sacrament, passed down through generation after generation of priests, has been entrusted also to us in the present moment of human and world history, which in Christ has become once and for all the history of salvation.

Today each one of us, dear brothers, retraces in his mind and heart the path which brought him to the priesthood, and then, his own path in the priesthood, a path of life and service which has come down to us from the Upper Room. All of us recall the day and the hour when, after we recited together the Litany of the Saints as we lay prostrate on the floor of the Church, the bishop imposed hands on each of us in profound silence. Since the time of the Apostles, the imposition of hands has been the sign of the bestowal of the Holy Spirit, who is the supreme author of the sacred power of the priesthood; sacramental and ministerial authority. The entire liturgy of the sacred triduum brings us nearer to the Paschal Mystery, from which this authority takes its origin, in order to become service and mission. We can apply here the words of the Book of Isaiah,[3] read by Jesus in the synagogue at Nazareth: "The Spirit of the Lord is upon me, because he has anointed me. . . . He has sent me."

2. Venerable and dear brothers: In my letter to you last Holy Thursday I sought to direct your attention to the meeting of the Synod of Bishops, which was to be devoted to the subject of priestly formation. The meeting took place last October, and we are currently preparing, together with the Council of the General Secretariat of the synod, the document which will present its results. But today, even before that document is published, I wish to tell you that the synod itself was a great blessing. For the Church, every synod is always a blessing because the collegiality of the bishops of the whole Church is expressed in a special way. This time the experience was particularly enriching, for at the synodal assembly we heard the voices of bishops from countries where the Church has only recently emerged, so to speak, from the catacombs.

Another grace of the synod was a new maturity in the way of looking at priestly service in the Church; a maturity which keeps pace with the times in which our mission is being carried out. This maturity finds expression in a more profound interpretation of the very essence of the sacramental priesthood and thus also of the personal life of each and every priest, that is to say, of each priest's participation in the saving mystery of Christ: *sacerdos alter Christus*. This is an expression which indicates how necessary it is that Christ be the starting point for interpreting the reality of the priesthood. Only in this way can we do full justice to the truth about the priest, who, having been "chosen from among men, is appointed to act on behalf of men in relation to God."[4] The human dimension of priestly service, in order to be fully authentic, must be rooted in God. Indeed, in every way that this service is "on behalf of men," it is also "in relation to God": It serves the manifold richness of this relationship. Without an effort to respond fully to that "anointing with the Spirit of the Lord" which establishes him in the ministerial priesthood, the priest cannot fulfill the expectations that people—the Church and the world—rightly place in him.

All of this is closely connected with the question of priestly identity. It is difficult to say why in the period following the council the awareness of this identity has in some quarters become less sure. The fact could depend on an incorrect reading of the Church's *conciliar magisterium* in the context of certain ideological premises inapplicable to the Church and of certain trends coming from the cultural environment. It appears that lately—even though the same premises and the same trends continue to operate—a significant transformation in the ecclesial communities themselves is taking place. Lay people are seeing the indispensable need for priests as a condition for their own authentic Christian life and their own apostolate. Likewise, this need is becoming obvious and indeed in many situations is becoming urgent, by reason of the lack or insufficient number of ministers of the divine mysteries. From another point of view, this need for priests is also felt in those countries where the gospel is being proclaimed for the first time, as was pointed out in the recent encyclical on the missions.

This need for priests—in some ways a growing phenomenon —should help to overcome the crisis of priestly identity. The experience of recent decades shows ever more clearly how much the priest is needed both in the Church and in the world, not in some "laicized" form, but in the form which is drawn from the gospel and from the rich tradition of the Church. The teaching of the Second Vatican Council is the expression and confirmation of this tradition, in the sense of a timely renewal (*accommodata renovatio*). This was the general tenor of the statements made by the bishops at the last synod and also by those who had been invited from different parts of the world to represent their fellow priests.

The gradual revival of priestly vocations only partially compensates for the shortage of priests. Even if this process is positive on a world-wide scale, nevertheless there are imbalances between different parts of the Church community throughout the world. The picture is very diversified.

During the synod this picture was analyzed in great detail not only for statistical purposes, but also with a view to a possible "exchange of gifts," that is to say, mutual assistance. The appropriateness of this kind of assistance is self-evident, since it is well known that there are places with one priest for several hundred Catholics and others where there is one priest for 10,000 Catholics or even more.

In this regard, I wish to recall a statement of the Second Vatican Council's Decree on the Ministry and Life of Priests: "The spiritual gift that priests have received in ordination prepares them not for any narrow and limited mission, but for the most universal and all-embracing mission of salvation 'to the end of the earth.'[5] . . . Priests, then, should bear in mind that they ought to care for all the churches."[6] Today the disturbing shortage of priests in some areas makes these words of the council more timely than ever. It is my hope that they will be meditated upon and implemented as generously as possible, particularly in dioceses with a relatively large number of clergy.

In any event, what is needed everywhere is to pray "the Lord of the harvest to send out laborers into his harvest."[7] This is a prayer for vocations and likewise a prayer that each priest will attain ever greater maturity in his vocation: in his life and in his service. This maturity contributes in a special way to an increase of vocations. We simply need to love our priesthood, to give ourselves completely to it, so that the truth about the ministerial priesthood may thus become attractive to others. In the life of each one of us, people should be able to discern the mystery of Christ, the mystery from which originates the reality of the *sacerdos* as *alter Christus*.

3.   Taking leave of the Apostles in the Upper Room, Christ promised them the Paraclete, another Counselor, the Holy Spirit "who proceeds from the Father and the Son." In fact he said: "It is to your advantage that I go away, for if I do not go away, the Counselor will not come to you; but if I go, I will send him to you."[8] These words give particular emphasis to the relationship existing between the Last Supper and Pentecost. At the cost of his "departure" through the sacrifice of the cross on Calvary (even before his "departure" to the Father on the 40th day after the Resurrection), Christ remains in the Church: He remains in the power of the Paraclete, the Holy Spirit, who "gives life."[9] It is the Holy Spirit who "gives" this divine life: a life which revealed itself in Christ's Paschal Mystery as stronger than death, a life which entered human history with Christ's resurrection.

The priesthood is completely at the service of this life: it bears witness to it through the service of the word; it generates it; it regenerates it and spreads it abroad through the service of the sacraments. Before all else the priest himself lives this life, which is the deepest source of his maturity and also the guarantee of the spiritual fruitfulness of his whole service! The Sacrament of Orders imprints on the soul of the priest a special character which, once it has been received, remains in him as a source of sacramental grace, and of all the gifts and charisms which correspond to the vocation to priestly service in the Church.

The liturgy of Holy Thursday is a special moment during the year in which we can and must renew and rekindle in ourselves the sacramental grace of the priesthood. We do this in union with the bishop and the entire presbyterate, with the mystery of the Upper Room before our eyes: the Upper Room of both Holy Thursday and the day of Pentecost. Entering deeply into the divine mystery of Christ's sacrifice, we open ourselves at the same time to the Holy Spirit, the Paraclete, whose gift to us is our special participation in the one Priesthood of Christ, the eternal Priest. It is by the power of the Holy Spirit that we are able to act *in persona Christi*, in the celebration of the Eucharist and in our entire sacramental service for the salvation of others.

Our witness to Christ is often very imperfect and deficient. How consoling it is for us to have the assurance that it is primarily he, the Spirit of Truth, who bears witness to Christ.[10] May our human witness be open above all to his witness! For it is the Spirit himself who "searches . . . the depths of God"[11] and alone can bring these "depths," these "mighty works of God"[12] to the minds and hearts of those to whom we are sent as servants of the gospel of salvation. The more overwhelmed we feel by our mission, the more open we must be to the action of the Holy Spirit, especially when the resistance of minds and hearts, the resistance of a culture begotten under the influence of"the spirit of the world,"[13] becomes particularly obvious and powerful.

"The Spirit helps us in our weakness . . . and intercedes for us with sighs too deep for words."[14] Despite the resistance of minds and hearts and of a culture steeped in "the spirit of the world," there nevertheless persists in all of creation the "longing" spoken of by St. Paul in the Letter to the Romans:"The whole creation has been groaning in travail together until now,"[15] that it May"obtain the glorious liberty of the children of God."[16] May this vision of St. Paul not fade from our priestly consciousness, and may it support us in our life and service! Then we shall better understand why the priest is necessary for the world and for mankind.

4.   "The Spirit of the Lord is upon me."Venerable and dear brothers in the ministerial priesthood: Before we receive the post-synodal exhortation on the theme of priestly formation, please accept this letter for Holy Thursday. May it be the sign and expression of the communion which unites all of us—bishops, priests and deacons as well—in a sacramental bond. May it help us, through the power of the Holy Spirit, to follow Jesus Christ,"the pioneer and perfecter of our faith."[17]

With my Apostolic Blessing.

From the Vatican, on March 10, the fourth Sunday of Lent, in the year 1991, the thirteenth of my Pontificate.

Endnotes

1. Lk 4: 18; Cf. Is 61: 1.
2. Lk 4: 18.
3. Cf. Is 61: 1.
4. Heb 5: 1.
5. Acts 1: 8.
6. *Presbyterorum ordinis*, 1.
7. Mt 9: 38.
8. Jn 16: 7.
9. Jn 6: 63.
10. Cf. Jn 15: 26.
11. 1 Cor 2: 10.
12. Acts 2: 11.
13. 1 Cor 2: 12.
14. Rom 8: 26.
15. Rom 8: 22.
16. Rom 8: 21.
17. Heb 12: 2.

1992

Fourteenth Year of Pontificate

The two most important papal documents of the year were the Post-Synodal Apostolic Exhortation *Pastores dabo vobis* on the formation of priests and the Apostolic Constitution *Depositum Fidei* on the publication of the *Catechism of the Catholic Church*.

The exhortation, dated March 25, was released April 7 at a press conference given by the Secretary General of the Synod of Bishops. "The title, taken from the first words of the exhortation," Archbishop Schotte said, "clearly and boldly indicates the meaning of the Ordinary General Assembly convoked to reflect on the theme of the formation of priests in circumstances of the present day. Beginning with the quotation from the Prophet Jeremiah 'I will give you shepherds after my own heart' (Jer 3: 15), the Holy Father refers to the most characteristic trait of the 1990 Synod Assembly: optimism based on faith in the Lord's promise." The exhortation is a beautiful and comprehensive document on priestly formation. It contains an introduction, six chapters, and a conclusion, ending, as it happens in other papal documents, with a prayer to the Blessed Virgin: "O Mary, Mother of Jesus Christ and Mother of Priests, accept this title which we bestow on you to celebrate your motherhood and to contemplate with you the Priesthood of your Son and of your sons, O Holy Mother of God. . . . Accept from the beginning those who have been called, protect their growth, in their life ministry accompany your sons, O Mother of Priests. Amen" (*Pastores dabo vobis*, n. 82).

Significantly, the Holy Thursday Letter for this year, dated March 29, the Fourth Sunday of Lent, was a very short letter to accompany the apostolic exhortation and released on the very same day. Referring to the allegory of the vine and the branches, the Holy Father wrote: "It is precisely to this text that I wish to refer on Holy Thursday in this year of the Lord 1992, as I offer to the Church the apostolic exhortation on priestly formation. . . . Today I wish to place this result of the synod Fathers' prayer and reflection at the feet of Christ the Priest and Pastor of our souls (cf. 1 Pt 2: 25). Together with you, I wish to receive this text from the altar of the one and eternal Priesthood of the Redeemer, which in a sacramental way became our portion at the Last Supper" (1992 Letter, nn. 1-2).

The Sacred Congregation for the Doctrine of the Faith published the Letter to the Bishops of the Catholic Church *Communionis notio* on some aspects of the Church understood as Communion, dated May 28 and presented by Cardinal Ratzinger on June 15.

The Apostolic Constitution *Depositum Fidei* on the publication of the *Catechism of the Catholic Church* was dated October 11, the thirtieth anniversary of the opening of Vatican II. "Guarding the deposit of faith," the document begins, "is the mission which the Lord has entrusted to his Church and which she fulfills in every age" (*Depositum fidei*, n. 1). The constitution summarizes the process and spirit of drafting the text (n. 2), the arrangement of the material (n. 3) and the doctrinal value of the text (n. 4).

Regarding the authority of the *Catechism*, the Holy Father says that it "is a statement of the Church's faith and of Catholic doctrine, attested to or illumined by Sacred Scripture, apostolic tradition and the Church's magisterium. I declare it to be a valid and legitimate instrument for ecclesial communion and a sure norm for teaching the faith" (n. 4). Regarding the intended audience, the pope states: "I ask the Church's pastors and the Christian faithful to receive this catechism in a spirit of communion and to use it assiduously in fulfilling their mission of proclaiming the faith and calling people to the gospel life. This catechism is given to them that it may be a sure and authentic reference text for teaching Catholic doctrine and particularly for preparing local catechisms. It is also offered to all the faithful who wish to deepen their knowledge of the unfathomable riches of salvation (cf. Jn 8: 32). It is meant to support ecumenical efforts. . . . The *Catechism of the Catholic Church*, lastly, is offered to every individual who asks us to give an account of the hope that is in us (cf. 1 Pt 3: 15) and who wants to know what the Catholic Church believes" (n. 4).

Pope John Paul officially presented the *Catechism* on December 7 in a special ceremony attended by cardinals, heads of dicasteries of the Roman Curia, the diplomatic corps accredited to the Holy See, representatives of the doctrinal commissions of episcopal conferences and members of the editorial commission. "The holy Church of God rejoices today," the Holy Father said, "because, as a special gift of divine providence, she can solemnly celebrate the promulgation of the new 'catechism,' presenting it officially to the faithful of the whole world. I give great thanks to the God of heaven and earth because he has allowed me to experience with you an event of incomparable richness and importance" (Address, December 7, n. 1). Speaking on behalf of the representatives from the doctrinal commissions, Bernard Cardinal Law, Archbishop of Boston, said: "Our most important task is to ensure that the gospel is proclaimed in its entirety. This new *Catechism of the Catholic Church* will be an invaluable and rich resource, as well as a clear norm."

The Holy Father spoke about the *Catechism* repeatedly and with great affection. "I would like to share with you an event of great importance for the life of the Church. I am referring to the publication of the *Catechism of the Catholic Church* which I approved last June. . . . It will be an event of historic importance because the new catechism is not just another book of theology or catechesis, but rather a general reference text for the catechetical activity of the whole People of God" (Angelus reflection, November 15). "I give thanks to the Lord for the wonderful 'symphony' of faith which has been shown once again and I express my wish that the new catechism will bear abundant fruit in the whole Church" (Angelus reflection, November 29). "This new text represents a privileged tool and a pressing invitation to an appropriate gospel formation in order to begin the new evangelization with firm conviction and apostolic foresight" (Angelus reflection, December 6). "The promulgation of the new catechism is not just an act of doctrinal regulation, but takes on the weight of an appeal addressed to all believers to work with greater commitment in the new evangelization" (Angelus reflection, December 13).

During this year the Holy Father made pastoral visits to Senegal, the Gambia, and Guinea (February 19-26); and later to Angola, Sao Tome, and Principe (June 4-10), the fifty-fifth apostolic visit outside of Italy; to the Dominican Republic (October 9-14) to celebrate the fifth centenary of America's evangelization. The liturgical high point of the visit was the Mass on Sunday, October 11, in Santo Domingo, commemorating the fifth centenary of the gospel's arrival in the New World. "The commemoration of the fifth centenary of the beginning of the evangelization of the New World is a great day for the Church," the pope said. "As the Successor of the Apostle Peter, I have the joy of celebrating this Eucharist . . . in this blessed land which five hundred years ago received Christ, the Light of the nations, and was marked with the sign of salvation" (Homily, October 11, n. 1). During the Mass the pope canonized Ezequiel Moreno, missionary and bishop, who was beatified by Paul VI in 1975. "What greater mark of glory for America than being able to present to everyone those witnesses of holiness who have helped keep the message of Jesus Christ alive in the New World throughout these five centuries? Behold this wonderful array of saints and blessed who adorn almost the whole of America's geography, whose lives are the most mature fruits of evangelization and the model and source of inspiration for the new evangelists. This mark of holiness is the setting for today's canonization of Blessed Ezequiel Moreno" (Homily, October 11, n. 4).

Holiness and evangelization were on the pope's lips as he addressed the Latin American bishops on the following day. "Under the guidance of the Spirit, whom we have fervently invoked to enlighten the work of this important ecclesial assembly, we are opening the Fourth General Congress of the Latin American Episcopate. . . . This conference is being held to celebrate Jesus Christ, to give thanks to God for his presence in these American lands where five hundred years ago the message of salvation began to be spread; it is being held to celebrate the planting of the Church which for five centuries has given the New World such abundant fruits of holiness and love. . . . Let us give thanks to God for the band of evangelists who left their country and gave their life to sow the new life of faith, hope and love in the New World" (Address, October 12, nn. 1-3).

Holiness and evangelization were in the pope's heart on many other occasions, as when he beatified Monsignor Josemaría Escrivá, priest and founder of Opus Dei, and Sister Josephine Bakhita on May 17. "With supernatural intuition," the pope said, "Blessed Josemaría untiringly preached the universal call to holiness and the apostolate. Christ calls everyone to become holy in the realities of everyday life. Hence, work too is a means of personal holiness and apostolate when it is lived in union with Jesus Christ" (Homily, May 17, n. 3).

In most of the General Audiences of the year John Paul II continued his catechetical reflections on the Church (nn. 266-294 in the series on the Creed, January 8-December 16). The Wednesday audiences were interrupted as the Holy Father recovered from surgery he underwent on July 15. Four days later the faithful listened on loudspeakers as the pope led the Angelus from his hospital room: "I entrust to the Lord, through the hands of Mary, the physical and spiritual suffering of all the world's sick people, and my suffering too, for the Church and for humanity" (Angelus reflection, July 19).

On July 22 the Secretary of State was the principal celebrant and homilist of a special Mass for the Holy Father's intentions. "On February 11, 1984, the pope gave us the wonderful Apostolic Letter *Salvifici doloris* on the Christian meaning of human suffering," Cardinal Sodano said. "The pope has illustrated that theme frequently in his discourses. . . . With his illness now, just as eleven years ago with his hospital stay after the attack which claimed him as a victim, the Holy Father is teaching us by his example, succeeding in reaching the heart of all believers. His catechesis from his bed in the Gemelli Polyclinic is a concrete catechesis, one easily understood. Released from the hospital on July 28, the following Sunday he made his first public appearance: "Today I have the joy of meeting you for the first time since my stay in the Gemelli, a time when I felt the solidarity and spiritual closeness of so many people. I thank the Lord for this and I thank everyone. . . . Today let us resume our spiritual pilgrimage to the American shrines in order to share with the ecclesial communities of that continent the 'singular year' which they are celebrating for the fifth centenary of their evangelization" (Angelus reflection, August 2). Before the year was over, as mentioned above, the pope visited Santo Domingo and promulgated the *Catechism of the Catholic Church*.

LETTER
OF THE HOLY FATHER
POPE JOHN PAUL II
TO ALL THE PRIESTS OF THE CHURCH
ON THE OCCASION OF HOLY THURSDAY 1992

Give Thanks for the Gift of the Priesthood

"I am the true vine, and my Father is the vinedresser."[1]

Dear Brother Priests!

1. Allow me to call to mind today the above words from the Gospel according to John. They are linked to the liturgy of Holy Thursday: "Before the feast of Passover, when Jesus knew that his hour had come,"[2] he washed his disciples' feet, and then spoke to them intimately and with great candor, as St. John tells us. This farewell discourse also contains the allegory of the vine and the branches: "I am the vine, you are the branches. He who abides in me, and I in him, he it is that bears much fruit, for apart from me you can do nothing."[3]

It is precisely to this text that I wish to refer on Holy Thursday in this year of the Lord 1992, as I offer to the Church the apostolic exhortation on priestly formation. It is the result of the collegial work of the 1990 Assembly of the Synod of Bishops, which was entirely devoted to that subject. We worked out together a much-needed and awaited document of the Church's magisterium, which brings together both the teaching of the Second Vatican Council and reflections on the experiences of the twenty-five years since the end of the council.

2. Today I wish to place this result of the synod Fathers' prayer and reflection at the feet of Christ the Priest and Pastor of our souls.[4] Together with you, I wish to receive this text from the altar of the one and eternal Priesthood of the Redeemer, which in a sacramental way became our portion at the Last Supper.

Christ is the true vine. If the Eternal Father cultivates his vineyard in this world, he does so in the power of the Truth and Life which are in the Son. Here are found the ever-new beginning and inexhaustible source of the formation of every Christian, and especially of every priest. On Holy Thursday let us try in a particular way to grow in our awareness of this reality and in the attitude needed for us to be able to remain, in Christ, open to the breath of the Spirit of Truth, and to bear abundant fruit in God's vineyard.

3. As we join in the Holy Thursday liturgy with all the pastors of the Church, let us give thanks for the gift of the priesthood which we share. At the same time let us pray that all those throughout the world who are offered the grace of a priestly vocation will respond to this gift, so that there will be no lack of laborers for the great harvest.[5]

As I express this hope I send to all of you an affectionate greeting and my Apostolic Blessing.

Given at the Vatican, on 29 March, the fourth Sunday of Lent, in the year 1992, the fourteenth of my Pontificate.

Endnotes

1. Jn 15: 1.
2. Jn 13: 1.
3. Jn 15: 5.
4. Cf. 1 Pt 2: 25.
5. Cf. Mt 9: 37.

1993

Fifteenth Year of Pontificate

A few days before Christmas the pope received members of the Curia for the traditional exchange of greetings. "The year 1993 was a rich year," he said, "and it is difficult for me not to refer to at least some of the 'treasures' which it has yielded" (Address, December 23, n. 3). Among the treasures he mentioned were the second Synod of the Church in Rome, some of his apostolic trips and the encyclical *Veritatis splendor*.

"Rome and her Bishop are at the service of the world's ecclesial communities: this has been confirmed by my numerous visits during the year, which is now coming to an end, in Italy, and I remember Sicily in particular, and abroad" (Address, December 21, n. 3). The trips abroad were to Benin, Uganda, and Sudan (February 3-10), the tenth apostolic visit to Africa; Albania (April 25); Spain (June 12-17); Jamaica, Mexico, and Denver, Colorado (August 9-16), the sixtieth outside Italy; Estonia, Latvia, and Lithuania (September 4-10).

The Holy Father was especially touched by the young people in Denver, and the young people were equally moved by the Holy Father's presence. In the General Audience following the trip the pope reflected on World Youth Day: "The stop in Denver was important, for it allowed me to meet thousands and thousands of people, more than expected. . . . This great pilgrimage of young people did not have a shrine for its destination, but a modern city. In the heart of this 'metropolis,' the world's young people proclaimed their identity as Catholics. . . . They gathered in Denver to say 'yes' to life and peace, against the threats of death that jeopardize the culture of life" (Address, August 18, nn. 4, 6). The impression was still deep in the pope's heart at the end of the year. "Denver was a great surprise overall, presented by the young people to society, and especially to American society. It was noted that during those few days people spontaneously behaved with exceptional kindness, and there were none of the usually frequent episodes of violence or aggression. . . . The Denver meeting discovered that young people are capable of 'surprising' the world by the wealth of their values, by their courage to live and by their witness to peace and solidarity" (Homily, December 14, nn. 5-6). "Denver was the big surprise of 1993. . . . Why did I find Denver the great surprise of 1993? Great opposition was expected, at least according to some sources of information, and instead World Youth Day was a tremendous achievement. Not an achievement of the pope or the Church, but first and foremost, Christ's achievement. And it was not the first time that the young people expressed so vigorously their desire to carry the gospel into the new millennium. Christ is the Way, the Truth and the Life (cf. Jn 14: 6); Christ is with them, and with an ardent youthful heart they yearn for his presence" (Address, December 21, n. 6).

The Holy Thursday Letter for this year focused on the new *Catechism*. "It is fitting to include in our thanksgiving this year," the pope wrote, "a particular element of gratitude for the gift of the *Catechism of the Catholic Church*. This text is a response to the mission which the Lord has entrusted to his Church: to guard the deposit of faith and to hand it down intact, with authority and loving concern, to coming generations." As he had done so many other times, the Holy Father reiterated the importance of the *Catechism*: "This *Catechism* is given to us as a sure point of reference for fulfilling the mission, entrusted to us in the Sacrament of Orders, of proclaiming the 'Good News' to all people in the name of Christ and of the Church.... In this summary of the deposit of faith, we can find an authentic and sure norm for teaching Catholic doctrine, for catechetical activity among the Christian people, for that 'new evangelization' of which today's world has such an immense need" (1993 Letter, n. 2).

As a means of encouraging further study of the problems associated with priestly spirituality in our time, the Holy Father directed that the Holy Thursday Letter be accompanied by the text of the reflections and prayer on priestly celibacy and vocations which he offered at the conclusion of his meeting with the presidents of the Episcopal Conferences of Europe held in the Vatican on December 1, 1992.

The Encyclical *Veritatis splendor*, dated August 6, Feast of the Transfiguration of the Lord, was officially presented on October 5. The previous Sunday, the Holy Father referred to it. "This document, greatly expected and prepared at length, is only now being published because it seemed appropriate that it be preceded by the *Catechism of the Catholic Church* which contains a complete, systematic exposition of Christian morality," the pope said (Angelus reflection, October 3, n. 1), linking the two documents, as he also does in the text of the encyclical (*Veritatis splendor*, n. 5). "The announcement of the encyclical's imminent publication has given rise to understandable interest in public opinion. I hope," John Paul II stated, "that when the text is read as a whole, it will be the object of calm consideration, and will thus be able to contribute to a better understanding of the demanding and liberating gospel message." And, as every so often in the pontificate, the act of entrustment: "I entrust this encyclical to the Blessed Virgin, whom we intend to honor particularly during this month of October with the prayer of the Holy Rosary" (Angelus reflection, October 3, nn. 2-3).

The document was presented by the prefect of the Congregation for the Doctrine of the Faith who explained the reasons behind it and gave a summary of its contents. "The structure of the encyclical is very simple," Joseph Cardinal Ratzinger said. "A short introduction explains the point of departure and goal of the text. Then follows the first chapter which is essentially biblical in character," including an extensive commentary on the conversation of the rich young man with Jesus. "The second chapter inserts these insights gleaned from Scripture and penetratingly explored by the Fathers into the current dispute over the foundation of moral conduct." Called the doctrinal chapter, it focuses on the relationship between freedom and truth—placing particular emphasis on freedom and law, conscience and truth, fundamental option and moral absolutes. "The third chapter places the insights of the first and second chapters into the vital context of Church and society. One could call it the pastoral chapter of the document. In this last part the reader perceives a passion for the cause of God and man which should touch him, the reader, immediately." The document concludes with a short prayer to Mary, Mother of Mercy.

At the end of the year the Holy Father commented on *Veritatis splendor*. "Regarding this," he said, "I feel a compelling need to give thanks to the Spirit of Truth, because . . . it was possible to publish this document which had been painstakingly prepared over a period of almost six years. Today it is impossible to deny that it was necessary. In the past we had to tell the truth about man to Eastern Europe. . . . It is now necessary to confirm this truth to the people living in the West" (Address, December 21, n. 8).

The year 1993 was again the year of *ad limina* visits by the American bishops. In his addresses to the different groups of bishops (March 20, April 24, May 28, June 5, June 8, July 2, September 21, October 2, October 15, November 11, and December 4), the Holy Father spoke often about the *Catechism of the Catholic Church*, the World Youth Day in Denver, and *Veritatis splendor*.

"While our private conversations deal with the situation of your individual dioceses, these group meetings," the pope told the first group of bishops, "give me an opportunity to share with you and your brother bishops in the United States some thoughts on more general aspects of your ministry and of the Church's life in your country. I wish to do so in the light of the *Catechism of the Catholic Church*. I consider its publication among the principal fruits of the Second Vatican Council and one of the most significant events of my Pontificate. It is an invaluable instrument of the genuine ecclesial renewal which the council intended. . . . It is my prayerful hope that the new catechism will provide the impetus for a national catechizing endeavor, of young and old alike. . . . I am confidently looking forward to the celebration of the World Youth Day in Denver, in August" (Address, March 20, nn. 1, 5, 6).

"This whole series of *ad limina* talks," the pope told another group, "is following the outline of the newly published *Catechism of the Catholic Church*. The *Catechism* is truly God's timely gift to the whole Church and to every Christian at the approach of the new millennium. Indeed I pray that the Church in the United States will recognize in the *Catechism* an authoritative guide to sound and vibrant preaching, an invaluable resource for parish adult formation programs, a basic text for the upper grades of Catholic high schools, colleges and universities. . . . My final thoughts this morning turn to Denver and the World Day of Youth, when I will have the opportunity to meet young men and women from all over America and the rest of the world. I wish to express my deep gratitude to the bishops and all those involved in preparing this event" (Address, June 5, nn. 2, 7).

"Today I wish to thank the whole Church in the United States, particularly the Archdiocese of Denver, for hosting the Eighth World Youth Day," the pope said in the fall. "I was moved many times by the young people's obvious and joyous love of God and of the Church. . . . I came away from Denver praising God who reveals to the young the secrets of his kingdom" (Address, September 21, n. 1).

"Indeed, the World Youth Day in Denver," John Paul told the last group of bishops, "offered us all a confirmation of the vitality of the Catholic community in the United States. The young especially are a lively and promising sign of God's life-giving presence in the heart of the world. . . . The thoughts which I have shared with the U.S. bishops during this year's *ad limina* visits have been guided by the outline and content of the *Catechism of the Catholic Church*. In your hands the *Catechism* will be an extremely effective help in making available to all the faithful the inexhaustible riches of what the Church believes, prays, celebrates and lives" (Address, December 4, nn. 2, 6).

In most of the General Audiences of the year, John Paul II continued his catechetical reflections on the Church (nn. 295-327 in the series on the Creed, January 13-December 15). These include eighteen addresses on the priesthood (nn. 301-318, March 31-September 29) which the Introduction to the Directory for the Life and Ministry of Priests, dated Holy Thursday, March 31, 1994, lists among recent magisterial documents on the priesthood.

LETTER
OF THE HOLY FATHER
POPE JOHN PAUL II
TO ALL THE PRIESTS OF THE CHURCH
ON THE OCCASION OF HOLY THURSDAY 1993

*The Catechism of the Catholic Church: An Authentic
and Sure Norm for Teaching Catholic Doctrine*

1. *"Jesus Christ is the same yesterday and today and forever."*[1]

Dear Brothers in the Priesthood of Christ! As we gather today in the many different cathedral churches throughout the world—members of the presbyteral communities of all the churches together with the pastors of the dioceses—there come back to our minds with new force these words about Jesus Christ which became the recurring theme of the 500th anniversary of the evangelization of the New World.

"Jesus Christ is the same yesterday and today and forever": these words refer to the *one eternal Priest,* who "entered once for all into the Holy Place, . . . with his own blood, thus securing an eternal redemption."[2] Now the days have come—the *Triduum Sacrum* of the Church's sacred liturgy—in which, with even deeper veneration and worship, we renew the Passover of Christ, "his hour,"[3] which is the blessed "fullness of time."[4]

Through the Eucharist, this "hour" of Christ's redemption continues, in the Church, to be salvific. Today especially the Church recalls the institution of the Eucharist at the Last Supper. "I will not leave you desolate; I will come to you."[5] The "hour" of the Redeemer, the "hour" of his going forth from this world to the Father, the "hour" of which he himself says: "I go away, and I will come to you."[6] Precisely though his "paschal going forth," Christ constantly comes to us and remains present among us, by the power of the Spirit, the Paraclete. He is present sacramentally. He is present through the Eucharist. He is really present.

Dear brothers, *after the Apostles we have received* this ineffable gift *so that we may be ministers* of Christ's *going forth* by way of the cross and, at the same time, of his *coming* in the Eucharist. How wonderful this holy triduum is for us! How wonderful for us is this day—the day of the Last Supper! We are ministers of the mystery of the redemption of the world, ministers of the body which was offered and of the blood which was shed so that sins might be forgiven. Ministers of that sacrifice by which he, alone, entered once for all into the Holy Place. "Having offered himself without blemish to God, he purifies our conscience from dead works to serve the living God."[7]

Although all the days of our life are marked by this great mystery of faith, today is even more so. This is our day with him.

2. On this day we gather together *in our priestly communities,* so that each one can contemplate more deeply the mystery of that sacrament whereby we have become ministers in the Church of Christ's priestly offering. We have likewise become servants of the royal priesthood of the whole People of God, of all baptized, so that we may proclaim the *magnalia Dei,* the "mighty works of God."[8]

It is fitting to include in our thanksgiving this year *a particular element of gratitude* for the gift of the *Catechism of the Catholic Church.* This text is a response to the mission which the Lord has entrusted to his Church: to guard the deposit of faith and to hand it down intact, with authority and loving concern, to coming generations.

The result of the fruitful cooperation of the bishops of the Catholic Church, the *Catechism* is entrusted above all to us, the pastors of God's People, in order to strengthen our deep bonds of communion in the same apostolic faith. *As a compendium of the one perennial Catholic faith,* it constitutes a trustworthy and authoritative means for bearing witness to and ensuring that unity in faith for which Christ himself prayed fervently to the Father as his "hour" drew near.[9]

The *Catechism* sets forth once more the fundamental and essential contents of Catholic faith and morality as they are believed, celebrated, lived and prayed by the Church today. It is thus *a special means* for deepening knowledge of the inexhaustible Christian mystery, for encouraging fresh enthusiasm for prayer intimately united with prayer of Christ and for strengthening the commitment of a consistent witness of life.

At the same time, this *Catechism* is given to us as a *sure point of reference* for fulfilling the mission, entrusted to us in the Sacrament of Orders, of proclaiming the "Good News" to all people *in the name of Christ and of the Church.* Thanks to it, we can put into practice in a constantly renewed way Christ's perennial command: "Go therefore and make disciples of all nations . . . teaching them to observe all that I have commanded you."[10]

Indeed, in this summary of the deposit of faith, we can find *an authentic and sure norm* for teaching Catholic doctrine, for catechetical activity among the Christian people, for that "new evangelization" of which today's world has such immense need.

Dear priests, our life and ministry will themselves become an eloquent catechesis for the entire community entrusted to us, provided that they are rooted in the Truth which is Christ. Then ours will not be an isolated witness, but a harmonious one, offered by people united in the same faith and sharing in the same cup. It is this sort of vital "infectiousness" that we must together aim at, in effective and affective communion, in order to carry out the ever more urgent "new evangelization."

3.   Gathered on Holy Thursday in all the priestly communities of the Church throughout the world, we give thanks for the gift of Christ's Priesthood which we share through the Sacrament of Holy Orders. In this thanksgiving we wish to include the theme of the *Catechism*, because its contents and its usefulness are *particularly linked with our priestly life and with the Church's pastoral ministry.*

In the journey towards the Great Jubilee of the Year 2000, the Church has succeeded in producing, after the Second Vatican Council, a compendium of her teaching on faith and morality, on sacramental life and prayer. This synthesis can support our priestly ministry in various ways. It can also enlighten the apostolic awareness of our brothers and sisters who, following their Christian vocation, desire together with us to account for that hope[11] which gives us life in Jesus Christ.

The *Catechism* presents the "*newness of the council,*" and at the same time situates it *in the whole of tradition.* The *Catechism* is so filled with the treasures found in Sacred Scripture and in the course of 2000 years that it will enable each of us to become like the man in the gospel parable "who brings out of his treasure what is new and what is old,"[12] the ancient and ever new riches of the divine deposit.

Rekindling the grace of the Sacrament of Orders, conscious of what the *Catechism of the Catholic Church* means for our priestly ministry, we confess with worship and love the One who is "the way, and the truth, and the life."[13]

"Jesus Christ is the same yesterday and today and forever."

From the Vatican, on 8 April, Holy Thursday, in the year 1993, the fifteenth of my Pontificate.

Endnotes

1. Heb 13: 8.
2. Cf. Heb 9: 12.
3. Cf. Jn 2: 4; 13: 1.
4. Cf. Gal 4: 4.
5. Jn 14: 18.
6. Jn 14: 28.
7. Cf. Heb 9: 14.
8. Acts 2: 11.
9. Cf. Jn 17: 21-23.
10. Mt 28: 19-20.
11. Cf. 1 Pt 3: 15.
12. Mt 13: 52.
13. Jn 14: 6.

1994

Sixteenth Year of Pontificate

From the very beginning this year was to have a particular flavor, the Year of the Family. During his homily on Trinity Sunday, June 6 of the previous year, the Holy Father announced 1994 as the International Year of the Family throughout the Church, thus associating the whole Church with the declaration made by the United Nations. "The Church gladly salutes this initiative," the pope said, "and joins in it with all the love she has for every human family. I want to announce . . . a special convocation for the whole Christian people. From the feast of the Holy Family of this year until the same feast in 1994, we shall also celebrate the International Year of the Family throughout the whole Catholic Church" (Homily, June 6, 1993, n. 5).

On the Feast of the Holy Family, December 26, 1993, Alfonso Cardinal López Trujillo, President of the Pontifical Council for the Family and papal legate, was the main celebrant at the Mass in Nazareth to inaugurate the Year of the Family.

In the last General Audience of 1993 the pope based his catechesis on the primacy of prayer for this year's goal. "The Year of the Family must above all be a year of prayer to implore from the Lord grace and blessings for all the families of the world. But the help we are asking from the Lord, as always, implies our commitment and demands our correspondence" (Address, December 29, n. 1).

The role of the family was the focus of the papal message for the twenty-seventh World Day of Peace: "I would like, on the occasion of the International Year of the Family, to devote this World Day of Peace message to a reflection on the close relationship between the family and peace. . . . Founded on love and open to the goal of life, the family contains in itself the very future of society; its most special task is to contribute effectively to a future of peace" (Message for the 1994 World Day of Peace, nn. 1-2).

The pope's wishes for this year were particularly expressed in his Letter to Families, dated February 2 and released February 22. "The celebration of the Year of the Family," the Holy Father says at the beginning of the letter, "gives me a welcome opportunity to knock at the door of your home, eager to greet you with deep affection and to spend time with you" (n. 1). The letter, which consists of an introduction (nn. 1-5) and two parts, called respectively "The Civilization of Love" (nn. 6-17) and "The Bridegroom Is with You" (nn. 18-23) is a rich meditation addressed "not to families in the abstract but to every particular family in every part of the world, wherever it is located and whatever the diversity and complexity of its culture and history" (n. 4). It confirms the role of the Church as mother and teacher: "While certainly showing maternal understanding for the many complex critical situations in which families are involved as well as for the moral frailty of every human being, the Church is convinced that she must remain absolutely faithful to the truth about human love. Otherwise she would betray herself" (n. 11). It is a call to fortitude and a reminder that Christ gives all the necessary means: "Do not be afraid of the risks! God's strength is always far more powerful than your difficulties! Immeasurably greater than the evil at work in the world is the power of the Sacrament of Reconciliation, which the Fathers of the Church rightly called a 'second Baptism.' Much more influential than the corruption present in the world is the divine power of the Sacrament of Confirmation. And incomparably greater than all is the power of the Eucharist" (n. 18).

Closely linked to the Letter to Families was the Holy Thursday Letter for this year, dated March 13, the Fourth Sunday of Lent and released March 22. "Today I wish to entrust to you, dear brothers, the letter which I have addressed to families in the year dedicated to the family" (1994 Letter, n. 2), the pope said. He sees this year as an exceptional opportunity to proclaim the gospel of the family proclaimed by Christ in his hidden life and taught by the Church throughout the centuries and in a very concrete way during this century through documents such as the pastoral constitution *Gaudium et spes* of Vatican II, Paul VI's encyclical *Humanæ vitæ* and John Paul II's Post-Synodal Apostolic Exhortation *Familiaris consortio* which the pope calls the Magna Carta of the apostolate to families. "It may be said," he continues, "that concern for the family, and particularly for married couples, children, young people and adults, requires of us, as priests and confessors, a deep appreciation and a constant promotion of the lay apostolate in this area. The pastoral care of the family—and I know this from personal experience—is in a way the quintessence of priestly activity at every level" (n. 2).

Comparing it to his 1985 Letter to Youth which prompted so many apostolic and pastoral initiatives, the Holy Father states that the Letter to Families "is not so much a doctrinal statement as a preparation for and an exhortation to prayer with families and for families. This is the first task through which you, dear brothers, can begin or carry forward the apostolate to families in your parish communities" (n. 2).

The pope also touches on the relationship between families and vocations: "While we owe our vocation to God, a significant role in it is also to be attributed to our parents" (n. 4), and on the Church as a family: "The Year of the Family is for all of us a call to make the Church ever more 'the household of God, in which his family lives.' . . . The

Church, in fidelity to the will of Christ, is striving to become ever more a 'family,' and the Apostolic See is committed to encouraging this growth. Bishops making their visits *ad limina Apostolorum* are well aware of this" (n. 3).

"On this occasion," the Holy Father points out, "I wish to mention the Directory prepared by the Congregation for the Clergy," released on the very same day as the Holy Thursday Letter, "which will be presented to bishops, priests' councils and all priests. It will certainly make a providential contribution to the renewal of their life and ministry" (n. 3).

The concern for families continued to be very present in the pope's apostolic service during this year, both in many positive comments and in some unavoidable critical comments. Among the positive comments are those he made in the Angelus reflections. "The family is indeed the sanctuary of human life, from its dawn to its natural setting. . . . The family is called to be a temple, that is, a house of prayer: a simple prayer, woven of toil and tenderness. A prayer that becomes life, so that the whole of life may become prayer!" (Angelus reflection, February 6, n. 3). "The family, the great workshop of love, is the first school, indeed, a lasting school where people are not taught to love with barren ideas, but with the incisive power of experience. May every family truly rediscover its own vocation to love!" (Angelus reflection, February 13, n. 2).

Among the positive comments are those he made to particular groups, for instance to the students and professors of the annual UNIV Congress, "marked this year by a particular note because of the recent death of your beloved Prelate, Bishop Alvaro del Portillo. . . . Before calling him to himself, God allowed him to make a pilgrimage to the places where Jesus spent his own earthly life. They were days of intense prayer that united him closely with Christ and prepared him as it were for his definitive meeting with the Holy Trinity." And in this context, he offered encouragement to reflect on the Letter to Families: "As Blessed Josemaría Escrivá clearly emphasized, personal holiness is inseparable from that of the family. Indeed the family is the way of the Church, as I wrote in my recent Letter to Families, on which I ask you to meditate attentively. The family must be at the heart of the new evangelization on the threshold of the third millennium. . . . I ask you to do all you can in your daily life to support the family as the basic cell of society" (Address, March 29, nn. 1-5).

There were the unavoidable critical comments because "unfortunately various programs backed by very powerful resources nowadays seem to aim at the breakdown of the family. At times it appears that concerted efforts are being made to present as normal and attractive, and even to glamorize, situations which are in fact 'irregular.' Indeed they contradict 'the truth and love' which should inspire and guide relationships between men and women, thus causing tensions and divisions in families, with grave consequences particularly for children. The moral conscience becomes darkened; what is true, good and beautiful is deformed; and freedom is replaced by what is actually enslavement. In view of all this, how relevant and thought-provoking are the words of the Apostle Paul about the freedom for which Christ has set us free, and the slavery which is caused by sin (cf. Gal 5: 1)" (Letter to Families, n. 5).

One of the apostolic concerns closest to the Holy Father's heart is the defense of the family, of every family everywhere, against the forces threatening to destroy it. In a March 19 letter sent to heads of state, including President Clinton, and to the secretary general of the United Nations the pope commented on the draft document for the International Conference on Population and Development scheduled for next September in Cairo. "The draft of the final document of the forthcoming Cairo Conference was of particular interest to me," the Holy Father said. "I found it a disturbing surprise. . . . There is reason to fear that it could cause a moral decline resulting in a serious setback for humanity, one in which man himself would be the first victim. . . . The idea of sexuality underlying this text is totally individualistic, to such an extent that marriage now appears as something outmoded. An institution as natural, fundamental and universal as the family cannot be manipulated by anyone. . . . The International Year of the Family should therefore be a special occasion for society and the State to grant the family the protection which the Universal Declaration recognizes it should have. Anything less would be a betrayal of the noblest ideals of the United Nations. Even more serious are the numerous proposals for a general international recognition of a completely unrestricted right to abortion. This goes well beyond what is already unfortunately permitted by the legislation of certain nations." At the end of a General Audience, the pope added: "Before passing to the Final Blessing . . . we should stress once again the importance of the Cairo Meeting during this Year of the Family. . . . We are concerned lest this Year of the Family become a Year against the Family. And it could easily become a Year against the Family if the plans, to which a response has already been given, were really to become the plans of the World Conference in Cairo, which is scheduled for September. We protest!" (At the end of the General Audience, April 6).

The Special Assembly for Africa of the Synod of Bishops opened its proceedings in the Vatican on April 11, in the presence of the Holy Father, and the concluding Mass was celebrated on Sunday, May 8. Presiding in the pope's name was Francis Cardinal Arinze, President of the Pontifical Council for Interreligious Dialogue, since the pope had been hospitalized for the treatment of a bone he had broken in an accident on April 28. The Holy Father spoke at the conclusion of the liturgy by radio link-up from his hospital room and also broadcast his weekly reflection before the *Regina cæli*: "I again express my thanks to all who are spiritually close to me during my physical recovery. I am gradually improving with God's help and with the expert, thoughtful care of my doctors, the sisters and the nursing staff. To each I express my sincerest gratitude" (*Regina cæli* reflection, May 8, n. 3).

LETTER
OF THE HOLY FATHER
POPE JOHN PAUL II
TO ALL THE PRIESTS OF THE CHURCH
ON THE OCCASION OF HOLY THURSDAY 1994

Priesthood and the Pastoral Care of the Family

1. Today we meet one another in the celebration of the Eucharist, in which, as the Second Vatican Council recalls, is contained the whole spiritual treasure of the Church.[1] As we commemorate the institution of the Eucharist in the liturgy of Holy Thursday, we see very clearly what Christ has left us in this wondrous sacrament: "Having loved his own who were in the world, he loved them to the end."[2] In a sense, these words of St. John contain the whole truth about the Eucharist: the truth which is at the same time the heart of the truth about the Church. In a certain sense the Church is daily born from the Eucharist, celebrated in so many places all over the world, in so many different situations, among such diverse cultures, and so the reenactment of the Eucharistic Mystery becomes as it were a daily "creation." Thanks to the celebration of the Eucharist, the evangelical awareness of the People of God grows ever more profound, both in nations of age-old Christian tradition and among peoples who have only recently entered the new dimension imparted to human culture in all times and places by the mystery of the incarnation of the Word and by the mystery of the Redemption accomplished by his death on the cross and his resurrection.

The sacred triduum leads us into this mystery in a way which is unique for the whole liturgical year. The liturgy of the institution of the Eucharist is a singular anticipation of Easter, which continues through Good Friday and the Easter Vigil, up to the Sunday of the Resurrection and its octave.

At the threshold of the celebration of this great mystery of faith, dear brothers in the priesthood, you gather today around your respective bishops in the cathedrals of the diocesan churches, in order to relive the institution of the sacrament of the priesthood and that of the Eucharist. The Bishop of Rome celebrates this liturgy surrounded by the presbyterate of his church, just as my brother bishops do with the priests of their diocesan communities.

This is the reason for today's letter. It is my wish on this occasion to address a special word to you, so that all of us together may live to the full the great gift which Christ has bestowed on us. For us priests the priesthood is the supreme gift, a particular calling to share in the mystery of Christ, a calling which confers on us the sublime possibility of speaking and acting in his name. Every time we offer the Eucharist, this possibility becomes a reality. We act *in persona Christi* when, at the moment of the consecration, we say the words: "This is my body which will be given up for you. . . . This is the cup of my blood, the blood of the new and everlasting covenant. It will be shed for you and for all so that sins may be forgiven. Do this in memory of me." We do precisely this: with deep humility and profound thanks. This exalted yet simple action of our daily mission as priests opens up our humanity, so to speak, to its furthermost limits.

We share in the mystery of the incarnation of the Word, "the first-born of all creation,"[3] who in the Eucharist restores to the Father the whole of creation: the world of the past and the world of the future, and above all the world of today. In this world he lives with us, he is present through us and precisely through us he offers to the Father the sacrifice of our redemption. We share in the mystery of Christ, "the firstborn from the dead,"[4] who by his Passover unceasingly transforms the world, bringing it ever closer to "the revealing of the sons of God."[5] In this way the whole of reality, in all its aspects, becomes present in our Eucharistic ministry, which at the same time embraces every concrete personal need, all suffering, expectation, joy or sadness, in accordance with the intentions which the faithful present for Holy Mass. We receive these intentions in a spirit of charity, thus introducing every human problem into the dimension of universal redemption.

Dear brothers in the priesthood! This ministry forms a new life in us and around us. The Eucharist evangelizes our surroundings and confirms us in the hope that Christ's words will not pass away.[6] His words will remain, for they are rooted in the sacrifice of the cross: We are special witnesses and privileged ministers of the permanence of this truth and of God's love. We can therefore rejoice together when people feel the need for the new catechism or are prompted to read the Encyclical *Veritatis splendor*. All of this strengthens us in the conviction that our ministry of the gospel becomes fruitful through the power of the Eucharist. As Jesus said to his Apostles at the Last Supper: "No longer do I call you servants . . . but I have called you friends. . . . You did not choose me, but I chose you and appointed you that you should go and bear fruit and that your fruit should abide."[7]

What unfathomable riches the Church offers us during the sacred triduum, and especially today, Holy Thursday, in the Chrism Mass! My words are but a partial reflection of the feelings which each of you undoubtedly experiences in his heart. Perhaps this Letter for Holy Thursday will help to ensure that the many different manifestations of Christ's gift implanted in so many hearts will come together before the majesty of the great "mystery of faith" in a meaningful sharing of what the priesthood is and will always be within the Church. May our union around the altar embrace all those who are marked by the indelible sign of this sacrament, including those brothers of ours who in some way or other have distanced themselves from the sacred ministry. I trust that this remembrance will lead each of us to live ever more deeply the excellence of the gift which is the Priesthood of Christ.

2.   Today I wish to entrust to you, dear brothers, the letter which I have addressed to families in the year dedicated to the family. I believe it to be providential that the United Nations organization has set aside 1994 as the International Year of the Family. The Church, fixing her gaze on the mystery of the Holy Family of Nazareth, is taking part in this initiative, seeing it as an exceptional opportunity to proclaim the "gospel of the family." Christ proclaimed this gospel by his hidden life in Nazareth in the bosom of the Holy Family. It was then proclaimed by the apostolic Church, as is clear from the New Testament, and it was later witnessed to by the post-apostolic Church, which has taught us to consider the family as the *ecclesia domestica*.

In our own century the "gospel of the family" has been taught by the Church through the voices of very many priests, pastors, confessors and bishops, and in particular through the voice of the successor of Peter. Almost all my predecessors have devoted a significant part of their "Petrine magisterium" to the family. The Second Vatican Council showed its love for the institution of the family in the Pastoral Constitution *Gaudium et spes*, in which it reaffirmed the need to uphold the dignity of marriage and of the family in today's world.

The 1980 Synod of Bishops inspired the Apostolic Exhortation *Familiaris consortio*, which can be considered the Magna Carta of the apostolate to families. The difficulties of the contemporary world, and particularly of the family, courageously faced by Pope Paul VI in his Encyclical *Humanæ vitæ*, demanded an overall examination of the human family and the *ecclesia domestica* in today's society. The apostolic exhortation sought to do precisely this. It was necessary to develop new methods of pastoral activity in order to meet the needs of the contemporary family. In a word, it may be said that concern for the family, and particularly for married couples, children, young people and adults, requires of us, as priests and confessors, a deep appreciation and a constant promotion of the lay apostolate in this area. The pastoral care of the family—and I know this from personal experience—is in a way the quintessence of priestly activity at every level. All of this is discussed in *Familiaris consortio*. The Letter to Families simply takes up and gives renewed expression to this heritage of the post-conciliar Church.

It is my wish that this letter may prove helpful to families both inside and outside the Church, and that it may assist you, dear priests, in your pastoral ministry to families. It is rather like my 1985 Letter to Youth, which prompted numerous apostolic and pastoral initiatives on behalf of young people in every part of the world. An expression of this movement is the World Youth Day celebrated in parishes and dioceses and at the level of the whole Church—like the one recently held in Denver, in the United States of America.

This Letter to Families is broader in scope. The problems of the family are in fact more complex and wide ranging. In preparing the letter, I was confirmed in my conviction that the magisterium of the Second Vatican Council, and the Pastoral Constitution *Gaudium et spes* in particular, represents a truly rich source of Christian thinking and life. I hope that the letter, inspired by the council's teaching, will be no less helpful to you than to all the families of goodwill to whom it is addressed.

For a correct approach to this letter, it will be useful to turn to that passage in the Acts of the Apostles where we read that the first communities devoted themselves "to the Apostles' teaching and fellowship, to the breaking of bread and the prayers."[8] The Letter to Families is not so much a doctrinal statement as a preparation for and an exhortation to prayer with families and for families. This is the first task through which you, dear brothers, can begin or carry forward the apostolate to families in your parish communities. If you find that you are asked, "How are we to attain the objectives of the Year of the Family?" the exhortation to prayer contained in the letter will show you the simplest direction in which to proceed. Jesus said to the Apostles: "Apart from me you can do nothing."[9] It is clear that we must "do as he does," that is, pray on bended knee. "For where two or three are gathered in my name, there I am in the midst of them."[10] These words of Christ should be translated into concrete initiatives in every community. A good pastoral program can be drawn from them, indeed a fruitful one, even when very few resources are available.

There are so many families in the world which pray! Children pray; they are the ones to whom the kingdom of heaven belongs before anyone else.[11] Thanks to them not only do mothers pray, but fathers too, and sometimes return to religious practice after having fallen away. Is this not often the case at the time of first holy communion? And do we not notice how there is a rise in the "spiritual temperature" of young people, and not merely young people, during pilgrimages to holy places? The age-old routes of pilgrimage in the East and West, whether those to Jerusalem, Rome and Santiago de Compostela, or those to the Marian shrines of Lourdes, Fatima, Jasna Gora and many others, have in the course of the centuries become a way for great numbers of believers and certainly many families to discover the Church. The Year of the Family should confirm, broaden and enrich this experience. Pastors, as well as all agencies responsible for the family apostolate, should be attentive to this, in cooperation with the Pontifical Council for the Family, which is entrusted with this apostolate at the level of the universal Church. As you know, the president of that council inaugurated the Year of the Family at Nazareth on the solemnity of the Holy Family, December 26, 1993.

3.   "They devoted themselves to the Apostles' teaching and fellowship, to the breaking of bread and the prayers."[12] According to the Constitution *Lumen gentium*, the Church is "the household of God,[13] in which his family lives, the dwelling place of God in the Spirit,[14] 'God's dwelling with men'(n. 6)."[15] The image of "God's household," among the many other biblical images, is used by the council to describe the Church. This image, moreover, is in some way contained in all the others. It figures in the Pauline analogy of the body of Christ,[16] to which Pope Pius XII referred in his historic Encyclical *Mystici Corporis*. It is also found in the notion of the People of God, to which the council made reference. The Year of the Family is for all of us a call to make the Church ever more "the household of God, in which his family lives."This is a call, an invitation, which could prove extraordinarily fruitful for the evangelization of the modern world. As I wrote in the Letter to Families, the fundamental dimen-

sion of human existence constituted by the family is under serious threat from various quarters in contemporary society.[17] And yet this aspect of life, which is "being a family," represents a great good for every individual. The Church wishes to be at its service. The Year of the Family thus represents an important opportunity for renewing the Church's "being a family" in all areas of her life.

Dear brothers in the priesthood! Each of you will surely find in prayer the light necessary for knowing how to make all this come to pass: you yourselves in your parishes and in your different fields of evangelical work; the bishops in their dioceses; and the Apostolic See through the Roman Curia, in accordance with the Apostolic Constitution *Pastor bonus*. The Church, in fidelity to the will of Christ, is striving to become ever more a "family," and the Apostolic See is committed to encouraging this growth. Bishops making their visits *ad limina Apostolorum* are well aware of this. Their visits, both to the Pope and to the different curial offices, while fulfilling what canon law prescribes, are less and less juridical-administrative in tone than was the case in the past. More and more there is the atmosphere of an "exchange of gifts," in accordance with the teaching of the Constitution *Lumen gentium*.[18] My brother bishops often mention this at our meetings.

On this occasion I wish to mention the Directory prepared by the Congregation for the Clergy which will be presented to bishops, priests' councils and all priests. It will certainly make a providential contribution to the renewal of their life and ministry.

4.   The call to pray with families and for families, dear brothers, concerns each one of you in a very personal way. We owe our lives to our parents, and we owe them a permanent debt of gratitude. Whether they are still alive or have already passed into eternity, we are united with them by a close bond which time does not destroy. While we owe our vocation to God, a significant role in it is also to be attributed to our parents. The decision of a son to dedicate himself to the priestly ministry, particularly in mission lands, is no small sacrifice for his parents. This was true also in the case of our own dear ones, yet they offered their feelings to God, letting themselves be guided by a deep faith. They then followed us with their prayer, just as Mary did with Jesus when he left the home at Nazareth in order to carry out his messianic mission.

What an experience it was for each of us, and at the same time for our parents, our brothers and sisters and those dear to us, when we celebrated our first holy Mass! What a great thing that celebration was for our parishes and the places where we grew up! Every new vocation makes the parish aware of the fruitfulness of its spiritual motherhood: The more often it happens, the greater the encouragement that results for others! Every priest can say of himself: "I am indebted to God and to others." There are many people who have accompanied us with their thoughts and prayers, just as there are many who by their thoughts and prayers accompany my own ministry in the See of Peter. This great prayerful solidarity is a source of strength for me. People really do place their trust in our vocation to serve God. The Church prays constantly for new priestly vocations and rejoices at their increase; she is saddened at the lack of vocations in certain places, regretting the lack of generosity of many people.

On this day every year we renew the promises we made in connection with the sacrament of the priesthood. These promises have great implications. What is at stake is the word we have given to Christ himself. Fidelity to our vocation builds up the Church, and every act of infidelity is a painful wound to the Mystical Body of Christ. And so, as we gather together and contemplate the mystery of the institution of the Eucharist and the priesthood, let us implore our High Priest who, as Sacred Scripture says, showed himself to be faithful,[19] that we too may remain faithful. In the spirit of this "sacramental brotherhood" let us pray for one another—priests for priests! May Holy Thursday become for us a renewed call to cooperate with the grace of the sacrament of the priesthood! Let us pray for our spiritual families, for those entrusted to our ministry. Let us pray particularly for those who in a special way expect our prayers and are in need of them. May our fidelity to prayer ensure that Christ will become ever more the life of our souls.

O great sacrament of faith, O holy Priesthood of the Redeemer of the world! Lord Jesus Christ, how grateful we are to you for having brought us into communion with you, for having made us one community around you, for allowing us to celebrate your unbloody sacrifice and to be ministers of the sacred mysteries in every place: at the altar, in the confessional, the pulpit, the sickroom, prisons, the classroom, the lecture hall, the offices where we work. All praise to the most holy Eucharist! I greet you, the Church of God, his priestly people,[20] redeemed by his precious blood!

From the Vatican, March 13, the fourth Sunday of Lent, in the year 1994, the sixteenth of my pontificate.

Endnotes

1. Cf. *Presbyterorum ordinis*, 5.
2. Jn 13: 1.
3. Col 1: 15.
4. Col 1: 18.
5. Rom 8: 19.
6. Cf. Lk 21: 33.
7. Jn 15: 15-16.
8. Acts 2: 42.
9. Jn 15: 5.
10. Mt 18: 20.
11. Cf. Mt 18: 2-5.
12. Acts 2: 42.
13. Cf. 1 Tm 3: 15.
14. Cf. Eph 2: 19-22.
15. Rv 21: 3, *Lumen gentium*, 6.
16. Cf. 1 Cor 12: 13, 27; Rom 12: 5.
17. Cf. *Lumen gentium*, 13.
18. Cf. *Ibid.*, 13.
19. Cf. Heb 2: 17.
20. Cf. 1 Pt 2: 9.

1995

Seventeenth Year of Pontificate

The year 1995 saw the Holy Father undertaking an extraordinary number of pastoral visits. Beginning with the tenth World Youth Day celebrations in Manila (January 12-16), he journeyed to Port Moresby, Papua New Guinea (January 16-18); to Sydney, Australia (January 18-20); and to Colombo, Sri Lanka (January 20-21).

In his address to youth gathered in Manila at the concluding Mass for the World Youth Day celebrations on January 15, using the theme of the tenth World Youth Day, *"As the Father sent me, so I am sending you,"* Pope John Paul II urged the gathered youth to base their lives on the truth of Christ's gospel. With the story of the young Jesus in the Temple as the basis for his homily, the pope reminded the gathered youth that it is the vocation of every Christian to share in Christ's mission of bringing the truth to every nation.

The pope's other pastoral visits during this year included Molise, Italy (March 19); Trent, Italy (April 29-30); the Czech Republic and Poland (May 20-22); Belgium (June 3-4); the Slovak Republic (June 30-July 3); Loreto, Italy (September 9-10); the African countries of Cameroon, South Africa, and Kenya (September 14-20); and the United States (October 4-8).

Important papal documents published this year included *Ut unum sint*, the encyclical letter on the Church's commitment to ecumenism; *Orientale lumen*, an apostolic letter marking the hundredth anniversary of Pope Leo XIII's letter *Orientalis dignitas*; and the Post-Synodal Apostolic Exhortation *Ecclesia in Africa* on the evangelizing mission of the Church in Africa towards the Year 2000. Most importantly, 1995 also saw the publication of one of the most important of the Holy Father's encyclicals, *Evangelium vitæ*, the pope's letter on the value and inviolability of human life.

Constant in his defense of human life and his condemnation of the approval which modern society increasingly affords abortion, contraception, and euthanasia, the pope in *Evangelium vitæ* forcefully presented the Church's teaching on the sacred character of human life and called on all Christians to defend it from conception to natural death.

Reaffirming the immeasurable worth of the human person, the Holy Father wrote that "Even in the midst of difficulties and uncertainties, every person sincerely open to truth and goodness can, by the light of reason and the hidden action of grace, come to recognize in the natural law written in the human heart (cf. Rom 2: 14-15) the sacred value of human life from its very beginning until its end, and can affirm the right of every human being to have this primary good respected to the highest degree" (n. 2). Recent scientific and technological advances, far from diminishing the threat to human life, seem rather to be expanding and new attacks on the dignity of human life flourish in a cultural climate in which public opinion justifies them in the name of individual freedom (n. 3). Moreover, far from simply justifying these attacks and seeking to exempt themselves from punishment, broad sectors in modern society seek authorization and assistance from the State so that these things can be done with total freedom. All of this, writes the Holy Father, is both a cause and a symptom of the grave moral decline from which modern society is suffering.

Against these trends the pope contrasts God's law, the Church's Faith in the incarnation of the Word of God, and her belief that this event reveals the profound dignity to which God has raised the human race by uniting himself to our nature (n. 2). Although the phrase "Gospel of Life" is not found in Sacred Scripture, the Holy Father carefully illuminates the progressive development of God's revelation of the dignity and inviolability of human life, beginning with the story of Cain's murder of his brother Abel and the slaughter of the Hebrew children in the Book of Genesis through the Christian message concerning life in the New Testament. Along the way, he presents the Church's response to the modern world's numerous errors regarding a distorted perception of human freedom (nn. 18-20), modern man's loss of the sense of God and his consequent alienation from himself and others, including the distortion of the meaning of human sexuality (nn. 21-24), the covenant and the commitment to which God has invited all men in Jesus Christ, who brings the meaning of human life to fulfillment (nn. 25-33), and the positive indications that the "culture of death" can be reversed.

Addressing the moral consequences of specific actions which contravene God's law and deny the sanctity of human life, the pope concludes his apostolic letter with an exposition of the challenges facing Christians seeking to build a "new culture of human life" (Ch. IV).

LETTER
OF THE HOLY FATHER
POPE JOHN PAUL II
TO ALL THE PRIESTS OF THE CHURCH
ON THE OCCASION OF HOLY THURSDAY 1995

The Importance of Women in the Life of the Priest

1. *"Honor to Mary, honor and glory, honor to the Blessed Virgin! . . . He who created the marvelous world honored in her his own Mother . . . He loved her as his Mother, he lived in obedience. Though he was God, he respected her every word."*

Dear Brother Priests!

Do not be surprised if I begin this letter, which I traditionally address to you on Holy Thursday, with the words of a Polish Marian hymn. I do so because this year I wish to speak to you *about the importance of women in the life of a priest,* and these verses which I have sung since my childhood can serve as a meaningful introduction to this subject.

The hymn speaks of Christ's love for his Mother. The first and most basic relationship which any human being establishes with a woman is precisely the relationship of the child to its mother. Each of us can express his love for his earthly mother just as the Son of God did and does for his. Our mother *is the woman to whom we owe our life.* She conceived us in her womb and brought us into the world amid the pains which are a part of the experience of every woman who gives birth. Through childbirth a special and almost *sacred* bond is established between a human being and his mother.

Having brought us into the world, our parents enabled us to become in Christ, through the *Sacrament of Baptism,* adopted children of God. All this further deepened the bond between us and our parents, and in particular between us and our mothers. *The prototype here is Christ himself, Christ the Priest,* who addresses the Eternal Father in these words: "Sacrifices and offerings you have not desired, but a body you have prepared for me. In burnt offerings and sin offerings you have taken no pleasure. Then I said, 'Lo, I have come to do your will, O God.'"[1] *These words in some way also involve his Mother,* since the Eternal Father formed Christ's body by the power of the Holy Spirit in the womb of the Virgin Mary, thanks also to her consent:"Let it be to me according to your word."[2]

How many of us also owe to our mothers our very vocation to the priesthood! Experience shows that very often it is the mother who for years nurtures in her own heart a desire for a priestly vocation for her son, and *obtains it by praying with persevering trust and deep humility.* Thus, without imposing her own will, she favors with the effectiveness typical of faith the blossoming of an aspiration to the priesthood in the soul of her son, an aspiration which will bear fruit in due season.

2. In this letter, I wish to reflect on the relationship between priests and women, taking as my point of departure the fact that *the subject of women calls for special attention this year,* just as last year the subject of the family did. In fact the important *International Conference called by the United Nations Organization Beijing* next September will be devoted to women. This is a new subject with respect to last year's, but closely related to it.

Dear brothers in the priesthood, with this letter I also wish to make reference to another document. Just as in the Holy Thursday message of last year I referred to my Letter to Families, so this time *I would like to redirect your attention* to the Apostolic Letter *Mulieris dignitatem,* issued on 15 August 1988. As you will recall, this text was prepared at the end of the Marian Year of 1987-1988, during which I published the Encyclical *Redemptoris Mater* (25 March 1987). It is my fervent hope that during this year you will reread *Mulieris dignitatem*, making it the subject of special meditation and giving particular consideration to its Marian aspects.

A link with the Mother of God is fundamental for Christian "thinking." This is true first of all on the theological level, because of the very special relationship of Mary with the Incarnate Word and the Church, his Mystical Body. But it is also true on the historical, anthropological and cultural levels. In Christianity, in fact, the figure of the Mother of God represents a great source of inspiration not only for the life of piety but also for Christian culture and even for love of country. Proofs of this exist in the history of many nations. In Poland for example the most ancient literary monument is the hymn *Bogurodzica* (Mother of God), which inspired our forefathers not only in shaping the life of the nation but even in defending the just cause on the battlefield. The Mother of God has become the "great inspiration" for individuals and for whole Christian nations. This too, in its own way, *tells us much about the importance of women in human life,* and, in a special way, *in the life of a priest.*

I have already had occasion to deal with this subject in the Encyclical *Redemptoris Mater* and in the Apostolic Letter *Mulieris dignitatem,* where I paid homage to those women—mothers, wives, daughters or sisters—who for their respective sons, husbands, parents and brothers were an effective inspiration for good. Not without reason do we speak of the "feminine genius," and what I have written thus far confirms the validity of this expression. However, in dealing with priestly life, the presence of women has a particular character and calls for a specific analysis.

3. But meanwhile let us return to Holy Thursday, the day when the words of the liturgical hymn take on special meaning:

Ave verum Corpus natum de Maria Virgine:
Vere passum, immolatum in cruce pro homine.

Cuius latus perforatum fluxit aqua et sanguine:
Esto nobis prægustatum mortis in examine.

Iesu dulcis! O Iesu pie! O Iesu, fili Mariæ!

These words, although they do not belong to the liturgy of Holy Thursday, are closely connected with it.

The Last Supper, at which Christ instituted the sacraments of the sacrifice and the priesthood of the New Covenant, is the beginning of the *Triduum Paschale. At its center is the body of Christ.* It is precisely this body which, before being subjected to suffering and death, is offered at the Last Supper as food in the institution of the Eucharist. Christ takes bread in his hands, breaks it and gives it to his Apostles with the words: "Take; eat: this is my body."[3] In this way he institutes the sacrament of his *body, that body which, as the Son of God, he had taken from his Mother, the Immaculate Virgin.* Then, taking the cup, he offers to the Apostles his own blood under the species of wine, saying: "Drink of it, all of you; for this is my blood of the covenant, which is poured out for many for the forgiveness of sins."[4] *Here too it is the blood which gave life to the body received from the Virgin Mother:* blood which had to be shed, in fulfillment of the mystery of the Redemption, in order that the body received from his Mother could—as *Corpus immolatum in cruce pro homine*—become for us and for all mankind the sacrament of eternal life, the viaticum for eternity. Thus in the *Ave verum,* which is at once a Eucharistic hymn and a Marian hymn, we ask: *Esto nobis prægustatum mortis in examine.*

Even though the Holy Thursday liturgy does not speak of Mary—
rather we find her on Good Friday at the foot of the cross with the
Apostle John—*it is difficult not to sense her presence at the institution of
the Eucharist,* the anticipation of the Passion and death of the body of
Christ, that body which the Son of God had received from the Virgin
Mother at the moment of the Annunciation.

For us, as priests, the Last Supper is an especially holy moment. Christ,
who says to the Apostles: "Do this in remembrance of me,"[5] institutes
the Sacrament of Holy Orders, With respect to our lives as priests,
this is *an eminently Christocentric moment:* for we receive the priesthood from Christ the Priest, the one Priest of the New Covenant. But
as we think of the Sacrifice of the Body and Blood, which we offer *in
persona Christi, we find it difficult not to recognize therein the presence
of the Mother.* Mary gave life to the Son of God so that he might offer himself, even as our mothers gave us life, that we too, through
the priestly ministry, might offer ourselves in sacrifice together with
him. Behind this mission there is the vocation received from God,
but there is also hidden the great love of our mothers, just as behind
the sacrifice of Christ in the Upper Room there was hidden the ineffable love of his Mother. *O how truly and yet discreetly is motherhood
and thus womanhood present in the Sacrament of Holy Orders* which we
celebrate anew each year on Holy Thursday!

4.   Christ Jesus is the *only son of Mary Most Holy.* We clearly understand the meaning of this mystery; it was fitting that he should
be such: a son so unique by reason of his divinity had to be the *only*
son of his Virgin Mother. But precisely *this uniqueness serves in some
way as the best "guarantee" of a spiritual "multiplicity."* Christ, true man
and yet eternal and only-begotten Son of the Heavenly Father, *has,
on the spiritual plane, a countless number of brothers and sisters.* For the
family of God includes everyone: not just those who through Baptism
become God's adopted children, but in a certain sense all mankind,
since Christ has redeemed all men and all women and offered them
the possibility of becoming adopted sons and daughters of the Eternal Father. Thus we have all become brothers and sisters in Christ.

At this point in our reflection on the relationship between priests
and women, beside the figure of the mother there emerges the figure of the *sister.* Thanks to the Redemption, the priest shares in a
special way in the *relationship of brotherhood* offered by Christ to all
the redeemed.

Many of us priests have sisters in our families. In any event, every priest from childhood onwards has met girls, if not in his own family at least in the neighborhood, in childhood games or at school. A type of mixed community has *enormous importance for the formation of the personalities of boys and girls.*

Here we encounter the original plan of the Creator, who in the beginning created man"male and female."[6] This divine creative act continues from generation to generation. The Book of Genesis speaks of it in the context of the vocation to marriage:"Therefore a man leaves his father and his mother and cleaves to his wife."[7] The vocation to marriage obviously assumes and requires that the environment in which one lives is made up of both men and women.

In this setting, however, there arise not only vocations to marriage but also *vocations to the priesthood and the consecrated life.* These do not develop in isolation. Every candidate for the priesthood, when he crosses the threshold of the seminary, has behind him the experience of his own family and of school, where he was able to meet many young people of his own age, of both sexes. In order to live as a celibate in a mature and untroubled way it seems particularly important that the priest should develop deep within himself *the image of women as sisters.* In Christ, men and women are brothers and sisters, independent of any bonds of family relationship. This is a universal bond, thanks to which the priest can be open to every new situation, even the most foreign from an ethnic or cultural standpoint, knowing that he must exercise towards the men and women to whom he is sent a ministry of authentic *spiritual fatherhood,* which gains him "sons" and "daughters" in the Lord.[8]

5.   Certainly"woman as sister" represents a *specific manifestation of the spiritual beauty of women;* but it is at the same time a revelation that they are in a certain sense"set apart."If the priest, with the help of divine grace and under the special protection of Mary, Virgin and Mother, gradually develops such an attitude towards women, he will see his ministry met by a *sense of great trust* precisely on the part of women whom he regards, in the variety of their ages and life situations, as sisters and mothers.

The figure of woman as sister has considerable importance in our Christian civilization, in which countless women have become *sisters to everyone,* thanks to their exemplary attitude towards their neighbor, especially to those most in need. A *"sister" is a guarantee of selflessness:* in the school, in the hospital, in prison and in other areas of social service. When a woman remains single, in her "gift of self as sister" by means of apostolic commitment or generous dedication to neighbor, she develops a particular *spiritual motherhood.* This self-less gift of femininity "as sister" lights up human existence, evokes the best sentiments of which human beings are capable and always leaves behind gratitude for the good freely offered.

Thus the dimensions of mother and sister *are the two fundamental dimensions* of the relationship between women and priests. If this relationship develops in a serene and mature way, women will find no particular difficulties in their contact with priests. For example they will not find difficulties in confessing their faults in the Sacrament of Penance. Even less will they encounter any in undertaking various kinds of *apostolic activities* with priests. Every priest thus has the great *responsibility of developing an authentic way of relating* to women *as a brother,* a way of relating which does not admit of ambiguity. In this perspective, St. Paul exhorts his disciple Timothy to treat "older women like mothers, younger women like sisters, in all purity."[9]

When Christ stated—as the Evangelist Matthew—that man can *remain celibate for the kingdom of God,* the Apostles were disturbed.[10] A little earlier Jesus had declared that marriage is indissoluble, and this truth had caused in them a significant reaction: "If such is the case of a man with his wife, it is expedient not to marry."[11] As is evident, their reaction went contrary to the notion of fidelity which Jesus had in mind. But the Master makes use even of this lack of understanding, in order to introduce into their narrow and limited way of thinking the perspective of celibacy for the sake of the kingdom of heaven. He thereby wishes to affirm that marriage has a specific dignity and sacramental holiness, and that nevertheless there exists another path for the Christian: a path which is not a flight from marriage but rather a *conscious choice of celibacy* for the sake of the kingdom of heaven.

In view of this, women can only be sisters for the priest, and their dignity as sister needs to be consciously fostered by him. The Apostle Paul, who lived a celibate life, writes in the First Letter to the Corinthians: "I wish that all were as I myself am. *But each one has his own special gift from God,* one of one kind and one of another."[12] For him there is no doubt: marriage and celibacy are both gifts of God, to be protected and fostered with great care.

While emphasizing the superiority of virginity, he does not in any way diminish the value of marriage. Each has its own specific *charism;*

each of them is a *vocation* which individuals, with the help of God's grace, must learn to discern in their own lives.

The vocation of celibacy needs to be consciously protected by keeping special watch over one's feelings and over one's whole conduct. In particular, it must be protected by those priests who, following the discipline in force in the Western Church and so highly esteemed by the Eastern Church, have chosen celibacy for the sake of the kingdom of God. If in a relationship with a woman the gift of celibacy should become endangered, the priest cannot but strive to earnestly remain faithful to his own vocation. Such a defense would not mean that marriage in itself is something bad, but that for him the path is a different one. For him to abandon that path would be to break the word he has given to God.

The Lord's prayer:"And lead us not into temptation, but deliver us from evil,"takes on a specific meaning in the context *of contemporary civilization,* steeped as it is in the elements of hedonism, self-centeredness and sensuality. Pornography is unfortunately rampant, debasing the dignity of women and treating them exclusively as objects of sexual pleasure. *These aspects of present-day civilization certainly do not favor either marital fidelity or celibacy for the sake of the kingdom of God.* Therefore if the priest does not foster in himself genuine dispositions of faith, hope and love of God, he can easily yield to the allurements coming to him from the world. On this Holy Thursday then, dear brother priests, how can I fail to address you in order to *exhort you to remain faithful to the gift of celibacy* which Christ has given us? In it is contained a spiritual treasure which belongs to each of us and to the whole Church.

Today our thoughts and prayers turn in a special way to *our brothers in the priesthood who meet with difficulties in this area,* and to all those who precisely because of a woman *have abandoned the priestly ministry.* Let us commend to Mary Most Holy, Mother of Priests, and to the intercession of the countless holy priests in the Church's history in the difficult time which they are experiencing, and let us implore them for them *the grace of a return to their first fervor.*[13] The experience of my own ministry, and I believe that this is true of every bishop, confirms that such returns do occur and that even today they are not rare. God remains faithful to his covenant with man in the Sacrament of Holy Orders.

6. At this point I would like to touch on the even wider issue of the role which women are called to play *in the building up of the Church.* The Second Vatican Council fully grasped the logic of the gospel, in chapters two and three of the Constitution *Lumen gentium,* when it presented the Church first as the People of God and only afterwards as a hierarchical structure. The Church is first and foremost the People of God, since all her members, men and women alike, *share*—each in his or her own specific way—*in the prophetic, priestly and royal mission of Christ.* While I invite you to reread those texts of the council, I will limit myself here to some brief reflections drawn from the gospel.

Just before his ascension into heaven, Christ commands the Apostles: "Go into all the world and preach the gospel to the whole creation."[14] To preach the gospel is to carry out the prophetic mission which has different forms in the Church, according to the charism granted to each individual.[15] In that circumstance, since it was a question of the Apostles and their own particular mission, this task was entrusted to certain men; but if we read the gospel accounts carefully, especially that of John, we cannot but be struck by the fact that *the prophetic mission,* considered in all its breadth and diversification, *is given to both men and women.* Suffice if to mention, for example, *the Samaritan woman* and her dialogue with Christ at Jacob's well in Sychar: [16] it is to her, a Samaritan woman and a sinner, that Jesus reveals the depths of the true worship of God, who is concerned not about the place but rather about the attitude of worship "in spirit and truth."

And what shall we say *of the sisters of Lazarus, Mary and Martha?* The Synoptics, speaking of the "contemplative" Mary, note the pre-eminence which Christ gives to contemplation over activity.[17] Still more important is what St. John writes in the context of the raising of their brother Lazarus. In this case it is to Martha, the more "active" of the two, that Jesus reveals the profound mysteries of his mission: "I am the resurrection and the life; he who believes in me, though he dies, yet shall he live, and whoever lives and believes in me shall never die."[18] The Paschal Mystery is summed up in these words addressed to a woman.

But let us proceed in the gospel account and enter into the Passion narrative. Is it not an incontestable fact that women were the ones closest to Christ along the way of the cross and at the hour of his death? A man, Simon of Cyrene, is forced to carry the cross;[19] but many women of Jerusalem spontaneously show him *compassion along* the *"via crucis."*[20] The figure of Veronica, albeit not biblical, expresses well the feelings of the of Jerusalem along the *via dolorosa.*

Beneath the cross there is only one Apostle, John, the son of Zebedee, whereas *there are several women:* [21] the Mother of Christ who, according to tradition, had followed him on his journey to Calvary; Salome, the mother of the sons of Zebedee, John and James; Mary, the mother of James the Less and Joseph; and Mary Magdalen. All these women were fearless witnesses of Jesus' agony; all were present at the anointing and the *laying of his body in the tomb.* After his burial, as the day before the Sabbath draws to a close, they depart, but with the intention of returning as soon as it is allowed. And it is they who will be the first to go to the tomb, early in the morning on the day after the feast. They will be *the first witnesses of the empty tomb,* and again they will be the ones to tell the Apostles and Christ's disciples.

Thus women too, together with men, have a part in the prophetic mission of Christ. The same can be said of their sharing in his priestly and royal mission. *The universal priesthood of the faithful and the royal dignity* belong to both men and women. Most enlightening in this regard is a careful reading of the passages of the First Letter of St. Peter[22] and of the Conciliar Constitution *Lumen gentium.*[23]

7.   In that dogmatic constitution, the chapter on the People of God is followed by the one on the hierarchical structure of the Church. Here reference is made to the *ministerial priesthood,* to which by the will of Christ only men are admitted. Today in some quarters the fact that women cannot be ordained priests is being interpreted as a form of discrimination. But is this really the case?

Certainly the question could be put in these terms if the hierarchical priesthood granted a social position of privilege characterized by the exercise of "power." But this is not the case: the ministerial priesthood, in Christ's plan, is an expression not of *domination* but of *service!* Anyone who interpreted it as "domination" would certainly be far from the intention of Christ, who in the Upper Room began the Last Supper by washing the feet of the Apostles. In this way he strongly emphasized the "ministerial" character of the priesthood which he instituted that very evening. "For the Son of Man came not to be served but to serve, and to give his life as a ransom for many."[24]

Yes, dear brothers, the priesthood which today we recall with such veneration as our special inheritance *is a ministerial priesthood! We are at the service of the People of God! We are at the service of its mission! This priesthood of ours must guarantee the participation of everyone*—men and women alike—in the threefold prophetic, priestly and royal mission of Christ. And not only is the Sacrament of Holy Orders ministerial: *above all else the Eucharist itself is ministerial.* When Christ affirms that:"This is my body which is given for you. . . . This cup which is poured out for you is the new covenant in my blood,"[25] he reveals his greatest service: *the service of the Redemption,* in which the only-begotten and eternal Son of God becomes the *Servant of man* in the fullest and most profound sense.

8.   Beside *Christ the Servant,* we cannot forget the one who is"the Handmaid,"Mary. St. Luke tells us that, at the decisive moment of the Annunciation, the Virgin expressed her"fiat"in these words:"Behold, I am the handmaid of the Lord."[26] The relationship of priests to women as mothers and sisters is enriched thanks to the *Marian tradition,* by another aspect: that of service in imitation of Mary *the Handmaid.* If the priesthood is by its nature ministerial, we must live it in union *with the Mother who is the Handmaid of the Lord.* Then our priesthood will be kept safe in her hands—indeed, in her heart—and we shall be able to open it to everyone. In this way our priesthood, in all its dimensions, will be fruitful and salvific.

May the Blessed Virgin look with special affection upon us all, her well-beloved sons, on this annual celebration of our priesthood. May she especially inspire in our hearts a burning desire for holiness. As I wrote in the Apostolic Exhortation *Pastores dabo vobis:* "The new evangelization needs new evangelizers, and these are the priests who are serious about living their priesthood as a specific path towards holiness."[27] Holy Thursday, by taking us back to the origins of our priesthood, reminds us also of the duty to strive for holiness, to be "ministers of holiness"to the men and women entrusted to our pastoral service. In this light we see how very fitting is the suggestion put forward by the Congregation for the Clergy that every diocese should celebrate a"Day for the Sanctification of Priests"on the Feast of the Sacred Heart or on another date better suited to local needs and pastoral usage. I make this suggestion my own, and I express my hope that this day will help priests to live in ever greater conformity to the heart of the Good Shepherd.

Upon you all I invoke the protection of Mary, the Mother of the Church, Mother of Priests, and with great affection I give you my blessing.

From the Vatican, 25 March 1995, the Solemnity of the Annunciation of the Lord.

Endnotes

1. Heb 10: 5-7.
2. Lk 1: 38.
3. Mt 26: 26.
4. Mt 26: 27-28.
5. 1 Cor 11: 24.
6. Cf. Gen 1: 27.
7. Gen 2: 24.
8. Cf. 1 Thes 2: 11; Gal 4: 19.
9. 1 Tm 5: 2.
10. Cf. Mt 19: 10-12.
11. Mt 19: 10.
12. 1 Cor 7: 7.
13. Cf. Rv 2: 4-5.
14. Mk 16: 15.
15. Cf. Eph 4: 11-13.
16. Cf. Jn 4: 1-42.
17. Cf. Lk 10: 42.
18. Jn 11: 25-26.
19. Cf. Mt 27: 32.
20. Cf. Lk 23: 27.
21. Cf. Mt 27: 55-56.
22. 1 Pt 2: 9-10.
23. *Lumen gentium*, 10-12; 34-36.
24. Mk 10: 45.
25. Lk 22: 19, 20.
26. Lk 1: 38.
27. *Pastores dabo vobis*, 82.

1996

Eighteenth Year of Pontificate

The Vatican officially made its debut on the internet on Christmas Day 1995, releasing the text of the pope's annual Christmas address to the world, with plans to add other papal speeches, documents from the Vatican library, and images of the art treasures in the Vatican museums to its web site as the year progressed.

The Holy Father celebrated the twenty-ninth annual World Day of Peace in St. Peter's Basilica. Praying for an end to violence in war-torn countries such as Bosnia and calling for the world's children to be protected from violence, the pope said, "The children of the earth, in this last part of the century, are the seeds of the third millennium. Let's not extinguish the hope in their hearts; let's not smother their expectations for peace."

Ecumenism continued to be of special concern to Pope John Paul II, who repeatedly called on believers to move towards full communion with one another as the Year 2000 approaches. During the Week of Prayer for Christian Unity, the pope reminded the faithful that "Barriers of division between Christians are a scandal that openly contradict the will of Christ."

In his Holy Thursday Letter for 1996, the Holy Father offered priests a meditation on the unique vocation of Christ the Priest, reminding them of the connection between Christ's Priesthood and the Sacrifice of the Cross, the relationship of the ministerial priesthood to the common priesthood of all the faithful, and challenging all priests to be faithful to their vocation of accompanying and guiding the faithful on their journey towards the fullness of life in God.

As part of his celebration of the anniversary of his ordination, the Holy Father published *Gift and Mystery*, a series of reflections on the meaning of the priesthood and his own vocation. Like previous papal books, such as *Crossing the Threshold of Hope*, the book was met with great interest and quickly became a bestseller.

The pope's 1996 travels included visits to Guatemala, Nicaragua, El Salvador, and Venezuela (February 5-12); Siena, Italy (March 30); Tunis, Tunisia (April 14); Como, Italy (May 4-5); Slovenia (May 17-19); Germany (June 21-23); Hungary (September 6-7); and France (September 19-22).

The visit to France presented a unique challenge for the pope. Prior to his arrival, opposition to the papal visit was stirred by a number of groups within France, who viewed the papal pilgrimage to some of the most important Christian shrines of their country as a contradiction of the pluralism that is characteristic of contemporary French society. Despite well-organized public protests, and even the threat of a bomb at the tomb of St. Louis de Montfort, where the Holy Father was scheduled to meet with representatives of various religious communities, the papal pilgrimage was a success. John Paul II won over even the most vocal opponents with his good humor, his patience, and his charity, as well as by surprising his critics in stressing the values of "liberty, equality, and fraternity," important to the French as the principal values of the French Revolution.

The most important papal documents of the year were *Universi Dominici gregis*, an apostolic constitution on the Vacancy of the Holy See and the Election of the Roman Pontiff, and *Vita consecrata*, the apostolic exhortation on the Consecrated Life and its mission.

The publication of *Universi Dominici gregis* came as a surprise to many people, updating the guidelines governing papal elections. Only minor changes were introduced to the procedures followed by the conclaves of cardinals who gather for this purpose, allowing for a new, more comfortable residence in the Vatican for the cardinal-electors and eliminating two ancient and seldom-used methods of election. The pope also reaffirmed the guidelines established in 1975 by Pope Paul VI: participation in the conclaves was limited to cardinals under the age of eighty, the number of cardinals participating was kept at the traditional 120, and the strict rules of secrecy which govern such conclaves were emphasized.

Vita consecrata was a pastoral document in which the pope emphasized the unique meaning and value of the consecrated life in the life of the Church. In it, the Holy Father reminded religious that religious life is a gift of God to his Church, that profession of the evangelical counsels is a vital part of the Church's life and that every mission within the Church finds its root in consecration to God. Additionally, the pope challenged religious to make their consecrated lives a prophetic witness to the modern world and emphasized that the promotion of religious vocations is a task for the whole Church.

Other important documents released by the Holy See in 1996 included the Pontifical Council for the Family's *Guidelines for Marriage Preparation* and the document on the *Truth and Meaning of Human Sexuality*, a document on guidelines for sexual education within the family.

The pope concluded the year by looking forward to 1997, reminding the Church that the coming year was designated to be the Year of God the Son, in preparation for the jubilee celebrations of the Year 2000.

LETTER
OF THE HOLY FATHER
POPE JOHN PAUL II
TO ALL THE PRIESTS OF THE CHURCH
ON THE OCCASION OF HOLY THURSDAY 1996

The Unique Vocation of Christ the Priest

Dear Brothers in the Priesthood!

"Let us consider our call, brethren."[1] The priesthood is a call, a particular vocation:"One does not take this honor upon himself, but he is called by God."[2] The Letter to the Hebrews harks back to the priesthood of the Old Testament in order to lead us to an understanding of the mystery of Christ the Priest:"Christ did not exalt himself to be made a high priest, but was appointed by him who said to him:'...You are a priest forever, after the order of Melchizedek.'"[3]

1.   Christ, the Son of one being with the Father, has been made priest of the New Covenant according to the order of Melchizedek: therefore he too was called to the priesthood. It is the Father who"calls" his own Son, whom he has begotten by an act of eternal love, to "come into the world"[4] and to become man. He wills that his only-begotten Son, by taking flesh, should become"a priest forever": the one Priest of the new, eternal Covenant. The Son's vocation to the priesthood expresses the depth of the Trinitarian mystery. For only the Son, the Word of the Father, in whom and through whom all things were created, can unceasingly offer creation in sacrifice to the Father, confirming that everything created has come forth from the Father and must become an offering of praise to the Creator. Thus the mystery of the priesthood has its beginning in the Trinity and is, at the same time, a consequence of the Incarnation. By becoming man, the only-begotten and eternal Son of the Father is born of a woman, enters into the created order and thus becomes a priest, the one eternal priest.

The author of the Letter to the Hebrews emphasizes that Christ's Priesthood is linked to the sacrifice of the cross:"Christ appeared as a high priest of the good things to come, then through the greater and more perfect tabernacle (not made with hands, that is, not of this creation), he entered once for all into the Holy Place, taking ... his own blood, thus securing an eternal redemption."[5] The Priesthood of Christ is rooted in the work of redemption. Christ is the priest of his own sacrifice:"Through the eternal spirit he offered himself without blemish to God."[6] The priesthood of the New Covenant, to which we are called in the Church, is thus a share in this unique Priesthood of Christ.

Common Priesthood and Ministerial Priesthood

2. The Second Vatican Council presents the idea of"vocation"in its broadest sense. It speaks of the vocation of mankind, the Christian vocation and the vocation to marriage and family life. In this context, the priesthood is one of many vocations, one of many possible ways of following Christ, who in the gospel frequently utters the invitation:"Follow me."

In the Dogmatic Constitution on the Church *Lumen gentium* the council teaches that all the baptized share in the Priesthood of Christ. But at the same time it clearly distinguishes between the priesthood of the People of God, common to all the faithful, and the hierarchical or the ministerial priesthood. In this regard, it is worthwhile quoting in full an instructive passage of the constitution:"Christ the Lord, High Priest taken from among men,"[7] "made a kingdom of priests to God his Father"[8] out of this new people. The baptized, by regeneration and the anointing of the Holy Spirit, are consecrated into a spiritual house and a holy priesthood. Thus through all those works befitting Christian men and women they can offer spiritual sacrifices and proclaim the power of him who has called them out of darkness into his marvelous light.[9] Therefore all the disciples of Christ, persevering in prayer and praising God,[10] should present themselves as a living sacrifice, holy and pleasing to God.[11] Everywhere on earth they must bear witness to Christ and give an answer to those who seek an account of that hope of eternal life which is in them.[12] Though they differ from one another in essence and not only in degree, the common priesthood of the faithful and the ministerial or hierarchical priesthood are nonetheless interrelated. Each of them in its own special way is a participation in the one Priesthood of Christ. The ministerial priest, by the sacred power he enjoys, molds and rules the priestly people. Acting in the person of Christ, he brings about the Eucharistic Sacrifice, and offers it to God in the name of all the people. For their part, the faithful join in the offering of the Eucharist by virtue of their royal priesthood. They likewise exercise that priesthood by receiving the sacraments, by prayer and thanksgiving, by the witness of a holy life, and by self-denial and active charity.

The ministerial priesthood is at the service of the common priesthood of the faithful. For when the priest celebrates the Eucharist and administers the sacraments, he leads the faithful to an awareness of their own particular sharing in the Priesthood of Christ.

The Personal Call to the Priesthood

3.   It is thus clear that, within the broader context of the Christian vocation, the priestly vocation is a specific call. And this tends to be borne out of our personal experience as priests: we received Baptism and Confirmation; we took part in catechesis, in celebrations of the liturgy and above all in the Eucharist. Our vocation to the priesthood first appeared in the context of the Christian life.

Nonetheless, every vocation to the priesthood has an individual history of its own, related to quite specific moments in the life of each one of us. When Christ called his Apostles, he said to each one of them: "Follow me!"[13] For 2000 years he has continued to address the same invitation to many men, especially young men. Sometimes he calls them in a surprising way, even though his call is never completely unexpected. Christ's call to follow him usually comes after a long preparation. Already present in the mind of the young person, even if later overshadowed by indecision or by the attraction of other possible paths, when the call makes itself felt once more it does not come as a surprise. No wonder then that this calling prevails over all others, and the young person is able to set out on the path shown him by Christ: he takes leave of his family and begins his specific preparation for the priesthood.

There is typology of vocation, which I would now like to sketch briefly. We find a first outline of this typology in the New Testament. With the words "follow me," Christ calls widely differing people: there are fishermen like Peter and the sons of Zebedee,[14] but there is also Levi, a publican, thereafter called Matthew. In Israel, the profession of tax-collector was considered sinful and despicable. And yet Christ calls a publican to join the group of Apostles.[15] Even more astonishing was the call of Saul of Tarsus,[16] a known and feared persecutor of Christians, who hated the name of Jesus. Yet this very Pharisee was called on the road to Damascus: the Lord wished to make him "a chosen instrument," destined to suffer much for his name.[17]

Each of us priests sees himself in the original typology of vocation found in the gospels. At the same time, each one knows that the story of his vocation, the path by which Christ guides him throughout his life, is in some sense unique.

Dear Brothers in the Priesthood, we must often pause in prayer and meditate on the mystery of our vocation, our hearts filled with wonder and gratitude to God for this ineffable gift.

The Priestly Vocation of the Apostles

4.   The image of vocation handed down to us by the gospels is particularly linked to the figure of the fisherman. Jesus called to himself some fishermen of Galilee, among them Simon Peter, and defined the apostolic mission by speaking of their trade. After the miraculous draught of fishes, when Peter threw himself at his feet and cried out: "Depart from me, for I am a sinful man, Lord," Christ replied: "Do not be afraid; henceforth you will be catching men."[18]

Peter and the other Apostles lived together with Jesus and traveled with him wherever his mission took him. They heard the words he spoke, marveled at his works and were astonished at the miracles he performed. They knew that Jesus was the Messiah, sent by God to show Israel and all humanity the way of salvation. But their faith had to pass through the mysterious saving event which he had several times foretold: "The Son of Man is to be delivered into the hands of men, and they will kill him, and he will be raised on the third day."[19] All this came about with his death and resurrection, in the days which the liturgy calls the *Triduum Sacrum*.

Precisely during that Paschal event Christ revealed to the Apostles that their vocation was to become priests like him and in him. This took place when, in the Upper Room, on the eve of his death on the cross, he took bread and then the cup of wine, and spoke over them the words of consecration. The bread and the wine became his body and blood, given in sacrifice and, through their hands, communicated it to the Church for all time. By entrusting to the Apostles the memorial of his sacrifice, Christ made them sharers in his priesthood. For there is a close and inseparable bond between the offering and the priest: the one who offers the sacrifice of Christ must have a share in the Priesthood of Christ. Consequently, the vocation to the priesthood is a vocation to offer *in persona Christi* his own sacrifice, by virtue of sharing in his priesthood. From the Apostles, then, we have inherited the priestly ministry.

The Priest Attains his Fulfillment
in a Constantly Renewed and Watchful Response

5.   "The Master is here and is calling you."[20] These words can be read with reference to the priestly vocation. God's call is at the origin of the journey which every person must make in life: it is the primary and fundamental aspect of vocation, but it is not the only one. Priestly ordination is in fact the beginning of a journey which continues until death, a journey which is "vocational" at every step. The Lord calls priests to a number of tasks and ministries deriving from this vocation. But there is a still deeper level. Over and above the tasks which are the expression of priestly ministry, there always remains the underlying reality of "being a priest." The situations and circumstances of life constantly call upon the priest to confirm his original choice, to respond ever anew to God's call. Our priestly life, like every authentic form of Christian existence, is a succession of responses to God who calls.

Emblematic in this regard is the parable of the servants who await their master's return. Because the master delays, they must stay awake in order to be found vigilant at his coming.[21] Could not this evangelical watchfulness be another way of defining a response to a vocation? For a vocation is lived out thanks to a vigilant sense of responsibility. Christ emphasizes this: "Blessed are those servants whom the master finds awake when he comes. . . . And if he comes in the second watch, or in the third, and finds them so, blessed are those servants!"[22]

Priests in the Latin Church take on the commitment to live in celibacy. If vocation is watchfulness, certainly a significant aspect of the latter is fidelity to this commitment throughout one's whole life. But celibacy is only one of the dimensions of a vocation—a vocation which is lived out, along the journey of life, as part of an overall commitment to the many different tasks which derive from the priesthood.

A vocation is not something static: it has an inherent dynamism. Dear brothers in the priesthood, we confirm and constantly fulfill our vocation to the extent that we live faithfully the *Mysterium* of God's covenant with mankind, and, in particular, the *Mysterium* of the Eucharist. We fulfill it to the extent that we love ever more intensely the priesthood and the priestly ministry which we are called to carry out. We then discover that we find our fulfillment in being priests, and thus we confirm the authenticity of our vocation, in accordance with God's unique and eternal plan for each one of us. This divine plan is realized to the extent that it is acknowledged and accepted by us as the plan and program of our lives.

Priesthood as *"Officium Laudis"*

6. *Gloria Dei vivens homo*. These words of St. Irenaeus profoundly link the glory of God and man's self-realization. "Not to us, O Lord, not to us, but to your name give glory."[23] Repeating often these words of the Psalmist, we come to understand that "realizing" ourselves in life has a point of reference and an end which are transcendent, both of them included in the concept of the "glory of God": we are called to make our life an *officium laudis*.

The priestly vocation is a special call to this *officium laudis*. When the priest celebrates the Eucharist, when he grants God's pardon in Penance or administers the other sacraments, always he is giving praise to God. The priest must therefore love the glory of the living God and proclaim, together with the community of believers, the divine glory which shines forth in creation and in redemption. The priest is called to be united in a special way to Christ, the Eternal Word and true Man, the Redeemer of the world: in the Redemption, in fact, is manifested the fullness of the glory which humanity and the whole of creation give to the Father in Jesus Christ.

Officium laudis includes not only the words of the Psalter, liturgical hymns, the songs of God's People lifted up in the sight of the Creator in all the different languages; *officium laudis* is above all the unceasing discovery of what is true, good and beautiful, which the world receives as a gift from the Creator. Along with that, it is the discovery of the meaning of human existence. The mystery of the Redemption has fully accomplished and revealed this meaning, bringing human life closer to the life of God. Redemption, definitively achieved in the Paschal Mystery through the passion, death and resurrection of Christ, reveals not only the transcendent holiness of God but also, as the Second Vatican Council teaches, reveals "man to himself."

God's glory is written in the order of creation and in the order of redemption; the priest is called to live this mystery in its fullness in order to participate in the great *officium laudis* which is unceasingly taking place in the universe. Only by living in depth the truth of the redemption of the world and of humanity can he come close to the sufferings and problems of individuals and families, and fearlessly face as well the reality of evil and sin, with the spiritual strength necessary to overcome them.

The Priest Accompanies the Faithful Towards the Fullness of Life in God

7.   *Gloria Dei vivens homo.* The priest, whose vocation is to give glory to God, is at the same time profoundly marked by the truth contained in the second part of the phrase from St. Irenaeus: *vivens homo.* Love for God's glory does not distance the priest from life and all that life entails; on the contrary, his vocation brings to him to discover its full meaning.

What does *vivens homo* mean? It means man in the fullness of his truth: man created by God in his own image and likeness; man to whom God has entrusted the earth in order that he might have dominion over it; man marked by the rich variety of nature and grace; man freed from the slavery of sin and raised to the dignity of an adopted child of God.

This is the man and the humanity which the priest has before him when he celebrates the divine mysteries: from the newborn infant brought by its parents for Baptism, to the children and youngsters he meets for catechism or religious instruction. And then there are the young people who in that most delicate period of life choose their path, their own vocation, and set out to form new families or to consecrate themselves to the kingdom of God by entering the seminary or institute of consecrated life. The priest must be very close to young people. At this stage of life they often turn to him for the support of his advice, for the help of his prayer, for wise vocational guidance. In this way the priest experiences how open and dedicated to people his vocation is. In coming close to young people he is meeting future fathers and mothers of families, future professionals or, at any event, people who will be able to contribute their own abilities to the building of tomorrow's society. Each of these many different vocations is close to his priestly heart, and he sees each one as a particular path along which God guides people and leads them to himself.

The priest thus becomes a sharer in many different life choices, sufferings and joys, disappointments and hopes. In every situation, his task is to show God to man as the final end of his personal existence. The priest becomes the one to whom people confide the things most dear to them and their secrets, which are sometimes very painful. He becomes the one whom the sick, the elderly and the dying wait for, aware as they are that only he, a sharer in the Priesthood of Christ, can help them in the final journey which is to lead them to God. As a witness to Christ, the priest is the messenger of man's supreme vocation to eternal life in God. And while he accompanies his brothers and sisters, he prepares himself: the exercise of the ministry enables him to deepen his own vocation to give glory to God in order to have a share in eternal life. He thus moves forward towards the day when Christ will say to him:"Well done, good and faithful servant, . . . enter into the joy of your master."[24]

The Priestly Jubilee: A Time of Joy and Thanksgiving

8.   "Consider your call, brethren."[25] Paul's exhortation to the Christians of Corinth takes on a particular meaning for us priests. We ought to "consider" our vocation often, and to discover anew its meaning and grandeur, which always surpass us. A special occasion for this is Holy Thursday, the day commemorating the institution of Holy Thursday and the Sacrament of Priesthood. Other fitting occasions are anniversaries of priestly ordination, and especially priestly jubilees.

Dear brother priests, as I share these reflections with you, I am thinking of my own 50th anniversary of ordination to the priesthood, which falls this year. I am thinking of my seminary classmates who, like myself, followed a path to the priesthood marked by the tragic period of the Second World War. At that time the seminaries were closed and seminarians were scattered here and there. Some of them lost their lives in the hostilities. For us, the priesthood, attained in those circumstances, took on a special value. I still cherish in my memory that great moment when, 50 years ago, the assembly invoked *Veni, Creator Spiritus* over us young deacons lying prostrate in the middle of the church, before we received ordination by the imposition of the bishop's hands. We give thanks to the Holy Spirit for that outpouring of grace which has marked our lives. And we continue to implore: *"Imple superna gratia, quæ tu creasti pectora."*

I wish to invite you, dear brothers in the priesthood, to share in my *Te Deum* of thanksgiving for the gift of my vocation. Jubilees, as you know, are important moments in a priest's life: they represent as it were milestones along the road of our calling. In the biblical tradition, a jubilee is a time of joy and thanksgiving. The farmer gives thanks to the Creator of the harvest; on the occasion of our jubilees, we wish to thank the Eternal Shepherd for the fruits of our priestly life, for the service we have rendered to the Church and to humanity in the different parts of the world, in the most varied conditions and in the different working situations to which Divine Providence has led us and wished us to be. We know that we are "unworthy servants,"[26] but we are grateful to the Lord for having wished to make us his ministers.

We are grateful also to people: most of all to those who helped us to reach the priesthood, and to those whom Divine Providence has placed on the path of our vocation. We thank them all, beginning with our parents, who in so many ways have been a gift of God for us: how many and how precious the teachings and the good examples they have given us!

As we give thanks, we also ask pardon of God, and of our brothers and sisters, for our negligence and failures, the results of human weakness. The jubilee, according to Sacred Scripture, could not be just thanksgiving for the harvest: it also involved the cancellation of debts. Let us therefore beg our merciful God to forgive the debts which we have accumulated in the course of our lives and in the exercise of our priestly ministry.

"Consider your call, brethren," the Apostle admonishes us. Prompted by his words, we "consider" the road which we have traveled up to this point, a road which has seen our call confirmed, deepened and consolidated. We "consider" it in order to become more clearly aware of God's loving action in our lives. At the same time, we cannot forget our brothers in the priesthood who have not persevered on the journey undertaken. We entrust them to the Father's love and assure each one of them of our prayers.

Thus, our "consideration" turns, almost without our realizing it, into prayer. It is in this perspective, dear brothers in the priesthood, that I wish to invite you to join in my thanksgiving for the gift of vocation and of the priesthood.

Thank you, O God, for the gift of the priesthood.

9.   *"Te Deum laudamus*
     Te Dominum confitemur . . ."
     We praise you and we thank you, O God:
     all the earth adores you.
     We your ministers, with the voices of the Prophets
     and the chorus of the Apostles,
     proclaim you as the Father and the Lord of life,
     of every form of life which comes from you alone.
     We recognize you, O Most Holy Trinity,
     as the birthplace and beginning of our vocation;

You, the Father, from eternity have thought of us,
wanted us and loved us;
You, the Son, have chosen us and called us to share
in your unique and eternal priesthood;
You, the Holy Spirit, have filled us with your gifts
and have consecrated us with your holy anointing.
You, the Lord of time and history,
have placed us on the threshold of
the third Christian millennium,
in order to be witnesses to the salvation
which you have accomplished for all humanity.
We, the Church which proclaims your glory, implore you:
let there never be lacking holy priests to serve the gospel;
let there solemnly resound in every cathedral
and in every corner of the world
the hymn *Veni, Creator Spiritus.*
Come, O Creator Spirit!
Come to raise up new generations of young people,
ready to work in the Lord's vineyard to spread the
kingdom of God to the furthermost ends of the earth.
And you, Mary, Mother of Christ,
who at the foot of the cross accepted us
as beloved sons with the Apostle John,
continue to watch over our vocation.
To you we entrust the years of ministry
which Providence will grant us yet to live.
Be near us to guide us along the paths of the world,
to meet the men and women
whom your Son redeemed with his blood.
Help us to fulfill completely the will of Jesus,
born of you for the salvation of humanity.
O Christ, you are our hope!
"In te, Domine, speravi, non confundar in æternum."

From the Vatican, on 17 March, the fourth Sunday of Lent, in the
year 1996, the eighteenth of my Pontificate.

Endnotes

1. Cf. 1 Cor 1: 26.
2. Heb 5: 4.
3. Heb 5: 5-6.
4. Heb 10: 5.
5. Heb 9: 14.
6. Heb 9: 14.
7. Cf. Heb 5: 1-5.
8. Rv 1: 6; cf. 5: 9-10.
9. Cf. 1 Pt 2: 4-10.
10. Cf. Acts 2: 42-47.
11. Cf. Rom 12: 1.
12. Cf. 1 Pt 3: 15.
13. Mt 4: 19; 9: 9; Mk 1: 17; 2: 14; Lk 5: 27; Jn 1: 43; 21: 19.
14. Cf. Mt 4: 19, 22.
15. Cf. Mt 9: 9.
16. Acts 9: 1-19.
17. Cf. Acts 9: 15-16.
18. Lk 5: 8, 10.
19. Mt 17: 22-23.
20. Cf. Jn 11: 28.
21. Cf. Lk 12: 35-40.
22. Lk 12: 37-38.
23. Ps 115: 1.
24. Mt 25: 21.
25. 1 Cor 1: 26.
26. Lk 17: 10.

1997

Nineteenth Year of Pontificate

As the pope stated in his Apostolic Letter *Tertio millennio adveniente*, "1997 will thus be devoted to reflection on Christ, the Word of God, made man by the power of the Holy Spirit." In order "to inspire in all the faithful a true longing for holiness," the year 1997 "will be the opportune moment for a renewed appreciation of catechesis . . . about the person of Jesus Christ and his mystery of salvation" (n. 42). In his Letter to Priests for 1997, the pope did not hesitate to remind all the priests of the universal Church that the preparation for the new millennium will be a "pilgrimage to the Father" and should begin with Christ. For "it is he, the eternal Son of God, made man and born of the Virgin Mary, who leads us to the Father" (1997 Letter, n. 2). For this reason, in the year dedicated to God the Son, the Holy Father offers to his brother priests an especially appropriate reflection on the eternal priesthood of Christ.

The pope recalls the Litany of Our Lord Jesus Christ, recited on the day before his own ordination, which "brings out in a particularly rich and profound way the Priesthood of Christ and our link with that Priesthood." It was Christ who "offered himself as a bloody sacrifice on the cross" and "also instituted its unbloody 'memorial' for all times." He "entrusted his sacrifice to the Church" so that now "the Church—and in the Church every priest—celebrates the one sacrifice of Christ." Therefore, it is in the words of consecration, whereby the bread and wine become Christ's true body and blood, that is expressed "the fullest realization of our priesthood" (1997 Letter, n. 3). The Holy Father reflected that it is only in this "fullest realization" that we can comprehend how truly Christ considered his Apostles "friends": "Could Jesus have expressed to us his friendship any more eloquently than by enabling us, as priests of the New Covenant, to act in his name, *in persona Christi*?" (n. 5). It is truly a great gift of Christ to his Church for the ministerial priesthood to have such an intimate share in his divine, eternal priesthood. In conclusion, the pope, in the words of St. John, wishes that all priests "May go and bear fruit, like the Apostles, and that our fruit may abide."

The two most significant events of this year devoted to God the Son focused on the youth and family. In August, the pope joined over one million young people from all over the world for the twelfth World Youth Day in Paris. His message was in keeping with preparation for the millennium: "Our worldwide gathering now takes on its fullest meaning through the celebration of Mass. Dear young friends, may your presence here mean a true commitment in faith! For Christ is now answering your own question and the questions of all those who seek the living God. He answers by offering an invitation: This is my body, take it and eat. To the Father he entrusts his supreme desire: that all those whom he loves may be one in the same communion. . . . Go forth now along the roads of the world, along the pathways of humanity, while remaining ever united in Christ's Church!" (Homily, August 24). It was most appropriate that here, before the youth of the world, the pope announced that he would declare St. Thérèse of Liseux a Doctor of the Church, a "holy young woman so present to our times . . . of particular interest to you young people."

In October, the pope traveled to Brazil for the Second World Meeting with Families. He stressed the crucial role that the family must play in the new millennium: "On the journey towards the Jubilee of the Year 2000, I invite all those listening to me to strengthen their faith and witness as Christians, so that with God's grace there may be true conversion and personal renewal in all the world's families" (Homily, October 5). His other pastoral trips of 1997 included his long-awaited visit to Sarajevo (April 12-13) as well as visits to the Czech Republic (April 25-27); Lebanon (May 10-11); his native Poland (May 31-June 10); and Bologna, Italy (September 28). The pope spent the final weeks of the year in Rome presiding over the Synod of American Bishops (November 16-December 12).

The most significant documents released during the year were the Apostolic Letter *Lætamur magnopere* promulgating the definitive Latin edition of the *Catechism of the Catholic Church* and the Apostolic Letter *Divinæ amoris scientia* which officially declared St. Thérèse to be a Doctor of the Church.

In his General Audiences throughout the year, the pope continued his long series of meditations on Mary (nn. 42-70). In particular, his discussions included Mary's new and distinct relationship with the Apostles after the resurrection, her unique participation in her Son's death and resurrection, her queenship, the importance of her intercession in obtaining the gifts of the Holy Spirit, and the necessity to accept her as our Mother.

LETTER
OF THE HOLY FATHER
POPE JOHN PAUL II
TO ALL THE PRIESTS OF THE CHURCH
ON THE OCCASION OF HOLY THURSDAY 1997

Dear Brothers in the Priesthood!

1. *Iesu, Sacerdos in æternum, miserere nobis!*

Continuing the tradition of addressing you on the day when you gather around your bishop to commemorate with joy the institution of the priesthood in the Church, I wish first of all to express once more my gratitude to the Lord for the jubilee celebrations which, on 1 and 10 November last, saw so many brother priests take part in my joy. I offer everyone my heartfelt thanks.

A special thought goes to those priests who like me celebrated the fiftieth anniversary of their ordination last year. Many of them did not hesitate, despite their years and the distance, to come to Rome to celebrate their Golden Jubilee with the Pope.

I thank the Cardinal Vicar, his auxiliary bishops, the priests and the faithful of the Diocese of Rome, who showed in various ways their union with the successor of Peter, praising God for the gift of the priesthood. My gratitude extends to the cardinals, archbishops, bishops, priests, consecrated men and women, and all the faithful of the Church for the gift of their closeness and of their prayer, and for the *Te Deum* of thanksgiving which we all sang together.

I also wish to thank all those working in the Roman Curia for everything that they did to make the Pope's Golden Jubilee a means of helping people appreciate better the great gift and mystery of the priesthood. It is my constant prayer that the Lord will continue to enkindle the spark of a priestly vocation in the souls of many young men.

During those days, I returned many times, in mind and heart, to the private chapel of the Archbishop of Krakow, where on 1 November 1946 in the unforgettable Metropolitan of Krakow, Archbishop and later Adam Stefan Cardinal Sapieha, imposed hands on me, transmitting to me the sacramental grace of the priesthood. With great emotion, I returned in spirit to the cathedral at Wawel, where I celebrated my first Holy Mass the day after my ordination. During those days of the Jubilee, we all experienced in a special way the presence of Christ the High Priest as we meditated on the words of the liturgy: "Behold the high priest who in his day pleased God and was found righteous." *Ecce Sacerdos magnus.* These words find their fullest application in Christ himself. He is the High Priest of the New and Eternal Covenant, the only Priest, from whom all other priests draw the grace of vocation and ministry. I rejoice in the fact that during the celebrations for the Jubilee of my ordination the Priesthood of Christ shone forth in its ineffable truth as gift and mystery for the people of all times, and until the end of time.

Fifty years after my priestly ordination, my thoughts turn every day, as always, to the priests of my own age, both from Krakow and from other local churches throughout the world who have not been able to reach this Jubilee. I pray that Christ, the Eternal Priest, will grant that they inherit their eternal reward, that he will welcome them into the glory of his kingdom.

2.   *Iesu, Sacerdos in æternum, miserere nobis!*

I write you this letter, dear brothers, during the first year of immediate preparation for the third millennium: *Tertio millennio adveniente.* In the apostolic letter which begins with these words, I indicated the significance of passing from the second to the third millennium after Christ's birth, and I directed that the three final years before the Year 2000 should be dedicated to the Holy Trinity. The first year, solemnly inaugurated on the First Sunday of Advent, is centered on Jesus Christ. For it is he, the eternal Son of God, made man and born of the Virgin Mary, who leads us to the Father. Next year will be dedicated to the Holy Spirit, the Paraclete, promised by Christ to the Apostles at the moment of his passing from this world to the Father. Finally, the year 1999 will be dedicated to the Father, to whom the Son wishes to lead us in the Holy Spirit, the Consoler.

Thus we shall conclude the second millennium in a great song of praise to the Holy Trinity. This journey will recall the trilogy of encyclicals which, by God's grace, I was able to publish at the beginning of my Pontificate: *Redemptor hominis, Dominum et vivificantem* and *Dives in misericordia.* I exhort you, dear brothers, to meditate on these once again during these three years. In our ministry, especially our liturgical ministry, we must always be aware that we are on pilgrimage to the Father, guided by the Son in the Holy Spirit. It is precisely to this awareness that we are called by the words with which we conclude every prayer: "Through our Lord Jesus Christ, your Son, who lives and reigns with you and the Holy Spirit, one God, forever and ever. Amen."

3. *Iesu, Sacerdos in æternum, miserere nobis!*

This invocation is taken from the Litany of our Lord Jesus Christ, Priest and Victim, which was recited in the seminary at Krakow on the day before ordinations to the priesthood. I included them as an appendix in my book *Gift and Mystery,* published on the occasion of my priestly jubilee. But I wish to highlight it in the present letter, for I think it brings out in a particularly rich and profound way the Priesthood of Christ and our link with that Priesthood. The words of the litany are based on the words of Sacred Scripture, particularly the Letter to the Hebrews, but not exclusively. When, for example, we pray: *Iesu, Sacerdos in æternum secundum ordinem Melchisedech,* our thoughts go back to the Old Testatment, to Psalm 110. We all know what it means that Christ is a priest like Melchizedek. His priesthood was expressed in the offering of his own body, "once for all."[1] He who offered himself as a bloody sacrifice on the cross also instituted its unbloody "memorial" for all times, under the species of bread and wine. And under these species he entrusted his sacrifice to the Church. In this way the Church—and in the Church every priest—celebrates the one sacrifice of Christ.

I remember vividly the impression made by the consecration when I uttered them for the first time together with the bishop who had just ordained me. I repeated them the following day in the Holy Mass celebrated in the Crypt of St. Leonard. And so many times since then—it is hard to count them—I have repeated these sacramental words in order to make Christ present, under the species of bread and wine, in the saving act of his self-sacrifice on the cross.

Let us together once more contemplate this sublime mystery. Jesus took the bread and gave it to his disciples saying: "Take this, all of you, and eat: this is my body." And then he took the cup filled with wine, blessed it, gave it to his disciples and said: "Take this, all of you, and drink: this is the cup of my blood, the blood of the new and everlasting covenant. It will be shed for you and for all, for the forgiveness of sins." And he added: "Do this in memory of me."

How could these wondrous words not be at the very heart of every priestly life? Let us repeat them every time as if it were the first! Let us take care that they are never said out of habit. They express the fullest realization of our priesthood.

4.   Celebrating the Sacrifice of Christ, we are constantly aware of the words which we read in the Letter to the Hebrews:"When Christ appeared as a high priest of the good things that have come, ... he entered once for all into the Holy Place, taking not the blood of goats and calves but his own blood, thus securing an eternal redemption. For if the sprinkling of defiled persons with the blood of goats and with the ashes of a heifer sanctifies for the purification of the flesh, how much more shall the blood of Christ, who through the eternal Spirit offered himself without blemish to God, purify your consciences from dead works to serve the living God? Therefore he is the mediator of a new covenant."[2]

The invocations of the Litany of Jesus Christ, Priest and Victim, in some way go back to these words or to others from the same letter:

> *Iesu,*
> *Pontifex ex hominibus assumpte,*
> *... pro hominibus constitute,*
> *Pontifex confessionis nostræ,*
> *... amplioris præ Moysi gloriæ,*
> *Pontifex tabernaculi veri,*
> *Pontifex futurorum bonorum,*
> *... sancte, innocens et impollute,*
> *Pontifex fidelis et misericors,*
> *... Dei et animarum zelo succense,*
> *Pontifex in æternum perfecte,*
> *Pontifex qui... cælos penetrasti...*

As we repeat these invocations, we see with the eyes of faith what is spoken of by the Letter to the Hebrews. As a Priest eternally consecrated by the Father in *Spritu Sancto et virtute,* Jesus now"is seated at the right hand of the Majesty on high."[3] And from there he intercedes for us as our Mediator—*semper vivens ad interpellandum pro nobis*—in order to blaze for us the path of a new, eternal life: *Pontifex qui nobis viam novam initiasti.* He loves us and shed his blood in order to wash away our sins—*Pontifex qui dilexisti nos et lavasti nos a peccatis in sanguine tuo.* He gave himself for us: *tradidisti temetipsum Deo oblationem et hostiam.*

Christ brings into the eternal Holy Place the self-sacrifice which is the price of our redemption. The offering—the victim—is inseparable from the priest. The Litany of Jesus Christ, Priest and Victim, recited in the seminary, helped me to understand all this better. I constantly return to this fundamental lesson.

5.   Today is Holy Thursday. The whole Church gathers in spirit in the Upper Room where the Apostles gathered with Christ for the Last Supper. Let us reread Christ's words of farewell in the Gospel of St. John. Among the many treasures of this text, I would like to pause at the following words spoken by Jesus to the Apostles: "Greater love has no man than this, that a man lay down his life for his friends. You are my friends if you do what I command you. No longer do I call you servants, for a servant does not know what his master is doing; but I have called you friends, for all that I have heard from my Father I have made known to you."[4]

"Friends": this is what Jesus calls the Apostles. This is what he also wishes to call us who, thanks to the Sacrament of Holy Orders, share in his Priesthood. Let us listen to these words with great emotion and humility. They contain the truth. First of all, the truth about friend-ship, but also a truth about ourselves who share in the priesthood of Christ as ministers of the Eucharist. Could Jesus have expressed to us his friendship any more eloquently than by enabling us, as priests of the New Covenant, to act in his name, *in persona Christi Capitis?* Precisely this takes place in all our priestly service, when we admin-ister the sacraments and especially when we celebrate the Eucharist. We repeat the words that he spoke over the bread and wine, and, through our ministry, the same consecration that he brought about takes place. Can there be a fuller expression of friendship than this? It goes to the very heart of our priestly ministry.

Christ says: "You did not choose me, but I chose you and appointed you that you should go and bear fruit and that your fruit should abide."[5] At the end of this letter, I offer these words to you as a wish. On the day of the institution of the sacrament of the priesthood, let us make this our wish for one another, dear brothers: that we may go and bear fruit, like the Apostles, and that our fruit may abide.

May Mary, the Mother of Christ the Eternal High Priest, sustain us with her constant protection along the path of our ministry, especially when the road becomes difficult and the work weighs more heavily upon us. May the faithful Virgin intercede with her Son, that we may never lack the courage to witness to him in the various fields of our apostolate, working with him so that the world may have life and have it in abundance.[6]

In the name of Christ, with great affection, I bless you all.

From the Vatican, on 16 March, the fifth Sunday of Lent, in the year 1997, the nineteenth of my Pontificate.

Endnotes

1. Heb 10: 10.
2. Heb 9: 11-15.
3. Heb 1: 3.
4. Jn 15: 13-15.
5. Jn 15: 16.
6. Cf. Jn 10: 10.

1998

Twentieth Year of Pontificate

In this Year of the Holy Spirit, the Holy Father focused on the close relationship between the Holy Spirit and the priesthood in his 1998 Letter to Priests: "An intimate bond unites our priesthood to the Holy Spirit and to his mission. On the day of our priestly ordination, by virtue of a unique outpouring of the Paraclete, the Risen One accomplished again in each of us what he accomplished in his disciples on the evening of Easter, and set us in the world as those who continue his mission" (1998 Letter, Introduction). While the 1997 Letter discussed the intimate relationship between God the Son and the ministerial priesthood by reflecting on his great gift to priests to act *in persona Christi*, this letter is an opportunity "for us priests to contemplate the work of the Holy Spirit in us and to implore his gifts in order to conform ourselves all the more to Christi, the Priest of the New Covenant" (1998 Letter, Introduction).

John Paul II's first major pastoral visit of 1998 turned out to be one of the most significant of his papacy. From January 21-25, the Holy Father visited Cuba, one of the world's last communist countries. While in Cuba, John Paul II met with President Fidel Castro and said Mass in José Martí Plaza. From his homily: "As I come among you, I wish to bring you the Good News of hope in God. As a servant of the gospel I bring you this message of love and solidarity which Jesus Christ, by his coming, offers to men and women in every age. In absolutely no way is this an ideology or a new economic or political system; rather it is a path of authentic peace, freedom, and justice."

On February 21, the Holy Father held a sacred consistory of his College of Cardinals in Rome, the first since 1994. He named twenty new cardinals from thirteen different countries "to help the Pope steer the barque of Peter towards that historic goal [of the new millennium]." With the vigor and fidelity of the Sacred College renewed, the pope foresees the fruition of the Second Vatican Council in the new millennium: "As I turn my gaze with you [cardinals] beyond the threshold of the Year 2000, I invoke from the Lord an abundance of gifts from the divine Spirit for the whole Church, so that the 'springtime' of the Second Vatican Council may find in the new millennium its 'summer,' that is to say, its full development" (Consistory Address, February 21).

Also significant was the Special Assembly for Asia of the Synod of Bishops, which met in Rome April 19–May 14. The pope wished to remind the prelates of the largest continent in the world that Asia is a vast land ripe for conversion: "How can we ignore the fact that *more than three fifths of the world's inhabitants are Asian* and that an important part of them are young people? To this vast portion of the humanity of our time, dwelling on the continent of Asia, we must bring with enthusiasm and vigor the Easter proclamation" (Homily, April 19). This rightly occurs in the Year of the Holy Spirit, who is the "principal agent of the new evangelization" and "builds the kingdom of God within the course of history and prepares its full manifestation in Jesus Christ" (*Tertio millennio adveniente*, n. 45).

Autumn marked a time of milestones for Pope John Paul II. On September 14, he signed his thirteenth encyclical, *Fides et ratio*, opening with one of the most memorable portions of his vast body of writings. "Faith and reason are like two wings on which the human spirit rises to the contemplation of truth; and God has placed in the human heart a desire to know the truth—in a word, to know himself—so that, by knowing and loving God, men and women may also come to the fullness of truth about themselves" (*Fides et ratio*, Introduction).

Then, on October 2-4, the pope visited Croatia, where he beatified Alojzije Cardinal Stepinac, followed on October 11 by the canonization of Sr. Teresa Benedicta of the Cross, better known to the world as Edith Stein.

Finally, on October 16, John Paul II celebrated the twentieth anniversary of his pontificate, the longest of the century. It was a time recognized by messages of thanks and good wishes from around the world. One of the highpoints of the events celebrating the anniversary was a Mass the Holy Father celebrated in St. Peter's Square to praise and thank the Lord for this pontificate. Concelebrating with the pope were forty cardinals, 100 archbishops and bishops, and 800 priests. In his homily, the pope rededicated himself to his unique ministry: "With all my heart, I once again entrust my life and ministry to the Virgin Mary, Mother of the Redeemer and Mother of the Church. To her I repeat with filial abandonment: *Totus tuus! Amen.*"

The year concluded with the Special Assembly of the Synod of Bishops for Oceania from November 22 to December 12, followed by a bull of indiction for the Holy Year 2000, *Incarnationis mysterium*.

LETTER
OF THE HOLY FATHER
POPE JOHN PAUL II
TO ALL THE PRIESTS OF THE CHURCH
ON THE OCCASION OF HOLY THURSDAY 1998

My Dear Brothers in the Priesthood!

With mind and heart turned to the Great Jubilee, the solemn celebration of the second millennium of the birth of Christ and the beginning of the third Christian millennium, I wish to join you in invoking the Spirit of the Lord, to whom we dedicate in a special way the second stage of the spiritual journey of immediate preparation for the Holy Year of 2000.

Docile to the Spirit's loving inspirations, we prepare ourselves to share intensely in this *favorable time*, imploring from *the Giver of gifts* the graces necessary to discern the signs of salvation and to respond with full fidelity to the call of God.

An intimate bond unites our priesthood to the Holy Spirit and to his mission. On the day of our priestly ordination, by virtue of a unique outpouring of the Paraclete, the Risen One accomplished again in each of us what he accomplished in his disciples on the evening of Easter, and set us in the world as those who continue his mission.[1] This gift of the Spirit, with its mysterious sanctifying power, is the source and root of the special task of evangelization and of sanctification which is entrusted to us.

On Holy Thursday, the day when we commemorate the Lord's Supper, we contemplate Jesus, the Servant "obedient unto death,"[2] who institutes the Eucharist and Holy Orders as the supreme sign of his love. He leaves us this extraordinary testament of love, so that always and everywhere the mystery of his body and blood may be perpetuated and people may approach the inexhaustible source of grace. Is there a more appropriate and evocative moment than this for us priests to contemplate the work of the Holy Spirit in us and to implore his gifts in order to conform ourselves all the more to Christ, the Priest of the New Covenant?

1. The Holy Spirit, Creator and Sanctifier

Veni, Creator Spiritus,
Mentes tuorum visita,
Imple superna gratia,
Quæ tu creasti pectora.

Come, O Creator Spirit,
visit our minds.
Fill with your grace
the hearts you have created.

This ancient liturgical hymn reminds every priest of his ordination day, recalling the commitment made in that unique moment to be completely open to the action of the Holy Spirit. It reminds him as well of the Paraclete's special assistance and of the many moments of grace, joy and intimacy which the Lord has granted him to enjoy on his life's journey.

In the Creed of the Councils of Nicaea and Constantinople the Church proclaims her faith in the Holy Spirit as *the Lord and Giver of Life*, which expresses well the role he plays in the events of human life, particularly in accompanying the Lord's disciples on the way to salvation.

He is the Creator Spirit, whom Scripture presents at the dawn of human history as *"moving over the face of the waters"*[3] and, at the dawn of the work of redemption, as the one through whom the Word of God took flesh.[4]

One in substance with the Father and the Son, "in the absolute mystery of the Triune God, he is the Person-love, the uncreated gift, who is the eternal source of every gift that comes from God in the order of creation, the direct principle and, in a certain sense, the subject of God's self-communication in the order of grace. The mystery of the Incarnation constitutes the climax of this giving, this divine self-communication."[5]

The Holy Spirit directs the earthly life of Jesus towards the Father. Through his mysterious intervention, the Son of God is conceived in the womb of the Virgin Mary[6] and becomes man. It is again the Spirit who, descending on Jesus in the form of a dove at the baptism in the Jordan,[7] shows him to be Son of the Father; and, immediately afterwards, it is the Spirit who drives him into the desert.[8] After his victory over the temptations, Jesus begins his mission "in the power of the Spirit";[9] Jesus rejoices in the Holy Spirit and blesses the Father for his providential plan;[10] and by the Spirit's power he drives out demons.[11] In the drama of the cross, Jesus offers himself "through the eternal Spirit,"[12] through whom he then rose[13] and was "designated Son of God in power."[14]

On the evening of Easter, the Risen Jesus said to the Apostles gathered in the Upper Room: "Receive the Holy Spirit";[15] and, after promising another outpouring, he sent them out on the roads of the world, entrusted with the salvation of their brothers and sisters: "Go . . . and make disciples of all nations, baptizing them in the name of the Father and of the Son and of the Holy Spirit, teaching them to observe all that I have commanded you; and lo, I am with you always, to the close of the age."[16]

The presence of Christ in the Church of all times and all places *becomes living and powerful in the hearts of the faithful through the work of the Consoler.*[17] For our time too the Spirit is the "principal agent of the new evangelization. . . . [He] builds the kingdom of God within the course of history and prepares its full manifestation in Jesus Christ, stirring people's hearts and quickening in our world the seeds of the full salvation which will come at the end of time."[18]

2. Eucharist and Orders, Fruits of the Spirit

Qui diceris Paraclitus,
Altissimi donum Dei,
Fons vivus, ignis, caritas
Et spiritalis unctio.

O you who are called Paraclete,
gift of the Most High God,
living spring, fire, love,
anointing of the soul.

With these words, the Church invokes the Holy Spirit as *spiritalis unctio*, anointing of the soul. Through the anointing of the Spirit in the immaculate womb of Mary, the Father consecrated Christ the Eternal High Priest of the New Covenant who wished to share his priesthood with us, calling us to be his presence in history for the salvation of our brothers and sisters.

On Holy Thursday, *feria quinta in Cena Domini*, we priests are invited to give thanks with the whole community of the faithful for the gift of the Eucharist and to renew our sense of the grace of our unique vocation. We are also inspired to entrust ourselves to the action of the Spirit with fresh heart and full receptiveness, allowing ourselves to be conformed day by day to Christ the Priest.

In tender and mysterious language, the Gospel of John tells the story of the first Holy Thursday, when the Lord, at table with his disciples in the Upper Room, "having loved his own who were in the world, loved them to the end."[19] *To the end!*: until, that is, the institution of the Eucharist, which anticipates not only Good Friday and the sacrifice of the cross but the entire Paschal Mystery. At the Last Supper, Jesus takes bread in his hands and for the first time utters the words of consecration: "This is my body which will be given up for you." Then, over the chalice filled with wine, he proclaims the words of consecration: "This is the cup of my blood, the blood of the new and everlasting covenant. It will be shed for you and for all so that sins may be forgiven," and he adds: "Do this in memory of me." Thus, in the Upper Room and without the shedding of blood, Christ completes the sacrifice of the New Covenant, which will be accomplished in blood on the following day, when he will say on the cross: "*Consummatum est*"—"It is accomplished."[20]

By the power of the Holy Spirit, this sacrifice, offered once and for all on Calvary, is entrusted to the Apostles as the most blessed sacrament of the Church. Seeking the mysterious intervention of the Spirit, the Church begs before the words of consecration: "And so, Father, we bring you these gifts. We ask you to make them holy by the power of your Holy Spirit, that they may become the Body and Blood of your Son, our Lord Jesus Christ, at whose command we celebrate this Eucharist."[21] Without the power of God's Spirit, how could human lips ever make of bread and wine the Body and Blood of the Lord, even to the end of time? It is only *because of the power of God's Spirit* that the Church can profess unceasingly the great mystery of faith: "Christ has died! Christ is risen! Christ will come again!"

The Eucharist and Orders are fruits of the same Spirit: "As in the Mass it is he who works the transubstantiation of bread and wine into the Body and Blood of Christ, so in the Sacrament of Orders it is he who works the consecration of bishop or priest."[22]

3. The Gifts of the Holy Spirit

Tu septiformis munere
Digitus paternæ dexteræ
Tu rite promissum Patris,
Sermone ditans guttura.

Finger of God's right hand,
the Savior's promise,
send forth your seven gifts,
stir in us the word.

How could we not reflect in a special way upon the gifts of the Holy Spirit, which the tradition of the Church, following the biblical and patristic sources, describes as *the sevenfold gift ("sacrum Septenarium")*? Scholastic theology gave thorough attention to this doctrine, amply illustrating its meaning and its characteristics.

"God has sent the Spirit of his Son into our hearts, crying, 'Abba! Father!'"[23] "All who are led by the Spirit are children of God. . . . It is that very Spirit bearing witness to our spirit that we are children of God."[24] The words of the Apostle Paul remind us that the fundamental gift of the Spirit is sanctifying grace (*gratia gratum faciens*), with which we receive the theological virtues—faith, hope and charity—and all the infused virtues (*virtutes infusæ*), which enable us to act under the influence of the Holy Spirit. Unlike the charisms, which are bestowed for the service of others, these gifts are offered to all, because they are intended to lead the person to sanctity and perfection.

The names of the gifts are familiar. The Prophet Isaiah mentions them in sketching the figure of the future Messiah: "The spirit of the Lord shall rest on him, the spirit of wisdom and understanding, the spirit of counsel and might, the spirit of knowledge and fear of the Lord. His delight shall be in the fear of the Lord."[25] The number will become seven in the translation of the Septuagint and the Vulgate, which add *piety* and eliminate from Isaiah's text the repetition of *fear of the Lord*.

St. Irenaeus also makes mention of *the sevenfold gift* and adds: "God gave this same Spirit to the Church [. . .] sending the Consoler upon the earth."[26] St. Gregory the Great in turn illustrates the supernatural dynamic which the Spirit imparts to the soul, listing the gifts in inverse order: "Through the fear of the Lord we rise to piety, from piety then to knowledge, from knowledge we derive strength, from strength counsel, with counsel we move towards understanding and with intelligence towards wisdom and thus, by the sevenfold grace of the Spirit, there opens to us at the end of the ascent the entrance to the life of heaven."[27]

The *Catechism of the Catholic Church* regards the gifts of the Holy Spirit as a special awakening of the human soul and its faculties to the action of the Paraclete, and as such "they complete and perfect the virtues of those who receive them. They make the faithful docile in readily obeying divine inspirations."[28] This means that the moral life of Christians is sustained by these "permanent dispositions which make man docile in following the promptings of the Holy Spirit."[29] These bring to maturity the supernatural life which grace works in every human being. Indeed, the gifts are wonderfully well adapted to our spiritual dispositions, perfecting them and opening them in a special way to the action of God.

4. The Influence of the Gifts of the Holy Spirit upon Man

Accende lumen sensibus
Infunde amorem cordibus
Infirma nostri corporis
Virtute firmas perpeti.

Be light to the mind,
burning love in the heart.
Heal our wounds
with the balm of your love.

Through the Spirit, God comes intimately to the person and penetrates the human world more and more: "The Triune God who 'exists' in himself as a transcendent reality of interpersonal gift, giving himself in the Holy Spirit as gift to man, *transforms the human world from within*, from inside hearts and minds."[30]

This truth leads the great Scholastic tradition to give a privileged place to the action of the Spirit in human affairs and to stress God's saving initiative in the moral life. Neither negating our personality nor depriving us of freedom, God saves us in a way which surpasses all our plans and expectations. A logic such as this reveals the gifts of the Holy Spirit as "perfections of man which dispose him to follow readily the promptings of God."[31]

With the *seven gifts*, the believer can enter into a personal and intimate relationship with the Father, with the freedom proper to the children of God. This is what St. Thomas underscores in noting how the Holy Spirit leads us to act not because we are compelled but because we love. "The Holy Spirit," he writes, "leads the children of God in freedom, through love, not by compulsion, through fear."[32] The Spirit renders Christian action *God-like*, in harmony, that is, with God's way of thinking, loving and acting, so that the believer becomes a visible sign of the Blessed Trinity in the world. Sustained by the friendship of the Paraclete, by the light of the Word and by the love of the Father, the believer can boldly set out to imitate the perfection of God.[33]

The Holy Spirit moves on two fronts, as my revered predecessor, the Servant of God Paul VI, recalled: "The first of these fronts is the individual soul . . . , that point where I am 'I.' Into this depth of our existence, mysterious even to ourselves, there comes the breath of the Holy Spirit; in the soul it spreads with this first and greatest charism, which we call *grace* and which is like new life, at once empowering the soul to act in ways which surpass its natural capacity.'""The power of Pentecost moves" on a second front which is "the visible body of the Church. . . . Of course *'Spiritus ubi vult spirat'*;[34] but, in the economy decreed by Christ, it is through the apostolic ministry that the Spirit moves." In virtue of this ministry, priests receive power to impart the Spirit to the faithful "as those authorized to proclaim the word of God with authority, as those who guide the Christian people and offer them the sacraments,[35] which are simply springs of grace, sources that is of the Paraclete's sanctifying power."[36]

5. The Gifts of the Spirit in the Life of the Priest

Hostem repellas longius
Pacemque dones protinus;
Ductore sic te prævio
Vitemus omne noxium.

From the enemy defend us,
bring forth the gift of peace.
With your invincible hand
keep us from all harm.

The Holy Spirit reestablishes in the human heart full harmony with God and, assuring man of victory over the Evil One, opens him to the boundless measure of divine love. Thus the Spirit draws man from love of self to love of the Trinity, leading him into the experience of inner freedom and peace, and prompting him to make his own life a gift. And so, by means of *the sevenfold gift*, the Spirit guides the baptized to the point where they are wholly configured to Christ and are in complete harmony with the horizon of the kingdom of God.

This is the path along which the Spirit gently urges each of the baptized; but, in order that they may exercise their demanding ministry with profit, the Spirit reserves a special attention for those who have received Holy Orders. With the gift of *wisdom*, therefore, the Spirit leads the priest to evaluate all things in the light of the gospel, helping him to read in his own experience and the experience of the Church the mysterious and loving plan of the Father. With the gift of *understanding*, the Spirit fosters in the priest a deeper insight into revealed truth, pressing him to proclaim with conviction and power the Good News of salvation. With the gift of *counsel*, the Spirit illuminates the ministry of Christ so that the priest may direct his activities according to the perspectives of Providence, never allowing himself to be swayed by the judgments of the world. With the gift of *strength*, the priest is sustained in the hardships of his ministry and provided with the boldness (*parrhesia*) required for the proclamation of the gospel.[37] With the gift of *knowledge*, the priest is able to understand and accept the sometimes mysterious interweaving of secondary causes with the First Cause in the turn of events in the universe. With the gift of *piety*, the Spirit revives in the priest the relationship of intimate communion with God and of trusting surrender to his providence. Finally, with the gift of *fear of the Lord*, last in the hierarchy of gifts, the Spirit gives the priest a stronger sense of his own human weakness and of the indispensable role of divine grace, since "neither the one who plants nor the one who waters is anything, but only God who gives the growth."[38]

6.   The Spirit Leads Us into the Life of the Trinity

Per te sciamus da Patrem
Noscamus atque Filium
Teque utriusque Spiritum
Credamus omni tempore.

Light of eternal wisdom,
unveil to us the great mystery
of God the Father and the Son
united in one single Love.

How evocative it is to imagine these words on the lips of the priest who, together with the faithful entrusted to his pastoral care, walks the path which leads to Christ! The priest yearns to come with them to a true knowledge of the Father and the Son, and so to pass from the experience of the Paraclete's action in history "*per speculum in ænigmate*"[39] to the contemplation of the living and pulsating reality of the Trinity *"facie ad faciem."*[40] He is well aware that he faces "a long crossing on little boats" and that he soars heavenwards "on little wings."[41] But he can also count on the One who sent himself to teach the disciples everything.[42]

Once he has learnt to read the signs of God's love in his personal story, the priest, as he comes closer to the moment of his final encounter with the Lord, prays with ever greater urgency and intensity. This is the sign of a mature faith which wants to obey the will of the Father, the Son and the Holy Spirit.

The Paraclete, "stairway of our ascent to God,"[43] draws the priest to the Father, stirring in his heart a burning desire to see God's face. The Paraclete makes known to him everything concerning the Son, drawing him to Christ with a deepening nostalgia; and the Paraclete illumines the priest about his own person, that the priest may come to see the Spirit in his own heart and in history.

Therefore, among the joys and anxieties, the sufferings and hopes of the ministry, the priest learns to put his trust in the final victory of love, thanks to the unfailing action of the Spirit who, despite the limitations of men and institutions, leads the Church to live the mystery of unity and truth in its fullness. This enables the priest to trust in the power of God's word, which surpasses every human word, and in the power of grace, which overcomes human sins and shortcomings. In time of trial, this makes the priest strong, despite his human weakness, and makes him ready to return with all his heart to the Upper Room where, persevering in prayer with Mary and the disciples, he can rekindle the enthusiasm he needs in order to resume the toil of apostolic service.

7. Prostrate in the Presence of the Spirit

Deo Patri sit gloria
Et Filio, qui a mortuis
Surrexit, ac Paraclito
In sæculorum sæcula. Amen.

To God the Father be glory,
to the Son who is risen
and to the Spirit, the Paraclete,
For ages unending. Amen.

As we ponder the birth of our priesthood on this Holy Thursday, each of us recalls that most evocative moment when, on the day of our priestly ordination, we prostrated ourselves on the sanctuary floor.

This gesture of deep humility and obedient openness was splendidly designed to ready our souls for the sacramental imposition of hands, through which the Holy Spirit entered us to accomplish his work. Once we had risen from the floor, we knelt before the bishop to be ordained priests and our hands were anointed by him for the celebration of the Holy Sacrifice, while the congregation chanted:"living spring, fire, love, anointing of the soul."

These symbolic gestures, which point to the presence and action of the Holy Spirit, invite us to renew this experience day by day in order to strengthen in ourselves the gifts of the Spirit. It is important that he should continue to work in us and that his influence should guide our way, but more important still that it should be the Spirit who acts through us. When temptation sets its trap and human strength grows weak, then is the moment to invoke the Spirit more urgently, that he come to help us in our weakness and grant us the strength and prudence which God wills. Our heart must always be open to this action of the Spirit which exalts and ennobles human efforts and leads to that spiritual depth where we find knowledge and love of the ineffable mystery of God.

Dearest brothers in the priesthood! Since the solemn invocation of the Holy Spirit and the eloquent gesture of humility during our priestly ordination, the *fiat* of the Annunciation has resounded through our lives. In the silence of Nazareth, Mary became ever more open to the will of the Lord and, by the power of the Holy Spirit, she conceived Christ, the salvation of the world. This first obedience pervades her entire life on earth and reaches its climax at the foot of the cross.

The priest is called to match the *fiat* of Mary at all times, allowing himself to be led by the Spirit as she was. The Virgin will support him in his choice of evangelical poverty and will prepare him to listen humbly and sincerely to his brothers and sisters, that he may recognize in the drama of their lives and in their aspirations the "groans of the Spirit."[44] She will enable the priest to serve them with enlightened discretion, that he may teach them the values of the gospel. She will make him diligent in searching for "the things that are above,"[45] that he may witness convincingly to the primacy of God. The Virgin will help the priest to welcome the gift of chastity as the expression of a greater love which the Spirit awakens so that the love of God may come to birth in a host of brothers and sisters. She will lead him down the ways of evangelical obedience, that the Paraclete may draw him, beyond all his own plans, towards total acceptance of the mind of God.

Accompanied by Mary, the priest will be able to renew his consecration day after day; and the time will come when, trusting the guidance of the Spirit whom he has invoked on his journey as man and as priest, he will set forth upon the ocean of light which is the Trinity.

Through the intercession of Mary, Mother of Priests, I invoke upon you all a special outpouring of the Spirit of love.

Come, Holy Spirit! Come, that our service to God and our brothers and sisters may yield a rich harvest!

Assuring you once more of my affection and wishing you the consolations of God in your ministry, I impart to you with all my heart a special Apostolic Blessing.

From the Vatican, on 25 March, Solemnity of the Annunciation of the Lord in the year 1998, the twentieth of my Pontificate.

Endnotes

1. Cf. Jn 20: 21-23.
2. Phil 2: 8.
3. Gen 1: 2.
4. Cf. Mt 1: 20; Lk 1: 35.
5. *Dominum et vivificantem*, 50.
6. Cf. Lk 1: 35.
7. Cf. Lk 3: 21-22.
8. Cf. Lk 4: 1.
9. Lk 4: 14.
10. Cf. Lk 10: 21.
11. Cf. Mt 12: 28; Lk 11: 20.
12. Heb 9: 14.
13. Cf. Rm 8: 11.
14. Rom 1: 4.
15. Jn 20: 22.
16. Mt 28: 19-20.
17. Cf. Jn 14: 26.
18. *Tertio millennio adveniente*, 45.
19. Jn 13: 1.
20. Jn 19: 30.
21. Eucharistic Prayer III.
22. *Gift and Mystery*, p. 53.
23. Gal 4: 6.
24. Rom 8: 14, 16.
25. Is 11: 2-3.
26. St. Irenaeus, *Adversus hæreses*, III, 17, 3.
27. St. Gregory the Great, *Hom. In Hezech.*, II, 7, 7.
28. CCC 1831.

29. CCC 1830.
30. *Dominum et vivificantem*, 59.
31. St. Thomas, *Summa Theologiæ* I-II, q. 68, a. 2.
32. St. Thomas, *Contra gentiles*, Book IV, 22.
33. Cf. Mt 5: 48.
34. Jn 3: 8.
35. Cf. 1 Cor 4: 1.
36. *Homily at Pentecost*, 25 May 1969.
37. Cf. Acts 4: 29, 31.
38. 1 Cor 3: 7.
39. 1 Cor 13: 12.
40. *Ibid.*
41. St. Gregory of Nazianzus, *Theological Poems*, 1.
42. Cf. Jn 14: 26.
43. St. Irenaeus, *Adversus hæreses*, III, 24, 1.
44. Cf. Rom 8: 26.
45. Col 3: 1.

1999

Twenty-first Year of Pontificate

The Holy Father opened the year with a pastoral visit—this time to Mexico and the United States. His first stop took him to Mexico City, on January 22, where he proceeded to sign the Post-Synodal Apostolic Exhortation *Ecclesia in America*, on the state of the Catholic Church in the New World. Many of the issues covered in the document were included in the addresses he gave while in Mexico. From, for example, his talk to the diplomatic corps assigned to Mexico: "This continent could be the 'Continent of Hope' if the human communities and their ruling classes which comprise it were to adopt a common ethical foundation. The Catholic Church and the other great religious confessions in America can contribute specific elements to this common ethic, elements which free consciences from being limited by ideas deriving from mere incidental consensus. America and all humanity need essential reference points for all citizens and their political leaders."

All of the pope's public audiences during this visit to the world's largest Catholic diocese were heavily attended. One of the highlights was the January 24 Mass celebrated at the Hermanos Rodríguez Racetrack, which drew over two million faithful. The closing Mass for the visit to Mexico City was celebrated at the Basilica of Our Lady of Guadalupe.

The Holy Father left Mexico City on January 26 for a visit to the Archdiocese of St. Louis, which was then under the guidance of Archbishop Justin Rigali, a longtime friend and confidant of the pope. Though the visit was short, His Holiness was able to accomplish much during his stay. He met privately with President Bill Clinton, prayed with young people at St. Louis' Kiel Center, visited hospitalized children, celebrated Mass with over 70,000 people, and led the recitation of Vespers before attending departure ceremonies on the 27th.

As always, John Paul II paid special attention to young people throughout his trip. During his meeting with young people in St. Louis, the pope told them to listen to St. Paul, who "tells Timothy: 'let no one have contempt for your youth' (1 Tm 4: 12). He says this because youth is a time of special energies, special opportunities and special responsibilities. Christ and the Church need your special talents. Use well the gifts the Lord has given you!" This visit seemed to be very much on the Holy Father's mind even after his return to Rome, where he noted the particular influence America has on the rest of the world.

The unity of Christians having been one of Pope John Paul II's constant themes, the pope welcomed a pilgrimage of Chicago-area leaders of the

Roman Catholic and Greek Orthodox Church on February 15. Leading the visit were Francis Cardinal George, archbishop of Chicago, and
Metropolitan Iakovos, Orthodox bishop of the same city. The pilgrimage first went to Constantinople, to visit Patriarch Bartholomew, head
of the Orthodox church. The group then visited Rome. Encouraged by
the visit, the pope said, "we look in hope to a future when love will be
perfect among us and the world will therefore know that we are Christ's
disciples."

This note of hope, though, was soon replaced with the pope's concern
with political affairs in Central Europe. When war broke out in the Bal-
kans, the pope was deeply troubled by the violence. Constant in his
hope for peaceful resolutions, in an Easter homily he asked, "How could
we not note the glaring contrast between the invitation to mercy and
forgiveness echoing in today's liturgy and the violence of the tragic conflicts which are soaking the Balkan region in blood? May peace prevail
at last! Here I renew the appeal dictated not only to faith, but first of
all by reason: May people be able to live together in harmony in their
lands; May weapons be silenced and dialogue resumed!"

Further proof of the warming relations between Catholics and Orthodox,
though, again came to the attention of many with the most significant
trip of the year for Pope John Paul II. From May 7-9 the Holy Father
made a pastoral visit to Romania: the first time a Roman pontiff has
visited a primarily Orthodox country since the schism in the Church
first occurred almost 1,000 years ago.

John Paul's next major pastoral visit would be to his homeland, Poland.
The pope's seventh trip to his native country, the Holy Father chose as
his theme for the trip, "God is Love."

John Paul II said a Mass near Gdansk, Poland, to commemorate
the 1,000[th] anniversary of the martyrdom of St. Adalbert, Poland's principal patron and chief evangelizer. The work of Adalbert would end up
uniting the Polish people and therefore, in a way, create Poland. The fact
that the Mass was said near the birthplace of the Solidarity labor movement, which played such a large role in the end of Communist rule, was
no coincidence. From the pope's homily:

"At the time [of the end of Communist rule in Poland] I heard you say
in Gdansk: 'There is no freedom without solidarity.' Today is the occasion
to say: 'There is no solidarity without love.' Indeed, there is no happiness, there is no future for the individual and the nation without love,
without that love which forgives yet does not forget, which is sensitive
to the misfortunes of others, which does not seek its own advantage but
seeks the good of the other person; that love which is ever ready to help,
which is selfless and disposed to give generously. We are therefore called

to build the future based on love of God and neighbor, establishing the 'civilization of love.' Today the world and Poland need great-hearted men who serve with humility and love, who bless and do not curse, who conquer the land with blessing."

In August and September, the Holy Father gave a series of talks during his General Audiences on penance and conversion. During these talks he spoke of the effect of an individual's sins upon society, as well as society giving scandal to individuals. He also spoke of the need to honestly look at the history of the Church, admitting the wrongdoing of individual members while at the same time recognizing the good she has done over the past 2,000 years. Also, from this series, a talk on the Sacrament of Penance: "The merciful Father who embraces the prodigal son is the definitive icon of God revealed by Christ. First and foremost he is Father. It is God the Father who extends his arms in blessing and forgiveness, always waiting, never forcing any of his children."

In September, the pope responded strongly to another instance of the type of violence that the Holy Father has so often addressed and he himself witnessed. When East Timor voted for independence from Indonesia, anti-independence factions began terrorizing and killing the people of East Timor. In a statement from September 12, the pope said, "I cannot fail to express my deep indignation at yet another defeat for all sense of humanity, when, on the dawn of the third millennium, fratricidal hands are again being raised to kill and destroy without pity."

In the closing moths of the 1999, the approaching Jubilee Year 2000 received much attention from the Vatican. In September, the Holy See released new guidelines on how to earn indulgences, an act that the Church encourages during Jubilee Years. Also in recognition of the Jubilee Year, the pope began a renewed push for the forgiveness of international debt owed by poor countries to rich countries. Recognizing that paying these debts, which often charged usurious interest, often forced countries to ignore the basic needs of their people, the debt relicf proposal was supported by several international organizations which often were on opposite sides of other debates. The pope's call was heeded by U.S. President Bill Clinton, who said he would forgive the debts of the world's poorest countries if these countries promised that the money saved would go toward providing for basic human needs.

Also in preparation for the new millennium, the pope asked the Pontifical Council for Justice and Peace to publish "an authorized synthesis of the social doctrine of the Church similar to the *Catechism of the Catholic Church.*"

On October 1, John Paul II proclaimed three new patron saints for Europe—Saints Catherine of Siena, Bridget of Sweden, and Teresa Benedicta of the Cross (better known as Edith Stein). In choosing three women saints the pope wished to demonstrate, "the providential tendency in the Church and in the society of our time, recognizing more clearly the dignity of women and their special gifts." The announcement of the new patronesses of Europe coincided with the opening of the Second Special Assembly for Europe of the Synod of Bishops, which also took place on October 1. The assembly was given the theme "Jesus Christ, Alive in His Church, Source of Hope for Europe."

On October 31, the pope hailed an accord between the Roman Catholic Church and the Lutherans as a "milestone" on the path to Christian unity. Signed at Augsburg, Germany, the accord ended a dispute which launched the Protestant Reformation in the sixteenth century. Focusing mainly on the question of justification, the accord recognized that "through faith in Christ's saving work and not because of any merit on our part, we are accepted by God and receive the Holy Spirit."

In early November, John Paul II continued his appeal to countries torn by political and ethnic strife to resolve their problems peacefully, by employing the use of dialogue rather than military power and violent force. The pope paid special attention to Chechnya and Burundi, calling upon those in power to allow humanitarian groups into these countries to aid the victims of war.

On November 5, the pope embarked on a monumental trip to India and to Georgia, a former Soviet republic. While in India, the Holy Father issued a key document to prepare the Roman Catholic Church in Asia for the new millennium with a fresh call for evangelization across the continent. The document, which came amid protests by Hindu extremists against the Church's evangelization in India, represented the final report by the Polish pontiff on last year's Synod of Asian Bishops held at the Vatican. The pope, during an open-air Mass on November 7, said that freedom to practice or change one's religion must be considered a basic human right. He later attended a meeting with representatives of other religions, describing it as a further sign that Roman Catholics seek dialogue with other faiths.

In Georgia, a predominantly Orthodox country, the pope was greeted by Georgian Orthodox Patriarch Ilia II and President Eduard Shevardnadze. Tens of thousands of people packed into a stadium in Tbilisi, the Georgian capital, for a papal Mass on November 9. Among the worshippers were several Orthodox Georgians, witnessing to the improving relations between Roman Catholics and Orthodox Christians.

"Poverty, hunger, and disease can no longer be regarded as either normal or inevitable," John Paul II said in a message to the Rome-based Food and Agriculture Organization on November 18. Expressing his long-standing, yet increasingly urgent commitment to the defense of human rights, the pontiff also urged the United Nations to take the lead in a renewed effort to rid the world of these problems. He called upon the international organization to recognize that human rights"transcend the will of individuals and nations."

Pope John Paul's main focus in the month of December was immediate preparation for the Jubilee Year 2000. He made several appeals to people of all nations to approach the new millennium with a spirit of interior conversion."How can we do other but open the heart to contrition; how can we lock in pride and hypocrisy there, precluding the possibility of true peace?" the pope asked, speaking in St. Peter's Square on December 5. The following day, the Holy Father spoke about the benefits and challenges of globalization in the third millennium. He reminded the more affluent and developed countries that it was their responsibility to assist less fortunate countries in their struggle against poverty and disease, not leaving them behind in the rapid process of globalization. On December 11, the pope inaugurated the Sistine Chapel at the end of a twenty-year restoration project. Throughout the final weeks of 1999, the Bishop of Rome dedicated much time to preparing his city for the millions of pilgrims that would visit in the Jubilee Year.

At midnight on December 24, the Jubilee Year officially began with the opening of the Holy Door at St. Peter's Basilica. In what would perhaps be the most important moment in his entire pontificate, the Holy Father stood on the threshold not only of St. Peter's but also of a new age for the Church, a springtime of evangelization, and a new era of hope. On this glorious Christmas Eve, the pope stood ready with his flock to welcome Christ into the world and into the hearts of all humanity. With the eyes of the world upon him, Pope John Paul II stepped through the bronze door, leading the Church into the third millennium.

LETTER
OF THE HOLY FATHER
POPE JOHN PAUL II
TO ALL THE PRIESTS OF THE CHURCH
ON THE OCCASION OF HOLY THURSDAY 1999

"Abba, Father!"

Dear Brothers in the Priesthood!

My Holy Thursday appointment with you in this year which immediately precedes the Great Jubilee of the Year 2000 focuses on this invocation in which, the exegetes tell us, we hear the *ipsissima vox Iesu.* It is an invocation which encloses the unfathomable mystery of the Word made flesh, sent by the Father into the world for the salvation of humanity.

The mission of the Son of God reaches its fulfillment when, offering himself, he brings about our adoption as sons and daughters and, by giving the Holy Spirit, makes it possible for human beings to share in the very communion of the Trinity. In the Paschal Mystery, through the Son and in the Holy Spirit, God the Father stoops down to every man and woman, offering the possibility of redemption from sin and liberation from death. By grace we are the ministers of this reality.

1.   In the Eucharistic celebration we conclude the Opening Prayer with the words:"Through our Lord Jesus Christ, your Son, who lives and reigns with you, and the Holy Spirit, one God, forever and ever." He lives and reigns with you, Father! This conclusion, we may say, has the nature of an ascent: through Christ, in the Holy Spirit, towards the Father. This is also the theological outline behind the three-year period of preparation, 1997-1999: first the year of the Son, then the year of the Holy Spirit and now the year of the Father. This *ascending* movement is rooted, as it were, in the *descent* described by the Apostle Paul in the Letter to the Galatians. We pondered this text with particular intensity in the liturgy of the Christmas season:"When the fullness of time had come, God sent forth his Son, born of a woman, born under the Law, to redeem those who were under the Law, so that they might receive adoption as sons and daughters."[1]

Here we find expressed the descending movement: God the Father sends the Son to make us, in him, his adopted children. In the Pas-

chal Mystery, Jesus accomplishes the Father's plan by giving his life
for us. The Father then sends the Spirit of the Son to enlighten us
with regard to this extraordinary privilege:"Because you are sons and
daughters, God has sent the Spirit of his Son into our hearts, crying,
Abba, Father! So through God you are no longer slaves but sons and
daughters, and if sons and daughters, then heirs."[2] How can we fail
to notice the uniqueness of what the Apostle writes? He declares
that it is precisely the Spirit who cries out: *Abba,* Father! Historically
in fact, through the mystery of the Incarnation and Redemption, the
witness to the fatherhood of God has been the Son of God: it was
he who taught us to turn to God and call him "Father." He himself
invoked God as "my Father," and he taught us to pray to God with the
affectionate name of "our Father."Yet St. Paul tells us that it is through
the inner instruction of the Holy Spirit that the Son's teaching must,
in a certain sense, be brought to life in the soul of those who listen
to him. In fact, only through the work of the Spirit are we able to
adore God in truth, invoking him as "*Abba,* Father."

2.   I write these words to you, dear brothers in the priesthood, with
Holy Thursday in mind, picturing you gathered around your bishops
for the Chrism Mass. It is my earnest wish that, as you meet in the
communion of your local presbyterates, you may feel united with
the whole Church as she lives the year of the Father, the year which
is the prelude to the end of the twentieth century and, at the same
time, of the second Christian millennium.

In this perspective, how can we fail to give thanks to God as we think
of the hosts of priests who, in this vast span of time, have spent their
lives in the service of the gospel, sometimes to the point of the supreme sacrifice of life itself? In the spirit of the coming Jubilee, while
confessing the limitations and shortcomings of past Christian generations, and therefore also of the priests of those times, we recognize with joy that a very significant part of the Church's inestimable
service to human progress is due to the humble and faithful work of
countless ministers of Christ who, in the course of the millennium,
have been generous builders of the civilization of love.

The immensity of time! If time is always a movement away from the
beginning, it is also, when we think of it, a return to the beginning.
And this is of fundamental importance: if time did no more than take
us ever further from the beginning, and if its final orientation—the
recovery of the origin—were not clear, then our whole existence in
time would lack a definite direction. It would have no meaning.

Christ, "the Alpha and Omega . . . the One who is, who was and who is to come,"[3] has given direction and meaning to our human passage through time. He said of himself: "I came from the Father and have come into the world; now I am leaving the world and going to the Father."[4] Thus the Christ-event pervades the passage of each one of us. It is with Christ that we pass through time, going in the same direction that he has taken: towards the Father.

This becomes even more evident during the Sacred Triduum, the holy days *par excellence* during which we share, through the Mystery, in Christ's return to the Father through his passion, death and resurrection. Faith assures us that this journey of Christ to the Father, his Passover, is not an event which involves him alone. We too are called to be part of it. His Passover is our Passover.

So then, together with Christ we journey towards the Father. We do so through the Paschal Mystery, reliving those crucial hours when Christ, dying on the cross, cried out: "My God, my God, why have you abandoned me?"[5] and then: "All is accomplished,"[6] "Father, into your hands I commit my spirit."[7] These expressions from the gospel are familiar to every Christian and in a particular way to every priest. They speak of our living and of our dying. At the end of each day, we say in the Liturgy of the Hours: "Into your hands, Lord, I commend my spirit," to prepare ourselves for the great mystery of our passage, our own personal Easter experience, when Christ, by virtue of his death and resurrection, will take us to himself in order to present us to the Heavenly Father.

3.   "I thank you, Father, Lord of heaven and earth, that you have hidden these things from the learned and clever and revealed them to little children. Yes, Father, for this was your gracious will. All things have been given to me by my Father; and no one knows the Son except the Father, and no one knows the Father except the Son and those to whom the Son chooses to reveal him."[8] Yes, the Son alone knows the Father. He who "is in the bosom of the Father"—as St. John writes in his Gospel[9]—has brought the Father close to us, has spoken to us of him, has revealed to us his face and heart. At the Last Supper, when the Apostle Philip asks, "Show us the Father,"[10] Christ replies: "Have I been with you so long and yet you do not know me, Philip? . . . Do you not believe that I am in the Father and the Father in me?"[11] With these words, Jesus bears witness to the Trinitarian mystery of his own eternal generation from the Father as Son, the mystery which is the deepest secret of his divine Person.

The Gospel is a continuous revelation of the Father. When the twelve-year-old Jesus is found by Joseph and Mary among the teachers in the Temple, he replies to his Mother's words "My son, why have you done this to us?"[12] by referring to the Father: "Did you not know that I must be about the things of my Father?"[13] Even at the age of twelve he already has a clear awareness of the meaning of his own life, of his mission, which, from the first moment to the last, is wholly dedicated to "the things of the Father." This mission reaches its high point on Calvary, with the sacrifice of the cross, accepted by Christ in a spirit of obedience and filial devotion: "My Father, if it be possible, let this cup pass from me! Yet not as I will, but as you will. . . . Your will be done!"[14] And the Father in turn accepts the sacrifice of the Son, for he so loved the world that he gave his only-begotten Son, that man might not die but have eternal life.[15] Yes, the Son alone knows the Father and therefore he alone can reveal him to us.

4. *"Per ipsum, et cum ipso, et in ipso . . ."* "Through him, with him and in him, in the unity of the Holy Spirit, all glory and honor is yours, Almighty Father, forever and ever."

Spiritually united and visibly gathered in our cathedral churches on this special day, we give thanks to God for the gift of the priesthood. We give thanks for the gift of the Eucharist which we celebrate as priests. The doxology with which the Canon ends has a fundamental importance in every Eucharistic celebration. In a certain sense it expresses the crowning moment of the *Mysterium Fidei*, of the central core of the Eucharistic Sacrifice, realized at the moment when, by the power of the Holy Spirit, we effect the changing of the bread and wine into the Body and Blood of Christ, just as he himself did for the first time in the Upper Room. When the great Eucharistic Prayer reaches its climax, the Church, at that precise moment, in the person of the ordained minister, addresses these words to the Father: "Through him, with him and in him, in the unity of the Holy Spirit, all glory and honor is yours, Almighty Father." *Sacrificium laudis!*

5. After the assembly has responded with the solemn acclamation "Amen," the celebrant intones the *Our Father*, the *Lord's Prayer*. The succession of these two moments is very significant. The gospel relates that the Apostles, marvelling at the Master's inner recollection in his dialogue with the Father, asked him: "Lord, teach us to pray."[16] Then, for the first time, he spoke the words which would become the principal and most frequently used prayer of the Church and of individual Christians: the *Our Father*. When we, as the liturgical assembly, make these words our own during the Eucharistic celebration, they take on a particular eloquence. It is as though we were professing at that moment that Christ taught us his own prayer to the Father in the fullest and most definitive way by explaining it through his sacrifice on the cross.

It is in the context of the Eucharistic Sacrifice that the *Our Father*, recited by the Church, discloses its whole meaning. Each of its invocations acquires a special ray of truth. On the cross the name of the Father is supremely "hallowed," and his kingdom irrevocably comes; in the *"consummatum est"* his will is definitively done. And is not the petition "Forgive us our trespasses, as we forgive those . . ." perfectly reflected in the words of the Crucified Jesus: "Father, forgive them; for they know not what they do"?[17] Asking for our daily bread becomes more meaningful than ever when, under the species of "broken bread," we receive the Body of Christ in Eucharistic Communion. And does not the prayer, "Lead us not into temptation, but deliver us from evil," attain its greatest efficacy at the very moment when the Church offers to the Father the ultimate price of our redemption and our deliverance from evil?

6.   In the Eucharist the priest personally draws near to the inexhaustible mystery of Christ and of his prayer to the Father. He can immerse himself daily in this mystery of redemption and grace by celebrating Holy Mass, which retains its meaning and value even when, for a just reason, it is offered without the participation of the faithful, yet always for the faithful and for the whole world. Precisely because of this indissoluble bond linking him to the priesthood of Christ, the priest is the teacher of prayer, and the faithful can rightly put to him the same request which the disciples put one day to Jesus: "Teach us to pray."

The Eucharistic liturgy is a preeminent school of Christian prayer for the community. The Mass opens up a wide variety of possibilities for a sound pedagogy of the spirit. One of these is Adoration of the Blessed Sacrament, which is a natural prolongation of the Eucharistic celebration. Through Adoration, the faithful can enjoy a particular experience of "abiding" in the love of Christ,[18] entering ever more deeply into his filial relationship with the Father.

It is precisely in this context that I exhort all priests to carry out with confidence and courage their duty of guiding the community to authentic Christian prayer. This is a duty which no priest may ever forsake, even though the difficulties caused by today's secularized mentality can at times make it extremely demanding for him.

The powerful missionary impulse which Providence has inspired in the Church in our time, especially through the Second Vatican Council, is a challenge above all to her ordained ministers, calling them first of all to conversion. They themselves must be converted in order to convert others or, in other words, they themselves must experience intensely that they are children of God in order to help all the baptized to discover the dignity and joy of belonging to our Heavenly Father.

7.   On Holy Thursday we shall renew, dear brothers, our priestly promises. In doing so, we desire that Christ may somehow enfold us once more in his holy priesthood, in his sacrifice, in his agony in Gethsemane and his death on Golgotha, and in his glorious resurrection. Retracing, as it were, the footsteps of Christ in all these saving events, we discover his profound openness to the Father. And it is for this reason that every Eucharist in a way repeats the request of the Apostle Philip in the Upper Room:"Lord, show us the Father," and, in the *Mysterium Fidei*, Christ seems to reply each time:"Have I been with you so long, and yet you do not know me? . . . Do you not believe that I am in the Father and the Father in me?"[19]

This Holy Thursday, dear priests throughout the world, as we recall the anointing with chrism received on the day of our ordination, we shall proclaim with one voice and with renewed gratitude:

> *Per ipsum, et cum ipso, et in ipso,*
> *est tibi Deo Patri omnipotenti,*
> *in unitate Spiritus Sancti,*
> *omnis honor et gloria*
> *per omnia sæcula sæculorum. Amen!*

From the Vatican, on 14 March, the fourth Sunday of Lent, in the year 1999, the twenty-first of my Pontificate.

Endnotes

1. Gal 4: 4-5.
2. Gal 4: 6-7.
3. Rv 1: 8.
4. Jn 16: 28.
5. Mk 15: 34.
6. Jn 19: 30.
7. Lk 23: 46.
8. Mt 11: 25-27.
9. Jn 1: 18.
10. Jn 14: 8.
11. Jn 14: 9-10.
12. Lk 2: 48.
13. Lk 2: 49.
14. Mt 26: 39, 42.
15. Cf. Jn 3: 16.
16. Lk 11: 1.
17. Lk 23: 34.
18. Cf. Jn 15: 9.
19. Jn 14: 9-10.

2000

Twenty-second Year of Pontificate

Pope John Paul II began the new year by blessing the thousands of faith-ful who had gathered in St. Peter's Square to greet the new millennium and celebrate the start of the Great Jubilee. This Holy Year had been the focus of the Holy Father for quite some time as evidenced by his desig-nation of the three preceding years to the three persons of the Blessed Trinity. The pontificate of John Paul II, second-longest in history, was filled with constant prayer and sacrifice. In his reign as pope, he had been an unconquerable force and an unfaltering voice, speaking out for basic human rights and solidarity.

Following the opening of the Holy Door at St. Peter's, the pope pro-ceeded to open the remainder of the Holy Doors in Rome, located at the three other major basilicas. At one such ceremony at the Basilica of St. Mary Major on January 1, the Holy Father, while meditating on the role of the Blessed Virgin Mary, said, "Every person's history is written first of all in his mother's heart. Today, on the threshold of a new year and a new millennium, the Church returns to this inner experience of the Mother of God." He also proclaimed a World Day of Peace on the first of the year, asking all people around the world to reflect on the mys-tery of Christ. "As we cross the threshold of the new year, I would like to knock at the door of every home. I ask Christ to bless this moment of festivity and good wishes, that it may be the promising beginning of a new millennium filled with peace and joy."

From the moment that John Paul II was elected, he has made interna-tional peace a focal point of his pontificate. The pope said in his homily on January 1, "May the Lord grant you peace! This is the Church's wish to all humanity on the first day of the year, a day dedicated to the cel-ebration of the World Day of Peace."

In February, the pope paid special tribute to Catholic missionary priests and nuns who "have paid for their loyalty to Christ and humanity with the supreme testimony of blood, without giving up and without compro-mising. To them goes our tribute, our recognition and our thanks." These remarks were given during a special Jubilee Mass in St. Peter's Square for more than 20,000 priests and nuns. Thirty-one Roman Catholic mis-sionaries were killed in 1999 on five different continents. Eight of these missionaries were killed on the island of Timor when anti-independence militias attacked various Church institutions. This sparked a meeting between the Holy Father and Indonesian president Abdunahman Wahid in which they discussed the inter-religious situations throughout Asia and especially in Timor.

The pope completed his ninetieth international trip in late February when he returned from Egypt, where the covenant between God and man was first established. He traveled to Mount Sinai, where Moses received the Ten Commandments from God. While in Egypt, John Paul II met with Islam and Coptic Orthodox leaders, strongly promoting greater inter-religious dialogue and international peace.

On March 12, John Paul II presided over a ceremony that caught the attention of the world. For the first time, a pope publicly asked God for forgiveness for wrongs committed throughout history by members of the Church. The papal *mea culpa* was among the most significant and controversial gestures of the pontificate. Aware of the confusion it could cause, the pope felt that the these concerns were outweighed by the possibilities that could be opened up for reconciliation, especially on the eve of his trip to the Holy Land.

In late March, the Holy Father embarked on his trip to Israel and the Holy Land, fulfilling his life-long desire to walk in the footsteps of Christ. While there, the pope was adamant about making an "unplanned" visit to the Chapel of Golgotha, the site of Christ's crucifixion. In Jerusalem, the pope placed a prayer on the Western Wall reading, "Asking your forgiveness, we wish to commit ourselves to genuine brotherhood with the people of the covenant." It had been one of the Holy Father's most fervent wishes to reestablish positive relations with the Jewish people, who along with many others suffered greatly in the twentieth century.

In May, the Holy Father paid tribute to all Christians who suffered in the twentieth century, whether in Nazi concentration camps, Soviet *gulags* or Chinese labor camps, remarking that the number of Christian martyrs in this century is possibly greater than that of the early Church during its persecutions in Rome. "In the twentieth century, and maybe even more than in the first period of Christianity, there has been a vast number of men and women who bore witness to the faith through sufferings that were often heroic."

On May 13, the eyes of the Church again turned toward Fatima, where the pope beatified Francisco and Jacinta, two of the children to whom the Blessed Virgin appeared in 1917. In an unexpected announcement, Cardinal Sodano, the Vatican Secretary of State, revealed on the pope's behalf part of the "third secret" of Fatima, which "concerns above all the war waged by atheist systems against the church and Christians, and it describes the immense suffering endured by the witnesses to the faith in the last century of the second millennium. It is an interminable Way of the Cross led by the Popes of the twentieth century." The pope himself again expressed his conviction that the Blessed Virgin had protected him from death when he was shot.

Thousands of priests were in Rome on May 18 to celebrate with the pope on his eightieth birthday. John Paul II thanked God for letting him reach another milestone and enthusiastically greeted the throngs of well-wishers who turned out to celebrate the occasion with him. Dario-Cardinal Castrillon Hoyos offered some moving words in a special tribute to the aging but ever-strong pontiff: "We feel guided by a man of God who has won love and respect beyond any human barrier. The Lord prepared an athlete to tirelessly walk the paths of the world." The cardinal offered thanks for "those white hairs, for the suffering that has made you even dearer in our eyes, for your physically tired steps so spiritually intrepid." By linking the Jubilee for Priests with his own birthday, John Paul emphasized the primacy of his priestly vocation in his life.

The event described by John Paul II as the "heart of the Jubilee Holy Year" was the weeklong International Eucharistic Congress that he opened with a prayer service on June 18, joined by 50,000 pilgrims. The pope said in a sermon that, "from this eucharistic congress comes the invitation to renew our faith in the real presence of Christ in the sacrament of the altar [and] at the same time it inspires an urgent appeal for the reconciliation and unity of all believers." John Paul II expressed his hope that the eucharistic spirituality displayed at the event would be shared by believers around the world. He closed the event by kneeling in silent adoration before the Eucharist.

Other papal activities in June exhibited the vast scope of the pontiff's ministry, and his ability to be at home with the most powerful people in the world as well as the most needy members of his flock. On June 5, the pope received in audience the president of the Russian Federation, Vladimir Putin, and on June 15 lunched with 200 poor and homeless people to celebrate the Jubilee. In July the pope celebrated the Jubilee in prisons and made a visit to the Regina Cæli Prison in Rome.

One of the most memorable events of the Jubilee Year was the celebration of the fifteenth World Youth Day. More than two million young people were present at the Campus of Tor Vergata outside Rome for the Jubilee with the pope. The concluding Mass on August 20 was the largest gathering of people in European history. In his homily, the pope challenged the youth to seek Christ in their own life and then work to transform society, to "carry the proclamation of Christ into the new millennium." The Holy Father also expressed his deep joy and gratitude elicited by the sight of so many young people, to whom are entrusted the future of the Church.

On September 3, Pope John Paul II beatified Pope Pius IX and Pope John XXIII at a ceremony in St. Peter's Square. These two popes had called the First and Second Vatican Councils, respectively, and each had a large following of devoted faithful. On September 5, the Congregation for the Doctrine of the Faith published the declaration *Dominus Iesus*. The document, signed by Pope John Paul II, re-stated the Church's teaching that Jesus Christ is Lord and that he is the only path to salvation. It was a powerful declaration of the Faith to help prepare the Church for the New Evangelization of the third millennium.

In October, the Holy Father celebrated the Jubilee of Bishops and the Jubilee of Families, and welcomed a visit from Queen Elizabeth II and Prince Philip of England. During the Jubilee of Bishops, the pope and the bishops consecrated the world to Mary. The Holy Father prayed that the Blessed Virgin would help the bishops to "bring their faithful to a new profession of faith in Christ." The pope also celebrated the Sports Jubilee this month, urging athletes to "not let themselves become obsessed with physical perfection, or allow themselves to be overtaken by the harsh rules of production and consumerism." He also renewed his call for peace in the Middle East, urging a return to negotiations and dialogue.

On November 5, the English martyr St. Thomas More was proclaimed the patron saint of statesmen and politicians on the occasion of the Jubilee of Government Leaders and Politicians. The Holy Father stressed that there needed to be a new understanding of politics and called on politicians to "live your involvement in politics as a service to others." The pope made further appeals for peace in the Middle East in November, telling both Jews and Muslims to strive for a peaceful coexistence that would respect the dignity of all persons. On November 11, the pope celebrated the Farmers' Jubilee, warning farmers of the potential dangers of biotechnology and denouncing the waste of natural resources and the "intolerable scandal" of hunger. Also in November the pope celebrated the Jubilee of the Military and the Jubilee of the Laity.

Of the Jubilee for the Disabled, celebrated December 3, Pope John Paul said: "This celebration is certainly among the most significant and dear to me of all the Jubilee celebrations." At the Mass celebrated at the Basilica of St. Paul Outside the Walls, the pope was visibly moved and told the pilgrims gathered that "through your presence, you reaffirm that a disability represents not only a need, but above all a stimulus and a challenge" to a society that often values "gratification, appearances, speed, and efficiency." That month the pope also continued his campaign for the relief of third world debt, peace in the Middle East, and the end of sanctions on Iraq. At the Jubilee for Catechists, the Holy Father told missionaries, parochial school teachers, and other religious workers that their "message to men and women of our time cannot betray the truth and the continuity of the doctrine of the faith." On December 17, the pope celebrated the Jubilee of Entertainment, meeting with actors and performers from around the globe.

Despite pouring rain, thousands gathered in St. Peter's Square for the first ever open-air midnight Mass on Christmas Eve. The papal *Urbi et orbi* message, usually delivered from the balcony of the basilica, was given by the pontiff from the steps of St. Peter's. He called for a continued struggle against the culture of death in its many forms, including abortion and euthanasia. The Holy Father especially emphasized the Jubilee theme of charity, urging people to engage in "charity in action, showing itself in openness to and support of our many brothers and sisters sorely tried by want and suffering."

At midnight on December 31, the Holy Father came to his window and read his New Year's message to the crowd below in St. Peter's Square. The next day, designated World Day for Peace, saw the pope emphasizing prayer in the new millennium and urging leaders toward dialogue while reminding them that "we cannot call for peace and at the same time disdain life." On January 6, Pope John Paul II brought an end to the Church's millennial Holy Year. He closed the Holy Door of St. Peter's and celebrated Mass for more than 100,000 faithful in the square. The pope also issued the Apostolic Letter *Novo millennio ineunte,* in which he offered a program for the New Evangelization, his vision for the Church in the third millennium.

LETTER
OF THE HOLY FATHER
POPE JOHN PAUL II
TO ALL THE PRIESTS OF THE CHURCH
ON THE OCCASION OF HOLY THURSDAY 2000

My Dear Brother Priests!

1.   Jesus, "having loved his own who were in the world, loved them to the end."[1] Here in Jerusalem, in the place where according to tradition Jesus and the Twelve were present for the Passover meal and the institution of the Eucharist, I am deeply moved as I read once again the words with which the Evangelist John introduces the account of the Last Supper.

I give praise to the Lord for enabling me, in this Jubilee Year of the Incarnation of his Son, to trace the earthly footsteps of Christ, following the paths which he took from his birth in Bethlehem to his death on Golgotha. Yesterday I spent time in Bethlehem, in the cave of the Nativity. In the days to come I will visit various places associated with the life and ministry of the Savior, from the house of the Annunciation to the Mount of the Beatitudes and the Garden of Olives. Finally on Sunday I will be at Golgotha and the Holy Sepulcher.

Today, this visit to the Upper Room gives me an opportunity to survey the entire mystery of the Redemption. It was here that Christ gave us the immense gift of the Eucharist. Here too our priesthood was born.

A Letter from the Upper Room

2.   From this Upper Room I would like to address this letter to you, as I have done for more than twenty years, on Holy Thursday, the day of the Eucharist and "our" day *par excellence*. I am indeed writing to you from the Upper Room, thinking back to all that took place within these walls on that evening charged with mystery. Spiritually, I see Jesus and the Apostles seated at table with him. I think of Peter especially: it is as if I can see him, with the other disciples, watching in amazement the Lord's actions, listening with deep emotion to his words and, for all the burden of his frailty, opening himself to the mystery proclaimed here and soon to be accomplished. These are the hours of the great battle between the love which gives itself without

reserve and the *mysterium iniquitatis* which is imprisoned in hostility. The betrayal of Judas appears emblematic of humanity's sin. "It was night," observes the Evangelist John: [2] the hour of darkness, an hour of separation and of infinite sadness. Yet in the emotion-filled words of Christ the light of dawn already shines forth: "I will see you again and your hearts will rejoice, and no one will take your joy from you."[3]

3. We must never cease meditating anew on the mystery of that night. We should often return in spirit to this Upper Room, where we priests especially can feel in a sense "at home." With regard to the Upper Room, it could be said of us what the Psalmist says of the peoples with regard to Jerusalem: "In the register of peoples, the Lord will write: These were born here."[4]

In this holy room I naturally find myself imagining you in all the various parts of the world, with your myriad faces, some younger, some more advanced in years, in all the different emotional states which you are experiencing: for many, thank God, joy and enthusiasm, for others perhaps suffering or weariness or discouragement. In all of you I honor the image of Christ which you received at your consecration, the "character" which marks each of you indelibly. It is a sign of the special love which every priest has come to know and upon which he can always rely, either to move ahead joyfully or to make a fresh start with renewed enthusiasm, in the hope of ever greater fidelity.

Born of Love

4. "Having loved his own who were in the world, Jesus loved them to the end." In contrast to the Synoptic Gospels, the Gospel of John does not relate the institution of the Eucharist, of which Jesus had already spoken at length in Capernaum;[5] instead it dwells upon the washing of the feet. Even more than an example of humility offered for our imitation, this action of Jesus, so disconcerting to Peter, is a revelation of the radicalness of God's condescension towards us. In Christ, God has "stripped himself," and has taken on "the form of a slave" even to the utter abasement of the Cross,[6] so that humanity might have access to the depths of God's very life. The great speeches which in John's Gospel follow the washing of the feet and are in some way commentaries upon it, serve as an introduction to the mystery of Trinitarian communion to which we are called by the Father who makes us sharers in Christ by the gift of the Spirit.

This communion must be lived in compliance with the new commandment:"Love one another as I have loved you."[7] It is not by chance that the priestly prayer is the culmination of this"mystagogy," since it shows us Christ in his oneness with the Father, ready to return to him through the sacrifice of himself, and wanting only that the disciples come to share his unity with the Father:"As you, Father, are in me and I in you, may they too be one in us."[8]

5.   From the small group of disciples who heard these words the whole Church was formed, growing through time and space as"a people gathered together by the unity of Father, Son and Holy Spirit."[9] The profound unity of this new people does not mean that there are not different and complementary tasks in its life. Those whose task it is to renew *in persona Christi* what Jesus did at the Last Supper when he instituted the Eucharistic Sacrifice,"the source and summit of the entire Christian life"[10]are thus linked in a special way to those first Apostles. The sacramental character which distinguishes them by virtue of their reception of Holy Orders ensures that their presence and ministry are unique, indispensable and irreplaceable.

Almost two thousand years have passed since that moment. How many priests have repeated what Jesus did! Often they were exemplary disciples, saints, martyrs. How can we forget, in this Jubilee Year, the many priests who have witnessed to Christ by their lives, even to the shedding of blood? Such martyrdom has accompanied the entire history of the Church; it has also marked the century just passed, a century characterized by different dictatorial regimes hostile to the Church. From the Upper Room, I wish to thank the Lord for the courage of these priests. Let us look to them and learn to follow them in the footsteps of the Good Shepherd who"lays down his life for his sheep."[11]

A Treasure in Earthen Vessels

6.   It is true that in the history of the priesthood, no less than in the history of the whole People of God, the dark presence of sin is also found. Many times, the human frailty of priests has made it hard to see in them the face of Christ. Here in the Upper Room why should this amaze us? Not only did the betrayal of Judas reach its climax here, but Peter himself had to reckon with his weakness as he heard the bitter prediction of his denial. In choosing men like the Twelve, Christ was certainly under no illusions: it was upon this human weakness that he set the sacramental seal of his presence.

And Paul shows us why: "We bear this treasure in earthen vessels, so that it might be clear that this extraordinary power comes from God and not from us."[12]

For all the frailties of their priests, then, the People of God have not ceased to put their faith in the power of Christ at work through their ministry. How can we fail in this regard to recall the splendid witness of Saint Francis of Assisi? Humility led him not to seek the priesthood, but in his Testament he expressed his faith in the mystery of Christ present in priests, declaring that he would turn to them even if they had persecuted him, taking no account of their sin. "And I do this," he explained, "because the only thing I see of the flesh of the most high Son of God in this world is his most holy Body and Blood which they alone consecrate and they alone administer to others."[13]

7. From this place where Christ spoke the words instituting the Eucharist, I invite you, dear priests, to rediscover the "gift" and the "mystery" which we have received. To go to the heart of it, we must reflect upon the priesthood of Christ. Certainly, the entire People of God participates in this priesthood by Baptism. But the Second Vatican Council reminds us that, in addition to the participation proper to all the baptized, there exists another specific, ministerial participation which, although intimately linked to the first, nonetheless differs from it in essence.[14]

In the context of the Jubilee of the Incarnation, we can approach the priesthood of Christ from a particular perspective. The Jubilee invites us to contemplate the intimate link between Christ's priesthood and the mystery of his person. The priesthood of Christ is not "incidental," a task which he might or might not have assumed: rather, it is integral to his identity as the Son Incarnate, as God-made-man. From now on, the relationship between mankind and God passes wholly through Christ: "No one comes to the Father, except through me."[15] This is why Christ is a priest endowed with an eternal and universal priesthood, of which the priesthood of the first Covenant was a prefigurement and a preparation.[16] He has exercised it fully from the moment he took his seat as High Priest "at the right hand of the throne of the Majesty in heaven."[17] From that time forth, the very nature of human priesthood changed: now there is but one priesthood, that of Christ, which can be shared and exercised in different ways.

Sacerdos et Hostiu

8.   At the same time, the meaning of sacrifice, the priestly act *par excellence,* was brought to perfection. On Golgotha, Christ made his own life an offering of eternal value, a "redemptive" offering which has reopened for ever the path of communion with God which had been blocked by sin.

The Letter to the Hebrews casts light upon this mystery by placing on the lips of Christ the words of Psalm 40: "You desired neither sacrifice nor offering, but instead you prepared a body for me . . . Here I am . . . I come to do your will, O God."[18] According to the author of the Letter, these prophetic words were spoken by Christ when he first came into the world. They express his mystery and his mission. They begin to be accomplished from the very moment of the Incarnation and reach their completion in the sacrifice of Golgotha. From that time forward, every priestly offering is but a representing to the Father of the one offering of Christ, made once for all.

Sacerdos et Hostia! Priest and Victim! This sacrificial aspect is a profound mark of the Eucharist; it is also an essential dimension of the priesthood of Christ and, therefore, of our own priesthood. In the light of this, let us read once again the words we speak every day, words which echoed for the first time here in the Upper Room: "Take this, all of you, and eat it: this is my Body which will be given up for you . . . Take this, all of you, and drink from it: this is the cup of my Blood, the Blood of the new and everlasting Covenant which will be shed for you and for all, so that sins may be forgiven."

These are the words we find in the Evangelists and in Paul, with largely converging redactional forms.

They were spoken in this Room in the late evening of Holy Thursday. By giving the Apostles his Body to eat and his Blood to drink, Jesus declared the deepest truth about what he would do shortly thereafter on Golgotha. For in the Bread of the Eucharist is present the very Body born of Mary and offered on the Cross:

> *Ave verum Corpus natum*
> *de Maria Virgine,*
> *Vere passum, immolatum*
> *in cruce pro homine.*

9. How can we not return ever anew to this mystery, which contains the entire life of the Church? For two thousand years, this Sacrament has given nourishment to countless believers. It has been the source of a great river of grace. How many saints have found in it not only the pledge, but as it were the foretaste of Heaven!

Let us allow ourselves to be carried along by the contemplative impulse, rich in poetry and theology, which inspired Saint Thomas Aquinas to sing of the mystery in the words of the hymn *Pange Lingua*. Today, in this Upper Room, these words come to me as an echo of the voice of so many Christian communities throughout the world, of so many priests, consecrated persons and lay faithful, who each day pause in adoration of the Eucharistic mystery:

> *Verbum caro, panem verum*
> *verbo carnem efficit,*
> *fitque sanguis Christi merum,*
> *et, si sensus deficit,*
> *ad firmandum cor sincerum*
> *sola fides sufficit.*

Do this in memory of me

10. The mystery of the Eucharist, which proclaims and celebrates the Death and Resurrection of Christ until he comes again, is the heart of the Church's life. For us it also has a very special meaning, for it stands at the center of our ministry. Our ministry is not of course limited to celebrating the Eucharist: it is a service which includes the proclamation of the Word, the sanctification of the faithful through the Sacraments, and the leadership of God's People in communion and service. But the Eucharist is the point from which everything else comes forth and to which it all returns. Our priesthood was born in the Upper Room together with the Eucharist.

"Do this in memory of me": [19] although addressed to the whole Church, the words of Christ are entrusted as a particular task to those who carry on the ministry of the first Apostles. It is to them that Jesus hands on the action which he has just performed—changing bread into his Body and wine into his Blood—the action in which he appears as Priest and Victim. It is the will of Christ that henceforth his action should also become sacramentally the action of the Church through the hands of priests. In saying "Do this," he refers not only to the action, but also to the one who is called to act; in other words, he institutes the ministerial priesthood, which thus becomes one of the essential elements of the Church.

11. This action is to be done "in his memory": these words are important. The Eucharistic action celebrated by priests will make present in every Christian generation, in every corner of the earth, the work accomplished by Christ. Wherever the Eucharist is celebrated, the bloody sacrifice of Calvary will be made present in an unbloody manner; there Christ himself, the Redeemer of the world, will be present.

"Do this in memory of me." Hearing these words once again within the walls of the Upper Room, it is natural to try to imagine what Christ felt. These were the dramatic hours which preceded the Passion. The Evangelist John evokes the intensity of the Master's words as he prepares the Apostles for his departure. What sadness was in their eyes: "Because I have said these things to you, sorrow has filled your hearts."[20] But Jesus reassures them: "I will not leave you orphans; I will come to you."[21] Although the Paschal Mystery will take him from their sight, he will be more present than ever in their life, "always, to the close of the age."[22]

A Memorial Which Makes Present

12. Christ's presence will be expressed in many ways. But of these his Eucharistic presence will certainly be supreme: no mere remembrance, but a "memorial" which makes present what it commemorates; not a symbolic evocation of the past, but the living presence of the Lord in the midst of his own. The enduring guarantee of this will be the Holy Spirit, constantly poured out in the Eucharistic celebration so that the bread and wine may become the Body and Blood of Christ. He is the same Spirit who on the evening of Easter, in this Upper Room, was "breathed" upon the Apostles,[23] and who found them here still, gathered with Mary, on the day of Pentecost. It was then that he came upon them as a strong wind and fire,[24] and impelled them to go to the ends of the earth to proclaim the Word and gather together the People of God in the "breaking of the bread."[25]

13. Two thousand years after the birth of Christ, in this Jubilee Year, we especially need to remember and ponder the truth of what we might call his "Eucharistic birth." The Upper Room is the place of this "birth." Here began a new presence of Christ for the world, a presence which constantly occurs wherever the Eucharist is celebrated and a priest lends his voice to Christ, repeating the sacred words of institution.

This Eucharistic presence has accompanied the two thousand years of the Church's history, and it will do so until the end of time. For us it is both a joy and a source of responsibility to be so closely linked to this mystery. Today we want to become more deeply aware of this presence, our hearts filled with wonder and gratitude, and in this spirit to enter the Easter Triduum of the Passion, Death and Resurrection of Christ.

What the Upper Room Hands On to Us

14. My dear brother priests, who on Holy Thursday gather in the Cathedrals around your Pastors, just as the presbyters of the Church in Rome gather around the Successor of Peter, please accept these reflections, my meditation in the evocative setting of the Upper Room! It would be hard to find a place better able to stir thoughts of both the Eucharistic mystery and the mystery of our priesthood.

Let us remain faithful to what the Upper Room "hands on" to us, to the great gift of Holy Thursday. May we always celebrate the Holy Eucharist with fervor. May we dwell long and often in adoration before Christ in the Eucharist. May we sit at the "school" of the Eucharist. Through the centuries, countless priests have found in the Eucharist the consolation promised by Jesus on the evening of the Last Supper, the secret to overcoming their solitude, the strength to bear their sufferings, the nourishment to make a new beginning after every discouragement, and the inner energy to bolster their decision to remain faithful. The witness which we give to the People of God in celebrating the Eucharist depends in large part upon our own personal relationship with the Eucharist.

15. Let us rediscover our priesthood in the light of the Eucharist! Let us help our communities to rediscover this treasure in the daily celebration of Holy Mass, and especially in the more solemn Sunday assembly. Through your apostolic labors, may love for Christ present in the Eucharist grow stronger. This is a particularly important goal in this Jubilee Year. I think of the International Eucharistic Congress to be held in Rome from June 18 to 25, which has as its theme Jesus Christ, the one Savior of the World, Bread for our Life. It will be a highlight of the Great Jubilee, which is meant to be "an intensely Eucharistic year."[26] The Congress will emphasize the profound link between the mystery of the Incarnation of the Word and the Eucharist, the Sacrament of Christ's Real Presence.

From the Upper Room, I embrace you in the Eucharist. May the image of Christ surrounded by his own at the Last Supper fill each of us with a vibrant sense of brotherhood and communion. Great painters have employed their finest gifts in depicting the face of Christ among his Apostles in the scene of the Last Supper: how can we forget Leonardo's masterpiece? But only the Saints, by the intensity of their love, can enter the depths of this mystery, leaning their head, as it were, like John, on the Lord's breast.[27] Here in fact we come to the height of love: "having loved his own who were in the world, he loved them to the end."

16. I would like to conclude these thoughts, which I affectionately entrust to your meditation, with the words of an ancient prayer:

"We thank you, our Father,
for the life and the knowledge
which you have revealed to us
through Jesus, your servant.
Glory to you through the ages!
As the bread we have broken
was scattered far and wide upon the hills,
but when harvested becomes one,
so may the Church be gathered
into your Kingdom
from the farthest reaches of the earth . . . .

Lord almighty, you created the universe
for the glory of your name;
you gave men food and drink
to strengthen them,
that they might give you thanks;
but to us you have given
spiritual food and drink,
and eternal life through your Son . . . .

Glory to you through the ages!"[28]

From the Upper Room, dear brother priests, I embrace all of you in spirit and I cordially impart my blessing.

From Jerusalem, 23 March, in the year 2000, the twenty-second of my Pontificate.

Endnotes

1. Jn 13: 1.
2. Jn 13: 30.
3. Jn 16: 22.
4. Ps 86: 6.
5. Cf. Jn 6: 26-65.
6. Cf. Phil 2: 7.
7. Jn 13: 34.
8. Jn 17: 21.
9. Saint Cyprian, *De Orat. Dom.*, 23.
10. *Lumen gentium*, 11.
11. Jn 10: 11.
12. 2 Cor 4: 7.
13. Fonti Francescane, 113.
14. Cf. *Lumen gentium*, 10.
15. Jn 14: 6.
16. Cf. Heb 9: 9.
17. Heb 8: 1.
18. Heb 10: 5-7; cf. Ps 40: 7-9.
19. Lk 22: 19.
20. Jn 16: 6.
21. Jn 14: 18.
22. Mt 28: 20.
23. Cf. Jn 20: 22.
24. Cf. Acts 2: 1-4.
25. Cf. Acts 2: 42.
26. *Tertio millennio adveniente*, 55.
27. Cf. Jn 13: 25.
28. *Didache* 9: 3-4; 10: 3-4.

2001

Twenty-third Year of Pontificate

Pope John Paul II began the year 2001 by issuing the Apostolic Letter *Novo millennio ineunte,* which embodied his vision for the future of the Church and provided a guide for Catholics in the new millennium. The pontiff said in the letter that the Church must be committed to promoting justice in the world and bringing the light of Christ to all nations. The apostolic letter provided a fitting transition from the celebration of the Great Jubilee of the year 2000 to the beginning of the New Evangelization. On January 1, the thirty-fourth World Day for Peace, the Holy Father petitioned for peace in the world, especially in the Holy Land, where the violence between Israelis and Palestinians continued to escalate.

On January 8, the United States House of Representatives awarded Pope John Paul II the Congressional Gold Medal, its highest civilian award. In an audience with American legislators in Rome, the pope was praised for using "his moral authority to hasten the fall of godless totalitarian regimes." In his yearly "state of the world" address, given a few days later, the pope denounced abortion, euthanasia, and other violence that continued around the globe. He also warned against the misuse of science and the neglect of the environment.

On January 21, the Holy Father announced the names of thirty-seven new cardinals. Among them were Edward Cardinal Egan, Archbishop of New York, Theodore Cardinal McCarrick, Archbishop of Washington, D.C., and Avery Cardinal Dulles, a prominent American Jesuit theologian. A week later, the pope announced an unprecedented seven more cardinals, raising the total number of voting cardinals to 135, the most there have ever been. The cardinals were officially installed at a consistory in Rome on February 21.

On February 18, the pope marked the 1700th anniversary of the Baptism of the Armenian People. The Divine Liturgy of the Armenian rite was celebrated on the occasion in St. Peter's Basilica and the pope issued the Apostolic Letter *Dio meraviglioso.* On March 11, the Holy Father beatified 233 Spanish martyrs who were killed from 1936 to 1939, during the Spanish Civil War. In his homily, the pope emphasized that the martyrs, who are an "example of courage and constancy in faith, aided by the grace of God," died for the Faith, not for politics. The Holy Father also made a special appeal for an end to the "perverse logic" of terrorism in Spain. Further appeals for peace were made by the pope when the bishops of Arab nations made their *ad limina* visit later in the month.

The bishops were urged to promote peace in their increasingly violent corner of the globe.

The Holy Father's annual Lenten retreat was preached by Francis Cardinal George, archbishop of Chicago. The cardinal's meditations drew from St. Luke's Gospel and centered on the themes of conversion, freedom, and communion and their role in the Church in the third millennium. After the retreat, the pope summed it up, saying that "faith in Christ is freedom borne from personal conversion, which opens to communion with all men."

In May, John Paul II made a historic and monumental trip to Greece and Damascus. In what was really the final action of the Holy Year 2000, the pope fulfilled his long-standing wish to "walk in the footsteps of St. Paul." Although there was strong resistance to the pope's trip among some of the Orthodox clergy in Greece, the pilgrimage took place without any major incidents. In Damascus, the Holy Father made history by being the first pope to enter an Islamic mosque. Although the Roman pontiff and the Muslim leaders did not pray together, they exchanged speeches and advanced the cause for improved relations between Islam and Catholicism. The pope also met with the president of Syria, Bashar Assad, and discussed peace in the Middle East.

In late May, all of the cardinals of the Church met in the Vatican for a special consistory. The pope summoned the cardinals, who are by tradition his advisors, in order to discuss the Apostolic Letter *Novo millennio ineunte*, issued by the pope at the beginning of the year. In charting the course of the Church in the third millennium, the consistory looked in particular at the role of the papacy and its implications for future efforts at re-unification with other Christian churches.

LETTER
OF THE HOLY FATHER
POPE JOHN PAUL II
TO ALL THE PRIESTS OF THE CHURCH
ON THE OCCASION OF HOLY THURSDAY 2001

Dear Brothers in the Priesthood!

1.   On the day when the Lord Jesus gave to the Church the gift of the Eucharist, and with it instituted our priesthood, I cannot but address to you — as is now traditional — a word of friendship and, I might say, of intimacy, wishing to join you in thanksgiving and praise.

Lauda Sion, Salvatorem, lauda ducem et pastorem, in hymnis et canticis! Great indeed is the mystery of which we have been made ministers. A mystery of love without limit, for "having loved his own who were in the world, he loved them to the end";[1] a mystery of unity, which from the source of Trinitarian life is poured out upon us in order to make us "one" in the gift of the Spirit;[2] a mystery of divine *diakonia* which prompts the Word made flesh to wash the feet of his creation, thus showing that service is the high road in all genuine relationships between people: "You also should do as I have done to you."[3]

Of this great mystery we have been made, in a special way, witnesses and ministers.

2.   This is the first Holy Thursday after the Great Jubilee. What we have experienced together with our communities, in that special celebration of mercy, two thousand years after the birth of Jesus, now becomes the incentive to continue the journey. *Duc in altum!* The Lord invites us to put out into the deep, with trust in his word. Let us learn from the Jubilee experience and persevere in the task of bearing witness to the Gospel with the enthusiasm that contemplating the face of Christ engenders in us!

As I in fact stressed in my Apostolic Letter *Novo millennio ineunte*, we must start out from Christ, in order to be open, in him, with the "ineffable" groanings of the Spirit,[4] to the embrace of the Father: "Abba! Father!"[5] Christ must be our point of departure in rediscovering the source and the profound rationale of our brotherhood: "As I have loved you, you also must love one another."[6]

3.   Today I wish to express to each of you my gratitude for all that you did during the Jubilee Year to ensure that the people entrusted to your care might experience more intensely the saving presence of the Risen Lord. At this time, I am also thinking of the work you do every day, work that is often hidden and, without making headlines, causes the Kingdom of God to advance in people's minds and hearts. I want you to know of my admiration for this ministry, discreet, tenacious and creative, even if it is sometimes watered by those tears of the soul which only God sees and "stores in his bottle."[7] Your ministry is all the more admirable when it is tested by the resistance of a widely secularized environment, which subjects priestly activity to the temptations of fatigue and discouragement. You well know that such daily commitment is precious in the eyes of God.

At the same time, I wish to echo the voice of Christ who continuously calls us to deepen our relationship with him. "Behold, I stand at the door and knock."[8] Chosen to proclaim Christ, we are first of all invited to live in intimacy with him: we cannot give to others what we ourselves do not have! There is a thirst for Christ which, despite many appearances to the contrary, emerges even in contemporary society; it is present among all the inconsistencies of new forms of spirituality; it can be seen even where, on important ethical issues, the Church's witness becomes a sign of contradiction. This thirst for Christ — whether conscious or not — cannot be quenched with empty words. Only authentic witnesses can communicate in a credible way the word that saves.

4.   In my Apostolic Letter *Novo millennio ineunte* I said that the true legacy of the Great Jubilee is the experience of a more intense encounter with Christ. From among the many aspects of this encounter, today I would like to choose for this reflection the theme of sacramental reconciliation: this too was a central feature of the Jubilee Year, also because it is closely connected with the gift of the Jubilee indulgence.

Here in Rome, and I am sure that you too had similar experiences in your local churches, one of the most visible manifestations of the Jubilee was certainly the exceptional numbers of people receiving the Sacrament of mercy. Even non-religious observers were impressed by this. The confessionals in Saint Peter's and in the other Basilicas were "stormed", as it were, by pilgrims, who often had to wait in long queues, patiently waiting their turn. The interest shown by young people in this Sacrament during the splendid week of their Jubilee was particularly significant.

5.   As you well know, in recent decades this Sacrament has passed through a certain crisis, for a number of reasons. Precisely in order to tackle this crisis, in 1984 a Synod was held, the conclusions of which were presented in the Post-Synodal Apostolic Exhortation *Reconciliatio et Pænitentia*.

It would be naive to think that the mere intensifying of the practice of the Sacrament of forgiveness during the Jubilee Year is proof of a definitive turnabout. It was nevertheless an encouraging sign. It impels us to recognize that the profound needs of the human spirit, to which God's saving plan responds, cannot be cancelled out by temporary crises. We should accept this Jubilee indication as a sign from on high, and make it a reason for renewed boldness in re-proposing the meaning and practice of this Sacrament.

6.   But it is not so much on pastoral problems that I wish to dwell. Holy Thursday, the special day of our vocation, calls us to reflect above all on "who we are," and in particular on our journey to holiness. It is from this source too that our apostolic zeal will flow.

So, as we gaze upon Christ at the Last Supper, as he becomes for us the "bread that is broken," as he stoops down in humble service at the feet of the Apostles, how can we not experience, together with Peter, the same feeling of unworthiness in the face of the greatness of the gift received? "You shall never wash my feet."[9] Peter was wrong to reject Christ's gesture. But he was right to feel unworthy of it. It is important, on this day of love *par excellence*, that we should feel the grace of the priesthood as a super-abundance of mercy.

Mercy is the absolutely free initiative by which God has chosen us: "You did not choose me but I chose you."[10]

Mercy is his deigning to call us to act as his representatives, though he knows that we are sinners.

Mercy is the forgiveness which he never refuses us, as he did not refuse it to Peter after his betrayal. The avowal that "there will be more joy in heaven over one sinner who repents than over ninety-nine righteous persons who need no repentance"[11] also holds true for us.

7.   Let us then rediscover our vocation as a "mystery of mercy." In the Gospel we find that Peter receives his special ministry with precisely this spiritual attitude. His experience is indicative for all those who have received the apostolic task in the different grades of the Sacrament of Orders.

Our thoughts turn to the scene of the miraculous catch of fish as described in the Gospel of Luke.[12] Jesus asks Peter for an act of trust in his word, inviting him to put out into the deep for a catch. A disconcerting request, humanly speaking: after a sleepless and exhausting night spent casting the nets with no result, how could one believe him? But trying again, "at Jesus' word," changes everything. The fish arrive in such quantities as to tear the nets. The Word reveals his power. The result is wonder, but also fear and trembling, as when we are unexpectedly struck by an intense beam of light which lays bare all our personal limits. Peter exclaims: "Depart from me, for I am a sinful man, O Lord."[13] But scarcely has he uttered his admission when the Master's mercy becomes for him the beginning of new life: "Do not be afraid; henceforth you will be catching men."[14] The "sinner" becomes a minister of mercy. From a fisher of fish to a "fisher of men"!

8.   Dear priests, this is a great mystery: Christ was not afraid to choose his ministers from among sinners. Is not this our own experience? It is Peter once again who will become more aware of this in his touching dialogue with Jesus after the Resurrection. Before entrusting him with the mandate to care for the flock, the Master asks the embarrassing question: "Simon, son of John, do you love me more than these?"[15] The one being questioned is the very man who a few days earlier had denied him three times. It is easy to understand the humble tone of his reply: "Lord, you know everything; you know that I love you."[16] And it is on the basis of this love, which knows all too well its own frailty, a love professed with both trust and hesitation, that Peter receives the commission: "Feed my lambs," "feed my sheep."[17] It will be on the basis of this love, strengthened by the fire of Pentecost, that Peter will be able to accomplish the ministry entrusted to him.

9.   And is it not within an experience of mercy that Paul's vocation too is born? No one experienced the gratuitousness of Christ's choice as vividly as he did. His past as a ferocious persecutor of the Church seared itself deep into his soul: "I am the least of the apostles, unfit to be called an apostle, because I persecuted the Church of God."[18]

Yet, far from stifling his enthusiasm, this memory made it soar. The more he was embraced by mercy, the more Paul felt the need to bear witness to it and to let it shine forth in his life. The "voice" which speaks to him on the road to Damascus leads him to the heart of the Gospel, and enables him to discover the Gospel as the merciful love of the Father who in Christ is reconciling the world to himself. On this basis, Paul will also understand apostolic service as the ministry of reconciliation: "All this is from God, who through Christ reconciled us to himself and gave us the ministry of reconciliation; that is, in Christ God was reconciling the world to himself, not counting men's trespasses against them, and entrusting to us the message of reconciliation."[19]

10. Dear priests, the witness of Peter and Paul contains valuable pointers for us. Their lives invite us to live the gift of the ministry with a sense of endless thanksgiving: nothing is due to our merits, all is grace! The experience of the two Apostles prompts us to abandon ourselves to the mercy of God, to give over to him in sincere repentance our frailties, and with his grace to set out again on our journey to holiness. In *Novo millennio ineunte* I indicated the commitment to holiness as the first element of all wise pastoral "planning." It is the basic task of all believers, so how much more must it be for us![20]

For this very reason it is important for us to rediscover the Sacrament of Reconciliation as a fundamental means of our sanctification. Approaching a brother priest in order to ask for the absolution that we so often give to the faithful enables us to live the great and consoling truth that, before being ministers, we are all members of the same people, a "saved" people. What Augustine said of his task as bishop is true also of the service of priests: "If I am anxious about being for you, I am consoled by being with you. For you I am a bishop, with you I am a Christian. . . . In the first there is danger, in the second there is salvation."[21] It is wonderful to be able to confess our sins, and to hear as a balm the word which floods us with mercy and sends us on our way again. Only those who have known the Father's tender embrace, as the Gospel describes it in the parable of the Prodigal Son —"he embraced him and kissed him"[22] — only they can pass on to others the same warmth, when after receiving pardon themselves they administer it to others.

11. On this holy day, therefore, let us ask Christ to help us to rediscover, for ourselves, the full beauty of this Sacrament. Did not Jesus
himself help Peter to make this discovery? "If I do not wash you, you
have no part in me."[23] Jesus of course was not referring directly to the
Sacrament of Reconciliation, but in some sense he was pointing to it,
alluding to that process of purification which would begin with his
redeeming Death, and to its sacramental application to individuals
down the ages.

Dear priests, let us make regular use of this Sacrament, that the Lord
may constantly purify our hearts and make us less unworthy of the
mysteries which we celebrate. Since we are called to show forth the
face of the Good Shepherd, and therefore to have the heart of Christ
himself, we more than others must make our own the Psalmist's
ardent cry: "A pure heart create for me, O God, put a steadfast spirit
within me."[24] The Sacrament of Reconciliation, essential for every
Christian life, is especially a source of support, guidance and healing
for the priestly life.

12. The priest who fully experiences the joy of sacramental reconciliation will find it altogether normal to repeat to his brothers and
sisters the words of Paul: "So we are ambassadors for Christ, God
making his appeal through us. We beseech you on behalf of Christ,
be reconciled to God."[25]

The crisis of the Sacrament of Reconciliation which I mentioned earlier is due to many factors from the diminished sense of sin to an in-
adequate realization of the sacramental economy of God's salvation.
But perhaps we should also recognize that another factor sometimes
working against the Sacrament has been a certain dwindling of our
own enthusiasm and availability for the exercise of this delicate and
demanding ministry.

Conversely, now more than ever the People of God must be helped
to rediscover the Sacrament. We need to declare with firmness and
conviction that the Sacrament of Penance is the ordinary means of
obtaining pardon and the remission of grave sins committed after
Baptism. We ought to celebrate the Sacrament in the best possible
way, according to the forms laid down by liturgical law, so that it may
lose none of its character as the celebration of God's mercy.

13. A source of renewed confidence in the revival of this Sacrament is not only the fact that, despite many incongruities, a new and urgent need for spirituality is becoming widespread in society. There is also a deeply-felt need for interpersonal contact, which is increasingly experienced as a reaction to the anonymous mass society which often leaves people interiorly isolated, even when it involves them in a flurry of purely functional relationships. Obviously sacramental confession is not to be confused with a support system or with psychotherapy. But neither should we underestimate the fact that the Sacrament of Reconciliation, when correctly celebrated, also has a "humanizing" effect, which is in perfect harmony with its primary purpose of reconciling the individual with God and the Church.

Here too, it is important that the minister of reconciliation should fulfil his role correctly. His ability to be welcoming, to be a good listener and to engage in dialogue, together with his ready accessibility, is essential if the ministry of reconciliation is to be seen in all its value. The faithful and uncompromising proclamation of the radical demands of God's word must always be accompanied by great understanding and sensitivity, in imitation of Jesus' own way of dealing with sinners.

14. The liturgical form of the Sacrament also needs to be given due attention. The Sacrament forms part of the structure of communion which is the mark of the Church. Sin itself cannot be properly understood if it is viewed in a purely "private" way, forgetting that it inevitably affects the entire community and lowers the level of holiness within it. Moreover, the offer of forgiveness expresses a mystery of supernatural solidarity, since its sacramental significance rests on the profound union between Christ the Head and the members of his Body.

It is extremely important to help people recover this "community" aspect of the Sacrament, also by means of community penance services which conclude with individual confession and absolution. This manner of celebration enables the faithful to appreciate better the two-fold dimension of reconciliation, and commits them more effectively to following the penitential path in all its revitalizing richness.

15. Then there is also the fundamental problem of catechetical teaching about the moral conscience and about sin, so that people can have a clearer idea of the radical demands of the Gospel. Unfortunately, there exists a minimalist tendency which prevents the Sacrament from producing all the benefits that we might hope for. Many of the faithful have an idea of sin that is not based on the Gospel but on common convention, on what is socially "acceptable." This makes them feel not particularly responsible for things that "everybody does," and all the more so if these things are permitted by civil law.

Evangelization in the third millennium must come to grips with the urgent need for a presentation of the Gospel message which is dynamic, complete and demanding. The Christian life to be aimed at cannot be reduced to a mediocre commitment to "goodness" as society defines it; it must be a true quest for holiness. We need to re-read with fresh enthusiasm the fifth chapter of *Lumen gentium*, which deals with the universal call to holiness. Being a Christian means to receive a "gift" of sanctifying grace which cannot fail to become a "commitment" to respond personally to that gift in everyday life. It is precisely for this reason that I have sought over the years to foster a wider recognition of holiness, in all the contexts where it has appeared, so that Christians can have many different models of holiness, and all can be reminded that they are personally called to this goal.

16. Dear Brother Priests, let us go forward in the joy of our ministry, knowing that we have at our side the One who called us and does not abandon us. May the certainty of his presence sustain and console us.

On Holy Thursday may we have an even more vivid sense of this presence, as we contemplate with deep emotion the hour when Jesus, in the Upper Room, gave himself to us under the signs of bread and wine, sacramentally anticipating the sacrifice of the Cross. Last year I wrote to you from the Upper Room itself, during my visit to the Holy Land. How can I forget that touching moment? I re-live it today, not without sorrow for the tragic situation which persists in the land of Christ.

Our spiritual meeting-place on Holy Thursday is still there, in the Upper Room, as we celebrate in union with the Bishops in the cathedrals of the whole world the mystery of the Body and Blood of Christ and gratefully recall the origins of our Priesthood.

In the joy of the immense gift which we have all received, I embrace you all and give you my blessing.

From the Vatican, on 25 March, the Fourth Sunday of Lent, in the year 2001, the twenty-third of my Pontificate.

Endnotes

1. Jn 13: 1.
2. Cf. Jn 17.
3. Jn 13: 15.
4. Cf. Rom 8: 26.
5. Gal 4: 6.
6. Jn 13: 34.
7. Ps 56: 8.
8. Rv 3: 20.
9. Jn 13: 8.
10. Jn 15: 16.
11. Lk 15: 7.
12. Lk 5: 1-11.
13. Lk 5: 8.
14. Lk 5: 10.
15. Jn 21: 15.
16. Jn 21: 17.
17. Jn 21: 15, 16, 17.
18. 1 Cor 15: 9.
19. 2 Cor 5: 18-19.
20. Cf. Novo millennio ineunte, 30-31.
21. Discourses, 340, 1.
22. Lk 15: 20.
23. Jn 13: 8.
24. Ps 51: 12.
25. 2 Cor 5: 20.

2002

Twenty-fourth Year of Pontificate

In the wake of the tragic events of September 11, 2001, and with the rise of violent conflict across the globe, John Paul II used the twenty-fourth year of his pontificate to urge the world toward peace and unity.

On January 24 he presided over a "Day of Peace in the World" in Assisi, Italy, where representatives of numerous religions and denominations gathered to make a united commitment to peace. Among those present were Christian, Buddhist, Muslim, and Jewish leaders from various parts of the world. Together with those present in Assisi, John Paul II denounced the use of religion as a justification for violence: "Once again, gathered here together, we declare that whoever uses religion to foment violence contradicts religion's deepest and truest inspiration" (Address of His Holiness Pope John Paul II to the representatives of the world religions, Assisi, January 24, 2002).

Less than three months after the conference in Assisi, with the Basilica of the Nativity in Bethlehem under siege, the Holy Father again summoned the world to pray for peace, asking that April 7 be a "Day of Prayer for Peace in the Holy Land."

Alongside and in addition to his pleas for peace in 2002, the Holy Father continued to work for unity among peoples, promoting dialogues between the Catholic Church and other religions, churches, and denominations. He especially reached out to Orthodox Churches, receiving a delegation from the Greek Orthodox Church in March and in October appearing in St. Peters Square with Teoctist, the Orthodox Patriarch of Romania. The two exchanged speeches and together signed a joint declaration.

The growing tension and violence in the Middle East and around the world did not distract the Holy Father from attending to the needs of his flock. He maintained his rigorous travel schedule and wrote profusely. He also continued to add new names to the canon of the Saints. Nine men and women were canonized in 2002, raised as examples of holiness to a troubled world. Among those canonized were Juan Diego Cuauhtlatoatzin, who received the image of the Virgin of Guadalupe in 1531; Pio da Pietrelcina, better known as Padre Pio; and Josemaría Escrivá de Balaguer, the founder of Opus Dei.

Despite his worsening health, the Holy Father continued to visit the faithful around the globe. In a period of only four months he made apostolic voyages to Ischia, Azerbaijan, Bulgaria, Toronto, Mexico City, Guatemala, and Poland.

In Toronto, the Holy Father appeared before millions at the seventeenth World Youth Day (July 23-29). Energized as always by the young people, he urged them to look to a brighter future, to a future in which the love of Christ prevails over violence and injustice: "You are the men and women of tomorrow. The future is in your hearts and in your hands. God is entrusting to you the task, at once difficult and uplifting, of working with him in the building of the *civilization of love*" (Evening Vigil with Young People, Toronto, Downsview Park, Saturday, July 27, 2002).

In August, he embarked on a pilgrimage to his native Poland for the dedication of the Shrine of Divine Mercy in Krakow-Lagiewniki. In a stirring farewell at the Balice Airport in Krakow he offered his final thanks and blessing to his Polish "brothers and sisters." Perhaps sensing that he would never again visit his homeland, he recalled not only his years as the first Polish pope but his early life as well, acknowledging the immeasurable worth of his heritage. "Grateful for everything, and with the entire ecclesial community in Poland, I repeat before the merciful Jesus: 'Jesus, in you I trust!' May these heartfelt words bring comfort to future generations in the new millennium. May God who is rich in mercy bless you! What can I say in the end? I am sorry to leave" (Farewell Ceremony at the International Airport of Kraków-Balice, August 19, 2002).

On October 16, to commemorate the start of his twenty-fifth year as the Roman Pontiff, John Paul II released the Apostolic letter *Rosarium Virginis Mariæ*. The document explores the rich history of the Marian devotion and affirms its immense importance to Christ's Church. It discusses its many uses and strengths as a form of truly *Christian* meditation, citing also its effectiveness as an instrument of peace: "The Rosary is by its nature a prayer for peace" (n. 40).

Most notably, the letter introduced the Luminous Mysteries, a fourth set of mysteries for meditating on Christ's public life from his Baptism to the institution of the Eucharist at the Last Supper.

Throughout his papacy John Paul II insisted that forgiveness is the basis of true peace. At the "Day of Peace in the World" in Assisi, he exhorted the delegates gathered there to embrace peace through a commitment to *Justice* and *Forgiveness*: "*Justice*, first of all, because there can be no true peace without respect for the dignity of persons and peoples, respect for the rights and duties of each person and respect for an equal distribution of benefits and burdens between individuals and in society as a whole. It can never be forgotten that situations of oppression and exclusion are often at the source of violence and terrorism. But *forgive-*

ness too, because human justice is subject to frailty and to the pressures of individual and group egoism. Forgiveness alone heals the wounds of the heart and fully restores damaged human relations" (Address of His Holiness Pope John Paul II to the representatives of the world religions, Assisi, January 24, 2002).

Given the violent state of the world in 2002 and John Paul II's recurring message of peace through forgiveness, it is no surprise that the 2002 Holy Thursday letter to priests focuses on the Sacrament of Reconciliation, the Church's precious gift of administering God's forgiveness.

LETTER
OF THE HOLY FATHER
POPE JOHN PAUL II
TO PRIESTS
FOR HOLY THURSDAY 2002

Dear Priests,

1.   With deep emotion I am sending you this traditional Holy Thursday Letter, taking my seat beside you as it were at the table in the Upper Room at which the Lord Jesus celebrated with his Apostles the first Eucharist: a gift to the whole Church, a gift which, although veiled by sacramental signs, makes him "really, truly and substantially" present (Council of Trent: *DS* 1651) in every tabernacle throughout the world. Before this unique presence, the Church bows down in adoration: "*Adoro te devote, latens Deitas*"; she is unceasingly moved by the spiritual raptures of the Saints and, as the Bride, she assembles in an intimate outpouring of faith and love: "*Ave, verum corpus natum de Maria Virgine*".

To the gift of this singular presence, which brings him to us in his supreme sacrifice and makes him our bread, Jesus, in the Upper Room, associated *a specific duty of the Apostles and their successors.* From that time on, to be an apostle of Christ, as are the Bishops and the priests sharing in their mission, has involved being able to act *in persona Christi Capitis.* This happens above all whenever the sacrificial meal of the Body and the Blood of the Lord is celebrated. For then the priest as it were lends Christ his own face and voice: "Do this in memory of me" (Lk 22: 19).

How marvellous is this vocation of ours, my dear Brother Priests! Truly we can repeat with the Psalmist: "What shall I render to the Lord for all his bounty to me? I will lift up the cup of salvation and call upon the name of the Lord" (Ps 116: 12-13).

2.   Joyfully meditating once again on this gift, I would like this year to speak to you about *an aspect of our mission* to which I called your attention last year at this same time. I believe that it warrants further reflection. I mean the mission which the Lord has given us to represent him not just in the *Eucharistic Sacrifice* but also *in the Sacrament of Reconciliation.*

Between the two sacraments there is a profound relationship. The Eucharist, the summit of the sacramental economy, is also its source: all the sacraments in a sense spring from the Eucharist and lead back to it. This is true in a special way of the sacrament charged with "mediating" the forgiveness of God, who welcomes the repentant sinner back into his embrace. It is true that as a re-enactment of Christ's Sacrifice, the Eucharist also serves to deliver us from sin. The *Catechism of the Catholic Church* reminds us: "The Eucharist cannot unite us to Christ without at the same time cleansing us from past sins and preserving us from future sins" (n. 1393). Nevertheless, in the economy of grace willed by Christ, this purifying power, while it directly cleanses from venial sins, only indirectly cleanses from mortal sins, which radically compromise the believer's relationship with God and his communion with the Church. "The Eucharist," the *Catechism* continues, "is not ordered to the forgiveness of mortal sins. That is proper to the Sacrament of Reconciliation. The Eucharist is properly the sacrament of those who are in full communion with the Church" (n. 1395).

In insisting on this truth, the Church in no way wishes to detract from the role of the Eucharist. Her intention is to grasp its significance in relation to the whole sacramental economy as instituted by God's saving wisdom. This, after all, is what Saint Paul clearly indicated when writing to the Corinthians: "Whoever eats the bread or drinks the cup of the Lord in an unworthy manner will be guilty of profaning the body and blood of the Lord. Let a man examine himself, and so eat of the bread and drink of the cup.

For any one who eats and drinks without discerning the body eats and drinks judgement upon himself" (1 Cor 11: 27-29). In line with this admonition of Saint Paul is the principle which states that "anyone conscious of a grave sin must receive the Sacrament of Reconciliation before coming to communion" (*Catechism of the Catholic Church*, n. 1385).

3.   My dear Brothers in the Priesthood: in recalling this truth, I feel a pressing need to urge you, as I did last year, to rediscover for yourselves and to help others to rediscover the beauty of the Sacrament of Reconciliation. In recent decades and for a variety of reasons, this sacrament has passed through something of a crisis. More than once I have drawn attention to this fact, even making it the theme of a gathering of the Synod of Bishops, whose reflections I then presented in the Apostolic Exhortation *Reconciliatio et Pænitentia*. On the other

hand, I cannot fail to acknowledge with deep joy the positive signs which, in the Jubilee Year especially, have shown that this sacrament, when suitably presented and celebrated, can have a broad appeal, even among the young. Its appeal is enhanced by the *need for personal contact*, something that is becoming increasingly scarce in the hectic pace of today's technological society, but which for this very reason is increasingly experienced as a vital need. Certainly, this need can be met in various ways. But how can we fail to recognize that the Sacrament of Reconciliation—without confusing it with any of the various forms of psychological therapy—offers an extraordinarily rich response to this need? It does so by bringing the penitent into contact with the merciful heart of God through the friendly face of a brother.

Yes, great indeed is the wisdom of God, who by instituting this sacrament has made provision for a profound and unremitting need of the human heart. We are meant to be loving and enlightened interpreters of this wisdom though the personal contact we are called to have with so many brothers and sisters in the celebration of Penance. In this regard, I wish to repeat that the usual form of administering this sacrament is its *individual* celebration, and only in "cases of grave necessity" is it lawful to employ the *communal* form with general confession and absolution. The conditions required for this form of absolution are well known; but perhaps we should remember that for absolution to be valid the faithful must have the intention of subsequently confessing their grave sins individually (cf. *Catechism of the Catholic Church*, n. 1483).

4.   With joy and trust let us rediscover this sacrament. Let us experience it above all for ourselves, as a deeply-felt need and as a grace which we constantly look for, in order to restore vigour and enthusiasm to our journey of holiness and to our ministry.

At the same time, let us make every effort to be *true ministers of mercy*. We know that in this sacrament, as in others, we are called to be agents of a grace which comes not from us but from on high and works by its own inner power. In other words—and this is a great responsibility—*God counts on us*, on our availability and fidelity, in order to work his wonders in human hearts. In the celebration of this sacrament, perhaps even more than in the others, it is important that the faithful have an intense experience of the face of Christ the Good Shepherd.

Allow me therefore to speak to you on this theme, imagining as it were all the places - cathedrals, parishes, shrines or elsewhere - in which you are daily engaged in administering this sacrament. Our minds turn to the pages of the Gospel which reveal most directly the merciful face of God. How can we fail to think of the *moving meeting between the prodigal son and his forgiving Father?* Or the image of the *sheep which was lost and then found,* and which the Shepherd joyfully lifts onto his shoulders? The Father's embrace and the Good Shepherd's joy must be visible in each one of us, dear Brothers, whenever a penitent asks us to become ministers of forgiveness.

In order to bring out certain specific aspects of the unique saving dialogue that is sacramental confession, I would like to use the "biblical icon" of *the meeting between Jesus and Zacchaeus* (cf. Lk 19: 1-10). To me it seems that what takes place between Jesus and the "chief tax collector" of Jericho resembles in a number of ways the celebration of the sacrament of mercy. As we follow this brief but powerful story, we try to capture in Christ's demeanour and in his voice all those nuances of wisdom, both human and supernatural, which we too must strive to communicate if the sacrament is to be celebrated in the best possible way.

5. The story, as we know, presents the meeting between Jesus and Zacchaeus as if it happened by chance. Jesus enters Jericho and moves through the city accompanied by the crowd (cf. Lk 19: 3). In climbing the sycamore tree, Zacchaeus seems prompted by curiosity alone. At times, God's meetings with man do appear to be merely fortuitous. But nothing that God does happens *by chance.* Surrounded by a wide variety of pastoral situations, we can sometimes lose heart and motivation because so many Christians pay too little attention to the sacramental life, and even when they do approach the sacraments, they often do so in a superficial way. Those who hear many confessions and see how people ordinarily approach the sacrament can be disconcerted by the way certain penitents come to confession without even a clear idea of what they want. Some come only because they feel the need to be listened to. Others because they want advice about something. Others have a psychological need to be released from burdensome feelings of guilt. Many, on the other hand, feel a real need to restore their relationship with God, but they confess without being really aware of the obligations which this entails. They may make a poor examination of conscience because they have little knowledge of the implications of a moral life inspired

by the Gospel. Is there any confessor who has not had this experience?

This is precisely the case of Zacchaeus. Everything that happens to
him is amazing. If there had not been, at a certain point, the "surprise" of Christ looking up at him, perhaps he would have remained
a silent spectator of the Lord moving through the streets of Jericho.

Jesus would have passed *by*, not *into*, his life. Zacchaeus had no
idea that the curiosity which had prompted him to do such an un-
usual thing was already the fruit of a mercy which had preceded
him, attracted him and was about to change him in the depths of
his heart.

Dear Priests, with so many of our penitents in mind, let us re-read
Luke's magnificent account of how Christ behaved: "When Jesus came
to the place, he looked up and said to him, `Zacchaeus, make haste
and come down; for I must stay at your house today'" (Lk 19: 5).

Every encounter with someone wanting to go to confession, even
when the request is somewhat superficial because it is poorly motivated and prepared, can become, through the surprising grace of
God, that "place" near the sycamore tree where Christ looked up at
Zacchaeus. How deeply Christ's gaze penetrated the Jericho publican's soul is impossible for us to judge. But we do know that that
same gaze looks upon each of our penitents. In the Sacrament of Reconciliation we are agents of a supernatural encounter with laws of its
own, an encounter which we have only to respect and facilitate. For
Zacchaeus, it must have been an stunning experience *to hear himself
called by his name*, a name which many of his townsmen spoke with
contempt. Now he hears it spoken in a tone of tenderness, expressing not just trust but familiarity, insistent friendship. Yes, Jesus speaks
to Zacchaeus like an old friend, forgotten maybe, but a friend who
has nonetheless remained faithful, and who enters with the gentle
force of affection into the life and into the home of his re-discovered
friend: "Make haste and come down; for I must stay at your house
today" (Lk 19: 5).

6.   Luke's account is remarkable for the tone of the language: everything is so personal, so tactful, so affectionate! Not only is the
text filled with humanity; it suggests insistence, an urgency to which
Jesus gives voice as the one offering the definitive revelation of God's
mercy. He says: "I must stay at your house", or to translate even more
literally: "I need to stay at your house" (Lk 19: 5). Following the mysterious road map which the Father has laid out for him, Jesus runs

into Zacchaeus along the way. He pauses near him as if the meeting had been planned from the beginning. Despite all the murmuring of human malice, the home of this sinner is about to become *a place of revelation*, the scene of a miracle of mercy. True, this will not happen if Zacchaeus does not free his heart from the ligatures of egoism and from his unjust and fraudulent ways. But mercy has already come to him as a gratuitous and overflowing gift. *Mercy has preceded him!*

This is what happens in every sacramental encounter. We must not think that it is the sinner, through his own independent journey of conversion, who earns mercy. On the contrary, it is mercy that impels him along the path of conversion. Left to himself, man can do nothing and he deserves nothing. Before being man's journey to God, confession is *God's arrival at a person's home.*

In confession, therefore, we can find ourselves faced with all kinds of people. But of one thing we must be convinced: anticipating our invitation, and even before we speak the words of the sacrament, the brothers and sisters who seek our ministry have already been touched by a mercy that works from within. Please God, we shall know how to cooperate with the mercy that welcomes and the love that saves. This we can do by our words and our attitude as pastors who are concerned for each individual, skilful in sensing people's problems and in delicately accompanying them on their journey, and knowing how to help them to trust in God's goodness.

7.   "I must stay at your house". Let us try to penetrate these words still more deeply. They are a proclamation. Before indicating a choice on the part of Christ, they proclaim the will of the Father. Jesus appears *as someone with a precise mandate.* There is a "law" which he too must observe: the will of the Father which he accomplishes with such love that it becomes his "food" (cf. Jn 4: 34). The words which Jesus speaks to Zacchaeus are not just a means of establishing a relationship but *the declaration of a plan drawn up by God.*

The meeting unfolds against the background of the Word of God, which is one with the Word and the Face of Christ. It is here too that the encounter which is at the heart of the celebration of Penance must begin. How poor if everything were reduced to the skills of human communication! Awareness of the laws of human communication can help and should not be overlooked, but it is the Word of God which must sustain everything. That is why the rite of the sacrament provides for the proclamation of this Word to the penitent.

This is a detail that should not be underestimated, even if it is not always easy to implement. Confessors very often find it hard to communicate what the Word demands to those who have only a superficial knowledge of it. Obviously, the actual celebration of the Sacrament is not the best time to make up for the lack. This should be done with pastoral insight during the time of preparation, by offering basic pointers that allow penitents to measure themselves against the truth of the Gospel. In any event, the confessor should not fail to use the sacramental encounter to lead penitents to some grasp of the way in which God is mercifully reaching down to them, stretching out his hand, not to strike but to save.

Who can deny that the dominant culture of our time creates very real difficulties in this regard? Even mature Christians are often hindered by it in their efforts to live by God's commandments and follow the guidelines set out on the basis of the commandments by the Church's magisterium. This is the case with many issues in the area of sexual and family morality, bio-ethics and professional and social morality; but it is also true of problems regarding obligations in the area of religious practice and participation in the life of the Church. For this reason there is a need for a catechesis which the confessor cannot offer at the moment of celebrating the sacrament. It would be best to make this catechesis part of a deeper preparation for confession. With this in mind, penitential celebrations with community preparation and individual confession can be very helpful.

To clarify all of this, the "biblical icon" of Zacchaeus provides *yet another important cue*. In the sacrament, the penitent first meets not "the commandments of God" but, in Jesus, "the God of the commandments". *To Zacchaeus, Jesus offers himself:* "I must stay at your house". He himself is the gift that awaits Zacchaeus, and he is also "God's law" for Zacchaeus. When we see our encounter with Jesus as a gift, even the most demanding features of the law assume the "lightness" of grace, in line with that supernatural dynamic which prompted Saint Paul to say: "If you are led by the Spirit, you are not under the law" (Gal 5: 18). Every celebration of Penance should cause the soul of the penitent to leap with the same joy that Christ's words inspired in Zacchaeus, who "made haste and came down and received him joyfully" (Lk 19: 6).

8.   The availability and superabundance of mercy should not how-ever obscure the fact that it is only *the premise of salvation*, which reaches fulfilment to the extent that it meets *a response in the human being*. In fact, the forgiveness granted in the Sacrament of Reconcili-ation is not some external action, a kind of legal "remission of the penalty", but *a real encounter of the penitent with God*, who restores the bond of friendship shattered by sin. The "truth" of this relation-ship requires that we welcome God's merciful embrace, overcoming all the resistance caused by sin.

This is what happens in the case of Zacchaeus. Aware that he is now being treated as a "son", he begins to think and act like a son, *and this he shows in the way he rediscovers his brothers and sisters*. Beneath the loving gaze of Christ, the heart of Zacchaeus warms to love of neighbour. From a feeling of isolation, which had led him to enrich himself without caring about what others had to suffer, he moves to an attitude of sharing. This is expressed in a genuine "division" of his wealth: "half of my goods to the poor". The injustice done to others by his fraudulent behaviour is atoned for by a fourfold restitution: "If I have defrauded any one of anything, I restore it fourfold" (Lk 19: 8). And it is only at this point that the love of God achieves its pur-pose, and salvation is accomplished: "Today salvation has come to this house" (Lk 19: 9).

Dear Priests, this journey of salvation, so clearly described in the story of Zacchaeus, should guide us and help us accomplish with wise pastoral balance our difficult work in the ministry of the confessional. It is a ministry always beset by two opposite extremes: *severity* and *laxity*. The first fails to take account of the early part of the story of Zacchaeus: mercy comes first, encouraging conversion and valuing even the slightest progress in love, because the Father wants to do the impossible to save the son who is lost: "The Son of Man came to seek and save the lost" (Lk 19: 10).

The other of the two extremes, laxity, fails to take into account the fact that the fullness of salvation, not just offered but also accepted, the salvation which truly heals and restores, involves a genuine con-version to the demands of God's love. If Zacchaeus had welcomed the Lord into his home without coming to an attitude of openness to love and reparation for the harm done, without a firm commit-ment to living a new life, he would not have received in the depths of his heart the forgiveness which the Lord had offered him with such concern.

We must always be careful to maintain a proper balance in order to avoid falling into one or the other of these extremes. *Severity* crushes people and drives them away. *Laxity* is misleading and deceptive. The minister of pardon, who exemplifies for penitents the face of the Good Shepherd, must express in equal measure the mercy already present and at work and the pardon which brings healing and peace. It is on the basis of these principles that the priest is deputed, in dialogue with the penitent, to discern whether he or she is ready for sacramental absolution. Undoubtedly, the delicacy of this meeting with souls, at such a personal and sometimes difficult moment, demands the utmost discretion. Unless it appears otherwise, the priest must assume that, in confessing his or her sins, the penitent is genuinely sorry and is determined to make amends. This can be more readily assumed if there are suitable pastoral aids for sacramental Reconciliation, including a time of preparation for the sacrament, in order to help penitents come to a more mature and satisfactory sense of what it is that they are looking for. Clearly, when there is no sorrow and amendment, the confessor is obliged to tell the penitent that he or she is not yet ready for absolution. If absolution were given to those who actually say that they have no intention of making amends, the rite would become a mere fiction; indeed, it would look almost like magic, capable perhaps of creating the semblance of peace, but certainly not that deep peace of conscience which God's embrace guarantees.

9.   In the light of what has been said, it is all the more evident why the *personal encounter* between confessor and penitent is the ordinary form of sacramental Reconciliation, while the practice of general absolution is only for exceptional circumstances. It is well known that the practice of the Church moved gradually to the private celebration of penance, after centuries in which public penance had been the dominant form. Not only did this development not change the substance of the sacrament - and how could it be otherwise! - but it actually expressed this substance more clearly and made it more effective. This happened not without the aid of the Holy Spirit, who here too fulfilled the mission of leading the Church "into all truth" (Jn 16: 13).

The ordinary form of Reconciliation not only expresses well *the truth of divine mercy* and the forgiveness which springs from it, but also sheds light on the *truth of man* in one of its most fundamental aspects. Although human beings live through a network of relationships and communities, the uniqueness of each person can never be lost in a shapeless mass. This explains the deep echo in our souls *when we hear ourselves called by name*. When we realize that we are known and accepted as we are, with our most individual traits, we feel truly alive. Pastoral practice needs to take this into greater account, in order to strike a wise balance between gatherings which emphasize the communion of the Church and other moments which attend to the needs of the individual. People ordinarily want to be recognized and looked after, and it is precisely this nearness to them that allows them to experience God's love more strongly.

Seen in these terms, the Sacrament of Reconciliation is *one of the most effective instruments of personal growth*. Here the Good Shepherd, through the presence and voice of the priest, approaches each man and woman, entering into a personal dialogue which involves listening, counsel, comfort and forgiveness. The love of God is such that it can focus upon each individual without overlooking the rest. All who receive sacramental absolution ought to be able to feel *the warmth of this personal attention*. They should experience the intensity of the fatherly embrace offered to the prodigal son: "His father . . . embraced him and kissed him" (Lk 15: 20). They should be able to hear that warm and friendly voice that spoke to the tax collector Zacchaeus, calling him by name to new life (cf. Lk 19: 5).

10. Accordingly, confessors too need *to be properly trained* for the celebration of this Sacrament. It must be celebrated in such a way that even in its external form it has all the liturgical dignity indicated in the norms laid down in the Rite of Penance. This does not exclude the possibility of adaptations for pastoral reasons, where the situation of the penitent truly calls for them, in light of the classical principle which holds that the *suprema lex* of the Church is the *salus animarum*. Let us make the wisdom of the Saints our guide. And let us move with courage in *proposing confession to young people*. We must be close to them, able to be with them as friends and fathers, confidants and confessors. They need to discover in us both of these roles, both dimensions.

While we remain firmly anchored in the discernment of the Church's magisterium, let us also make every effort to keep our theological training truly up-to-date, especially where emerging ethical issues are concerned. It can happen that in the face of complex contemporary ethical problems the faithful leave the confessional with somewhat confused ideas, especially if *they find that confessors are not consis-*

tent in their judgments. The truth is that those who fulfil this delicate ministry in the name of God and of the Church have a specific duty not to promote and, even more so not to express in the confessional, personal opinions that do not correspond to what the Church teaches and professes. Likewise, *a failure to speak the truth because of a misconceived sense of compassion should not be taken for love.* We do not have a right to minimize matters of our own accord, even with the best of intentions. Our task is to be God's witnesses, to be spokesmen of a mercy that saves even when it shows itself as judgment on man's sin. "Not everyone who says to me, `Lord, Lord', shall enter the kingdom of heaven, but he who does the will of my Father who is in heaven" (Mt 7: 21).

11. Dear Priests! Know that I am especially close to you as you gather with your Bishops on this Holy Thursday of the year 2002. We have all experienced a new momentum in the Church at the dawn of the new millennium, in the sense of "starting afresh from Christ" (*Novo millennio ineunte*, 29 ff.). We had all hoped that this momentum might coincide with a new era of brotherhood and peace for all humanity. Instead we have seen more bloodshed. Once again we have been witnesses of wars. We are distressed by the tragedy of the divisions and hatreds which are devastating relations between peoples.

At this time too, as priests we are personally and profoundly afflicted by the sins of some of our brothers who have betrayed the grace of Ordination in succumbing even to the most grievous forms of the *mysterium iniquitatis* at work in the world. Grave scandal is caused, with the result that a dark shadow of suspicion is cast over all the other fine priests who perform their ministry with honesty and integrity and often with heroic self-sacrifice. As the Church shows her concern for the victims and strives to respond in truth and justice to each of these painful situations, all of us—conscious of human weakness, but trusting in the healing power of divine grace—are called *to embrace the "mysterium Crucis"* and to commit ourselves more fully to the search for holiness. We must beg God in his Providence to prompt a whole-hearted reawakening of those ideals of total self-giving to Christ which are the very foundation of the priestly ministry.

It is precisely our faith in Christ which gives us the strength to look trustingly to the future. We know that the human heart has always been attracted to evil, and that man will be able to radiate peace and love to those around him only if he meets Christ and allows himself to be "overtaken" by him. As ministers of the Eucharist and of sacramental Reconciliation, we in particular have the task of communicating hope, goodness and peace to the world.

My wish is that you will live this most holy day in peace of heart, in profound communion among yourselves, with your Bishop and your communities, when we recall, with the institution of the Eucharist, our own "birth" as priests. With the words of Christ to the Apostles in the Upper Room after the Resurrection, and calling upon the Blessed Virgin Mary, *Regina Apostolorum* and *Regina pacis*, I warmly embrace you all as brothers: Peace, peace to each and every one of you. Happy Easter!

From the Vatican, on 17 March, the Fifth Sunday of Lent, in the year 2002, the twenty-fourth of my Pontificate.

2003

Twenty-fifth Year of Pontificate

The twenty-fifth year of John Paul II's Pontificate was marked by his continuing call for peace and unity in the world and by the celebration of Europe's deep Christian roots. In the midst of the Church's struggles and celebrations, the Holy Father placed the Eucharist: "This year, the twenty-fifth of my Pontificate, I wish to involve the whole Church more fully in this Eucharistic reflection" (*Ecclesia de Eucharistia*, n. 7).

On April 17, the Holy Father published his first encyclical in over four years: *Ecclesia de Eucharistia*. The work delves into the many aspects of the Eucharist and stresses its unique presence within the Catholic Church. Appropriately released on Holy Thursday, April 17, 2003, the encyclical is addressed not only to bishops and priests but to all consecrated men and women and to the whole laity. Given the special relationship between the consecrated priesthood and the Eucharist (a matter discussed at length in the encyclical), *Ecclesia de Eucharistia* replaced the pope's usual letter to priests and is subsequently printed here.

In January the Holy Father met via television linkup with Manila for the fourth World Meeting of Families. He urged families to be foundations of peace and unity in the world, reminding them of their enormous importance in spreading the Gospel: "The future of humanity passes by way of the family" (cf. *Familiaris consortio*, n. 86).

The pope continued his efforts for peace in 2003 by paying particular attention to the conflicts in the Middle East. During March he exhorted American and Iraqi leaders to avoid war and work for a peaceful resolution. In the same month, at the beginning of the Lenten season, he asked that Ash Wednesday be "a day of fasting for the cause of peace, above all in the Middle East," a plea further revealing his great concern for the wellbeing of those lands. In November, during an appearance to say the Sunday Angelus, the pope again voiced his concern for the region, saying: "The Holy Land does not need walls but bridges."

Throughout 2003 the pope fearlessly continued his apostolic visits to various countries. Between June and September he visited Croatia, Bosnia and Herzegovina, and Slovakia. He brought a message of hope to those countries that have seen the horrors of war and oppression: "I remember your distress because of the war that still marks your faces and your lives, and I feel close to all who are suffering its tragic consequences. However, I also know your strength, your courage and your hope, and I know that your constant perseverance will enable you to see better days" (Forum Square, Zadar, Croatia, Monday, June 9, 2003).

As was his practice throughout his papacy, John Paul II called out in a special way to the youth of these countries, sighting them as the harbingers of peace to a troubled world. "Dear young friends, you are the hope of the Church and of society; you are the hope of the Pope! Do not be afraid to become true friends of Jesus" (Bratislava, Esplanade of Petržalka, Sunday, September 14, 2003).

In addition to his visits to several Eastern European countries, the Holy Father also visited Spain in May and canonized a number of martyrs killed during the Spanish civil war. In June the Holy Father released the Apostolic Exhortation *Ecclesia in Europa*, in which he rejoices in Europe's deep Christian roots while issuing a stern warning to the peoples of Europe to combat the hopelessness that accompanies the "silent apostasy" of a culture where unbelief is considered "self-explanatory." Following the release of the document, the pope dedicated the meditations of the weekly Sunday Angelus to the Christian roots of Europe.

In October John Paul II made a pilgrimage to the shrine of Our Lady of the Rosary of Pompeii as a means of closing the Year of the Rosary. Later in the month he celebrated his twenty-fifth anniversary as the Roman pontiff and held his ninth consistory, creating thirty-one new cardinals, including one *in pectore*.

Throughout 2003 the Holy Father continued to name new saints, canonizing twelve men and women from various European countries. On October 19, the Holy Father beatified Mother Teresa of Calcutta, barely five years after her death.

In addition to his new encyclical, Pope John Paul II continued to write for the benefit of the Church. He released two letters in December: one on sacred music for the first centenary of *Tra le Sollecitudini* (November 22, 1903), the other on Sacred Liturgy for the fortieth anniversary of *Sacrosanctum consilium*. On March 6 he surprised and delighted the Church by publishing a book of his poems called "Roman Triptych-Meditations."

ENCYCLICAL LETTER
ECCLESIA DE EUCHARISTIA
OF HIS HOLINESS
POPE JOHN PAUL II
TO THE BISHOPS, PRIESTS AND DEACONS
MEN AND WOMEN IN THE CONSECRATED LIFE
AND ALL THE LAY FAITHFUL
ON THE EUCHARIST
IN ITS RELATIONSHIP TO THE CHURCH

INTRODUCTION

1. The Church draws her life from the Eucharist. This truth does not simply express a daily experience of faith, but recapitulates *the heart of the mystery of the Church*. In a variety of ways she joyfully experiences the constant fulfilment of the promise: "Lo, I am with you always, to the close of the age" (Mt 28: 20), but in the Holy Eucharist, through the changing of bread and wine into the body and blood of the Lord, she rejoices in this presence with unique intensity. Ever since Pentecost, when the Church, the People of the New Covenant, began her pilgrim journey towards her heavenly homeland, the Divine Sacrament has continued to mark the passing of her days, filling them with confident hope.

The Second Vatican Council rightly proclaimed that the Eucharistic sacrifice is "the source and summit of the Christian life".[1] "For the most holy Eucharist contains the Church's entire spiritual wealth: Christ himself, our passover and living bread. Through his own flesh, now made living and life-giving by the Holy Spirit, he offers life to men".[2] Consequently the gaze of the Church is constantly turned to her Lord, present in the Sacrament of the Altar, in which she discovers the full manifestation of his boundless love.

2. During the Great Jubilee of the Year 2000 I had an opportunity to celebrate the Eucharist in the Cenacle of Jerusalem where, according to tradition, it was first celebrated by Jesus himself. *The Upper Room was where this most holy Sacrament was instituted.* It is there that Christ took bread, broke it and gave it to his disciples, saying: "Take this, all of you, and eat it: this is my body which will be given up for you" (cf. Mk 26: 26; Lk 22: 19; 1 Cor 11: 24). Then he took the cup of wine and said to them:"Take this, all of you and drink from it: this is the cup of my blood, the blood of the new and everlasting covenant. It will be shed for you and for all, so that sins may be forgiven" (cf. Mt 14: 24; Lk 22: 20; 1 Cor 11: 25). I am grateful to the Lord Jesus for allowing me to repeat in that same place, in obedience to his command:"Do this in memory of me" (Lk 22: 19), the words which he spoke two thousand years ago.

Did the Apostles who took part in the Last Supper understand the meaning of the words spoken by Christ? Perhaps not. Those words would only be fully clear at the end of the *Triduum sacrum*, the time from Thursday evening to Sunday morning. Those days embrace the *mysterium paschale*; they also embrace the *mysterium eucharisticum*.

3. The Church was born of the paschal mystery. For this very reason the Eucharist, which is in an outstanding way the sacrament of the paschal mystery, *stands at the centre of the Church's life*. This is already clear from the earliest images of the Church found in the Acts of the Apostles:"They devoted themselves to the Apostles' teaching and fellowship, to the breaking of bread and the prayers" (2: 42). The "breaking of the bread" refers to the Eucharist. Two thousand years later, we continue to relive that primordial image of the Church. At every celebration of the Eucharist, we are spiritually brought back to the paschal Triduum: to the events of the evening of Holy Thursday, to the Last Supper and to what followed it. The institution of the Eucharist sacramentally anticipated the events which were about to take place, beginning with the agony in Gethsemane. Once again we see Jesus as he leaves the Upper Room, descends with his disciples to the Kidron valley and goes to the Garden of Olives. Even today that Garden shelters some very ancient olive trees. Perhaps they witnessed what happened beneath their shade that evening, when Christ in prayer was filled with anguish"and his sweat became like drops of blood falling down upon the ground" (cf. Lk 22: 44). The blood which shortly before he had given to the Church as the drink of salvation in the sacrament of the Eucharist, *began to be shed*; its outpouring would then be completed on Golgotha to become the means of our redemption:"Christ . . . as high priest of the good things to come. . . , entered once for all into the Holy Place, taking not the blood of goats and calves but his own blood, thus securing an eternal redemption" (Heb 9: 11- 12).

4.   *The hour of our redemption.* Although deeply troubled, Jesus does not flee before his "hour". "And what shall I say? 'Father, save me from this hour?' No, for this purpose I have come to this hour" (Jn 12: 27). He wanted his disciples to keep him company, yet he had to experience loneliness and abandonment: "So, could you not watch with me one hour? Watch and pray that you may not enter into temptation" (Mt 26: 40- 41). Only John would remain at the foot of the Cross, at the side of Mary and the faithful women. The agony in Gethsemane was the introduction to the agony of the Cross on Good Friday. *The holy hour*, the hour of the redemption of the world. Whenever the Eucharist is celebrated at the tomb of Jesus in Jerusalem, there is an almost tangible return to his "hour", the hour of his Cross and glorification. Every priest who celebrates Holy Mass, together with the Christian community which takes part in it, is led back in spirit to that place and that hour.

"He was crucified, he suffered death and was buried; he descended to the dead; on the third day he rose again". The words of the profession of faith are echoed by the words of contemplation and proclamation: *"This is the wood of the Cross, on which hung the Saviour of the world. Come, let us worship".* This is the invitation which the Church extends to all in the afternoon hours of Good Friday. She then takes up her song during the Easter season in order to proclaim: *"The Lord is risen from the tomb; for our sake he hung on the Cross, Alleluia".*

5.   *"Mysterium fidei!* - The Mystery of Faith!".* When the priest recites or chants these words, all present acclaim: "We announce your death, O Lord, and we proclaim your resurrection, until you come in glory".

In these or similar words the Church, while pointing to Christ in the mystery of his passion, *also reveals her own mystery: Ecclesia de Eucharistia.* By the gift of the Holy Spirit at Pentecost the Church was born and set out upon the pathways of the world, yet a decisive moment in her taking shape was certainly the institution of the Eucharist in the Upper Room. Her foundation and wellspring is the whole *Triduum paschale*, but this is as it were gathered up, foreshadowed and "concentrated' for ever in the gift of the Eucharist. In this gift Jesus Christ entrusted to his Church the perennial making present of the paschal mystery. With it he brought about a mysterious "oneness in time" between that *Triduum* and the passage of the centuries.

The thought of this leads us to profound amazement and gratitude. In the paschal event and the Eucharist which makes it present throughout the centuries, there is a truly enormous"capacity"which embraces all of history as the recipient of the grace of the redemption. This amazement should always fill the Church assembled for the celebration of the Eucharist. But in a special way it should fill the minister of the Eucharist. For it is he who, by the authority given him in the sacrament of priestly ordination, effects the consecration. It is he who says with the power coming to him from Christ in the Upper Room:"This is my body which will be given up for you This is the cup of my blood, poured out for you . . .". The priest says these words, or rather *he puts his voice at the disposal of the One who spoke these words in the Upper Room* and who desires that they should be repeated in every generation by all those who in the Church ministerially share in his priesthood.

6.   I would like to rekindle this Eucharistic "amazement" by the present Encyclical Letter, in continuity with the Jubilee heritage which I have left to the Church in the Apostolic Letter *Novo millennio ineunte* and its Marian crowning, *Rosarium Virginis Mariæ*. To contemplate the face of Christ, and to contemplate it with Mary, is the"programme"which I have set before the Church at the dawn of the third millennium, summoning her to put out into the deep on the sea of history with the enthusiasm of the new evangelization. To contemplate Christ involves being able to recognize him wherever he manifests himself, in his many forms of presence, but above all in the living sacrament of his body and his blood. *The Church draws her life from Christ in the Eucharist*; by him she is fed and by him she is enlightened. The Eucharist is both a mystery of faith and a"mystery of light".[3] Whenever the Church celebrates the Eucharist, the faithful can in some way relive the experience of the two disciples on the road to Emmaus:"their eyes were opened and they recognized him" (Lk 24: 31).

7.   From the time I began my ministry as the Successor of Peter, I have always marked Holy Thursday, the day of the Eucharist and of the priesthood, by sending a letter to all the priests of the world. This year, the twenty-fifth of my Pontificate, I wish to involve the whole Church more fully in this Eucharistic reflection, also as a way of thanking the Lord for the gift of the Eucharist and the priesthood:"Gift and Mystery".[4] By proclaiming the Year of the Rosary, I wish to put this, my twenty-fifth anniversary, under the *ægis of the contemplation of Christ at the school of Mary*. Consequently, I cannot let this Holy Thursday 2003 pass without halting before the

"Eucharistic face" of Christ and pointing out with new force to the Church the centrality of the Eucharist.

From it the Church draws her life. From this "living bread" she draws her nourishment. How could I not feel the need to urge everyone to experience it ever anew?

8.   When I think of the Eucharist, and look at my life as a priest, as a Bishop and as the Successor of Peter, I naturally recall the many times and places in which I was able to celebrate it. I remember the parish church of Niegowic, where I had my first pastoral assignment, the collegiate church of Saint Florian in Krakow, Wawel Cathedral, Saint Peter's Basilica and so many basilicas and churches in Rome and throughout the world. I have been able to celebrate Holy Mass in chapels built along mountain paths, on lakeshores and seacoasts; I have celebrated it on altars built in stadiums and in city squares . . . This varied scenario of celebrations of the Eucharist has given me a powerful experience of its universal and, so to speak, cosmic character. Yes, cosmic! Because even when it is celebrated on the humble altar of a country church, the Eucharist is always in some way celebrated *on the altar of the world*. It unites heaven and earth. It embraces and permeates all creation. The Son of God became man in order to restore all creation, in one supreme act of praise, to the One who made it from nothing. He, the Eternal High Priest who by the blood of his Cross entered the eternal sanctuary, thus gives back to the Creator and Father all creation redeemed. He does so through the priestly ministry of the Church, to the glory of the Most Holy Trinity. Truly this is the *mysterium fidei* which is accomplished in the Eucharist: the world which came forth from the hands of God the Creator now returns to him redeemed by Christ.

9.   The Eucharist, as Christ's saving presence in the community of the faithful and its spiritual food, is the most precious possession which the Church can have in her journey through history. This explains the *lively concern* which she has always shown for the Eucharistic mystery, a concern which finds authoritative expression in the work of the Councils and the Popes. How can we not admire the doctrinal expositions of the Decrees on the Most Holy Eucharist and on the Holy Sacrifice of the Mass promulgated by the Council of Trent? For centuries those Decrees guided theology and catechesis, and they are still a dogmatic reference-point for the continual renewal and growth of God's People in faith and in love for the Eucharist. In times closer to our own, three Encyclical Letters should be

mentioned: the Encyclical *Miræ caritatis* of Leo XIII (28 May 1902),[5] the Encyclical *Mediator Dei* of Pius XII (20 November 1947)[6] and the Encyclical *Mysterium Fidei* of Paul VI (3 September 1965).[7]

The Second Vatican Council, while not issuing a specific document on the Eucharistic mystery, considered its various aspects throughout its documents, especially the Dogmatic Constitution on the Church *Lumen gentium* and the Constitution on the Sacred Liturgy *Sacrosanctum concilium*.

I myself, in the first years of my apostolic ministry in the Chair of Peter, wrote the Apostolic Letter *Dominicæ cenæ* (24 February 1980),[8] in which I discussed some aspects of the Eucharistic mystery and its importance for the life of those who are its ministers. Today I take up anew the thread of that argument, with even greater emotion and gratitude in my heart, echoing as it were the word of the Psalmist:"What shall I render to the Lord for all his bounty to me? I will lift up the cup of salvation and call on the name of the Lord" (Ps 116: 12-13).

10. The Magisterium's commitment to proclaiming the Eucharistic mystery has been matched by interior growth within the Christian community. Certainly *the liturgical reform inaugurated by the Council* has greatly contributed to a more conscious, active and fruitful participation in the Holy Sacrifice of the Altar on the part of the faithful. In many places, *adoration of the Blessed Sacrament* is also an important daily practice and becomes an inexhaustible source of holiness. The devout participation of the faithful in the Eucharistic procession on the Solemnity of the Body and Blood of Christ is a grace from the Lord which yearly brings joy to those who take part in it.

Other positive signs of Eucharistic faith and love might also be mentioned.

Unfortunately, alongside these lights, *there are also shadows*. In some places the practice of Eucharistic adoration has been almost completely abandoned. In various parts of the Church abuses have occurred, leading to confusion with regard to sound faith and Catholic doctrine concerning this wonderful sacrament. At times one encounters an extremely reductive understanding of the Eucharistic mystery. Stripped of its sacrificial meaning, it is celebrated as if it were simply a fraternal banquet. Furthermore, the necessity of the ministerial priesthood, grounded in apostolic succession, is at times obscured and the sacramental nature of the Eucharist is reduced to its mere effectiveness as a form of proclamation. This has led here and there to ecumenical initiatives which, albeit well-intentioned, indulge in Eucharistic practices contrary to the discipline by which the Church expresses her faith. How can we not express profound grief at all this? The Eucharist is too great a gift to tolerate ambiguity and depreciation.

It is my hope that the present Encyclical Letter will effectively help to banish the dark clouds of unacceptable doctrine and practice, so that the Eucharist will continue to shine forth in all its radiant mystery.

CHAPTER ONE:

THE MYSTERY OF FAITH

11. "The Lord Jesus on the night he was betrayed" (1 Cor 11: 23) instituted the Eucharistic Sacrifice of his body and his blood. The words of the Apostle Paul bring us back to the dramatic setting in which the Eucharist was born. The Eucharist is indelibly marked by the event of the Lord's passion and death, of which it is not only a reminder but the sacramental re-presentation. It is the sacrifice of the Cross perpetuated down the ages.[9] This truth is well expressed by the words with which the assembly in the Latin rite responds to the priest's proclamation of the "Mystery of Faith": "*We announce your death, O Lord*".

The Church has received the Eucharist from Christ her Lord not as one gift—however precious - among so many others, but as *the gift par excellence*, for it is the gift of himself, of his person in his sacred humanity, as well as the gift of his saving work. Nor does it remain confined to the past, since "all that Christ is—all that he did and suffered for all men—participates in the divine eternity, and so transcends all times".[10]

When the Church celebrates the Eucharist, the memorial of her Lord's death and resurrection, this central event of salvation becomes really present and "the work of our redemption is carried out".[11] This sacrifice is so decisive for the salvation of the human race that Jesus Christ offered it and returned to the Father only *after he had left us a means of sharing in it* as if we had been present there. Each member of the faithful can thus take part in it and inexhaustibly gain its fruits. This is the faith from which generations of Christians down the ages have lived. The Church's Magisterium has constantly reaffirmed this faith with joyful gratitude for its inestimable gift.[12] I wish once more to recall this truth and to join you, my dear brothers and sisters, in adoration before this mystery: a great mystery, a mystery of mercy. What more could Jesus have done for us? Truly, in the Eucharist, he shows us a love which goes "to the end" (cf. Jn 13: 1), a love which knows no measure.

12. This aspect of the universal charity of the Eucharistic Sacrifice is based on the words of the Saviour himself. In instituting it, he did not merely say: "This is my body", "this is my blood", but went on to add: "which is given for you", "which is poured out for you" (Lk 22: 19-20). Jesus did not simply state that what he was giving them to eat and drink was his body and his blood; he also expressed *its sacrificial meaning* and made sacramentally present his sacrifice which would soon be offered on the Cross for the salvation of all. "The Mass is at the same time, and inseparably, the sacrificial memorial in which the sacrifice of the Cross is perpetuated and the sacred banquet of communion with the Lord's body and blood".[13]

The Church constantly draws her life from the redeeming sacrifice; she approaches it not only through faith-filled remembrance, but also through a real contact, since *this sacrifice is made present ever anew*, sacramentally perpetuated, in every community which offers it at the hands of the consecrated minister. The Eucharist thus applies to men and women today the reconciliation won once for all by Christ for mankind in every age. "The sacrifice of Christ and the sacrifice of the Eucharist are *one single sacrifice*".[14] Saint John Chrysostom put it well: "We always offer the same Lamb, not one today and another tomorrow, but always the same one. For this reason the sacrifice is always only one . . . Even now we offer that victim who was once offered and who will never be consumed".[15]

The Mass makes present the sacrifice of the Cross; it does not add to that sacrifice nor does it multiply it.[16] What is repeated is its *memorial* celebration, its "commemorative representation" (*memorialis demonstratio*),[17] which makes Christ's one, definitive redemptive sacrifice always present in time. The sacrificial nature of the Eucharistic mystery cannot therefore be understood as something separate, independent of the Cross or only indirectly referring to the sacrifice of Calvary.

13. By virtue of its close relationship to the sacrifice of Golgotha, the Eucharist is *a sacrifice in the strict sense,* and not only in a general way, as if it were simply a matter of Christ's offering himself to the faithful as their spiritual food. The gift of his love and obedience to the point of giving his life (cf. Jn 10: 17-18) is in the first place a gift to his Father. Certainly it is a gift given for our sake, and indeed that of all humanity (cf. Mt 26: 28; Mk 14: 24; Lk 22: 20; Jn 10: 15), yet it is *first and foremost a gift to the Father*:"a sacrifice that the Father accepted, giving, in return for this total self-giving by his Son, who 'became obedient unto death' (Phil 2: 8), his own paternal gift, that is to say the grant of new immortal life in the resurrection".[18]

In giving his sacrifice to the Church, Christ has also made his own the spiritual sacrifice of the Church, which is called to offer herself in union with the sacrifice of Christ. This is the teaching of the Second Vatican Council concerning all the faithful:"Taking part in the Eucharistic Sacrifice, which is the source and summit of the whole Christian life, they offer the divine victim to God, and offer themselves along with it".[19]

14. Christ's passover includes not only his passion and death, but also his resurrection. This is recalled by the assembly's acclamation following the consecration:"*We proclaim your resurrection*". The Eucharistic Sacrifice makes present not only the mystery of the Saviour's passion and death, but also the mystery of the resurrection which crowned his sacrifice. It is as the living and risen One that Christ can become in the Eucharist the"bread of life" (Jn 6: 35, 48), the"living bread"(Jn 6: 51). Saint Ambrose reminded the newly-initiated that the Eucharist applies the event of the resurrection to their lives:"Today Christ is yours, yet each day he rises again for you".[20] Saint Cyril of Alexandria also makes clear that sharing in the sacred mysteries"is a true confession and a remembrance that the Lord died and returned to life for us and on our behalf".[21]

15. The sacramental re-presentation of Christ's sacrifice, crowned by the resurrection, in the Mass involves a most special presence which—in the words of Paul VI—"is called 'real' not as a way of excluding all other types of presence as if they were 'not real', but because it is a presence in the fullest sense: a substantial presence whereby Christ, the God-Man, is wholly and entirely present".[22] This sets forth once more the perennially valid teaching of the Council of Trent:"the consecration of the bread and wine effects the change of the whole substance of the bread into the substance of the body of Christ our Lord, and of the whole substance of the wine into the substance of his blood. And the holy Catholic Church has fittingly and properly called this change transubstantiation".[23] Truly the Eucharist is a *mysterium fidei*, a mystery which surpasses our understanding and can only be received in faith, as is often brought out in the catechesis of the Church Fathers regarding this divine sacrament: "Do not see—Saint Cyril of Jerusalem exhorts—in the bread and wine merely natural elements, because the Lord has expressly said that they are his body and his blood: faith assures you of this, though your senses suggest otherwise".[24]

Adoro te devote, latens Deitas, we shall continue to sing with the Angelic Doctor. Before this mystery of love, human reason fully experiences its limitations. One understands how, down the centuries, this truth has stimulated theology to strive to understand it ever more deeply.

These are praiseworthy efforts, which are all the more helpful and insightful to the extent that they are able to join critical thinking to the "living faith" of the Church, as grasped especially by the Magisterium's "sure charism of truth" and the "intimate sense of spiritual realities"[25] which is attained above all by the saints. There remains the boundary indicated by Paul VI: "Every theological explanation which seeks some understanding of this mystery, in order to be in accord with Catholic faith, must firmly maintain that in objective reality, independently of our mind, the bread and wine have ceased to exist after the consecration, so that the adorable body and blood of the Lord Jesus from that moment on are really before us under the sacramental species of bread and wine".[26]

16. The saving efficacy of the sacrifice is fully realized when the Lord's body and blood are received in communion. The Eucharistic Sacrifice is intrinsically directed to the inward union of the faithful with Christ through communion; we receive the very One who offered himself for us, we receive his body which he gave up for us on the Cross and his blood which he "poured out for many for the forgiveness of sins" (Mt 26: 28). We are reminded of his words: "As the living Father sent me, and I live because of the Father, so he who eats me will live because of me" (Jn 6: 57). Jesus himself reassures us that this union, which he compares to that of the life of the Trinity, is truly realized. *The Eucharist is a true banquet*, in which Christ offers himself as our nourishment. When for the first time Jesus spoke of this food, his listeners were astonished and bewildered, which forced the Master to emphasize the objective truth of his words: "Truly, truly, I say to you, unless you eat the flesh of the Son of Man and drink his blood, you have no life within you" (Jn 6: 53). This is no metaphorical food: "My flesh is food indeed, and my blood is drink indeed" (Jn 6: 55).

17. Through our communion in his body and blood, Christ also grants us his Spirit. Saint Ephrem writes:"He called the bread his living body and he filled it with himself and his Spirit . . .

He who eats it with faith, eats Fire and Spirit . . . Take and eat this, all of you, and eat with it the Holy Spirit. For it is truly my body and whoever eats it will have eternal life".[27] The Church implores this divine Gift, the source of every other gift, in the Eucharistic epiclesis. In the *Divine Liturgy* of Saint John Chrysostom, for example, we find the prayer:"We beseech, implore and beg you: send your Holy Spirit upon us all and upon these gifts . . . that those who partake of them may be purified in soul, receive the forgiveness of their sins, and share in the Holy Spirit".[28] And in the *Roman Missal* the celebrant prays:"grant that we who are nourished by his body and blood may be filled with his Holy Spirit, and become one body, one spirit in Christ".[29] Thus by the gift of his body and blood Christ increases within us the gift of his Spirit, already poured out in Baptism and bestowed as a"seal"in the sacrament of Confirmation.

18. The acclamation of the assembly following the consecration appropriately ends by expressing the eschatological thrust which marks the celebration of the Eucharist (cf. 1 Cor 11: 26):"*until you come in glory*". The Eucharist is a straining towards the goal, a foretaste of the fullness of joy promised by Christ (cf. Jn 15: 11); it is in some way the anticipation of heaven, the"pledge of future glory".[30] In the Eucharist, everything speaks of confident waiting"in joyful hope for the coming of our Saviour, Jesus Christ".[31] Those who feed on Christ in the Eucharist need not wait until the hereafter to receive eternal life: *they already possess it on earth*, as the first-fruits of a future fullness which will embrace man in his totality. For in the Eucharist we also receive the pledge of our bodily resurrection at the end of the world:"He who eats my flesh and drinks my blood has eternal life, and I will raise him up at the last day" (Jn 6: 54). This pledge of the future resurrection comes from the fact that the flesh of the Son of Man, given as food, is his body in its glorious state after the resurrection. With the Eucharist we digest, as it were, the"secret"of the resurrection. For this reason Saint Ignatius of Antioch rightly defined the Eucharistic Bread as"a medicine of immortality, an antidote to death".[32]

19. The eschatological tension kindled by the Eucharist *expresses and reinforces our communion with the Church in heaven*. It is not by chance that the Eastern Anaphoras and the Latin Eucharistic Prayers honour Mary, the ever-Virgin Mother of Jesus Christ our Lord and God, the angels, the holy apostles, the glorious martyrs and all the saints. This is an aspect of the Eucharist which merits greater attention: in celebrating the sacrifice of the Lamb, we are united to the heavenly "liturgy" and become part of that great multitude which cries out: "Salvation belongs to our God who sits upon the throne, and to the Lamb!" (Rv 7: 10). The Eucharist is truly a glimpse of heaven appearing on earth. It is a glorious ray of the heavenly Jerusalem which pierces the clouds of our history and lights up our journey.

20. A significant consequence of the eschatological tension inherent in the Eucharist is also the fact that it spurs us on our journey through history and plants a seed of living hope in our daily commitment to the work before us. Certainly the Christian vision leads to the expectation of "new heavens" and "a new earth" (Rv 21: 1), but this increases, rather than lessens, *our sense of responsibility for the world today*.[33] I wish to reaffirm this forcefully at the beginning of the new millennium, so that Christians will feel more obliged than ever not to neglect their duties as citizens in this world. Theirs is the task of contributing with the light of the Gospel to the building of a more human world, a world fully in harmony with God's plan.

Many problems darken the horizon of our time. We need but think of the urgent need to work for peace, to base relationships between peoples on solid premises of justice and solidarity, and to defend human life from conception to its natural end. And what should we say of the thousand inconsistencies of a "globalized" world where the weakest, the most powerless and the poorest appear to have so little hope! It is in this world that Christian hope must shine forth! For this reason too, the Lord wished to remain with us in the Eucharist, making his presence in meal and sacrifice the promise of a humanity renewed by his love. Significantly, in their account of the Last Supper, the Synoptics recount the institution of the Eucharist, while the Gospel of John relates, as a way of bringing out its profound meaning, the account of the "washing of the feet", in which Jesus appears as the teacher of communion and of service (cf. Jn 13: 1-20). The Apostle Paul, for his part, says that it is "unworthy" of a Christian community to partake of the Lord's Supper amid division and indifference towards the poor (cf. 1 Cor 11: 17-22, 27-34).[34]

Proclaiming the death of the Lord "until he comes" (1 Cor 11: 26) entails that all who take part in the Eucharist be committed to changing their lives and making them in a certain way completely "Eucharistic". It is this fruit of a transfigured existence and a commitment to transforming the world in accordance with the Gospel which splendidly illustrates the eschatological tension inherent in the celebration of the Eucharist and in the Christian life as a whole: "Come, Lord Jesus!" (Rv 22: 20).

CHAPTER TWO:

THE EUCHARIST
BUILDS THE CHURCH

21. The Second Vatican Council teaches that the celebration of the Eucharist is at the centre of the process of the Church's growth. After stating that "the Church, as the Kingdom of Christ already present in mystery, grows visibly in the world through the power of God",[35] then, as if in answer to the question: "How does the Church grow?", the Council adds: "as often as the sacrifice of the Cross by which 'Christ our pasch is sacrificed' (1 Cor 5: 7) is celebrated on the altar, the work of our redemption is carried out. At the same time in the sacrament of the Eucharistic bread, the unity of the faithful, who form one body in Christ (cf. 1 Cor 10: 17), is both expressed and brought about".[36]

A causal influence of the Eucharist is present at the Church's very origins. The Evangelists specify that it was the Twelve, the Apostles, who gathered with Jesus at the Last Supper (cf. Mt 26: 20; Mk 14: 17; Lk 22: 14). This is a detail of notable importance, for the Apostles "were both the seeds of the new Israel and the beginning of the sacred hierarchy".[37] By offering them his body and his blood as food, Christ mysteriously involved them in the sacrifice which would be completed later on Calvary. By analogy with the Covenant of Mount Sinai, sealed by sacrifice and the sprinkling of blood,[38] the actions and words of Jesus at the Last Supper laid the foundations of the new messianic community, the People of the New Covenant.

The Apostles, by accepting in the Upper Room Jesus' invitation: "Take, eat", "Drink of it, all of you" (Mt 26: 26-27), entered for the first time into sacramental communion with him. From that time forward, until the end of the age, the Church is built up through sacramental communion with the Son of God who was sacrificed for our sake: "Do this is remembrance of me . . . Do this, as often as you drink it, in remembrance of me" (1 Cor 11: 24-25; cf. Lk 22: 19).

22. Incorporation into Christ, which is brought about by Baptism, is constantly renewed and consolidated by sharing in the Eucharistic Sacrifice, especially by that full sharing which takes place in sacramental communion. We can say not only that *each of us receives Christ*, but also that *Christ receives each of us*. He enters into friendship with us:"You are my friends" (Jn 15: 14). Indeed, it is because of him that we have life:"He who eats me will live because of me" (Jn 6: 57). Eucharistic communion brings about in a sublime way the mutual"abiding" of Christ and each of his followers:"Abide in me, and I in you" (Jn 15: 4).

By its union with Christ, the People of the New Covenant, far from closing in upon itself, becomes a"sacrament"for humanity,[39] a sign and instrument of the salvation achieved by Christ, the light of the world and the salt of the earth (cf. Mt 5: 13-16), for the redemption of all.[40] The Church's mission stands in continuity with the mission of Christ:"As the Father has sent me, even so I send you" (Jn 20: 21). From the perpetuation of the sacrifice of the Cross and her communion with the body and blood of Christ in the Eucharist, the Church draws the spiritual power needed to carry out her mission. The Eucharist thus appears as both *the source* and *the summit* of all evangelization, since its goal is the communion of mankind with Christ and in him with the Father and the Holy Spirit.[41]

23. Eucharistic communion also confirms the Church in her unity as the body of Christ. Saint Paul refers to this *unifying power* of participation in the banquet of the Eucharist when he writes to the Corinthians:"The bread which we break, is it not a communion in the body of Christ? Because there is one bread, we who are many are one body, for we all partake of the one bread" (1 Cor 10: 16-17). Saint John Chrysostom's commentary on these words is profound and perceptive:"For what is the bread? It is the body of Christ. And what do those who receive it become? The Body of Christ - not many bodies but one body. For as bread is completely one, though made of up many grains of wheat, and these, albeit unseen, remain nonetheless present, in such a way that their difference is not apparent since they have been made a perfect whole, so too are we mutually joined to one another and together united with Christ".[42] The argument is compelling: our union with Christ, which is a gift and grace for each of us, makes it possible for us, in him, to share in the unity of his body which is the Church. The Eucharist reinforces the incorporation into Christ which took place in Baptism though the gift of the Spirit (cf. 1 Cor 12: 13, 27).

The joint and inseparable activity of the Son and of the Holy Spirit, which is at the origin of the Church, of her consolidation and her continued life, is at work in the Eucharist. This was clearly evident to the author of the *Liturgy of Saint James*: in the epiclesis of the Anaphora, God the Father is asked to send the Holy Spirit upon the faithful and upon the offerings, so that the body and blood of Christ "May be a help to all those who partake of it . . . for the sanctification of their souls and bodies".[43] The Church is fortified by the divine Paraclete through the sanctification of the faithful in the Eucharist.

24. The gift of Christ and his Spirit which we receive in Eucharistic communion superabundantly fulfils the yearning for fraternal unity deeply rooted in the human heart; at the same time it elevates the experience of fraternity already present in our common sharing at the same Eucharistic table to a degree which far surpasses that of the simple human experience of sharing a meal. Through her communion with the body of Christ the Church comes to be ever more profoundly "in Christ in the nature of a sacrament, that is, a sign and instrument of intimate unity with God and of the unity of the whole human race".[44]

The seeds of disunity, which daily experience shows to be so deeply rooted in humanity as a result of sin, are countered by *the unifying power* of the body of Christ. The Eucharist, precisely by building up the Church, creates human community.

25. The *worship of the Eucharist outside of the Mass* is of inestimable value for the life of the Church. This worship is strictly linked to the celebration of the Eucharistic Sacrifice. The presence of Christ under the sacred species reserved after Mass—a presence which lasts as long as the species of bread and of wine remain[45]—derives from the celebration of the sacrifice and is directed towards communion, both sacramental and spiritual.[46] It is the responsibility of Pastors to encourage, also by their personal witness, the practice of Eucharistic adoration, and exposition of the Blessed Sacrament in particular, as well as prayer of adoration before Christ present under the Eucharistic species.[47]

It is pleasant to spend time with him, to lie close to his breast like the Beloved Disciple (cf. Jn 13: 25) and to feel the infinite love present in his heart. If in our time Christians must be distinguished above all by the "art of prayer",[48] how can we not feel a renewed need to spend time in spiritual converse, in silent adoration, in heartfelt love before Christ present in the Most Holy Sacrament? How often, dear brother and sisters, have I experienced this, and drawn from it strength, consolation and support!

This practice, repeatedly praised and recommended by the Magisterium,[49] is supported by the example of many saints. Particularly outstanding in this regard was Saint Alphonsus Liguori, who wrote: "Of all devotions, that of adoring Jesus in the Blessed Sacrament is the greatest after the sacraments, the one dearest to God and the one most helpful to us".[50] The Eucharist is a priceless treasure: by not only celebrating it but also by praying before it outside of Mass we are enabled to make contact with the very wellspring of grace. A Christian community desirous of contemplating the face of Christ in the spirit which I proposed in the Apostolic Letters *Novo millennio ineunte* and *Rosarium Virginis Mariæ* cannot fail also to develop this aspect of Eucharistic worship, which prolongs and increases the fruits of our communion in the body and blood of the Lord.

CHAPTER THREE:

THE APOSTOLICITY OF THE EUCHARIST AND OF THE CHURCH

26. If, as I have said, the Eucharist builds the Church and the Church makes the Eucharist, it follows that there is a profound relationship between the two, so much so that we can apply to the Eucharistic mystery the very words with which, in the Nicene-Constantinopolitan Creed, we profess the Church to be "one, holy, catholic and apostolic". The Eucharist too is one and catholic. It is also holy, indeed, the Most Holy Sacrament. But it is above all its apostolicity that we must now consider.

27. The *Catechism of the Catholic Church*, in explaining how the Church is apostolic—founded on the Apostles—sees *three meanings* in this expression. First, "she was and remains built on 'the foundation of the Apostles' (Eph 2: 20), the witnesses chosen and sent on mission by Christ himself".[51] The Eucharist too has its foundation in the Apostles, not in the sense that it did not originate in Christ himself, but because it was entrusted by Jesus to the Apostles and has been handed down to us by them and by their successors. It is in continuity with the practice of the Apostles, in obedience to the Lord's command, that the Church has celebrated the Eucharist down the centuries.

The second sense in which the Church is apostolic, as the *Catechism* points out, is that "with the help of the Spirit dwelling in her, the Church keeps and hands on the teaching, the 'good deposit', the salutary words she has heard from the Apostles".[52] Here too the Eucharist is apostolic, for it is celebrated in conformity with the faith of the Apostles. At various times in the two-thousand-year history of the People of the New Covenant, the Church's Magisterium has more precisely defined her teaching on the Eucharist, including its proper terminology, precisely in order to safeguard the apostolic faith with regard to this sublime mystery. This faith remains unchanged and it is essential for the Church that it remain unchanged.

28. Lastly, the Church is apostolic in the sense that she "continues to be taught, sanctified and guided by the Apostles until Christ's return, through their successors in pastoral office: the college of Bishops assisted by priests, in union with the Successor of Peter, the Church's supreme pastor".[53] Succession to the Apostles in the pastoral mission necessarily entails the sacrament of Holy Orders, that is, the uninterrupted sequence, from the very beginning, of valid episcopal ordinations.[54] This succession is essential for the Church to exist in a proper and full sense.

The Eucharist also expresses this sense of apostolicity. As the Second Vatican Council teaches, "the faithful join in the offering of the Eucharist by virtue of their royal priesthood",[55] yet it is the ordained priest who, "acting in the person of Christ, brings about the Eucharistic Sacrifice and offers it to God in the name of all the people".[56] For this reason, the Roman Missal prescribes that only the priest should recite the Eucharistic Prayer, while the people participate in faith and in silence.[57]

29. The expression repeatedly employed by the Second Vatican Council, according to which "the ministerial priest, acting in the person of Christ, brings about the Eucharistic Sacrifice",[58] was already firmly rooted in papal teaching.[59] As I have pointed out on other occasions, the phrase *in persona Christi* "means more than offering 'in the name of' or 'in the place of' Christ. *In persona* means in specific sacramental identification with the eternal High Priest who is the author and principal subject of this sacrifice of his, a sacrifice in which, in truth,

nobody can take his place".[60] The ministry of priests who have received the sacrament of Holy Orders, in the economy of salvation
chosen by Christ, makes clear that the Eucharist which they celebrate
is *a gift which radically transcends the power of the assembly* and is in
any event essential for validly linking the Eucharistic consecration to
the sacrifice of the Cross and to the Last Supper. The assembly gathered together for the celebration of the Eucharist, if it is to be a truly
Eucharistic assembly, absolutely requires the presence of an ordained
priest as its president. On the other hand, the community is by itself
incapable of providing an ordained minister. This minister is a gift
which the assembly *receives through episcopal succession going back
to the Apostles.* It is the Bishop who, through the Sacrament of Holy
Orders, makes a new presbyter by conferring upon him the power
to consecrate the Eucharist. Consequently, "the Eucharistic mystery
cannot be celebrated in any community except by an ordained priest,
as the Fourth Lateran Council expressly taught".[61]

30. The Catholic Church's teaching on the relationship between
priestly ministry and the Eucharist and her teaching on the Eucharistic Sacrifice have both been the subject in recent decades of a
fruitful dialogue *in the area of ecumenism.* We must give thanks to the
Blessed Trinity for the significant progress and convergence achieved
in this regard, which lead us to hope one day for a full sharing of
faith. Nonetheless, the observations of the Council concerning the
Ecclesial Communities which arose in the West from the sixteenth
century onwards and are separated from the Catholic Church remain fully pertinent: "The Ecclesial Communities separated from us
lack that fullness of unity with us which should flow from Baptism,
and we believe that especially because of the lack of the sacrament
of Orders they have not preserved the genuine and total reality of
the Eucharistic mystery. Nevertheless, when they commemorate the
Lord's death and resurrection in the Holy Supper, they profess that
it signifies life in communion with Christ and they await his coming
in glory".[62]

The Catholic faithful, therefore, while respecting the religious con-
victions of these separated brethren, must refrain from receiving the
communion distributed in their celebrations, so as not to condone an
ambiguity about the nature of the Eucharist and, consequently, to fail
in their duty to bear clear witness to the truth. This would result in
slowing the progress being made towards full visible unity. Similarly,
it is unthinkable to substitute for Sunday Mass ecumenical celebra-

tions of the word or services of common prayer with Christians from the aforementioned Ecclesial Communities, or even participation in their own liturgical services. Such celebrations and services, however praiseworthy in certain situations, prepare for the goal of full communion, including Eucharistic communion, but they cannot replace it.

The fact that the power of consecrating the Eucharist has been entrusted only to Bishops and priests does not represent any kind of belittlement of the rest of the People of God, for in the communion of the one body of Christ which is the Church this gift redounds to the benefit of all.

31. If the Eucharist is the centre and summit of the Church's life, it is likewise the centre and summit of priestly ministry. For this reason, with a heart filled with gratitude to our Lord Jesus Christ, I repeat that the Eucharist "is the principal and central *raison d'être* of the sacrament of priesthood, which effectively came into being at the moment of the institution of the Eucharist".[63]

Priests are engaged in a wide variety of pastoral activities. If we also consider the social and cultural conditions of the modern world it is easy to understand how priests face the very real *risk of losing their focus* amid such a great number of different tasks. The Second Vatican Council saw in pastoral charity the bond which gives unity to the priest's life and work. This, the Council adds, "flows mainly from the Eucharistic Sacrifice, which is therefore the centre and root of the whole priestly life".[64] We can understand, then, how important it is for the spiritual life of the priest, as well as for the good of the Church and the world, that priests follow the Council's recommendation to celebrate the Eucharist daily: "for even if the faithful are unable to be present, it is an act of Christ and the Church".[65] In this way priests will be able to counteract the daily tensions which lead to a lack of focus and they will find in the Eucharistic Sacrifice - the true centre of their lives and ministry - the spiritual strength needed to deal with their different pastoral responsibilities. Their daily activity will thus become truly Eucharistic.

The centrality of the Eucharist in the life and ministry of priests is the basis of its centrality in the *pastoral promotion of priestly vocations*. It is in the Eucharist that prayer for vocations is most closely united to the prayer of Christ the Eternal High Priest. At the same time the diligence of priests in carrying out their Eucharistic ministry, together with the conscious, active and fruitful participation of the faithful in the Eucharist, provides young men with a powerful example and incentive for responding generously to God's call. Often it is the example of a priest's fervent pastoral charity which the Lord uses to sow and to bring to fruition in a young man's heart the seed of a priestly calling.

32. All of this shows how distressing and irregular is the situation of a Christian community which, despite having sufficient numbers and variety of faithful to form a parish, does not have a priest to lead it. Parishes are communities of the baptized who express and affirm their identity above all through the celebration of the Eucharistic Sacrifice. But this requires the presence of a presbyter, who alone is qualified to offer the Eucharist *in persona Christi*. When a community lacks a priest, attempts are rightly made somehow to remedy the situation so that it can continue its Sunday celebrations, and those religious and laity who lead their brothers and sisters in prayer exercise in a praiseworthy way the common priesthood of all the faithful based on the grace of Baptism. But such solutions must be considered merely temporary, while the community awaits a priest.

The sacramental incompleteness of these celebrations should above all inspire the whole community to pray with greater fervour that the Lord will send labourers into his harvest (cf. Mt 9: 38). It should also be an incentive to mobilize all the resources needed for an adequate pastoral promotion of vocations, without yielding to the temptation to seek solutions which lower the moral and formative standards demanded of candidates for the priesthood.

33. When, due to the scarcity of priests, non-ordained members of the faithful are entrusted with a share in the pastoral care of a parish, they should bear in mind that—as the Second Vatican Council teaches—"no Christian community can be built up unless it has its basis and centre in the celebration of the most Holy Eucharist".[66] They have a responsibility, therefore, to keep alive in the community a genuine "hunger" for the Eucharist, so that no opportunity for the celebration of Mass will ever be missed, also taking advantage of the occasional presence of a priest who is not impeded by Church law from celebrating Mass.

CHAPTER FOUR:

THE EUCHARIST
AND ECCLESIAL COMMUNION

34. The Extraordinary Assembly of the Synod of Bishops in 1985 saw in the concept of an "ecclesiology of communion" the central and fundamental idea of the documents of the Second Vatican Council.[67] The Church is called during her earthly pilgrimage to maintain and promote communion with the Triune God and communion among the faithful. For this purpose she possesses the word and the sacraments, particularly the Eucharist, by which she "constantly lives and grows"[68] and in which she expresses her very nature. It is not by chance that the term *communion* has become one of the names given to this sublime sacrament.

The Eucharist thus appears as the culmination of all the sacraments in perfecting our communion with God the Father by identification with his only-begotten Son through the working of the Holy Spirit. With discerning faith a distinguished writer of the Byzantine tradition voiced this truth: in the Eucharist "unlike any other sacrament, the mystery [of communion] is so perfect that it brings us to the heights of every good thing: here is the ultimate goal of every human desire, because here we attain God and God joins himself to us in the most perfect union".[69] Precisely for this reason it is good to *cultivate in our hearts a constant desire for the sacrament of the Eucharist*. This was the origin of the practice of "spiritual communion", which has happily been established in the Church for centuries and recommended by saints who were masters of the spiritual life. Saint Teresa of Jesus wrote: "When you do not receive communion and you do not attend Mass, you can make a spiritual communion, which is a most beneficial practice; by it the love of God will be greatly impressed on you".[70]

35. The celebration of the Eucharist, however, cannot be the starting-point for communion; it presupposes that communion already exists, a communion which it seeks to consolidate and bring to perfection. The sacrament is an expression of this bond of communion both in its *invisible* dimension, which, in Christ and through the working of the Holy Spirit, unites us to the Father and among ourselves, and in its *visible* dimension, which entails communion in the teaching of the Apostles, in the sacraments and in the Church's hierarchical order. The profound relationship between the invisible and the visible elements of ecclesial communion is constitutive of the Church as the sacrament of salvation.[71] Only in this context can there be a legitimate celebration of the Eucharist and true participation in it. Consequently it is an intrinsic requirement of the Eucharist that it should be celebrated in communion, and specifically maintaining the various bonds of that communion intact.

36. Invisible communion, though by its nature always growing, pre-supposes the life of grace, by which we become "partakers of the divine nature" (2 Pt 1: 4), and the practice of the virtues of faith, hope and love. Only in this way do we have true communion with the Father, the Son and the Holy Spirit. Nor is faith sufficient; we must persevere in sanctifying grace and love, remaining within the Church "bodily" as well as "in our heart";[72] what is required, in the words of Saint Paul, is "faith working through love" (Gal 5: 6).

Keeping these invisible bonds intact is a specific moral duty incumbent upon Christians who wish to participate fully in the Eucharist by receiving the body and blood of Christ. The Apostle Paul appeals to this duty when he warns: "Let a man examine himself, and so eat of the bread and drink of the cup" (1 Cor 11: 28). Saint John Chrysostom, with his stirring eloquence, exhorted the faithful: "I too raise my voice, I beseech, beg and implore that no one draw near to this sacred table with a sullied and corrupt conscience. Such an act, in fact, can never be called 'communion', not even were we to touch the Lord's body a thousand times over, but 'condemnation', 'torment' and 'increase of punishment'".[73]

Along these same lines, the *Catechism of the Catholic Church* rightly stipulates that "anyone conscious of a grave sin must receive the sacrament of Reconciliation before coming to communion".[74] I therefore desire to reaffirm that in the Church there remains in force, now and in the future, the rule by which the Council of Trent gave concrete expression to the Apostle Paul's stern warning when it affirmed that, in order to receive the Eucharist in a worthy manner, "one must first confess one's sins, when one is aware of mortal sin".[75]

37. The two sacraments of the Eucharist and Penance are very closely connected. Because the Eucharist makes present the redeeming sacrifice of the Cross, perpetuating it sacramentally, it naturally gives rise to a continuous need for conversion, for a personal response to the appeal made by Saint Paul to the Christians of Corinth: "We beseech you on behalf of Christ, be reconciled to God" (2 Cor 5: 20). If a Christian's conscience is burdened by serious sin, then the path of penance through the sacrament of Reconciliation becomes necessary for full participation in the Eucharistic Sacrifice.

The judgment of one's state of grace obviously belongs only to the person involved, since it is a question of examining one's conscience. However, in cases of outward conduct which is seriously, clearly and steadfastly contrary to the moral norm, the Church, in her pastoral concern for the good order of the community and out of respect for the sacrament, cannot fail to feel directly involved. The *Code of Canon Law* refers to this situation of a manifest lack of proper moral disposition when it states that those who "obstinately persist in manifest grave sin" are not to be admitted to Eucharistic communion.[76]

38. Ecclesial communion, as I have said, is likewise *visible*, and finds expression in the series of "bonds" listed by the Council when it teaches: "They are fully incorporated into the society of the Church who, possessing the Spirit of Christ, accept her whole structure and all the means of salvation established within her, and within her visible framework are united to Christ, who governs her through the Supreme Pontiff and the Bishops, by the bonds of profession of faith, the sacraments, ecclesiastical government and communion".[77]

The Eucharist, as the supreme sacramental manifestation of communion in the Church, demands to be celebrated in *a context where the outward bonds of communion are also intact*. In a special way, since the Eucharist is "as it were the summit of the spiritual life and the goal of all the sacraments",[78] it requires that the bonds of communion in the sacraments, particularly in Baptism and in priestly Orders, be real. It is not possible to give communion to a person who is not baptized or to one who rejects the full truth of the faith regarding the Eucharistic mystery. Christ is the truth and he bears witness to the truth (cf. Jn 14: 6; 18: 37); the sacrament of his body and blood does not permit duplicity.

39. Furthermore, given the very nature of ecclesial communion and its relation to the sacrament of the Eucharist, it must be recalled that "the Eucharistic Sacrifice, while always offered in a particular community, is never a celebration of that community alone. In fact, the community, in receiving the Eucharistic presence of the Lord, receives the entire gift of salvation and shows, even in its lasting visible particular form, that it is the image and true presence of the one, holy, catholic and apostolic Church".[79] From this it follows that a truly Eucharistic community cannot be closed in upon itself, as though it were somehow self-sufficient; rather it must persevere in harmony with every other Catholic community.

The ecclesial communion of the Eucharistic assembly is a communion with its own *Bishop* and with the *Roman Pontiff.* The Bishop, in effect, is the *visible* principle and the foundation of unity within his particular Church.[80] It would therefore be a great contradiction if the sacrament *par excellence* of the Church's unity were celebrated without true communion with the Bishop. As Saint Ignatius of Antioch wrote: "That Eucharist which is celebrated under the Bishop, or under one to whom the Bishop has given this charge, may be considered certain".[81] Likewise, since "the Roman Pontiff, as the successor of Peter, is the perpetual and visible source and foundation of the unity of the Bishops and of the multitude of the faithful",[82] communion with him is intrinsically required for the celebration of the Eucharistic Sacrifice. Hence the great truth expressed which the Liturgy expresses in a variety of ways: "Every celebration of the Eucharist is performed in union not only with the proper Bishop, but also with the Pope, with the episcopal order, with all the clergy, and with the entire people. Every valid celebration of the Eucharist expresses this universal communion with Peter and with the whole Church, or objectively calls for it, as in the case of the Christian Churches separated from Rome".[83]

40. The Eucharist *creates communion* and *fosters communion.* Saint Paul wrote to the faithful of Corinth explaining how their divisions, reflected in their Eucharistic gatherings, contradicted what they were celebrating, the Lord's Supper. The Apostle then urged them to reflect on the true reality of the Eucharist in order to return to the spirit of fraternal communion (cf. 1 Cor 11: 17-34). Saint Augustine effectively echoed this call when, in recalling the Apostle's words: "You are the body of Christ and individually members of it" (1 Cor 12: 27), he went on to say: "If you are his body and members of him, then you will find set on the Lord's table your own mystery. Yes, you receive your own mystery".[84] And from this observation he concludes: "Christ the Lord . . . hallowed at his table the mystery of our peace and unity. Whoever receives the mystery of unity without preserving the bonds of peace receives not a mystery for his benefit but evidence against himself".[85]

41. The Eucharist's particular effectiveness in promoting communion is one of the reasons for the importance of Sunday Mass. I have already dwelt on this and on the other reasons which make Sunday Mass fundamental for the life of the Church and of individual believers in my Apostolic Letter on the sanctification of Sunday *Dies Domini*.[86] There I recalled that the faithful have the obligation to attend Mass, unless they are seriously impeded, and that Pastors have the corresponding duty to see that it is practical and possible for all to fulfil this precept.[87] More recently, in my Apostolic Letter *Novo millennio ineunte*, in setting forth the pastoral path which the Church must take at the beginning of the third millennium, I drew particular attention to the Sunday Eucharist, emphasizing its effectiveness for building communion. "It is" - I wrote - "the privileged place where communion is ceaselessly proclaimed and nurtured. Precisely through sharing in the Eucharist, *the Lord's Day* also becomes *the Day of the Church*, when she can effectively exercise her role as the sacrament of unity".[88]

42. The safeguarding and promotion of ecclesial communion is a task of each member of the faithful, who finds in the Eucharist, as the sacrament of the Church's unity, an area of special concern. More specifically, this task is the particular responsibility of the Church's Pastors, each according to his rank and ecclesiastical office. For this reason the Church has drawn up norms aimed both at fostering the frequent and fruitful access of the faithful to the Eucharistic table and at determining the objective conditions under which communion may not be given. The care shown in promoting the faithful observance of these norms becomes a practical means of showing love for the Eucharist and for the Church.

43. In considering the Eucharist as the sacrament of ecclesial communion, there is one subject which, due to its importance, must not be overlooked: I am referring to the *relationship of the Eucharist to ecumenical activity*. We should all give thanks to the Blessed Trinity for the many members of the faithful throughout the world who in recent decades have felt an ardent desire for unity among all Christians. The Second Vatican Council, at the beginning of its Decree on Ecumenism, sees this as a special gift of God.[89] It was an efficacious grace which inspired us, the sons and daughters of the Catholic Church and our brothers and sisters from other Churches and Ecclesial Communities, to set forth on the path of ecumenism.

Our longing for the goal of unity prompts us to turn to the Eucharist, which is the supreme sacrament of the unity of the People of God, in as much as it is the apt expression and the unsurpassable source of that unity.[90] In the celebration of the Eucharistic Sacrifice the Church prays that God, the Father of mercies, will grant his children the fullness of the Holy Spirit so that they may become one body and one spirit in Christ.[91] In raising this prayer to the Father of lights, from whom comes every good endowment and every perfect gift (cf. Jas 1: 17), the Church believes that she will be heard, for she prays in union with Christ her Head and Spouse, who takes up this plea of his Bride and joins it to that of his own redemptive sacrifice.

44. Precisely because the Church's unity, which the Eucharist brings about through the Lord's sacrifice and by communion in his body and blood, absolutely requires full communion in the bonds of the profession of faith, the sacraments and ecclesiastical governance, it is not possible to celebrate together the same Eucharistic liturgy until those bonds are fully re-established. Any such concelebration would not be a valid means, and might well prove instead to be *an obstacle, to the attainment of full communion,* by weakening the sense of how far we remain from this goal and by introducing or exacerbating ambiguities with regard to one or another truth of the faith. The path towards full unity can only be undertaken in truth. In this area, the prohibitions of Church law leave no room for uncertainty,[92] in fidelity to the moral norm laid down by the Second Vatican Council.[93]

I would like nonetheless to reaffirm what I said in my Encyclical Letter *Ut unum sint* after having acknowledged the impossibility of Eucharistic sharing: "And yet we do have a burning desire to join in celebrating the one Eucharist of the Lord, and this desire itself is already a common prayer of praise, a single supplication. Together we speak to the Father and increasingly we do so 'with one heart'".[94]

45. While it is never legitimate to concelebrate in the absence of full communion, the same is not true with respect to the administration of the Eucharist *under special circumstances, to individual persons* belonging to Churches or Ecclesial Communities not in full communion with the Catholic Church. In this case, in fact, the intention is to meet a grave spiritual need for the eternal salvation of an individual believer, not to bring about an *intercommunion* which remains impossible until the visible bonds of ecclesial communion are fully re-established.

This was the approach taken by the Second Vatican Council when it gave guidelines for responding to Eastern Christians separated in good faith from the Catholic Church, who spontaneously ask to receive the Eucharist from a Catholic minister and are properly disposed.[95] This approach was then ratified by both Codes, which also consider - with necessary modifications - the case of other non-Eastern Christians who are not in full communion with the Catholic Church.[96]

46. In my Encyclical *Ut unum sint* I expressed my own appreciation of these norms, which make it possible to provide for the salvation of souls with proper discernment:"It is a source of joy to note that Catholic ministers are able, in certain particular cases, to administer the sacraments of the Eucharist, Penance and Anointing of the Sick to Christians who are not in full communion with the Catholic Church but who greatly desire to receive these sacraments, freely request them and manifest the faith which the Catholic Church professes with regard to these sacraments. Conversely, in specific cases and in particular circumstances, Catholics too can request these same sacraments from ministers of Churches in which these sacraments are valid".[97]

These conditions, from which no dispensation can be given, must be carefully respected, even though they deal with specific individual cases, because the denial of one or more truths of the faith regarding these sacraments and, among these, the truth regarding the need of the ministerial priesthood for their validity, renders the person asking improperly disposed to legitimately receiving them. And the opposite is also true: Catholics may not receive communion in those communities which lack a valid sacrament of Orders.[98]

The faithful observance of the body of norms established in this area[99] is a manifestation and, at the same time, a guarantee of our love for Jesus Christ in the Blessed Sacrament, for our brothers and sisters of different Christian confessions—who have a right to our witness to the truth—and for the cause itself of the promotion of unity.

CHAPTER FIVE:

THE DIGNITY
OF THE EUCHARISTIC CELEBRATION

47. Reading the account of the institution of the Eucharist in the Synoptic Gospels, we are struck by the simplicity and the "solemnity" with which Jesus, on the evening of the Last Supper, instituted this great sacrament. There is an episode which in some way serves as its prelude: *the anointing at Bethany*. A woman, whom John identifies as Mary the sister of Lazarus, pours a flask of *costly ointment* over Jesus' head, which provokes from the disciples—and from Judas in particular (cf. Mt 26: 8; Mk 14: 4; Jn 12: 4)—an indignant response, as if this act, in light of the needs of the poor, represented an intolerable "waste". But Jesus' own reaction is completely different. While in no way detracting from the duty of charity towards the needy, for whom the disciples must always show special care—"the poor you will always have with you" (Mt 26, 11; Mk 14: 7; cf. Jn 12: 8) - he looks towards his imminent death and burial, and sees this act of anointing as an anticipation of the honour which his body will continue to merit even after his death, indissolubly bound as it is to the mystery of his person.

The account continues, in the Synoptic Gospels, with Jesus' charge to the disciples to *prepare carefully the "large upper room"* needed for the Passover meal (cf. Mk 14: 15; Lk 22: 12) and with the narration of the institution of the Eucharist. Reflecting at least in part the *Jewish rites* of the Passover meal leading up to the singing of the Hallel (cf. Mt 26: 30; Mk 14: 26), the story presents with sobriety and solemnity, even in the variants of the different traditions, the words spoken by Christ over the bread and wine, which he made into concrete expressions of the handing over of his body and the shedding of his blood. All these details are recorded by the Evangelists in the light of a praxis of the "breaking of the bread" already well-established in the early Church. But certainly from the time of Jesus on, the event of Holy Thursday has shown visible traces of a liturgical "sensibility" shaped by Old Testament tradition and open to being reshaped in Christian celebrations in a way consonant with the new content of Easter.

48. Like the woman who anointed Jesus in Bethany, *the Church has feared no "extravagance"*, devoting the best of her resources to expressing her wonder and adoration before the *unsurpassable gift of the Eucharist*. No less than the first disciples charged with preparing the "large upper room", she has felt the need, down the centuries and in her encounters with different cultures, to celebrate the Eucharist in a setting worthy of so great a mystery. In the wake of Jesus' own words and actions, and building upon the ritual heritage of Judaism, the *Christian liturgy was born*. Could there ever be an adequate means of expressing the acceptance of that self-gift which the divine Bridegroom continually makes to his Bride, the Church, by bringing the Sacrifice offered once and for all on the Cross to successive generations of believers and thus becoming nourishment for all the faithful? Though the idea of a "banquet" naturally suggests familiarity, the Church has never yielded to the temptation to trivialize this "intimacy" with her Spouse by forgetting that he is also her Lord and that the "banquet" always remains a sacrificial banquet marked by the blood shed on Golgotha. *The Eucharistic Banquet is truly a "sacred" banquet*, in which the simplicity of the signs conceals the unfathomable holiness of God: *O sacrum convivium, in quo Christus sumitur!* The bread which is broken on our altars, offered to us as wayfarers along the paths of the world, is *panis angelorum*, the bread of angels, which cannot be approached except with the humility of the centurion in the Gospel: "Lord, I am not worthy to have you come under my roof" (Mt 8: 8; Lk 7: 6).

49. With this heightened sense of mystery, we understand how the faith of the Church in the mystery of the Eucharist has found historical expression not only in the demand for an interior disposition of devotion, but also *in outward forms* meant to evoke and emphasize the grandeur of the event being celebrated. This led progressively to the development of *a particular form of regulating the Eucharistic liturgy*, with due respect for the various legitimately constituted ecclesial traditions. On this foundation *a rich artistic heritage* also developed. Architecture, sculpture, painting and music, moved by the Christian mystery, have found in the Eucharist, both directly and indirectly, a source of great inspiration.

Such was the case, for example, with architecture, which witnessed the transition, once the historical situation made it possible, from the first places of Eucharistic celebration in the *domus* or "homes" of Christian families to the solemn *basilicas* of the early centuries, to the imposing *cathedrals* of the Middle Ages, and to the *churches*, large and small, which gradually sprang up throughout the lands touched by Christianity. The designs of altars and tabernacles within Church interiors were often not simply motivated by artistic inspiration but also by a clear understanding of the mystery. The same could be said for *sacred music*, if we but think of the inspired Gregorian melodies and the many, often great, composers who sought to do justice to the liturgical texts of the Mass. Similarly, can we overlook the enormous quantity of *artistic production*, ranging from fine craftsmanship to authentic works of art, in the area of Church furnishings and vestments used for the celebration of the Eucharist?

It can be said that the Eucharist, while shaping the Church and her spirituality, has also powerfully affected "culture", and the arts in particular.

50. In this effort to adore the mystery grasped in its ritual and aesthetic dimensions, a certain "competition" has taken place between Christians of the West and the East. How could we not give particular thanks to the Lord for the contributions to Christian art made by the great architectural and artistic works of the Greco-Byzantine tradition and of the whole geographical area marked by Slav culture? In the East, sacred art has preserved a remarkably powerful sense of mystery, which leads artists to see their efforts at creating beauty not simply as an expression of their own talents, but also as *a genuine service to the faith*. Passing well beyond mere technical skill, they have shown themselves docile and open to the inspiration of the Holy Spirit.

The architectural and mosaic splendours of the Christian East and West are a patrimony belonging to all believers; they contain a hope, and even a pledge, of the desired fullness of communion in faith and in celebration. This would presuppose and demand, as in Rublëv's famous depiction of the Trinity, *a profoundly Eucharistic Church* in which the presence of the mystery of Christ in the broken bread is as it were immersed in the ineffable unity of the three divine Persons, making of the Church herself an "icon" of the Trinity.

Within this context of an art aimed at expressing, in all its elements, the meaning of the Eucharist in accordance with the Church's teaching, attention needs to be given to the norms regulating *the construction and decor of sacred buildings*. As history shows and as I emphasized in my Letter to Artists,[100] the Church has always left ample room for the creativity of artists. But sacred art must be outstanding for its ability to express adequately the mystery grasped in the fullness of the Church's faith and in accordance with the pastoral guidelines appropriately laid down by competent Authority. This holds true both for the figurative arts and for sacred music.

51. The development of sacred art and liturgical discipline which took place in lands of ancient Christian heritage is also taking place *on continents where Christianity is younger*. This was precisely the approach supported by the Second Vatican Council on the need for sound and proper "inculturation". In my numerous Pastoral Visits I have seen, throughout the world, the great vitality which the celebration of the Eucharist can have when marked by the forms, styles and sensibilities of different cultures. By adaptation to the changing conditions of time and place, the Eucharist offers sustenance not only to individuals but to entire peoples, and it shapes cultures inspired by Christianity.

It is necessary, however, that this important work of adaptation be carried out with a constant awareness of the ineffable mystery against which every generation is called to measure itself. The "treasure" is too important and precious to risk impoverishment or compromise through forms of experimentation or practices introduced without a careful review on the part of the competent ecclesiastical authorities. Furthermore, the centrality of the Eucharistic mystery demands that any such review must be undertaken in close association with the Holy See. As I wrote in my Post-Synodal Apostolic Exhortation *Ecclesia in Asia*, "such cooperation is essential because the Sacred Liturgy expresses and celebrates the one faith professed by all and, being the heritage of the whole Church, cannot be determined by local Churches in isolation from the universal Church".[101]

52. All of this makes clear the great responsibility which belongs to priests in particular for the celebration of the Eucharist. It is their responsibility to preside at the Eucharist *in persona Christi* and to provide a witness to and a service of communion not only for the community directly taking part in the celebration, but also for the universal Church, which is a part of every Eucharist. It must be lamented that, especially in the years following the post-conciliar liturgical reform, as a result of a misguided sense of creativity and adaptation there have been a number of *abuses* which have been a source of suffering for many. A certain reaction against "formalism" has led some, especially in certain regions, to consider the "forms" chosen by the Church's great liturgical tradition and her Magisterium as non-binding and to introduce unauthorized innovations which are often completely inappropriate.

I consider it my duty, therefore to appeal urgently that the liturgical norms for the celebration of the Eucharist be observed with great fidelity. These norms are a concrete expression of the authentically ecclesial nature of the Eucharist; this is their deepest meaning. Liturgy is never anyone's private property, be it of the celebrant or of the community in which the mysteries are celebrated. The Apostle Paul had to address fiery words to the community of Corinth because of grave shortcomings in their celebration of the Eucharist resulting in divisions (*schismata*) and the emergence of factions (*haireseis*) (cf. 1 Cor 11: 17-34). Our time, too, calls for a renewed awareness and appreciation of liturgical norms as a reflection of, and a witness to, the one universal Church made present in every celebration of the Eucharist. Priests who faithfully celebrate Mass according to the liturgical norms, and communities which conform to those norms, quietly but eloquently demonstrate their love for the Church. Precisely to bring out more clearly this deeper meaning of liturgical norms, I have asked the competent offices of the Roman Curia to prepare a more specific document, including prescriptions of a juridical nature, on this very important subject. No one is permitted to undervalue the mystery entrusted to our hands: it is too great for anyone to feel free to treat it lightly and with disregard for its sacredness and its universality.

CHAPTER SIX:

AT THE SCHOOL OF MARY, "WOMAN OF THE EUCHARIST"

53. If we wish to rediscover in all its richness the profound relationship between the Church and the Eucharist, we cannot neglect Mary, Mother and model of the Church. In my Apostolic Letter *Rosarium Virginis Mariæ*, I pointed to the Blessed Virgin Mary as our teacher in contemplating Christ's face, and among the mysteries of light I included *the institution of the Eucharist*.[102] Mary can guide us towards this most holy sacrament, because she herself has a profound relationship with it.

At first glance, the Gospel is silent on this subject. The account of the institution of the Eucharist on the night of Holy Thursday makes no mention of Mary. Yet we know that she was present among the Apostles who prayed "with one accord" (cf. Acts 1: 14) *in the first community which gathered after the Ascension in expectation of Pentecost*. Certainly Mary must have been present at the Eucharistic celebrations of the first generation of Christians, who were devoted to "the breaking of bread" (Acts 2: 42).

But in addition to her sharing in the Eucharistic banquet, an indirect picture of Mary's relationship with the Eucharist can be had, beginning with her interior disposition. *Mary is a "woman of the Eucharist" in her whole life.* The Church, which looks to Mary as a model, is also called to imitate her in her relationship with this most holy mystery.

54. *Mysterium fidei!* If the Eucharist is a mystery of faith which so greatly transcends our understanding as to call for sheer abandonment to the word of God, then there can be no one like Mary to act as our support and guide in acquiring this disposition. In repeating what Christ did at the Last Supper in obedience to his command:"Do this in memory of me!", we also accept Mary's invitation to obey him without hesitation:"Do whatever he tells you"(Jn 2: 5). With the same maternal concern which she showed at the wedding feast of Cana, Mary seems to say to us:"Do not waver; trust in the words of my Son. If he was able to change water into wine, he can also turn bread and wine into his body and blood, and through this mystery bestow on believers the living memorial of his passover, thus becoming the'bread of life'".

55. In a certain sense Mary lived her *Eucharistic faith* even before the institution of the Eucharist, by the very fact that *she offered her virginal womb for the Incarnation of God's Word.* The Eucharist, while commemorating the passion and resurrection, is also in continuity with the incarnation. At the Annunciation Mary conceived the Son of God in the physical reality of his body and blood, thus anticipating within herself what to some degree happens sacramentally in every believer who receives, under the signs of bread and wine, the Lord's body and blood.

As a result, there is a profound analogy between the *Fiat* which Mary said in reply to the angel, and the *Amen* which every believer says when receiving the body of the Lord. Mary was asked to believe that the One whom she conceived"through the Holy Spirit"was"the Son of God"(Lk 1: 30-35). In continuity with the Virgin's faith, in the Eucharistic mystery we are asked to believe that the same Jesus Christ, Son of God and Son of Mary, becomes present in his full humanity and divinity under the signs of bread and wine.

"Blessed is she who believed"(Lk 1: 45). Mary also anticipated, in the mystery of the incarnation, the Church's Eucharistic faith. When, at the Visitation, she bore in her womb the Word made flesh, she became in some way a "tabernacle" - the first "tabernacle" in history - in which the Son of God, still invisible to our human gaze, allowed himself to be adored by Elizabeth, radiating his light as it were through the eyes and the voice of Mary. And is not the enraptured gaze of Mary as she contemplated the face of the newborn Christ and cradled him in her arms that unparalleled model of love which should inspire us every time we receive Eucharistic communion?

56. Mary, throughout her life at Christ's side and not only on Calvary, made her own *the sacrificial dimension of the Eucharist*. When she brought the child Jesus to the Temple in Jerusalem "to present him to the Lord" (Lk 2: 22), she heard the aged Simeon announce that the child would be a "sign of contradiction" and that a sword would also pierce her own heart (cf. Lk 2: 34-35). The tragedy of her Son's crucifixion was thus foretold, and in some sense Mary's *Stabat Mater* at the foot of the Cross was foreshadowed. In her daily preparation for Calvary, Mary experienced a kind of "anticipated Eucharist" - one might say a "spiritual communion" - of desire and of oblation, which would culminate in her union with her Son in his passion, and then find expression after Easter by her partaking in the Eucharist which the Apostles celebrated as the memorial of that passion.

What must Mary have felt as she heard from the mouth of Peter, John, James and the other Apostles the words spoken at the Last Supper: "This is my body which is given for you" (Lk 22: 19)? The body given up for us and made present under sacramental signs was the same body which she had conceived in her womb! For Mary, receiving the Eucharist must have somehow meant welcoming once more into her womb that heart which had beat in unison with hers and reliving what she had experienced at the foot of the Cross.

57. "Do this in remembrance of me" (Lk 22: 19). In the "memorial" of Calvary all that Christ accomplished by his passion and his death is present. Consequently *all that Christ did with regard to his Mother* for our sake is also present. To her he gave the beloved disciple and, in him, each of us: "Behold, your Son!". To each of us he also says: "Behold your mother!" (cf. Jn 19: 26-27).

Experiencing the memorial of Christ's death in the Eucharist also means continually receiving this gift. It means accepting - like John - the one who is given to us anew as our Mother. It also means taking on a commitment to be conformed to Christ, putting ourselves at the school of his Mother and allowing her to accompany us. Mary is present, with the Church and as the Mother of the Church, at each of our celebrations of the Eucharist. If the Church and the Eucharist are inseparably united, the same ought to be said of Mary and the Eucharist. This is one reason why, since ancient times, the commemoration of Mary has always been part of the Eucharistic celebrations of the Churches of East and West.

58. In the Eucharist the Church is completely united to Christ and his sacrifice, and makes her own the spirit of Mary. This truth can be understood more deeply by *re-reading the Magnificat* in a Eucharistic key. The Eucharist, like the Canticle of Mary, is first and foremost praise and thanksgiving. When Mary exclaims: "My soul magnifies the Lord and my spirit rejoices in God my Saviour", she already bears Jesus in her womb. She praises God "through" Jesus, but she also praises him "in" Jesus and "with" Jesus. This is itself the true "Eucharistic attitude".

At the same time Mary recalls the wonders worked by God in salvation history in fulfilment of the promise once made to the fathers (cf. Lk 1: 55), and proclaims the wonder that surpasses them all, the redemptive incarnation. Lastly, the *Magnificat* reflects the eschatological tension of the Eucharist. Every time the Son of God comes again to us in the "poverty" of the sacramental signs of bread and wine, the seeds of that new history wherein the mighty are "put down from their thrones" and "those of low degree are exalted" (cf. Lk 1: 52), take root in the world. Mary sings of the "new heavens" and the "new earth" which find in the Eucharist their anticipation and in some sense their programme and plan. The *Magnificat* expresses Mary's spirituality, and there is nothing greater than this spirituality for helping us to experience the mystery of the Eucharist. The Eucharist has been given to us so that our life, like that of Mary, may become completely a *Magnificat!*

CONCLUSION

59. *Ave, verum corpus natum de Maria Virgine!* Several years ago I celebrated the fiftieth anniversary of my priesthood. Today I have the grace of offering the Church this Encyclical on the Eucharist on the

Holy Thursday which falls *during the twenty-fifth year of my Petrine ministry*. As I do so, my heart is filled with gratitude. For over a half century, every day, beginning on 2 November 1946, when I celebrated my first Mass in the Crypt of Saint Leonard in Wawel Cathedral in Krakow, my eyes have gazed in recollection upon the host and the chalice, where time and space in some way "merge" and the drama of Golgotha is re-presented in a living way, thus revealing its mysterious "contemporaneity". Each day my faith has been able to recognize in the consecrated bread and wine the divine Wayfarer who joined the two disciples on the road to Emmaus and opened their eyes to the light and their hearts to new hope (cf. Lk 24: 13-35).

Allow me, dear brothers and sisters, to share with deep emotion, as a means of accompanying and strengthening your faith, my own testimony of faith in the Most Holy Eucharist. *Ave verum corpus natum de Maria Virgine, vere passum, immolatum, in cruce pro homine!* Here is the Church's treasure, the heart of the world, the pledge of the fulfilment for which each man and woman, even unconsciously, yearns. A great and transcendent mystery, indeed, and one that taxes our mind's ability to pass beyond appearances. Here our senses fail us: *visus, tactus, gustus in te fallitur*, in the words of the hymn *Adoro te devote*; yet faith alone, rooted in the word of Christ handed down to us by the Apostles, is sufficient for us. Allow me, like Peter at the end of the Eucharistic discourse in John's Gospel, to say once more to Christ, in the name of the whole Church and in the name of each of you: "Lord to whom shall we go? You have the words of eternal life" (Jn 6: 68).

60. At the dawn of this third millennium, we, the children of the Church, are called to undertake with renewed enthusiasm the journey of Christian living. As I wrote in my Apostolic Letter *Novo millennio ineunte*, "it is not a matter of inventing a 'new programme'. The programme already exists: it is the plan found in the Gospel and in the living Tradition; it is the same as ever. Ultimately, it has its centre in Christ himself, who is to be known, loved and imitated, so that in him we may live the life of the Trinity, and with him transform history until its fulfilment in the heavenly Jerusalem". [103] The implementation of this programme of a renewed impetus in Christian living passes through the Eucharist.

Every commitment to holiness, every activity aimed at carrying out the Church's mission, every work of pastoral planning, must draw the strength it needs from the Eucharistic mystery and in turn be directed to that mystery as its culmination. In the Eucharist we have Jesus, we have his redemptive sacrifice, we have his resurrection, we have the gift of the Holy Spirit, we have adoration, obedience and love of the Father. Were we to disregard the Eucharist, how could we overcome our own deficiency?

61. The mystery of the Eucharist—sacrifice, presence, banquet—*does not allow for reduction or exploitation*; it must be experienced and lived in its integrity, both in its celebration and in the intimate converse with Jesus which takes place after receiving communion or in a prayerful moment of Eucharistic adoration apart from Mass. These are times when the Church is firmly built up and it becomes clear what she truly is: one, holy, catholic and apostolic; the people, temple and family of God; the body and bride of Christ, enlivened by the Holy Spirit; the universal sacrament of salvation and a hierarchically structured communion.

The path taken by the Church in these first years of the third millennium is also a *path of renewed ecumenical commitment*. The final decades of the second millennium, culminating in the Great Jubilee, have spurred us along this path and called for all the baptized to respond to the prayer of Jesus *"ut unum sint"* (Jn 17: 11). The path itself is long and strewn with obstacles greater than our human resources alone can overcome, yet we have the Eucharist, and in its presence we can hear in the depths of our hearts, as if they were addressed to us, the same words heard by the Prophet Elijah: "Arise and eat, else the journey will be too great for you" (1 Kgs 19: 7). The treasure of the Eucharist, which the Lord places before us, impels us towards the goal of full sharing with all our brothers and sisters to whom we are joined by our common Baptism. But if this treasure is not to be squandered, we need to respect the demands which derive from its being the sacrament of communion in faith and in apostolic succession.

By giving the Eucharist the prominence it deserves, and by being careful not to diminish any of its dimensions or demands, we show that we are truly conscious of the greatness of this gift. We are urged to do so by an uninterrupted tradition, which from the first centuries on has found the Christian community ever vigilant in guarding this "treasure". Inspired by love, the Church is anxious to hand on to future generations of Christians, without loss, her faith and teaching with regard to the mystery of the Eucharist. There can be no danger of excess in our care for this mystery, for "in this sacrament is recapitulated the whole mystery of our salvation".[104]

62. Let us take our place, dear brothers and sisters, *at the school of the saints,* who are the great interpreters of true Eucharistic piety. In them the theology of the Eucharist takes on all the splendour of a lived reality; it becomes "contagious" and, in a manner of speaking, it "warms our hearts". Above all, let us *listen to Mary Most Holy,* in whom the mystery of the Eucharist appears, more than in anyone else, as a mystery of light. Gazing upon Mary, we come to know *the transforming power present in the Eucharist.* In her we see the world renewed in love. Contemplating her, assumed body and soul into heaven, we see opening up before us those "new heavens" and that "new earth" which will appear at the second coming of Christ. Here below, the Eucharist represents their pledge, and in a certain way, their anticipation: "*Veni, Domine Iesu!*" (Rv 22: 20).

In the humble signs of bread and wine, changed into his body and blood, Christ walks beside us as our strength and our food for the journey, and he enables us to become, for everyone, witnesses of hope. If, in the presence of this mystery, reason experiences its limits, the heart, enlightened by the grace of the Holy Spirit, clearly sees the response that is demanded, and bows low in adoration and unbounded love.

Let us make our own the words of Saint Thomas Aquinas, an eminent theologian and an impassioned poet of Christ in the Eucharist, and turn in hope to the contemplation of that goal to which our hearts aspire in their thirst for joy and peace:

> *Bone pastor, panis vere,*
> *Iesu, nostri miserere . . .*
>
> *Come then, good Shepherd, bread divine,*
> *Still show to us thy mercy sign;*
> *Oh, feed us, still keep us thine;*
> *So we may see thy glories shine*
> *in fields of immortality.*
>
> *O thou, the wisest, mightiest, best,*
> *Our present food, our future rest,*
> *Come, make us each thy chosen guest,*
> *Co-heirs of thine, and comrades blest*
> *With saints whose dwelling is with thee.*

Given in Rome, at Saint Peter's, on 17 April, Holy Thursday, in the year 2003, the Twenty-fifth of my Pontificate, the Year of the Rosary.

Endnotes

1. Second Vatican Ecumenical Council, Dogmatic Constitution on the Church *Lumen gentium*, 11.
2. Second Vatican Ecumenical Council, Decree on the Ministry and Life of Priests *Presbyterorum ordinis*, 5.
3. Cf. John Paul II, Apostolic Letter *Rosarium Virginis Mariæ* (16 October 2002), 21: AAS 95 (2003), 19.
4. This is the title which I gave to an autobiographical testimony issued for my fiftieth anniversary of priestly ordination.
5. *Leonis XIII P.M. Acta*, XXII (1903), 115-136.
6. AAS 39 (1947), 521-595.
7. AAS 57 (1965), 753-774.
8. AAS 72 (1980), 113-148.
9. Cf. Second Vatican Ecumenical Council, Constitution *Sacrosanctum concilium*, 47:". . . our Saviour instituted the Eucharistic Sacrifice of his body and blood, in order to perpetuate the sacrifice of the Cross throughout time, until he should return".
10. *Catechism of the Catholic Church*, 1085.
11. Second Vatican Ecumenical Council, Dogmatic Constitution on the Church *Lumen gentium*, 3.
12. Cf. Paul VI, *Solemn Profession of Faith*, 30 June 1968, 24: AAS 60 (1968), 442; John Paul II, Apostolic Letter *Dominicæ cenæ* (24 February 1980), 12: AAS 72 (1980), 142.
13. *Catechism of the Catholic Church*, 1382.
14. *Catechism of the Catholic Church*, 1367.
15. *In Epistolam ad Hebraeos Homiliæ, Hom.* 17,3: PG 63, 131.
16. Cf. Ecumenical Council of Trent, Session XXII, *Doctrina de ss. Missæ Sacrificio*, Chapter 2: DS 1743:"It is one and the same victim here offering himself by the ministry of his priests, who then offered himself on the Cross; it is only the manner of offering that is different".
17. Pius XII, Encyclical Letter *Mediator Dei* (20 November 1947): AAS 39 (1947), 548.
18. John Paul II, Encyclical Letter *Redemptor hominis* (15 March 1979), 20: AAS 71 (1979), 310.
19. Dogmatic Constitution on the Church *Lumen gentium*, 11.
20. *De Sacramentis*, V, 4, 26: CSEL 73, 70.
21. *In Ioannis evangelium*, XII, 20: PG 74, 726.
22. Encyclical Letter *Mysterium Fidei* (3 September 1965): AAS 57 (1965), 764.
23. Session XIII, *Decretum de ss. Eucharistia*, Chapter 4: DS 1642.
24. *Mystagogical Catecheses*, IV, 6: SCh 126, 138.
25. Second Vatican Ecumenical Council, Dogmatic Constitution on Divine Revelation *Dei Verbum*, 8.
26. *Solemn Profession of Faith*, 30 June 1968, 25: AAS 60 (1968), 442-443.
27. *Sermo IV in Hebdomadam Sanctam*: CSCO 413/Syr. 182, 55.
28. Anaphora.
29. Eucharistic Prayer III.
30. Solemnity of the Body and Blood of Christ, Second Vespers, Antiphon to the *Magnificat*.
31. *Missale Romanum*, Embolism following the Lord's Prayer.
32. *Ad Ephesios*, 20: PG 5, 661.
33. Cf. Second Vatican Ecumenical Council, Pastoral Constitution on the Church in the Modern World *Gaudium et spes*, 39.

34. "Do you wish to honour the body of Christ? Do not ignore him when he is naked. Do not pay him homage in the temple clad in silk, only then to neglect him outside where he is cold and ill-clad. He who said:'This is my body' is the same who said:'You saw me hungry and you gave me no food', and 'Whatever you did to the least of my brothers you did also to me'... What good is it if the Eucharistic table is overloaded with golden chalices when your brother is dying of hunger. Start by satisfying his hunger and then with what is left you may adorn the altar as well": Saint John Chrysostom, *In Evangelium S. Matthaei, hom.* 50: 3-4: PG 58, 508-509; cf. John Paul II, Encyclical Letter *Sollicitudo rei socialis* (30 December 1987), 31: AAS 80 (1988), 553-556.
35. Dogmatic Constitution *Lumen gentium*, 3.
36. *Ibid.*
37. Second Vatican Ecumenical Council, Decree on the Missionary Activity of the Church *Ad gentes*, 5.
38. "Moses took the blood and threw it upon the people, and said:'Behold the blood of the Covenant which the Lord has made with you in accordance with all these words'" (Ex 24: 8).
39. Cf. Second Vatican Ecumenical Council, Dogmatic Constitution on the Church *Lumen gentium*, 1.
40. Cf. *ibid.*, 9.
41. Cf. Second Vatican Ecumenical Council, Decree on the Life and Ministry of Priests *Presbyterorum ordinis*, 5. The same Decree, in n. 6, says:"No Christian community can be built up which does not grow from and hinge on the celebration of the most holy Eucharist".
42. *In Epistolam I ad Corinthios Homiliæ*, 24, 2: PG 61, 200; Cf. *Didache*, IX, 4: F.X. Funk, I, 22; Saint Cyprian, *Ep.* LXIII, 13: PL 4, 384.
43. PO 26, 206.
44. Second Vatican Ecumenical Council, Dogmatic Constitution on the Church *Lumen gentium*, 1.
45. Cf. Ecumenical Council of Trent, Session XIII, *Decretum de ss. Eucharistia*, Canon 4: DS 1654.
46. Cf. *Rituale Romanum: De sacra communione et de cultu mysterii eucharistici extra Missam*, 36 (n. 80).
47. Cf. *ibid.*, 38-39 (nn. 86-90).
48. John Paul II, Apostolic Letter *Novo millennio ineunte* (6 January 2001), 32: AAS 93 (2001), 288.
49. "In the course of the day the faithful should not omit visiting the Blessed Sacrament, which in accordance with liturgical law must be reserved in churches with great reverence in a prominent place. Such visits are a sign of gratitude, an expression of love and an acknowledgment of the Lord's presence": Paul VI, Encyclical Letter *Mysterium Fidei* (3 September 1965): AAS 57 (1965), 771.
50. *Visite al SS. Sacramento e a Maria Santissima*, Introduction: *Opere Ascetiche*, Avellino, 2000, 295.
51. N. 857.
52. *Ibid.*
53. *Ibid.*
54. Cf. Congregation for the Doctrine of the Faith, Letter *Sacerdotium Ministeriale* (6 August 1983), III.2: AAS 75 (1983), 1005.
55. Second Vatican Ecumenical Council, Dogmatic Constitution on the Church *Lumen gentium*, 10.
56. *Ibid.*
57. Cf. *Institutio Generalis*: Editio typica tertia, n. 147.
58. Cf. Dogmatic Constitution on the Church *Lumen gentium*, 10 and 28; Decree on the Ministry and Life of Priests *Presbyterorum ordinis*, 2.

59. "The minister of the altar acts in the person of Christ inasmuch as he is head, making an offering in the name of all the members": Pius XII, Encyclical Letter *Mediator Dei* (20 November 1947): AAS 39 (1947), 556; cf. Pius X, Apostolic Exhortation *Hærent animo* (4 August 1908): *Acta Pii X*, IV, 16; Pius XI, Encyclical Letter *Ad Catholici sacerdotii* (20 December 1935): AAS 28 (1936), 20.
60. Apostolic Letter *Dominicæ cenæ* (24 February 1980), 8: AAS 72 (1980), 128-129.
61. Congregation for the Doctrine of the Faith, Letter *Sacerdotium Ministeriale* (6 August 1983), III.4: AAS 75 (1983), 1006; cf. Fourth Lateran Ecumenical Council, Chapter 1, Constitution on the Catholic Faith *Firmiter Credimus*: DS 802.
62. Second Vatican Ecumenical Council, Decree on Ecumenism *Unitatis redintegratio*, 22.
63. Apostolic Letter *Dominicæ cenæ* (24 February 1980), 2: AAS 72 (1980), 115.
64. Decree on the Life and Ministry of Priests *Presbyterorum ordinis*, 14.
65. *Ibid.*, 13; cf. *Code of Canon Law*, Canon 904; *Code of Canons of the Eastern Churches*, Canon 378.
66. Decree on the Ministry and Life of Priests *Presbyterorum ordinis*, 6.
67. Cf. Final Report, II.C.1: *L'Osservatore Romano*, 10 December 1985, 7.
68. Second Vatican Ecumenical Council, Dogmatic Constitution on the Church *Lumen gentium*, 26.
69. Nicolas Cabasilas, *Life in Christ*, IV, 10: SCh 355, 270.
70. *Camino de Perfección*, Chapter 35.
71. Cf. Congregation for the Doctrine of the Faith, Letter to the Bishops of the Catholic Church on Some Aspects of the Church Understood as Communion *Communionis notio* (28 May 1992), 4: AAS 85 (1993), 839-840.
72. Cf. Second Vatican Ecumenical Council, Dogmatic Constitution on the Church *Lumen gentium*, 14.
73. *Homiliæ in Isaiam*,6, 3: PG 56, 139.
74. N. 1385; cf. *Code of Canon Law*, Canon 916; *Code of Canons of the Eastern Churches*, Canon 711.
75. Address to the Members of the Sacred Apostolic Penitentiary and the Penitentiaries of the Patriarchal Basilicas of Rome (30 January 1981): AAS 73 (1981), 203. Cf. Ecumenical Council of Trent, Sess. XIII, *Decretum de ss. Eucharistia*, Chapter 7 and Canon 11: DS 1647, 1661.
76. Canon 915; *Code of Canons of the Eastern Churches*, Canon 712.
77. Dogmatic Constitution on the Church *Lumen gentium*, 14.
78. Saint Thomas Aquinas, *Summa Theologiæ*, III, q. 73, a. 3c.
79. Congregation for the Doctrine of the Faith, Letter to the Bishops of the Catholic Church on Some Aspects of the Church Understood as Communion *Communionis notio* (28 May 1992), 11: AAS 85 (1993), 844.
80. Cf. Second Vatican Ecumenical Council, Dogmatic Constitution on the Church *Lumen gentium*, 23.
81. *Ad Smyrnæos*, 8: PG 5, 713.
82. Second Vatican Ecumenical Council, Dogmatic Constitution on the Church *Lumen gentium*, 23.
83. Congregation for the Doctrine of the Faith, Letter to the Bishops of the Catholic Church on Some Aspects of the Church Understood as Communion *Communionis notio* (28 May 1992), 14: AAS 85 (1993), 847.
84. *Sermo*272: PL 38, 1247.
85. *Ibid.*, 1248.
86. Cf. nn. 31-51: AAS 90 (1998), 731-746.
87. Cf. *ibid.*, nn. 48-49: AAS 90 (1998), 744.
88. N. 36: AAS 93 (2001), 291-292.
89. Cf. Decree on Ecumenism *Unitatis redintegratio*, 1.
90. Cf. Dogmatic Constitution on the Church *Lumen gentium*, 11.
91. "Join all of us, who share the one bread and the one cup, to one another in the communion of the one Holy Spirit": *Anaphora of the Liturgy of Saint Basil.*

92. Cf. *Code of Canon Law*, Canon 908; *Code of Canons of the Eastern Churches*, Canon 702; Pontifical Council for the Promotion of Christian Unity, *Ecumenical Directory*, 25 March 1993, 122-125, 129-131: AAS 85 (1993), 1086-1089; Congregation for the Doctrine of the Faith, Letter *Ad Exsequendam*, 18 May 2001: AAS 93 (2001), 786.
93. "Divine law forbids any common worship which would damage the unity of the Church, or involve formal acceptance of falsehood or the danger of deviation in the faith, of scandal, or of indifferentism": Decree on the Eastern Catholic Churches *Orientalium Ecclesiarum*, 26.
94. N. 45: AAS 87 (1995), 948.
95. Decree on the Eastern Catholic Churches *Orientalium Ecclesiarum*, 27.
96. Cf. *Code of Canon Law*, Canon 844 §§ 3-4; *Code of Canons of the Eastern Churches*, Canon 671 §§ 3-4.
97. N. 46: AAS 87 (1995), 948.
98. Cf. Second Vatican Ecumenical Council, Decree on Ecumenism *Unitatis redintegratio*, 22.
99. *Code of Canon Law*, Canon 844; *Code of Canons of the Eastern Churches*, Canon 671.
100. Cf. AAS 91 (1999), 1155-1172.
101. N. 22: AAS 92 (2000), 485.
102. Cf. n. 21: AAS 95 (2003), 20.
103. N. 29: AAS 93 (2001), 285.
104. Saint Thomas Aquinas, *Summa Theologiæ*, III, q. 83, a. 4c.

2004

Twenty-sixth Year of Pontificate

During the twenty-sixth year of his pontificate, John Paul II continued to emphasize the importance of the Eucharist in Christian life, declaring 2004-2005 to be the Year of the Eucharist. The letter to priests for Holy Thursday 2004 echoed the Holy Father's encyclical from the previous year in its explanation of the relationship between the priesthood and the Eucharist: "There is a particular interplay between the Eucharist and the priesthood, an interplay which goes back to the Upper Room: these two Sacraments were born together and their destiny is indissolubly linked until the end of the world" (2004 Letter, n. 3).

Pope John Paul II wrote about the Year of the Eucharist in the Apostolic Letter *Mane nobiscum Domine*, in which he offers "some basic guidelines" on how the year should be celebrated. The Year of the Eucharist officially opened on October 17 when the Holy Father met, via television linkup, with the forty-eighth International Eucharist Congress convened in Guadalajara, Mexico.

Throughout 2004 the Holy Father continued his efforts to promote dialogue between the Roman Catholic Church and the Eastern Orthodox Churches. On June 29 he met with Bartholomew I, Ecumenical Patriarch of Constantinople, and the two signed a joint declaration. In August, he had the Kazan Icon of the Mother of God delivered to Alexei II, Patriarch of the Russian Orthodox Church. The icon, said to have brought miraculous protection to Moscow in 1612, was stolen from Russia several hundred years ago and was recently discovered in a small chapel in Portugal. With the icon the Holy Father sent a letter in which he voiced his desire for future unity: "The Bishop of Rome has prayed before this sacred Icon, asking that the day may come when we will all be united and able to proclaim to the world, with one voice and in visible communion, the salvation of our one Lord and his triumph over the evil and impious forces which seek to damage our faith and our witness of unity" (Letter to His Holiness Patriarch Alexei II on the occasion of the return to Russia of the Icon of Our Lady of Kazan)

In November the Holy Father sent the relics of the Saints John Chrysostom and Gregory of Nazianen to the Ecumenical Patriarch of Constantinople, Bartholomew I. In the letter accompanying the relics, Pope John Paul II voiced his own determination to be a "servant of communion": "I will never tire of searching out, steadfastly and with determination, this communion between Christ's disciples" (Ecumenical celebration of the occasion of the transferal from Rome to Constantinople of the relics of Sts. Gregory of Nazianen and John Chrysostom).

Despite his worsening physical condition, Pope John Paul II journeyed to Bern, Switzerland, for the National Meeting of Young Catholics in June. In August he made a pilgrimage to Lourdes, France, for the one hundred-fiftieth anniversary of the promulgation of the Dogma of the Immaculate Conception. There he prayed to the Virgin Mary for peace in the world: "May forgiveness and brotherly love take root in human hearts. May every weapon be laid down, and all hatred and violence put aside" (*Accueil Notre-Dame*, August 14, 2004).

During the course of his twenty-sixth year as the Roman pontiff, Pope John Paul beatified eighteen men and women.

On May 16 the Holy Father canonized six men and women, among them Gianna Beretta Molla, a mother who willingly gave her own life so that her child might be born.

Just two days later, on May 18, John Paul II released his fourth book, *Rise, Let Us Be On Our Way!* in which he discusses his forty-five years as a bishop. In addition to being a veritable manual for the episcopate, the book is highly philosophical and includes discussions on courage and the relationship between truth and love.

LETTER
OF THE HOLY FATHER
POPE JOHN PAUL II
TO PRIESTS
FOR HOLY THURSDAY 2004

Dear Priests!

1.   It is with great joy and affection that I write you this Holy Thursday Letter, following a tradition which began with my first Easter as the Bishop of Rome twenty-five years ago. Our annual encounter through this Letter is a particularly fraternal one, thanks to our common sharing in the Priesthood of Christ, and it takes place in the liturgical setting of this holy day marked by its two significant celebrations: the morning Chrism Mass, and the evening Mass *in Cena Domini.*

I think of you first as you gather in the cathedrals of your different Dioceses around your respective Ordinaries for the renewal of your priestly promises. This eloquent rite (which) takes place before the blessing of the Holy Oils, especially the Chrism, and is a most fitting part of the Chrism Mass, which highlights the image of the Church as a priestly people made holy by the sacraments and sent forth to spread throughout the world the good odour of Christ the Saviour (2 Cor 2: 14-16).

At dusk I see you entering the Upper Room for the beginning of the Easter Triduum. It is precisely to that *"large room upstairs"* (Lk 22: 12) that Jesus invites us to return each Holy Thursday, and it is there above all that I most cherish meeting you, my dear brothers in the priesthood. At the Last Supper, *we were born as priests*: for this reason it is both a pleasure and a duty to gather once again in the Upper Room and to remind one another with heartfelt gratitude of the lofty mission which we share.

2.   We were born from the Eucharist. If we can truly say that the whole Church lives from the Eucharist (*"Ecclesia de Eucharistia vivit"*), as I reaffirmed in my recent Encyclical, we can say the same thing about the ministerial priesthood: it is born, lives, works and bears fruit *"de Eucharistia"* (cf. Council of Trent, Sess. XXII, canon 2: DS 1752). "There can be no Eucharist without the priesthood, just as there can be no priesthood without the Eucharist" (cf. *Gift and Mystery.*

On the Fiftieth Anniversary of My Priestly Ordination, New York, 1996, pp. 77-78).

The ordained ministry, which may never be reduced to its merely functional aspect since it belongs on the level of"being", enables the priest to act *in persona Christi* and culminates in the moment when he consecrates the bread and wine, repeating the actions and words of Jesus during the Last Supper.

Before this extraordinary reality we find ourselves amazed and overwhelmed, so deep is the humility by which God"stoops"in order to unite himself with man! If we feel moved before the Christmas crib, when we contemplate the Incarnation of the Word, what must we feel before the altar where, by the poor hands of the priest, Christ makes his Sacrifice present in time? We can only fall to our knees and silently adore this supreme mystery of faith.

3. *"Mysterium fidei"*, the priest proclaims after the consecration. The Eucharist is a mystery of faith, yet the priesthood itself, by reflection, is also a mystery of faith (cf. *ibid.*, p. 78). The same mystery of sanctification and love, the work of the Holy Spirit, which makes the bread and wine become the Body and Blood of Christ, is at work in the person of the minister at the moment of priestly ordination. There is a particular interplay between the Eucharist and the priesthood, an interplay which goes back to the Upper Room: these two Sacraments were born together and their destiny is indissolubly linked until the end of the world.

Here we touch on what I have called the"*apostolicity of the Eucharist*" (cf. Encyclical *Ecclesia de Eucharistia*, 26-33). The sacrament of the Eucharist—like the sacrament of Reconciliation—was entrusted by Christ to the Apostles and has been passed down by them and their successors in every generation. At the beginning of his public life, the Messiah called the Twelve, appointed them"*to be with him*"and sent them out on mission (cf. Mk 3: 14-15). At the Last Supper, this"being with"Jesus on the part of the Apostles reached its culmination. By celebrating the Passover meal and instituting the Eucharist, the divine Master brought their vocation to its fulfilment. By saying"*Do this in memory of me*", he put a Eucharistic seal on their mission and, by uniting them to himself in sacramental communion, he charged them to perpetuate that most holy act in his memory.

As he pronounced the words"*Do this . . .*"Jesus' thoughts extended to the successors of the Apostles, to those who would continue their mission by distributing the food of life to the very ends of the earth.

In some way, then, dear brother priests, in the Upper Room we too were called personally, each one of us, "with brotherly love" (*Preface of the Chrism Mass*), to receive from the Lord's sacred hands the Eucharistic Bread and to break it as food for the People of God on their pilgrim way through time towards our heavenly homeland.

4. The Eucharist, like the priesthood, is a gift from God "which radically transcends the power of the assembly" and which the assembly "receives through episcopal succession going back to the Apostles" (Encyclical *Ecclesia de Eucharistia*, 29). The Second Vatican Council teaches that "the ministerial priest, by the sacred power that he enjoys . . . effects the Eucharistic Sacrifice in the person of Christ and offers it to God in the name of all the people" (Dogmatic Constitution *Lumen gentium*, 10). The assembly of the faithful, united in faith and in the Spirit and enriched by a variety of gifts, even though it is the place where Christ "is present in his Church, especially in her liturgical celebrations (Constitution *Sacrosanctum concilium*, 7), is not by itself able to celebrate the Eucharist or to provide the ordained minister.

Quite rightly, then, the Christian people gives thanks to God for the gift of the Eucharist and the priesthood, while praying unceasingly that priests will never be lacking in the Church. The number of priests is never sufficient to meet the constantly increasing demands of evangelization and the pastoral care of the faithful. In some places of the world the shortage of priests is all the more urgently felt since today the number of priests is dwindling without sufficient replacements from the younger generation. In other places, thank God, we see a promising spring-time of vocations. There is also a growing awareness among the People of God of the need to pray and work actively to promote vocations to the priesthood and to the consecrated life.

5. Vocations are indeed a gift from God for which we must pray unceasingly. Following the invitation of Jesus, we need to pray the Lord of the harvest to send out labourers into his harvest (cf. Mt 9: 37). Prayer, enriched by the silent offering of suffering, remains the first and most effective means of *pastoral work for vocations*. To pray means to keep our gaze fixed on Christ, confident that from him, the one High Priest, and from his divine oblation, there will be an abundant growth, by the work of the Holy Spirit, of the seeds of those vocations needed in every age for the Church's life and mission.

Let us pause in the Upper Room and contemplate the Redeemer who instituted the Eucharist and the priesthood at the Last Supper.

On that holy night he *called by name* each and every priest in every time. He looked at each one of them with the same look of loving encouragement with which he looked at Simon and Andrew, at James and John, at Nathanael beneath the fig tree, and at Matthew sitting at the tax office. Jesus has called us and, along a variety of paths, he continues to call many others to be his ministers.

From the Upper Room Christ tirelessly seeks and calls. Here we find the origin and the perennial source of an authentic pastoral promotion of priestly vocations. Let us consider ourselves, my brothers, the first ones responsible in this area, ready to help all those whom Christ wishes to associate to his priesthood to respond generously to his call.

First, however, and more than any other effort on behalf of vocations, our personal fidelity is indispensable. What counts is our personal commitment to Christ, our love for the Eucharist, our fervour in celebrating it, our devotion in adoring it and our zeal in offering it to our brothers and sisters, especially to the sick. Jesus the High Priest continues personally to call new workers for his vineyard, but he wishes from the first to count on our active cooperation. Priests in love with the Eucharist are capable of communicating to children and young people that *"Eucharistic amazement"* which I have sought to rekindle with my Encyclical *Ecclesia de Eucharistia* (cf. n. 6). Generally these are the priests who lead them to the path of the priesthood, as the history of our own vocations might easily show.

6.   In the light of this, dear brother priests, I would ask you, among other initiatives, to *show special care for altar servers*, who represent a kind of "garden" of priestly vocations. The group of altar servers, under your guidance as part of the parish community, can be given a valuable experience of Christian education and become a kind of pre-seminary. Help the parish, as a family made up of families, to look upon the altar servers as their own children, like *"olive shoots around the table"* of Jesus Christ, the Bread of Life (cf. Ps 127: 3).

With the help of the families most involved and catechists, be particularly concerned for the group of servers so that, through their service at the altar, each of them will learn to grow in love for the Lord Jesus, to recognize him truly present in the Eucharist and to experience the beauty of the liturgy. Initiatives for altar servers on the diocesan or local level should be promoted and encouraged, with attention to the different age groups. During my years of episcopal ministry in Krakow I was able to see the great benefits which can

accrue from a concern for their human, spiritual and liturgical training. When children and young people serve at the altar with joy
and enthusiasm, they offer their peers an eloquent witness to the
importance and beauty of the Eucharist. Thanks to their own lively
imagination and the explanations and example given by priests and
their older friends, even very young children can grow in faith and
develop a love for spiritual realities.

Finally, never forget that you yourselves are the first "Apostles" of
Jesus the High Priest. Your own witness counts more than anything
else. Altar servers see you at the regular Sunday and weekday celebrations; in your hands they see the Eucharist "take place", on your
face they see its mystery reflected, and in your heart they sense the
summons of a greater love. May you be for them fathers, teachers
and witnesses of Eucharistic piety and holiness of life!

7.   Dear brother priests, your particular mission in the Church requires that you be "friends" of Christ, constantly contemplating his
face with docility at the school of Mary Most Holy. Pray unceasingly,
as the Apostle exhorts (cf. 1 Thes 5: 17), and encourage the faithful to
pray for vocations, for the perseverance of those called to the priestly
life and for the sanctification of all priests. Help your communities
to love ever more fully that unique "gift and mystery" which is the
ministerial priesthood.

In the prayerful setting of Holy Thursday, I would recall once again
some invocations of the Litany of Jesus Christ Priest and Victim
(cf. *Gift and Mystery*, pp. 108-114), which I have recited for many
years with great spiritual profit:

> *Iesu, Sacerdos et Victima,*
> *Iesu, Sacerdos qui in novissima Cena formam sacrificii*
>   *perennis instituisti,*
> *Iesu, Pontifex ex hominibus assumpte,*
> *Iesu, Pontifex pro hominibus constitute,*
> *Iesus, Pontifex qui tradidisti temetipsum Deo oblationem*
>   *et hostiam,*
> *miserere nobis!*

> *Ut pastores secundum cor tuum populo tuo providere digneris,*
> *ut in messem tuam operarios fideles mittere digneris,*
> *ut fideles mysteriorum tuorum dispensatores multiplicare*
>   *digneris,*
> *Te rogamus, audi nos!*

8. I entrust each of you and your daily ministry to Mary, Mother of Priests. During the recitation of the Rosary, the fifth *mystery of light* leads us to contemplate with Mary's eyes the gift of the Eucharist, to marvel at the love that Jesus showed *"to the end"* (Jn 13: 1) in the Upper Room, and at his humble presence in every tabernacle. May the Blessed Virgin obtain for you the grace never to take for granted the mystery put in your hands. With endless gratitude to the Lord for the amazing gift of his Body and Blood, may you persevere faithfully in your priestly ministry.

Mary, Mother of Christ our High Priest, pray that the Church will always have numerous and holy vocations, faithful and generous ministers of the altar!

Dear brother priests, I wish you and your communities a Holy Easter and to all of you I affectionately impart my blessing.

From the Vatican, on 28 March, the Fifth Sunday of Lent, in the year 2004, the twenty-sixth of my Pontificate.

2005

Twenty-seventh Year of Pontificate

Pope John Paul's final year as the Roman pontiff was marked by his immense courage in dealing with his own physical suffering. Once a vigorous and athletic man, the Holy Father aged with such humility and fortitude that he became a living testament to the dignity of human life, no matter how frail.

Pope John Paul II continued to write until the end, releasing his final book *Memory and Identity* in late February of 2005. In *Memory* the pope discusses an array of issues, interspersing philosophical rejections of Nazism and Communism with meditative poetry, and refuting modern relativism. The book is perhaps best known for containing the pope's first printed reflections on the attempt made on his life in 1981.

In his final years, Pope John Paul II's message seemed to gravitate toward the center of Christian life: the Eucharist. His final Letter to Priests, released on March 13 from Gemelli Hospital in Rome, uses the words of the consecration as a guide to meditate on both the Eucharist and the priesthood, sacraments he considered to be intimately united and complementary.

On February 1, 2005, the pope was hospitalized for ten days after having breathing trouble and voice box spasms. Despite his illness the Holy Father appeared in his hospital window to give a blessing to well-wishers. After being released he continued to make public appearances until returning to the hospital on February 24 because of breathing trouble and a fever. He returned to the Vatican on March 13 though he was unable to preside over the Holy Week activities. Throughout the week he made appearances at his window and via television despite his condition. On April 2, after suffering septic shock, the pope passed away in his Vatican Apartment. He was surrounded by his closest aides while thousands kept vigil in St. Peter's Square, praying and singing for their beloved Holy Father.

Hundreds of thousands from around the globe attended the funeral Mass of Pope John Paul II. During the Mass' homily, Cardinal Joseph Ratzinger, who would become Pope Benedict XVI only a few weeks later, eloquently recalled the priestly nature of the pope's life: "The Holy Father was a priest to the last, for he offered his life to God for his flock and for the entire human family, in a daily self-oblation for the service of the Church, especially amid the sufferings of his final months. And in this way he became one with Christ, the Good Shepherd who loves his sheep."

LETTER
OF THE HOLY FATHER
JOHN PAUL II
TO PRIESTS
FOR HOLY THURSDAY 2005

Dear Priests!

1.   In this Year of the Eucharist, I particularly welcome our annual spiritual encounter for Holy Thursday, the day when Christ's love was manifested "to the end" (cf. Jn 13: 1), the day of the Eucharist, the day of our priesthood.

My thoughts turn to you, dear priests, as I spend this time recuperating in hospital, a patient alongside other patients, uniting in the Eucharist my own sufferings with those of Christ. In this spirit I want to reflect with you on some aspects of our priestly spirituality.

I will take as my inspiration the words of Eucharistic consecration, which we say every day *in persona Christi* in order to make present on our altars the sacrifice made once and for all on Calvary. These words provide us with illuminating insights for priestly spirituality: if the whole Church draws life from the Eucharist, all the more then must the life of a priest be "shaped" by the Eucharist. So for us, the words of institution must be more than a formula of consecration: they must be a "formula of life".

A life of profound "gratitude"

2.   *"Tibi gratias agens benedixit"*. At every Mass we remember and relive the first sentiment expressed by Jesus as he broke the bread: that of *thanksgiving*. Gratitude is the disposition which lies at the root of the very word "Eucharist". This expression of thanksgiving contains the whole Biblical spirituality of praise for the *mirabilia Dei*. God loves us, he goes before us in his Providence, he accompanies us with his continuous saving acts.

In the Eucharist Jesus thanks the Father with us and for us. How could this thanksgiving of Jesus fail to shape the life of a priest? He knows that he must cultivate *a constant sense of gratitude* for the many gifts he has received in the course of his life: in particular, for the gift of faith, which it is his task to proclaim, and for the gift of the priesthood, which consecrates him totally to the service of the Kingdom of God. We have our crosses to bear — and we are certainly not the only ones! — but the gifts we have received are so great that we cannot fail to sing from the depths of our hearts our own *Magnificat*.

A life that is "given"

3.   *"Accipite et manducate. Accipite et bibite"*. Christ's self-giving, which has its origin in the Trinitarian life of the God who is Love, reaches its culmination in the sacrifice of the Cross, sacramentally anticipated in the Last Supper. It is impossible to repeat the words of consecration without *feeling oneself caught up in this spiritual movement*. In a certain sense, when he says the words: "take and eat", the priest must learn to apply them also to himself, and to speak them with truth and generosity. If he is able to offer himself as a gift, placing himself at the disposal of the community and at the service of anyone in need, his life takes on its true meaning.

This is exactly what Jesus expected of his apostles, as the Evangelist John emphasizes in his account of the washing of the feet. It is also what the People of God expect of a priest. If we think about it more fully, the priest's promise of *obedience*, which he made on the day of Ordination and is asked to renew at the Chrism Mass, is illuminated by this relationship with the Eucharist. Obeying out of love, sacrificing even a certain legitimate freedom when the authoritative discernment of the Bishop so requires, the priest lives out in his own flesh that "take and eat" with which Christ, in the Last Supper, gave himself to the Church.

A life that is "saved" in order to save

4.   *"Hoc est enim corpus meum quod pro vobis tradetur."* The body and the blood of Christ are given for the salvation of man, of the *whole* man and of *all* men. This salvation is *integral* and at the same time *universal*, because no one, unless he freely chooses, is excluded from the saving power of Christ's blood: *"qui pro vobis et pro multis effundetur"*. It is a sacrifice offered for "many", as the Biblical text says (Mk 14: 24; Mt 26: 28; cf. Is 53: 11-12); this typical Semitic expression refers to the multitude who are saved by Christ, the one Redeemer, yet at the same time it implies *the totality of human beings* to whom salvation is offered: the Lord's blood is *"shed for you and for all"*, as some translations legitimately make explicit. Christ's flesh is truly given "for the life of the world" (Jn 6: 51; cf. 1 Jn 2: 2).

Repeating Christ's venerable words in the recollected silence of the liturgical assembly, we priests become *privileged heralds* of this mystery of salvation. Yet unless we sense that we ourselves are saved, how can we be convincing heralds? We are the first to be touched inwardly by the grace which raises us from our frailty and makes us cry "Abba, Father" with the confidence of God's children (cf. Gal 4: 6; Rom 8: 15). This in turn commits us to advance along the path of perfection. *Holiness*, in fact, is the full expression of *salvation*. Only if our lives manifest the fact that we are saved do we become credible heralds of salvation. Moreover, a constant awareness of Christ's will to offer salvation *to all* cannot fail to inspire us with fresh *missionary fervour*, spurring each of us on to become "all things to all men, in order to save at least some of them" (1 Cor 9: 22).

A life that "remembers"

5. *"Hoc facite in meam commemorationem."* These words of Jesus have been preserved for us not only by Luke (22: 19) but also by Paul (1 Cor 11: 24). We should keep in mind that they were spoken in the context of the Paschal meal, which for the Jews was indeed a "memorial" (in Hebrew, *zikkarôn*). On that occasion the Israelites relived the Exodus first and foremost, but also the other important events of their history: the call of Abraham, the sacrifice of Isaac, the Covenant of Sinai, the many acts of God in defence of his people. For Christians too, the Eucharist is a "memorial", but of a unique kind: it not only commemorates, but sacramentally makes present the death and resurrection of the Lord.

Jesus said: "Do this in memory *of me*". The Eucharist does not simply commemorate a fact; it commemorates Him! Through his daily repetition *in persona Christi* of the words of the "memorial", the priest is invited to develop a "spirituality of remembrance". At a time when rapid social and cultural changes are weakening the sense of tradition and leading the younger generation especially to risk losing touch with their roots, the priest is called to be, within the community entrusted to him, the *man who faithfully remembers* the entire mystery of Christ: prefigured in the Old Testament, fulfilled in the New, and understood ever more deeply, under the guidance of the Spirit, as Jesus explicitly promised: "He will teach you all things and *bring to your remembrance* all that I have said to you" (Jn 14: 26).

A "consecrated" life

6. *"Mysterium fidei!"* Every time he proclaims these words after consecrating the bread and wine, the priest expresses his *ever-renewed amazement* at the extraordinary miracle worked at his hands. It is a miracle which only the eyes of faith can perceive. The natural elements do not lose their external characteristics, since the "species" remain those of bread and wine; but their "substance", through the power of Christ's word and the action of the Holy Spirit, is changed into the substance of the body and blood of Christ. On the altar, then, Christ crucified and risen is "truly, really and substantially" present in the fullness of his humanity and divinity. What an *eminently sacred reality*! That is why the Church treats this mystery with such great reverence, and takes such care to ensure the observance of the liturgical norms intended to safeguard the sanctity of so great a sacrament.

We priests are the *celebrants*, but also the *guardians* of this most sacred mystery. It is our relationship to the Eucharist that most clearly challenges us to lead a "sacred" life. This must shine forth from our whole way of being, but above all from the way we celebrate. Let us sit at the school of the saints! The Year of the Eucharist invites us to rediscover those saints who were vigorous proponents of Eucharistic devotion (cf. *Mane nobiscum Domine*, 31). Many beatified and canonized priests have given exemplary testimony in this regard, enkindling fervour among the faithful present at their celebrations of Mass. Many of them were known for their prolonged Eucharistic adoration. To place ourselves before Jesus in the Eucharist, to take advantage of our ``moments of solitude" and to fill them with this Presence, is to enliven our consecration by our personal relationship with Christ, from whom our life derives its joy and its meaning.

A life centred on Christ

7. *"Mortem tuam annuntiamus, Domine, et tuam resurrectionem confitemur, donec venias."* Every time we celebrate the Eucharist, the remembrance of Christ in his Paschal Mystery leads to the desire for a full and definitive encounter with Him. We live in *expectation of his coming*! In priestly spirituality, this expectation must be lived out *through pastoral charity*, which impels us to live in the midst of God's People, so as to direct their path and to nourish their hope. This task requires from the priest an interior attitude similar to that of the Apostle Paul: *"Forgetting what lies behind and straining forward to what lies ahead, I press on towards the goal"* (Phil 3: 13-14). The priest is someone who, despite the passing of years, continues to radiate youthfulness, spreading it almost"contagiously"among those he meets along the way. His secret lies in his "passion" for Christ. As Saint Paul said: *"For me, to live is Christ"* (Phil 1: 21).

Particularly in the context of the new evangelization, the people have a right to turn to priests in the hope of"seeing" Christ in them (cf. Jn 12: 21). The young feel the need for this especially; Christ continues to call them, to make them his friends and to challenge some to give themselves completely for the sake of the Kingdom. Vocations will certainly not be lacking if our manner of life is truly priestly, if we become more holy, more joyful, more impassioned in the exercise of our ministry. A priest "won" by Christ (cf. Phil 3: 12) more easily"wins" others, so that they too decide to set out on the same adventure.

A "Eucharistic" life at the school of Mary

8. The relationship between the Blessed Virgin Mary and the Eucharist is a very close one, as I pointed out in the Encyclical *Ecclesia de Eucharistia* (cf. nn. 53-58). In its own sober liturgical language, every Eucharistic Prayer brings this out. Thus in the Roman Canon we say:"In union with the whole Church we honour Mary, the ever-virgin Mother of Jesus Christ our Lord and God". In the other Eucharistic Prayers, honour leads to petition, as for example in Prayer II:"Make us worthy to share eternal life with Mary, the virgin Mother of God."

In recent years, I have warmly recommended the contemplation of the face of Christ, especially in my Letters *Novo millennio ineunte* (cf. nn. 23ff.) and in *Rosarium Virginis Mariæ* (cf. nn. 9ff.), and I have pointed to Mary as our great teacher. In the Encyclical on the Eucharist I then spoke of her as the"Woman of the Eucharist" (cf. n. 53). Who more than Mary can help us taste the greatness of the Eucharistic mystery? She more than anyone can teach us how to celebrate the sacred mysteries with due fervour and to commune with her Son, hidden in the Eucharist. I pray to her, then, for all of you, and I entrust to her especially the elderly, the sick, and those in difficulty. This Easter, in the Year of the Eucharist, I gladly repeat to each of you the gentle and consoling words of Jesus:"Behold your Mother" (Jn 19: 27).

With these sentiments, I send you my heartfelt blessing, and I wish you the profound joy of Easter.

From Gemelli Hospital in Rome, on 13 March, the Fifth Sunday of Lent, in the year 2005, the twenty-seventh of my Pontificate.

Index

aware of the mission of the laity 158
a priest forever 164
being the model of Christ 134, 277
comes from Christ's priesthood 72, 279, 281
common priesthood of the faithful 10, 11, 12, 18, 120, 127, 143, 153, 154, 156, 166, 279, 333
cornerstone of prayer 133
daily commitment 289, 325
differs from the priesthood of the laity 279
discover the charism of the laity 157
example of the Curé of Ars 113, 123
gift for the sake of the Eucharist 78
gift to the Church 279, 283, 360, 362, 365
Holy Spirit, author of the power of priesthood 177
Holy Thursday: the birthday of our priesthood 84, 102, 112, 277, 280, 281
inscribed in the mystery of Christ's redemption 88, 94, 133, 155, 280
instituted by Christ 83, 281
integrity of life and service 12
intimacy with Christ 289
in persona Christi 102, 140, 141, 146, 153, 158, 278, 300, 330, 333, 344, 359, 367
is a "social" sacrament 155
is the love of the Heart of Jesus 114
linked to the Eucharist 128, 133, 278, 280, 281, 282, 283
means special friendship with Christ 84, 146, 147, 164, 327
mystery of mercy 290
not laiziced priests 179
of Christ 132, 279, 281, 358
of the redemptive sacrifice of Christ 153
our holiest task: ministers of the Eucharist 127
our nearness to the Mother of Christ 24
pastoral power and charism from the Church 102
priestly personality 15
priests as teachers of truth 87
priests as teachers of truth and morality 22
qualities of the priest 15, 114, 294
recognizing vocation to the priesthood 108
rooted in prayer 131
sacerdos alter Christus 178, 179
sharing in the Trinitarian Communion 277
solicitude for the salvation of our neighbor 13, 74
started at Last Supper 148, 276, 281, 358
stewards of the mysteries of God 134, 155, 158
the way priests should preside 157, 344
to be stewards of God 156
trials 289
triple dimension of the hierarchical priesthood 10, 12, 18
unity with the priesthood of Christ 5, 279, 358
vocation and service 128, 366